Jump Up!

AMERICAN MUSICSPHERES

Series Editor
Mark Slobin

Fiddler on the Move
Exploring the Klezmer World
Mark Slobin

The Lord's Song in a Strange Land
Music and Identity in Contemporary Jewish Worship
Jeffrey A. Summit

Lydia Mendoza's Life in Music
Yolanda Broyles-González

Four Parts, No Waiting
A Social History of American Barbershop Harmony
Gage Averill

Louisiana Hayride
Radio and Roots Music Along the Red River
Tracey E. W. Laird

Balkan Fascination
Creating an Alternative Music Culture in America
Mirjana Lauševič

Polkabilly
How the Goose Island Ramblers Redefined American Folk Music
James P. Leary

Cajun Breakdown
The Emergence of an American-Made Music
Ryan André Brasseaux

Claiming Diaspora
Music, Transnationalism, and Cultural Politics in Asian/Chinese America
Su Zheng

Bright Star of the West
Joe Heaney, Irish Song-Man
Sean Williams and Lillis Ó Laire

Romani Routes
Cultural Politics and Balkan Music in Diaspora
Carol Silverman

Voices from the Canefields
Folksongs from Japanese Immigrant Workers in Hawai'i
Franklin Odo

Greeted With Smiles
Bukharian Jewish Music and Musicians in New York
Evan Rapport

Resounding Afro Asia
Interracial Music and the Politics of Collaboration
Tamara Roberts

Singing God's Words
The Performance of Biblical Chant in Contemporary Judaism
Jeffrey Summit

JUMP UP!

Caribbean Carnival Music in New York City

Ray Allen

OXFORD
UNIVERSITY PRESS

OXFORD
UNIVERSITY PRESS

Oxford University Press is a department of the University of Oxford. It furthers the University's objective of excellence in research, scholarship, and education by publishing worldwide. Oxford is a registered trade mark of Oxford University Press in the UK and certain other countries.

Published in the United States of America by Oxford University Press
198 Madison Avenue, New York, NY 10016, United States of America.

© Oxford University Press 2019

Library of Congress Cataloging-in-Publication Data
Names: Allen, Ray, author.
Title: Jump up! Caribbean carnival music in New York City / Ray Allen.
Description: New York, NY : Oxford University Press, 2019. |
Series: American musicspheres | Includes bibliographical references and index.
Identifiers: LCCN 2018057149 | ISBN 9780190656843 (hardcover : alk. paper) |
ISBN 9780190656850 (pbk. : alk. paper)
Subjects: LCSH: Popular music—New York (State)—New York—
History and criticism. | Steel bands (Music)—New York (State)—New York. |
Soca—History and criticism. | Popular music—Caribbean Area—
History and criticism. | Caribbean Americans—New York (State)—New York—
Music—History and criticism. | Carnival—New York (State)—New York.
Classification: LCC ML3477.8.N48 A55 2019 |
DDC 781.62/9697298307471—dc23
LC record available at https://lccn.loc.gov/2018057149

Contents

Acknowledgments

The efforts of many have made *Jump Up!* possible. I am deeply indebted to the scores of Carnival singers, musicians, arrangers, and promoters who offered up their stories that form the foundation of much of this book. I am especially grateful to the journalist Leslie Slater and Carnival historian Ray Funk for their assistance in setting up and conducting interviews. Ray Funk, the late anthropologist Donald Hill and sound archivist Zeke Runyon, generously shared materials from their personal Carnival archival collections that proved indispensable to this work.

Special thanks to my Oxford University Press series editor Mark Slobin and my longtime friend and Caribbean scholar Stephen Stuempfle for their encouragement in the early stages of my research and for reviewing sections of my manuscript. Appreciation to my fellow Caribbean scholars Andrew Martin, Philip Kasinitz, Dale Byam, Kendall Williams, and Don Robotham, and to *Everybody's Caribbean Magazine* editor Herman Hall, for their helpful comments along the way, and to Michael Serrill for his editorial advice.

It was a privilege to collaborate with Yvette Rennie of J'Ouvert City International, Martin Douglas of the United States Steelband Association, Michael Manswell of Something Positive, Chris Mulé of the Brooklyn Arts Council, Steve Zeitlin of City Lore, and Brooklyn College alumnus and soca arranger extraordinaire Frankie McIntosh to bring a public programing component to my research.

I am grateful to my home institution, Brooklyn College, for granting me a sabbatical in 2014 to pursue my field research in Brooklyn and Trinidad, and to the Advanced Research Collaborative at the Graduate Center, CUNY, for awarding me a research fellowship in 2017 to complete the initial draft of this book. Thanks also to the PSC CUNY Research Foundation for their manuscript preparation award, and to Suzanne Ryan and her Oxford University Press editing team for shepherding the work through the production process.

And finally, to my lifelong partner EL Russell I can only say—without you my dearest, none of this would have been possible.

Introduction

Carnival Music and Diasporic Transnationalism

Inside these two buildings called calypso tents, it is tropic hot. Forty or more calypsonians are entertaining as part of the buildup for the upcoming Labor Day Caribbean Carnival in Brooklyn. People brush against one another as they dance and applaud to the tantalizing, titillating tempo of authentic calypso music. The action is tight.
          —Herman Hall, *Everybody's Caribbean Magazine*, 1982[1]

So chronicled Herman Hall, a longtime Carnival observer and editor of the popular Caribbean publication *Everybody's Caribbean Magazine*. In the week prior to Brooklyn's 1982 Labor Day Carnival, Hall attended calypso shows at the Rainbow Terrace and B's Calypso Castle, clubs located around the corner from one another in central Brooklyn's Crown Heights neighborhood. Throughout the early 1980s, these two venues featured "clashes" between the world's leading calypsonians. Among the scores of singers to grace the stages of the Terrace and the Castle were the Mighty Sparrow, Calypso Rose, Shadow, and Lord Nelson.

Sparrow, indisputably the most popular Trinidadian calypso singer of the era, had been splitting his time between Trinidad and New York for more than a decade, using the city as a base for touring and recording. In addition to winning numerous Trinidad Road March and Calypso Monarch titles in the 1960s and 1970s, he established the Madison Square Garden Caribbean show in 1969, headlined the Brooklyn Carnival Labor Day shows throughout the 1970s, and recorded for the Brooklyn-based Caribbean labels Straker's, Charlie's, and B's Records.

Calypso Rose, a native Tobagonian known as the "Queen of Calypso," had won fame in the Port of Spain Carnival before relocating to New York in the late 1970s to tour and record. She wrote her biggest hit, "Give Me Tempo," in New York while riding on the subway. Released on Charlie's Records, the song won her the prestigious Trinidad Carnival Road March title in 1977, marking the first time a woman had accomplished such a feat.

Shadow was a frequent visitor to Brooklyn's Labor Day Carnival. His calypso hit "Bass Man," which won the Trinidad Carnival Road March in 1974, helped launch Granville Straker's Brooklyn-based record label, and served as an early prototype for the emerging soca (soul/calypso) style.

Nelson, a native of Tobago, was often referred to as the "Yankee Calypsonian" following his permanent move to New York in the 1950s. He recorded for Charlie's and B's Records and was considered a soca music pioneer in the late 1970s and early 1980s for his innovative blending of calypso with African American soul, funk, and disco styles. Nelson's musical arranger, Clive Bradley, was another musician who shuttled between Trinidad and New York in the 1980s, working with Nelson and other singers while winning Panorama titles with his arrangements for Trinidad's fabled Desperadoes Steel Orchestra and Brooklyn's Metro Steel Orchestra.

Nelson, Rose, Shadow, and Sparrow had all recorded for Tobago-born Rawlston Charles, the founder of Charlie's Records. Located on Fulton Street just a few blocks from the Rainbow Terrace and Calypso Castle, Charles's company was, by the early 1980s, the leading producer and distributor of calypso and soca music in the United States and the Caribbean. The Rainbow Terrace tent was organized by Count Robin, yet another Trinidadian expatriate. He joined Rudy King's popular Tropicans steelband shortly after arriving in Brooklyn in 1967, and several years later he helped found the Sonatas Steel Orchestra, one of the first steelbands to participate in Brooklyn's Eastern Parkway Carnival parade. When Robin

Figure I.1. Shadow at the Rainbow Terrace Calypso Tent, Brooklyn, 1981. Photo by Kevin Burke.

wasn't beating pan, he was busy composing and recording calypso songs for Straker's Records. He traveled back to Trinidad every year for Carnival to sing and help manage the calypso tent run by Shadow (see Figure I.1), and to scout out talent for the Terrace in Brooklyn.

Sparrow, Rose, Shadow, Nelson, Bradley, Charles, and Robin are among the scores of Afro-Caribbean musicians and cultural entrepreneurs who plied their crafts within a transnational network, circulating musical ideas, styles, repertoires, and recordings among New York's diasporic Caribbean[2] communities and their island homelands. *Jump Up! Caribbean Carnival Music in New York City* tells their stories, recounting their contributions to the emergence of Brooklyn's Labor Day Carnival in the late 1960s, and those of their predecessors who took part in the original Harlem Carnival back in the 1940s and 1950s.

Jump Up! is the first comprehensive history of Trinidadian calypso/soca and steelband music in the diaspora. Previous studies have given ample coverage to Carnival music in the context of Trinidad, but paid nominal attention to the migration and significance of this music outside of the Caribbean.[3] Brooklyn Carnival has been the subject of several informative sociological, anthropological, and historical investigations, which have concentrated primarily on cultural politics and identity while offering only cursory treatments of the music.[4] Likewise, works exploring the globalization of Trinidadian-style Carnivals have focused on the intersection of resistance, hegemony, and cultural agency in diasporic communities, while offering little discussion of music.[5] Seeking to fill this void, *Jump Up!* addresses the interplay of music, migration, and transnational identity in the context of diasporic Carnivals.

Carnival, transplanted from Trinidad to Harlem in the 1930s, and to Brooklyn in the late 1960s, provides the cultural setting. The story begins in New York recording studios in the late 1920s, when Trinidad calypsonians and dance orchestras arrived to make records that were marketed to Harlem's expanding Caribbean community and for export back home. By the mid-1930s those same orchestras and singers were staging annual Carnival dances and masquerades for homesick Trinidadians. Calypso music would eventually spill out of the Caribbean dance halls and fetes into the streets of Harlem to provide the soundtrack for New York's 1947 inaugural Labor Day Carnival parade. Recently arrived steelband men, beating single pans suspended around their necks as they progressed down the street, vied for the crowd's attention with popular calypsonians who were perched on floats, singing the latest songs from Trinidad. Together, they provided lively music for the mas (masquerade) bands to jump up to on Harlem's Seventh Avenue.

During the 1950s, street Carnival rose to prominence in Harlem, only to have its permit revoked in the early 1960s amid an atmosphere of growing racial unrest. In the late 1960s the celebration resurfaced in the central Brooklyn Caribbean neighborhoods, which were expanding rapidly following immigration law reform. By the early 1970s, steelbands were again joining mas bands as the main attractions of a massive Carnival parade that took place on Brooklyn's grand boulevard, Eastern Parkway, each Labor Day afternoon.

Re-creating a decades-old Trinidad practice, the Brooklyn bands engaged in heated competition during the annual Panorama contest, held behind the nearby Brooklyn Museum. As Carnival grew, it attracted prominent calypso/soca singers, musicians, and arrangers from Trinidad and adjacent islands. In turn, migrant entrepreneurs opened independent record companies that would, by the early 1980s, establish Brooklyn as the primary center of production and distribution of modern calypso and soca music. In the mid-1990s the *J'Ouvert* (Break of Day) procession was added to Brooklyn's Labor Day Carnival, completing the structural format of the multiday celebration to loosely mirror its Trinidadian parent.

The turn of the millennium offers an appropriate endpoint for the narrative arc of this study. By that time, Caribbean Carnival, with its Eastern Parkway Road March parade, steelband Panorama contest, Dimanche Gras concerts, and J'Ouvert celebration, was fully established as a New York institution. Brooklyn calypso and soca record production, having reached its zenith in the late 1980s, had by 2000 suffered a radical decline due to sweeping changes in the music business.

Jump Up! draws on a substantial body of scholarship that views diaspora, transnationalism, globalization, hybridity, and heritage as key to understanding the flow of music across geographic and cultural borders. Not surprisingly, the concept of diaspora looms large, given the historical circumstances of New York's Afro-Caribbean migrants. Stuart Hall has identified such New World African communities as consisting of "twice-diasporized" people, for whom, according to Christine Ho and Keith Nurse, the Caribbean served as "both a point of arrival and departure in the long-term process of globalization and diasporisation."[6] Paul Gilroy has demonstrated convincingly that diaspora is the crucible in which transatlantic African identity was forged. Music, he argues, is most illustrative of the centuries-old hybridizing process of African and European styles, and of more recent exchanges of expressive culture between Africa and the African societies of the Caribbean and North America.[7] Hall's and Gilroy's formulations are particularly useful for understanding the development of Caribbean Carnival in New York, where hybridized African/European Carnival traditions from Trinidad were rehybridized with black American expressions by the twice-diasporized descendants of the original island slaves now relocated to urban North America.

Gilroy's work, along with globalization models developed by the anthropologist Arjun Appadurai stressing the disjunctive flows of people, media, commerce, and cultural expressions across national borders, inspired ethnomusicologists to reassess their approach to the study of music and migration.[8] Mark Slobin, a pioneer in this movement, coined the term "diasporic interculture" in his call for the study of "the linkages that (musical) subcultures set up across national boundaries."[9] For Slobin, diaspora was more than a simple demographic category marking a population geographically separated from its homeland—he also argued for its exist-ence as a "sort of consciousness of a separation, a gap, a disjuncture" that could be articulated through music.[10]

More recent studies of transplanted migrant music cultures in the United States have built on Slobin's theorizing, employing the concept of "diasporic transnationalism" to describe the cyclical flow of musical expressions among multiple sites.[11] This approach supplanted outmoded Eurocentric models that envisioned migrants as homogenous folk groups who, finding themselves completely cut off from their Old World enclaves, would naturally assimilate to the norms of their New World host cultures. By contrast, diasporic transnationalism involves transmigrant musicians who span borders, linking home and host societies through hybrid mu-sical expressions that mediate the migration experience. For instance, as Gage Averill observed, Haitian popular music formed the "connecting tissue of the Haitian transnation," joining the Haitian homeland with overseas communities in New York and Paris.[12]

Averill is not alone in employing the concept of diasporic transnation-alism to describe the music cultures of Caribbean migrants who arrived in New York in the post-1965 era. Scholars have parsed the transna-tional dimensions of Cuban/Nuyorican salsa, Dominican merengue, and Jamaican reggae, in addition to Haitian *konpa* (or *kompa*) explored by Averill, as well as a plethora of folk and religious musical expressions.[13] The model is pertinent for the study of overseas Carnival music, as Trinidadian migrants have remained closely tethered to their home culture in general, and to their Carnival in particular. As Jocelyne Guilbault notes in her study of Trinidadian soca music, the ease and frequency of international travel and phone communication, coupled with advances in mass media, have blurred "the traditional meaning of 'home' [for Trinidadians in the diaspora] defined by specific place or locality."[14]

Jump Up! will dig deeper into this phenomenon of deterritorialization, seeking to elucidate how, in the context of Labor Day Carnival, the perfor-mance of calypso/soca and steelband music contributed to an emergent sense of transnation among Caribbean New Yorkers. Guilbault further reminds us that the heterogeneous nature of New York's large English-speaking Caribbean population has resulted in Carnival rituals and music that "have catered simultaneously to both a pan–West Indian and Trinidadian identity."[15] This assessment will be fleshed out by probing the attitudes of New York's Caribbean musicians, promoters, and audiences regarding their island-specific affiliations and how those relationships have shaped their broader sense of pan-Caribbean identity.

Central to diasporic transnationalism is hybridization—the dynamic mixing that takes place during cross-cultural contact. The concept of hybridity has become increasingly fashionable in the field of cultural studies in reference to phenomena resulting from the recent amalgama-tion and recombination of seemingly unrelated cultural forms, sometimes instigated and often accelerated by electronic media and a postmodern zeitgeist.[16] Anthropologists and linguists, however, have long understood that the prolonged, often centuries-old process of intercultural exchange, described as creolization (by linguists) and syncretism (by anthropologists studying religion), has been the central trope of Caribbean culture and the broader black Atlantic since the first European contact and importation of African forced labor into the region.

Regardless of what term we apply, cultural miscegenation between African and European traditions has been a hallmark of vernacular New World music practices, including Trinidadian calypso and steelband music.[17] But, as Jan Nederveen Pieterse has warned, interpreting hybridity demands careful interrogation of the production and control of culture, taking into account both aesthetic and financial considerations in the context of power relations between home and host societies. Otherwise, cultural hybridity can turn into a vapid "multiculturalism lite" that simply celebrates diversity while ignoring inequity, exploitation, and appropriation.[18] *Jump Up!* turns a critical eye to the production, distribution, and audience marketing of calypso and steelband music in New York, focusing on the way these hybridized expressive forms have constructed and negotiated cultural boundaries while simultaneously reinforcing and challenging cultural hierarchies.

Works addressing the issues of Carnival and globalization theory have also informed this study. Keith Nurse's comparative investigation of overseas Carnivals in Brooklyn, Toronto, and London reprised Hall's notion of the twice diasporized by positing the globalization of Trinidad Carnival as a dual process—as the *"localization of global influence"* (i.e., the hybrid development of the early Trinidad Carnival from African and European antecedents) and the *"globalization of local impulses"* (i.e., the exportation of Carnival to diasporic communities). As overseas Carnivals expanded, they began to impact their host societies, leading Nurse to pose a provocative query: "Who is globalizing whom?"[19] *Jump Up!* addresses this question, examining the flows and counterflows of steelband and calypso/soca between the Caribbean and New York, drawing upon past scholarship that has challenged traditional globalization models based on simple, unidirectional, center-periphery cultural exchange.[20]

The concept of heritage is useful in illuminating the deeper cultural meanings of New York Carnival music. Here the work of Barbara Kirshenblatt-Gimblett is indispensable. In her examination of tourism and museums, she has identified "heritage" as a "new mode of cultural production in the present that has recourse to the past."[21] In reference to the resurgence of interest in Jewish klezmer music in the late 1970s, she coined the term "heritage music" to distinguish "music that has been singled out for preservation, protection, enshrinement, and revival."[22] The implication of self-conscious selection is critical as Kirshenblatt-Gimblett moves us away from debates on authenticity and invented tradition to refocus on how and why certain musical styles and genres are imbued with cultural significance and power. Steelband music and calypso were promoted as symbols of Trinidadian nationalism in the early days of independence, but they took on new cultural implications as they were incorporated into

Brooklyn's Carnival parade and J'Ouvert celebrations. How and why these particular expressive forms were selected for enshrinement shed light on their meanings and functions in the diaspora.

Moving from broad, cultural globalization and heritage theories to actual grassroots music-making, Thomas Turino's work on the cultural politics of performance provides a conceptual framework for exploring a variety of social contexts in which Carnival music is practiced and the fluid nature of artist-audience interaction in different settings. In his study of global vernacular music practices, Turino identifies "participatory" musical performances as those unfolding in situations where distinctions between artists and audience members tend to evaporate, with all in attendance expected to participate in the shared experience of music-making and dance. A second trope of performance practices, deemed "presentational," occurs in social situations where a group of specified musicians presents their art to a separate group of nonparticipants. Turino recognizes a third field, "high fidelity," as the production of musical recordings that reference live performances.[23] Practitioners of Carnival music, both in the Caribbean and in the diaspora, have participated in all three of these modes: on-the-road processions that are highly participatory in nature, sit-down calypso tents and steelband competitions that lean toward the presentational, and making calypso/soca recordings that provide mediated sound that often intertwines with live participatory and presentational performances.

At this juncture it should be clear that Caribbean Carnival music, or for that matter any other vernacular music tradition recently arrived from outside the borders of the United States, can no longer be studied in isolation from its immediate neighbors or its international place of origin. In multicultural urban centers like New York, special attention must be paid to potential interaction with the musical practices of nearby native-born black and local transmigrant communities. Equally important in the modern, globalized era, connections back to the source society must be thoroughly fleshed out. This latter point is essential for this study, which explores the reciprocal flow of musicians, arrangers, producers, cultural entrepreneurs, and audiences across the political and cultural borders separating the Caribbean and New York City.

Jump Up! draws on a number of primary sources, including oral history interviews, written archival documents, newspaper reports, and sound recordings, as well as my own ethnographic observations of Brooklyn Carnival. Interviews with Brooklyn's Caribbean musicians, arrangers, record producers, and cultural workers were conducted in two stages—the first between 1995 and 1998, as part of my initial research on Brooklyn's steelband movement and J'Ouvert celebration; the second between 2013 and 2017, as part of my current project. The journalist and longtime Brooklyn Carnival observer Leslie Slater was instrumental in helping conduct the first set of interviews, and Carnival historian Ray Funk collaborated with me on the second round. Also important were the archival collections of the Brooklyn Museum (host to Panorama and related Carnival events since 1973), the Brooklyn

Historical Society (coordinators of an extensive Carnival oral history project in the 1990s), and the Schomburg Center for Research in Black Culture. These institutions, along with the personal collections of the late anthropologist Don Hill, journalist Herman Hall, and Ray Funk, were key repositories of historical documents and clippings that informed this study.Sound recordings and discographies were essential to this project. Dmitri Subotsky's discography of postwar calypso and soca recordings helped make organizational sense of the thousands of commercial recordings by scores of calypso and soca singers from the late 1960s through the early 1990s.[24] Thanks to the magic of YouTube and the many anonymous calypso and soca fans who took time to upload their favorite recordings, nearly all the calypso and soca songs discussed in this work are available for streaming. Brooklyn steelband recordings are more difficult to come by, as Brooklyn Panorama was not officially recorded until the 1990s, and the early winners, with few exceptions, did not make commercial recordings. Fortunately, Donald Hill's bootleg tape recordings of the 1975 and 1976 Brooklyn Panorama contests provide a window into the sonic world of early Brooklyn Carnival.

I received my first taste of Brooklyn Carnival on Labor Day 1984, when, as a graduate student, I stumbled upon the Eastern Parkway parade. I recall being mesmerized by the massive Sonatas Steel Orchestra, with its scores of players on two-story mobile racks being wheeled down Eastern Parkway by exuberant fans, by the thundering truck-mounted sound systems powered by deejays spinning Arrow's "Hot, Hot, Hot" and Sparrow's "Don't Back Back," and by the dozens of dazzling mas bands who "chipped" (shuffle stepped) and "wined" (danced) to the music. Over the past thirty-plus years I have regularly attended the parade, the J'Ouvert celebration, the Brooklyn Museum Labor Day Panorama and Dimanche Gras shows, and a variety of calypso/soca tents and dances during Carnival season. I have also spent time in numerous pan yards observing and occasionally recording rehearsals.[25] While this work depends primarily on archival and oral-history sources, I occasionally interject my own observations from the late 1980s and 1990s regarding the Eastern Parkway parade, Panorama, and the emergence of J'Ouvert, as well as my account of Brooklyn Carnival 2017.

Jump Up! is organized chronologically as an interpretive historical narrative. The first chapter offers a brief history of Carnival music in Trinidad and the emergence of diasporic Carnival celebrations in New York, London, and Toronto. The tangled transnational origins of calypso and steelband, along with their development as expressions of cultural identity and resistance for Afro-Trinidadians, set the stage for the music's migration to North America and Europe. The next two chapters focus on Harlem, beginning with the early dance orchestras and calypsonians who brought Carnival music to New York in the 1930s and 1940s, and moving into the story of the Seventh Avenue Labor Day Carnival parade. Initially staged in 1947, the event would grow into one of the city's most prominent cultural festivals.

The study turns next to the establishment of Brooklyn Carnival. Chapter 4 recounts the mass in-migration of English-speaking Caribbean people to the borough in the wake of the new 1965 immigration laws. In 1971 the West Indian American Day Carnival Association (WIADCA) launched a Labor Day Carnival parade down Eastern Parkway, establishing Brooklyn as the new center of New York Carnival. The rise of steelbands on the Parkway and the establishment of WIADCA's Brooklyn Panorama steelband competition during the 1970s and 1980s are the subjects of chapter 5. New York's complex multiethnic political landscape served as a backdrop for WIADCA's struggle to deploy various Carnival expressions, particularly steelband and calypso music, in hopes of uniting Brooklyn's diverse island populations under a single pan-Caribbean banner, while also encouraging greater social integration of Caribbean culture into mainstream American urban society.

Chapters 6 and 7 focus on the rise of Brooklyn soca, beginning with the story of the early Bronx-based independent record company Camille Records, before shifting to the three most important Brooklyn-based labels: Straker's Records, Charlie's Records, and B's Records. These migrant, Caribbean-owned businesses, along with a cadre of influential calypso/soca singers and the music arrangers with whom they collaborated, played a crucial role in the evolution of modern calypso and soca music during the 1970s and 1980s. The style, structure, and themes of Brooklyn-produced songs are examined and positioned within the broader context of Caribbean and world music recordings of the period. An alternative history of soca is proposed, one emphasizing transnational roots resulting from the confluence of Trinidadian and American musical influences.

Chapter 8 describes the emergence of Brooklyn's J'Ouvert celebration in the 1990s. With its steelband and percussion-only policy, which strictly forbade deejays and amplified bands, J'Ouvert reflected a conscious attempt to preserve and revitalize older Carnival musical practices as forms of cultural heritage, in response to their near disappearance from the more commercial Eastern Parkway parade. Finally, chapter 9 offers a brief survey of recent developments in Brooklyn Carnival and the current status of its steelband and calypso/soca scenes. A description of Labor Day Carnival 2017, marking the 50th anniversary of the celebration, serves as a final coda.

Thirty years prior to this writing, the anthropologist Constance Sutton used the term "cross-roads" to describe the "continuous and intense bidirectional flow of peoples, ideas, practices, and ideologies between the Caribbean region and New York City."[26] Nowhere was her conjecture more evident than in the realm of music. By the time Sutton was writing in the late 1980s, a potpourri of Caribbean styles, including Cuban/Nuyorican mambo and salsa, Dominican merengue, Jamaican reggae, Haitian konpa, and Trinidadian calypso/soca had transformed the city's musical landscape. These genres all shared similar neo-African roots in addition to a proclivity for hybridizing with African American jazz and related popular music styles. Transnational Caribbean musicians and promoters took advantage of the city's advanced recording and broadcast media, seeking to capitalize on rapidly expanding diasporic markets, cycling their music between the Big Apple and the islands of the Caribbean. Along the way these musics became powerful symbols of culture-specific group identity for many transplanted Caribbean New Yorkers, while simultaneously opening up channels of exchange among the various island groups, and among Caribbean migrants and members of the city's African American and white communities.

These shared aesthetic sensibilities and cultural practices notwithstanding, each of these Caribbean musics took a different developmental path once they reached New York. What proved crucial was the historical relationship of the migrants to their respective homelands, as well as the unique social and economic conditions that shaped the production, distribution, and eventual exportation of each island's music. Trinidad calypso/ soca and steelband, the subjects of this study, occupied unique positions in the pantheon of Caribbean New York musics, given their affiliations with seasonal Carnival events both locally and back home. *Jump Up!* aims to illuminate the role that Carnival music played in negotiating the complex migrant/host/home relationship, exploring the contours of the transnational arc that connected Trinidad and the Caribbean to their New York diasporic communities. This phenomenon is best understood through the experiences of the transmigrants who brought Carnival music to the streets, the clubs, the concert stages, and the local music shops of Harlem and Brooklyn, and then back to the Caribbean. But before recounting their stories, we must first return to the source—Caribbean Carnival in nineteenth-century Trinidad.

Notes

1. Herman Hall, "Inside Brooklyn Carnival," *Everybody's Caribbean Magazine* 6, no. 7 (1982): 12.

2. The term "Caribbean" will be used in this study in reference to New York City's Afro-Caribbean transmigrants who trace their ancestries to the Anglophone islands of the Caribbean, including Jamaica, Trinidad and Tobago, Barbados, Grenada, St. Vincent, Monserrat, St. Kitts, Antigua, St. Lucia, and the US Virgin Islands, as well as the South American coastal country of Guyana. This particular demographic was commonly identified as "West Indian" in the past, but the term has increasingly come into disfavor, given its imperialistic and colonial connotations. For this study the designation "Caribbean" does not apply to New York's sizeable communities of Spanish-speaking migrants form Puerto Rico and immigrants from the Dominican Republic and Cuba.

3. The most concise history of steelband, calypso, and soca music in Trinidad is Shannon Dudley, *Carnival Music in Trinidad: Experiencing Music, Expressing Culture* (Oxford University Press, 2004). Indispensable works on the history and practice of steelband music in Trinidad are Shannon Dudley, *Music from Behind the Bridge: Steelband Spirit and Politics in Trinidad and Tobago* (Oxford University Press, 2008); and

Stephen Stuempfle, *The Steelband Movement: The Forging of a National Art in Trinidad and Tobago* (University of Pennsylvania Press, 1995). Three critical works on calypso and soca music in Trinidad are Donald Hill, *Calypso Calaloo: Early Carnival Music in Trinidad* (University Press of Florida, 1993); Gordon Rohlehr, *A Scuffling of Islands: Essays on Calypso* (Lexicon Trinidad Ltd., 2004); and Jocelyne Guilbault, *Governing Sound: The Cultural Politics of Trinidad's Carnival Musics* (University of Chicago Press, 2007). Hill's book contains several chapters on prewar calypso in New York City, while Guilbault's work includes a brief but informative section on soca in the diaspora (pp. 196–201).

4. The earliest scholarly account of Brooklyn Carnival is found in the sociologist Philip Kasinitz's *Caribbean New York: Black Immigrants and the Politics of Race* (Cornell University Press, 1992), pp. 133–159. The cultural historian Rachel Buff examines identity politics in Brooklyn Carnival in *Immigration and the Political Economy of Home: West Indian Brooklyn and American Indian Minneapolis, 1945–1992* (University of California Press, 2001). She includes a chapter on Brooklyn pan yards, but her emphasis is sociological rather than musical. A dual-sight ethnography connecting Trinidad and Brooklyn Carnival in a transnational framework is offered in the anthropologist Philip Scher's *Carnival and the Formation of a Caribbean Transnation* (University Press of Florida, 2003). Scher's observations on the formation of transnational identity are useful, but his evidence is drawn primarily from his work with Carnival masquerade bands rather than steelband musicians or calypso singers. A comparative study of Brooklyn's and London's Notting Hill Carnival is found in the historian Joshua Guild's "You Can't Go Home Again: Migration, Citizenship, and Black Community in Postwar New York and London" (PhD diss., Yale University, 2007). Guild's focus is migration and cultural politics, but he makes some useful observations about the role of Carnival music in the process.

Three studies offering preliminary but incomplete accounts of the Brooklyn's steelband movement in the context of Labor Day Carnival are Gage Averill, "'Pan Is We Ting': West Indian Steelbands in Brooklyn," in *Musics of Multicultural America*, edited by Kip Lornell and Anne Rasmussen (Schirmer Books, 1997), pp. 101–130; Ray Allen and Les Slater, "Steel Pan Grows in Brooklyn: Trinidadian Music and Cultural Identity," in *Island Sounds in the Global City: Caribbean Popular Music and Identity in New York*, edited by Ray Allen and Lois Wilcken (University of Illinois Press, 1998), pp. 114–137; and Ray Allen, "*J'Ouvert* in Brooklyn Carnival," *Western Folklore* 58 (Summer/Fall, 1999): 255–277.

5. For discussions of diasporic Carnivals and globalization theory, see Frank Manning, "Overseas Caribbean Carnivals: The Art and Politics of a Transnational Celebration," *Plantation Society in the Americas* 3, no. 1 (1990): 47–62; and Keith Nurse, "Globalization and Trinidad Carnival: Diaspora, Hybridity and Identity in Global Culture," *Cultural Studies* 13, no. 4 (1999): 661–690. See also Christine Ho and Keith Nurse's "Introduction" in their co-edited volume, *Globalisation, Diaspora and Caribbean Popular Culture* (Ian Randle, 2005), pp. vii–xxiv.

6. Quoted in Ho and Nurse, *Globalisation, Diaspora, and Caribbean Popular Culture*, p. ix. Stuart Hall's initial discussion of "twice diasporized" Caribbean societies is found in Hall, *Myths of Caribbean Identity* (University of Warwick, Center for Caribbean Studies, 1991).

7. Paul Gilroy's landmark study, *The Black Atlantic: Modernity and Double Consciousness* (Harvard University Press, 1993), is an informative discussion of diaspora and New World African culture. See in particular his sections on black music and authenticity (pp. 72–110) and tradition and diaspora (pp. 187–221).

8. Arjun Appadurai's often-quoted essay, "Disjuncture and Difference in the Global Cultural Economy," *Public Culture* 2, no. 2 (1990): 1–24, offers a provocative critique of traditional center-periphery models of globalization.

9. Mark Slobin, *Subcultural Sounds: Micromusics of the West* (Wesleyan University Press, 1993), p. 64.

10. Mark Slobin, "The Destiny of 'Diaspora' in Ethnomusicology," in *The Cultural Study of Music*, edited by Martin Clayton, Trevor Herbert, and Charles Middleton (Routledge, 2003), p. 288.

11. See, for example, Su Zheng, *Claiming Diaspora: Music, Transnationalism, and Cultural Politics in Asian/Chinese America* (Oxford University Press, 2010). Zheng's introduction and second chapter, titled "The Formation of a Diasporic Musical Culture as a Site of Contradiction," together offer an informative overview of how theories of diaspora, transnationalism, and globalization have shaped recent studies in the field of music and migration. Carol Silverman's *Romani Routes: Cultural Politics and Balkan Music in Diaspora* (Oxford University Press, 2012) also includes a useful review of the subject in the chapter titled "Dilemmas of Diaspora, Hybridity, and Identity."

12. Gage Averill, "'Mezanmi, Kouman Nou Ye?': Musical Constructions of the Haitian Transnation," in *Ethnomusicology: A Contemporary Reader*, edited by Jennifer Post (Routledge, 2006), p. 272.

13. Works that discuss the transnational connections between Caribbean musical practices at home and in the diaspora, particularly between the islands and Caribbean communities in New York City, include Peter Manuel, *Caribbean Currents: Caribbean Music from Rumba to Reggae* (Temple University Press, 1995); Gage Averill, *A Day for the Hunter, A Day for the Prey: Popular Music and Power in Haiti* (University of Chicago Press, 1997); Paul Austerlitz, *Merengue: Dominican Music and Dominican Identity* (Temple University Press, 1997); Allen and Wilcken, *Island Sound in the Global City*; Lise Waxer, ed., *Situating Salsa: Global Markets and Local Meaning in Latin Popular Music* (Routledge, 2002); and Guilbault, *Governing Sound*.

14. Guilbault, *Governing Sound*, p. 198.

15. Ibid., p. 199.

16. The use of the concept of hybridity in contemporary scholarship, and its relationship to terms such as creolization and syncretism, are discussed in Jan Nederveen Pieterse, *Globalization and Culture: Global Mélange*, 3rd ed. (Rowman & Littlefield, 2015), pp. 101–105.

17. For further background on the process of hybridization between African and European musical practices in the Caribbean, see Manuel, *Caribbean Currents*, pp. 5–16.

18. Pieterse, *Globalization and Culture*, p. 102. See also Carol Silverman's critique of hybridity and world music in *Romani Routes*, pp. 44–47.

19. Nurse, "Globalization and Trinidadian Carnival," p. 683.

20. For a discussion of the limitations of global center-periphery theory with regard to the migration of world musics, see Jocelyn Guilbault, "On Redefining the 'Local' Through World Music," *Worlds of Music* 35, no. 2

(1993): 140; and Ian Chambers, "Travelling Sounds: Whose Center, Whose Periphery?" *Popular Music Perspectives* 3 (1992): 141–146.

21. Barbara Kirshenblatt-Gimblett, "Theorizing Heritage," *Ethnomusicology* 3 (Fall 1995): 369.

22. Barbara Kirshenblatt-Gimblett, "Sounds of Sensibility," in *American Klezmer: Its Roots and Offshoots*, edited by Mark Slobin (University of California Press, 2002), p. 133.

23. Thomas Turino, *Music as Social Life: The Politics of Participation* (University of Chicago Press, 2008), p. 26.

24. The most complete discography of postwar calypso and soca recordings is Dmitri Subotsky's Calypso Archives, which can be accessed via the archive's website, Wayback Machine, at https://web.archive.org/web/20080513092643/http://www.calypsoarchives.co.uk/. See also Discogs, at http://www.discogs.com/sell/list?format=Vinyl.

25. In August 2000, I oversaw the recording of the tune "My Time" by the CASYM Steel Orchestra in their Brooklyn pan yard. The tune, arranged by Arddin Herbert, won the 2000 Brooklyn Panorama and can be heard on the CD compilation *New York: Global Beat of the Boroughs: Music from NYC's Ethnic & Immigrant Communities* (Smithsonian Folkways Records SFW 40493, 2001).

26. Constance Sutton, "The Caribbeanization of New York City and the Emergence of a Transnational Sociocultural System," in *Caribbean Life in New York City: Sociocultural Dimensions*, edited by Constance Sutton and Elsa Chaney (Center for Migration Studies, 1987), p. 19.

1

Carnival Music in Trinidad and into the Diaspora

The small south Caribbean island nation of Trinidad and Tobago is home to one of the world's most robust and emulated Carnival celebrations. Rivaling Brazil's Rio Carnival and New Orleans's Mardi Gras in size and stature, Port of Spain's annual pre-Lenten festival has gone international, serving as a model for scores of modern urban Carnivals around the Caribbean, North America, and Europe. Calypso and steelband, the two defining musical practices to emerge from twentieth-century Carnival and the primary subjects of this book, are recognized today as Trinidad's most distinctive contributions to the world's musics. The histories of Trinidad Carnival and attendant calypso and steelband musics have been amply chronicled elsewhere and will not be reprised here in depth. Instead, this chapter provides the necessary background for understanding this music's migration and life outside the Caribbean in Harlem and Brooklyn. Guideposts are offered for approaching Trinidad Carnival and its musics as distinctive transnational expressions that are hybrid and protean in nature, at once ritual and commodity, both cultural and political display, and ripe for exportation back into the black Atlantic diaspora.

Carnival Music as Transnational Expression

Calypso and steelband music are the unique creations of the Trinidad people. They are transnational expressions whose roots lie across the Atlantic in the celebratory practices and expressive forms brought to the island by the Africans and Europeans who settled and worked in the original colony. Trinidad developed a polyglot culture in the centuries following its 1498 "discovery" and naming by Columbus. The island's indigenous people and early Spanish settlers were eventually joined by a substantial French planter and free colored population, who together transformed the neglected eighteenth-century outpost into a thriving agricultural colony that produced sugar, tobacco, cocoa, cotton, and coffee. The labor-intensive nature of these crops prompted the French to engage in the forced importation of Africans in the late 1700s to work their plantations. By the 1820s the enslaved African and free colored populations accounted for nearly 90 percent of the island's inhabitants.

The British took possession of Trinidad in 1797, but the colony remained heavily French Catholic in terms of culture, with a majority of the population speaking French or *patois* (a vernacular form of French that incorporated African linguistic elements) throughout the nineteenth century. In the decades following the 1834–1838 emancipation of the African slaves, East Indians were brought in as indentured servants to work the plantations, adding significantly to the cultural mix. By the late nineteenth century, Africans and Europeans from other Caribbean islands, along with Venezuelans of Spanish descent and migrants of Chinese, Portuguese, and Middle Eastern ancestry, migrated to Port of Spain in search of opportunity in the growing port city.[1]

European Carnival, the boisterous celebration that occurs just prior to Ash Wednesday and the austere Lenten season that follows it, was introduced to Trinidad by French-Catholic planters in the late eighteenth century. Back in Europe, Carnival was a time when social mores were relaxed, allowing for excessive eating, drinking, dancing, music, and masquerading. The latter often involved satirical displays in which the upper and lower classes would impersonate and lampoon one another. In Trinidad, the French planters held elegant costume balls and house-to-house parties, engaging in elaborate forms of masquerade that included dressing as slaves and performing African-like songs and dances alongside their European quadrilles and aristocratic garb.

Meanwhile, quite apart from the French and British elites, the African slaves practiced their own set of complex ceremonies based on West African cultural memories. African-derived drumming, dancing, call-and-response singing, masquerading, and *kalinda* stick fighting were vital components of the slave's funeral, ancestor worship, and *cannes brûlées* (ritual reenactments of cane burning) ceremonies. These expressions would become central to their midsummer Canboulay emancipation celebrations following the cessation of slavery. As the Europeans retreated from outdoor Carnival following emancipation, the Africans took over, folding their Canboulay music, dance, and masquerading traditions into the two-day, pre-Lenten celebration period. The result, according to Errol Hill, bore little resemblance to "a European-inspired nature festival," but was rather a "celebration of freedom from slavery . . . a deeply meaningful anniversary of deliverance from the most hateful form of human bondage."[2] By the turn of the twentieth century, when the colonial government and the ruling elites had become more tolerant of the celebration that some factions had tried but failed to eradicate, Trinidad's Carnival/Canboulay street festivities had drifted from its earlier Euro-Catholic moorings. What emerged was a uniquely creolized celebration shaped by the creative sensibilities of the descendants of African slaves, who drew on multiple African, European, Latin American, and other Caribbean cultural sources.[3]

Hollis Liverpool has noted that there is substantial historical evidence from the post-emancipation period to conclude that "the majority of the customs [music, dance, and masquerading] associated with the [Trinidad] festival are African in form and function."[4] There is no question that modern, twentieth-century Carnival, with its emphasis on processional and competitive performance, groove-based rhythms, call-and-response singing, and masquerade themes referencing Africa, slavery, and emancipation, bears the heavy stamp of African tradition in terms of style and content. The festival did, however, retain vestiges of the European celebration beyond its pre-Lenten calendrical setting. European aristocratic, military, clowning, and satirical themes remained popular among masqueraders, and early twentieth-century Venezuelan-derived string bands (of Spanish origin) frequently provided music for dance and outdoor processions. Most importantly for this study, the calypso and steelband traditions that became the soundtrack for modern Carnival developed as Afro-Euro hybrid expressions. As discussed below, they were deeply rooted in West African musical practices while drawing freely on a variety of European and other creolized island and Latin forms.

From these multifarious roots, Trinidadians of African descent created a unique Caribbean Carnival/Canboulay celebration that was a protean admixture of transatlantic expressions. Forged in the diverse and cosmopolitan crucible of Port of Spain, Carnival and its musics were well suited for adaptation and further transformation when carried north to Harlem and Brooklyn.

Carnival Music as Hybridity

The calypso and steelband traditions associated with the twentieth-century Carnival are best understood as products of musical hybridity—the process of mixing various musical practices to forge new expressions related to but not identical to their antecedents. Comparative studies have determined that, despite their differences, African and European vernacular musics shared enough in terms of melodic and harmonic structure to intermingle with relative comfort. Thus, as Richard Waterman notes, it was "easy and inevitable" for "many varieties of Euro-African musical syncretism to be observed in the New World."[5] This was especially true across the Caribbean, where a number of Afro-Euro creolized music styles emerged, including Trinidadian calypso, Jamaican mento, Cuban son, Puerto Rican plena, and Dominican merengue, as well as an array of Afro-Christian musical expressions.[6]

This blending of cultural forms took place because, in addition to the overall structural compatibility of their musical systems, Africans and Europeans did listen to and appreciate one another's music, albeit most often in social contexts marked by asymmetrical power relations that inexorably privileged European cultural forms. In any case, the Afro-Trinidadians who dominated Carnival drew on multiple musical resources. They were steeped in various West African drum and dance traditions that prized complex rhythmic patterns, repetitive call-and-response figures, vocal and instrumental improvisation, and open-ended participatory performance. But they also were familiar with European hymnody, American popular songs, and marching-band music grounded in simple duple-meter rhythms, diatonic melodies, harmony singing with progressive chordal accompaniment, verse/chorus structures, and closed forms. They played African-derived drums and percussion instruments similar to those of their ancestors, but also the Spanish guitars, cuatros, and violins from nearby Venezuela, and the fixed-pitch brass, reed, and keyboard instruments of their former French and English overlords. Many played by ear, but some learned to read European notation, which was necessary to arrange music for marching bands and dance orchestras. They adapted creolized folk songs and dance melodies from nearby English- and French-speaking islands, and when electronic recordings from the United States and other parts of the globe began circulating in the 1920s, new worlds of musical possibilities opened for them.

The development of Trinidadian calypso is a case study in Caribbean musical hybridity. Nineteenth-century Carnival street processions often involved African-derived drumming, dancing, and *kalinda* stick-fighting, led by a chantwell who improvised sung or chanted lines of praise and insult to the response of a chorus. These call-and-response vocal figures gradually developed into more fixed melodic and stanzaic structures that came to be known as *lavways* or *kaiso* songs. From these emerged the earliest calypsos, which were strophic in form, built around four- or eight-line stanzas with choruses, and increasingly sung in English rather than the older Afro-French *patois*. In the early decades of the twentieth century, as chantwells morphed into calypsonians, older Carnival-band tents transformed into calypso tents, where the most talented singers would perform for seated, paying audiences.[7] There they honed their compositional and oratory skills, writing clever topical songs based on satirical, humorous, and bawdy themes that were delivered with extraordinary verbal dexterity. In the tents, the drums and bamboo percussion favored by street chantwells gradually gave way to Venezuelan-style string-band accompaniment with guitars and cuatros that provided elementary chordal progressions. While calypso's drift toward more closed forms, English-language lyrics, and string-instrument accompaniment was a clear reflection of European and Euro-American influences, the music retained a pulsing groove, and the best singers demonstrated verbal improvisational skills in keeping with their African heritage.

Early calypso proved to be an extremely flexible form, as its practitioners creatively remixed multiple African, European, North American, and creolized Latin/Caribbean musical resources.[8] This may account for calypso's proclivity, in the words of Gordon Rohlehr, to continue to "reinvent itself" as it moved from the streets to the dance halls and tents, and eventually into the diaspora, where it would further absorb elements of ragtime, jazz, rock, soul, and funk (the latter three under the guise of "soca").[9] Born of early Afro-Euro hybridization in Trinidad, calypso would continue to transform throughout the twentieth century, accelerated by electronic media and its migration to Harlem and Brooklyn.

Trinidadian steelband music evolved through a similar process of hybridization. Following the banning of African drums in Carnival by the British authorities in the 1880s, tamboo bamboo bands, consisting of individuals who beat and stamped bamboo tubes, provided rhythmic accompaniment for chantwells and their masqueraders. The tamboo bamboo bands began experimenting with metal containers such as paint cans and biscuit drums that could produce several pitches when struck in different areas. By the 1930s, mixed bamboo and metallic percussion bands had become increasingly common in street Carnival. Eventually, musicians discovered they could produce multiple pitches by pounding the bottoms of their containers into various shapes and striking them with sticks, spurring the transformation of metal percussion devices into melody-producing instruments.

In the early postwar years, steel pan tuners (builders) began to fashion instruments from oil drums cut into different sizes to produce a range of tonal pitches. More sophisticated techniques were developed for grooving out notes, leading to pans capable of producing full diatonic and chromatic scales and, when played in tandem, Western chordal harmonies. By the early 1950s these innovations allowed steelbands to play more complex instrumental arrangements of calypsos as well as Latin dance pieces, American popular songs, and even European classical compositions.[10] Stephen Stuempfle has described the early steelband as "an instrument of creolization," drawing rhythmically on African-derived drumming and bamboo traditions, European marching band cadences, and East Indian tassa drumming practices. Pan players incorporated melodic and harmonic patterns from calypsos, European hymns and classical compositions, Venezuelan parang songs, and American popular tunes. On the road for Carnival, the new steelbands had become "percussion ensemble(s) with melodic and harmonic dimensions," capable of providing full musical accompaniment for singers and dancing masqueraders.[11]

As steelbands increased in size and complexity in the 1950s, they became organized into sections based on the melodic range and timbral variations produced by the differently sized pans. The overall ensemble resembled a Western classical orchestra, consisting of high-, mid-, and low-range pan sections, as well as a large percussion section of various drum and metallic instruments—dubbed the "engine room"—that produced densely textured African-inflected rhythms. The complex Panorama arrangements that emerged in the late 1960s were similar to Western orchestral compositions in their closed form, theme/variation/coda structures, and harmonic modulations, but were always undergirded by the pulsing rhythms of the engine room and syncopated bass lines.[12] Within modern steelbands, African- and European-derived musical practices nested comfortably together.

When the first steel pans appeared in Harlem in the late 1940s, they were still relatively unknown in New York's Caribbean community. Over the ensuing decades, steelbands would mirror developments in Trinidad, emerging as a mainstay of the Brooklyn Carnival parade and eventually as the centerpiece of the popular Panorama competition. In addition, the steelband's hybrid roots and the players' penchant for embracing a broad range of musical genres—especially American popular songs and dance music—tendered the possibility for a musical and cultural dialogue among Trinidad migrants and their black and white North American neighbors.

Carnival Music as Participatory Ritual

At its core, early Trinidad Carnival was ritual—a liminal festivity marked by the suspension of everyday time, activity, and social norms. For the colony's African underclass, the annual celebration marked a special time of coming together in public space to reaffirm a common ancestry and shared values, to celebrate emancipation, and to set aside the travails of everyday life by engaging in highly creative and possibly subversive play. At the height of street Carnival, participants sought to achieve a state of social interconnectedness and existential immediacy akin to what Victor Turner termed "spontaneous *communitas*," in which individuals interacting with one another "become totally absorbed into a single, synchronized, fluid event."[13] Music was the siren's call that pulled revelers in, uniting them around a pulsating beat.

Early Carnival street music is illustrative of Thomas Turino's aforementioned "participatory performance." Such performances, Turino explains, can lead to flashes of deep cultural connectedness, as "differences among participants melt away as attention is focused on the seamlessness of sound and motion. At such moments, moving together and sounding together in a group creates a direct sense of *being* together and of deeply felt similarity, and hence identity, among participants."[14] Socially, participatory performances are associated with dance, ritual, and ceremony; musically, they tend to be organized around open forms while employing short, repetitive (and relatively easy to learn) motifs, dense textures, and strong rhythmic grooves meant to engage the body in motion and dance.[15]

Outdoor Carnival processions, dating back to the nineteenth century when chantwells sang over skin drums and tamboo bamboo ensembles, were ritualistic and participatory by nature. The music was structured around compact, repetitive, call-and-response vocal lines anchored by a steady rhythmic drive. All present were encouraged to join in with the chantwell and percussionists by masquerading, dancing, singing, clapping, or playing additional hand percussion instruments. The practice continued in the twentieth century when steelbands replaced drum and bamboo ensembles as the primary music-makers for the road march.

The earliest pan players suspended single pans around their necks and shoulders (dubbed "pan-around-the-neck"), and, by the late 1950s rolling wagons and racks allowed multiple pans on stands to be "pushed and pulled" down the road by their most avid followers. This physical configuration allowed for the commingling of musicians, singers, dancers, and masqueraders in the public space of the road. The unspoken goal was to create a transcendent moment of *communitas* when participants could unite around shared cultural expressions and feel a flash of sublime camaraderie with their fellow revelers.

This sense of unity, pride, and assertiveness was particularly significant for the Afro-Trinidadian underclass who made up the bulk of Carnival celebrators, and whose everyday lives were severely constricted under British colonial rule. Such a Carnival throng, unified through participatory performance that enabled them to assert control over public space, portended resistance against those authorities. Trinidadian Carnival, of course, was not the only participatory cultural practice that fostered a sense of unity, shared social identity, and possible resistance among Afro-diasporic people. As Paul Gilroy has observed, the "ubiquity of antiphonal" during these sorts of neo-African ritualized performances across the black Atlantic provided a space where "a relationship of identity is enacted in the way that the performer dissolves into the crowd."[16]

Carnival Music as Presentation and Commodity

As Trinidad modernized in the twentieth century, practitioners of both calypso and steelband music began to embrace more prescribed presentational modes of performance that contributed to the commodification of their music. Such presentational performances, according to Turino, are most often associated with formal stage and concert events, where the lines between performers and audiences are sharply demarcated.[17] In contrast to participatory practices, presentational performances favor music that is closed and scripted in form, with organized beginnings and endings. Thematic contrasts, transparent textures, variable rhythms, and individual virtuosity are emphasized.[18]

In Trinidad Carnival, the shift from participatory to presentational performance began in the early 1900s with the establishments of the previously mentioned calypso tents. In those semi-interior spaces, chantwells-turned-calypsonians composed and sang lyrically complex songs for seated audiences who had paid admission to be entertained. These new breeds of calypsonians were esteemed for their highly individual vocal virtuosity and poetic prowess. Backing musical ensembles of string, brass, and reed players were expected to produce tight arrangements that would include composed instrumental introductions, thematic interludes between sung verses, and codas. The calypsonians and musicians considered themselves to be professionals, and they demanded remuneration for their services. Audiences were not passive, as would be the case during a Western

20   *Jump Up!*

classical concert—they no doubt swayed, clapped, and occasionally sang along with choruses. But the modern tents were not dances, and their configurations maintained an artist-audience separation that was foreign to road march and earlier drum/dance performances. The growing popularity of calypso contests in the tents, along with the eventual establishment of a National Calypso King competition on the main Port of Spain Savannah stage in 1953, further pushed live calypso performance toward presentational display.[19]

A somewhat similar progression unfolded with steelband performance. During the 1950s and 1960s, a period often referred to as the golden era of pan-on-the-road, steelbands were pushed and pulled on racks and wagons through the streets of Port of Spain, providing the musical accompaniment for most of the large mas bands. But by the early 1970s, calypso orchestras and deejays mounted on large trucks began to replace the steelbands, which could not compete with the recorded music delivered over high-volume sound systems. While steelbands maintained an active presence on the road during J'Ouvert, their roles in the daytime Carnival road festivities and at evening fetes were diminished, and they found themselves increasingly channeled into the large Panorama competition that was established in 1963, and that would become the centerpiece of the big Port of Spain Savannah stage shows. Playing for a ticket-holding, seated audience and a panel of judges, and competing for prize money, Panorama steelbands found themselves gradually becoming part of what Shannon Dudley identified as "a pervasive staging of culture."[20] Such formal presentations called for longer, more complex musical arrangements that would become the sole focus of the bands' rehearsing during Carnival season, often leading to more limited repertories.

A number of critics were troubled by the decline of participatory calypso and steelband on the road, along with the increasing commercialization and tourism that came to characterize Carnival in the decades following Trinidad's independence. For the author Earl Lovelace, the diminished presence of pan-on-the-road threatened the essence of the "Emancipation-Jouvay" spirit he saw as central to the transgressive Carnival ethos.[21] Others, however, perceived benefits to the music moving into more formal, presentational settings. Performing for tent audiences prompted the best and most competitive calypsonians to write more lyrically complex and provocative songs, emphasizing both storytelling and sophisticated oration.[22] Steelband aficionados contended that Panorama competition encouraged the production of more elaborate, multi-themed arrangements as well as experimentation with new harmonies, textures, and rhythmic patterns.[23] Carnival music simultaneously mirrored and contributed to the transformation of Trinidad Carnival as it vacillated between its participatory ritual roots and its more official, commodified presentational modes.

The survival of ritualized, participatory street Carnival and its music would eventually become a matter of concern for Carnival organizers in Trinidad and in Brooklyn. By the mid-1990s, attempts were being made (with limited success) to bring the steelbands back to daytime road marches in Port of Spain. At the same time, the nostalgic desire to preserve old-time pan and masquerading traditions in Brooklyn spawned the establishment of a "pan-only" J'Ouvert celebration that became more traditional than its contemporaneous Trinidad parent.

Turino's third field of performance, "high fidelity," involves capturing the sound of live music-making for later consumption by a group not present in the original face-to-face performance.[24] Such commercial recordings, particularly of calypso, played a vital role in the development of the music's form and style, as well as the way it was consumed in various Carnival settings. By the 1920s, Trinidad dance orchestras and calypsonians were traveling to New York to record, thrusting the singers and musicians deeper into the international arena, where they would absorb elements of black American jazz and contemporary Latino vernacular styles. American record companies sent mobile crews to Trinidad to record, and studios were eventually established in and around Port of Spain. Recordings turned the sounds of street Carnival, tent shows, and fetes into commercial commodities and hastened the professionalization of the first generation of calypsonians, including Houdini, Executor, Roaring Lion, Atilla the Hun, and Growling Tiger. The early calypso records made in New York were circulated back to Trinidad and to other islands, establishing the primacy of calypso song throughout the English-speaking Caribbean.[25]

In the 1970s and 1980s, a new generation of singers and musicians from Trinidad and adjacent islands would migrate to Brooklyn to record with the producers Rawlston Charles and Granville Straker, who helped shape the new soca sound. Record-spinning deejays, aided by high-volume sound systems, would use calypso and soca recordings to engage masqueraders on the road and dancers at fetes in Port of Spain and Brooklyn, adding fresh energy to the tradition of participatory performance, but this time with the assistance of mediated sound.

Trinidad steelband music was recorded as early as the 1940s, but commercial recordings played a relatively minor role in the music's development and dissemination. The music was, and continues to be, consumed primarily in live settings on the road, at dances and fetes, in the pan yards, or at competitions. The reasons for this are both acoustic and social. "The omnidirectional nature of the sounds created by [live] steelbands swirls around and produces a single cohesive tonal fabric that is both sweet and powerful," explains Andrew Martin.[26] Stuempfle concludes that Trinidadians "have always preferred to hear steelbands in live performance," due to the music's affiliation with Carnival and the fact that it was not easy to record.[27] To the chagrin of many steel pan players, it was the deejay-broadcast calypso and soca recordings that usurped their role at the Carnival road marches and fetes. However, the relationship between recorded calypso/soca and live steelband music was by no means totally adversarial. Calypsonians, from Lord Kitchener to David Rudder, wrote and recorded songs in praise of legendary steelband heroes, and their annual records were often the source for steelband tunes, especially for Panorama. During the Port of Spain competition, the prerecorded calypso/soca piece upon which the upcoming Panorama arrangement is based is broadcast at high volume while the steelband is pushed up the ramp and set up to perform on stage.

Turino's model is useful in conceptualizing the diverse musical practices found in Carnival music, but clearly there is a good deal of overlap in his three fields of musical performance. In the twentieth century, an array of live and recorded sounds, performed through participatory and presentational modes, intermingled to form the multifaceted soundscape of modern Trinidad Carnival. Music has always been fundamental to Carnival's paradoxical stature as traditional ritual and commodified spectacle, both in Port of Spain and in the diaspora.

Carnival Music as Resistance and Identity

Historically, Trinidad Carnival has been a time for extraordinary creative expression and play. Nevertheless, since its inception, it has provided an arena for social commentary, resistance to authority, and the formation of ethnic and national identities. This is not unexpected, given European Carnival's proclivity for satire and subversive play and African Canboulay's ethos of liberation and struggle against oppression. The forging of identity involved protracted struggles between the island's African working-class populace and the colonial authorities who tended to see Carnival and its attendant musics as threats to civic and moral order, and later between grassroots communities and post-independence leaders who sought to unite Trinidadians under a perceived shared national culture.

The torch-bearing, stick-fighting, African-drumming masqueraders who paraded through the streets of Port of Spain on J'Ouvert morning, reenacting their emancipation, were of considerable concern to the nineteenth-century British ruling elite who feared insurrection. On various occasions they tried to shut down, or at least curtail, street Carnival. Tensions came to a head in the early 1880s when police clashed with bands of stick fighters in the now legendary Canboulay riots that led to the banning of drumming and stick fighting during Carnival.[28]

Eventually the British regime and the aspiring middle-class Creoles, realizing that Carnival was too ingrained in the culture to be abolished, sought to control the more offensive and possibly dangerous practices. By the 1920s, committees were formed to "improve" calypso lyrics, and tent contests with cash prizes were encouraged to reward the most sophisticated songs. Following independence, sponsorship of the decade-old National Calypso King contest and the newly inaugurated Panorama competition were taken over by Eric Williams and his People's National Movement (PNM) party. These events were promoted as celebrations of Trinidad heritage and national identity, as well as opportunities for tourism and commerce.[29] In an attempt to maintain the authenticity of the national art, rules were established limiting participants to singers who actually lived in Trinidad, thereby excluding calypsonians from other islands and returning expatriates.[30] Despite the state's efforts to control the calypso competition and to cast the music as a unifying force among all Trinidadians, many calypsonians, including multiple-crown winners Sparrow, Chalkdust, and Black Stalin, exercised their own agency by lampooning corrupt politicians and business leaders in their songs. Even the most heralded maintained their status as the voice of the Afro-Trinidadian working class. Exactly where Trinidad's East Asian population fit into the nationalist Carnival equation was not clear, and it was not until the establishment of a Chutney Soca Monarch competition in the mid-1990s that they became more visibly active in Carnival.[31]

The offspring of African-derived drumming and bamboo ensembles, the early steelbands were initially viewed as disruptive and dangerous, especially given their strong presence in the raucous predawn J'Ouvert gatherings. In the early postwar Carnivals, clashes between rival steelbands occasionally erupted into violence, reinforcing middle-class perceptions that pan players and their followers represented a disreputable element who posed a threat to orderly society. However, the working class and unemployed steelband men, who felt ignored and disparaged by the ruling and middle classes, demanded their right to the streets during Carnival as a means of displaying their culture and asserting their resistance to the colonial authorities.[32] Then, in the years leading up to independence, the newly constituted PNM sought to use steel pan as a unifying force, promoting it as a national cultural symbol and looking to steelbands for help in rallying support for their cause.[33] In 1963 the newly constituted government established an official Panorama competition, with significant prize money, in part to channel the steelband energy away from the chaotic streets into the more controllable environment of the official Savannah stage.[34] The move to control the steelbands and to promote the steel pan as the national instrument of Trinidad was partially successful. Violence gradually decreased, and as growing numbers of middle-class men and women took up the instrument, the steelband was re-envisioned as a respectable music practice. But as Stuempfle points out, there remained a degree of ambiguity regarding steelband as a signifier of class, national, and ethnic identity. The steel pan evoked "expressions of both national consensus and of grass-roots, street-based assertion and struggle."[35]

The spirit of resistance and struggles over class and ethnic identity would follow Trinidad Carnival musicians when they migrated to New York. As a large, public display of Caribbean migrant culture, Carnival provided a space for underlying community tensions to surface. Issues of neighborhood racial violence, community policing, gentrification, and strained relations with African Americans (in Harlem) and the Hasidic Jewish community (in Crown Heights, Brooklyn) came to the forefront during Carnival season. Regarding identity, Brooklyn's West Indian American Day Carnival Association (WIADCA) sought to use calypso and steel pan music to unite Brooklyn's diverse Caribbean constituents—of which Trinidadians were neither the only nor the largest group—under a single pan-Caribbean banner. The results were mixed, underscoring the difficulty in controlling Carnival and deploying its music in the service of specific political and cultural agendas.

Carnival Music as Diasporic Expression

Trinidad could not contain the Carnival to which it gave birth. Throughout the twentieth century, Trinidad-style Carnivals and music spread to other English-speaking Caribbean islands. Migrants from Trinidad and adjacent islands carried the celebration to diasporic communities in North America and Europe, where vibrant calypso and steelband scenes took hold. Given the transnational and transcultural history of the island and its music, it is not surprising that Port of Spain's Carnival would migrate and thrive in other culturally diverse metropoles where Caribbean migrants had established communities.

By some estimates there were, by the early 2000s, as many as sixty Trinidad-inspired urban Carnivals in the United States, Canada, and the United Kingdom.[36] Most exhibited significant similarities, drawing on the three principal Trinidad art forms of mas, calypso, and steelband music. A masquerade road-march parade was generally the centerpiece of a multiday festival that often included staged concerts of calypso, soca, reggae, and other Caribbean musics, as well as steelband and costume competitions. Diasporic Carnivals became political as well as cultural displays, affording marginalized migrant communities the opportunity to unite in their struggle for social justice and to negotiate the terms of integration into their new host societies. Moreover, there were economic considerations. As the larger diasporic Carnivals became more firmly institutionalized through state and private support, often under the guise of celebrating multiculturalism, they were increasingly perceived as tourist attractions capable of drawing huge crowds of Caribbean and non-Caribbean spectators.[37] Some were troubled by this drift away from cultural roots and resistance in migrant communities where Caribbean people were not always treated as equal citizens.

There was, however, one major structural difference between the larger overseas Carnivals and their Trinidadian parent. In Port of Spain, J'Ouvert and the daytime Carnival road marches were loosely organized, with mas bands, steelbands, and sound trucks proceeding across the city over multiple, circuitous routes toward the Savannah and downtown areas. In keeping with the Carnival spirit, revelers were not bound to official routes or time schedules, and the entire city embraced a "no business as usual" Carnival consciousness that presumed and tolerated a degree of public disorder.[38] In contrast, most diasporic Carnivals were forced to adhere to prescribed parade routes and strict timetables, given the participants' position as minority populations in large urban centers whose officials and residents generally showed little interest or support for their activities.

Restrictions on Carnival processions were often flashpoints of dispute between Carnival participants, event organizers, and the local police. The oldest and most esteemed of these overseas Carnivals are New York's Harlem and Brooklyn Labor Day celebrations, the subjects of this study. The two other most prominent celebrations are held in London's Notting Hill neighborhood and as part of Toronto's Caribana festival. During the postwar years, Notting Hill became home to London's burgeoning English-speaking Caribbean communities. In the mid-1950s, homesick Trinidadians began to hold indoor Carnival celebrations, which by the late 1960s had evolved into an annual outdoor festival held on the last weekend of August. The Notting Hill Carnival grew into a sprawling event centered on a masquerade parade fueled by steelbands and calypso/soca trucks. By the 1990s the London Carnival was attracting upward to a million and a half participants.[39]

The Notting Hill Carnival was marred, however, by violent clashes between police and the steelbands in 1976, and again in 1987 and 1988. Tensions between Trinidadian soca and Jamaica reggae crowds occasionally contributed to the discord.[40] Heated debates over what constituted "authentic" Carnival and Caribbean culture unfolded, with one side advocating for an orthodox Trinidad model, and the other for a broader multicultural festival. The former lobbied Carnival organizers for more resources for Trinidadian steelband and calypso, with the British Association of Steelbands calling for limitations on the size and power of mobile sound trucks as well as a "pan only" J'Ouvert event. The latter, which included the British Association of Sound Systems, pushed for a wider variety of musical offerings from around the Caribbean, including reggae, zouk, and salsa, as well as other "black" styles of world music.[41] Ironically, efforts by city officials to close down Carnival backfired by rallying the Trinidadians, Jamaicans, and other island groups to coalesce around a movement to save the event.[42] Carnival eventually became more institutionalized and multicultural as Latin American, Asian, and African migrants, along with white British youth, integrated into the mix. By the turn of the millennium, the Notting Hill celebration was being touted as Europe's largest outdoor ethnic festival, drawing crowds of over two million, and with an estimated economic impact of 93 million pounds.[43]

Toronto's Caribana Carnival, a two-week festival held in early August, began as a component of Canada's 1967 Centennial celebration meant to celebrate the city's multicultural diversity. In addition to multiple music performances, dances, island picnics, and boat cruises, a huge Parade of the Bands wound through downtown Toronto to City Hall, where masquerade bands competed for prize money. Unlike the neighborhood-based Carnivals in the United States and the United Kingdom, Caribana's parade proceeded down fashionable University Avenue past major government and corporate centers, reflecting widespread government, private, and media support of the event.[44] Caribana aimed to be pan-Caribbean, but rivalries between Trinidadian and non-Trinidadian (particularly Jamaican) factions plagued the administration of the event throughout the 1970s. As in Notting Hill, disputes flared over exactly which genres of music were representative of Caribbean culture in general, and of Carnival in particular. Predictably, Trinidad purists argued that musical performances should highlight calypso and steelband, while other factions pushed for the inclusion of reggae, dance hall, and even black American R&B and hip-hop.[45] These divisions aside, Caribana continued to grow, and by the early 2000s it was attracting audiences of over a million, with an estimated economic impact of $200 million for the two-week festival.[46]

Music has, and continues to be, central to the cultural and political dimensions of overseas Carnivals. As Tina Ramnarine concludes in her study of Notting Hill and Caribana, Caribbean music in the diaspora serves as a "medium for creative expression, empowerment, and political visibility," while also providing migrants an opportunity for "claiming major urban spaces as their own."[47] Debates over whose music was deemed an authentic representation of Caribbean culture (and whose was not), and how that music should be presented during public Carnival celebrations, exposed cultural cleavages among the various island groups—as well as attempts to bridge those divides.

Exactly how Carnival music and masquerading traditions became integral to these celebrations and interwoven into migrant cultural politics was site-specific. Although a thorough comparative history of the three major overseas Carnivals has yet to be written, Frank Manning's work provides a useful starting point for considering the respective roles that music and related art forms played in each of the big three overseas Carnivals. Based on his observations in the 1980s, Manning claimed that Caribana's mas costumes were the most elaborate and the mas bands were the driving force of the festival. In Notting Hill, he surmised, it was the steelbands that dominated by providing the primary structure for the outdoor parade and the first line of resistance against the police. In Brooklyn, calypso ruled, with international luminaries cycling in and out to perform and record throughout the year.[48]

While Manning's model is somewhat cursory and certainly dated, his latter observation regarding the dominance of calypso in New York provides a window into the ways in which Harlem and Brooklyn Carnivals, and particularly their musical expressions, stood apart from their competitors. Unlike Toronto or London, Harlem had a large native African American community as well as significant numbers of Afro-Latino and English-speaking Caribbean migrants prior to the arrival of calypso singers and musicians in the 1920s and the staging of the first outdoor Carnival in 1947. New York's black and Latino musicians had established an extensive network of clubs, dance halls, and theaters from which they launched their popular jazz, blues, ragtime, and Latin styles. From the 1920s on, the major New York–based record companies, including Victor, Columbia, and Decca, were eager to record a range of vernacular black and Latin genres. Predictably, New York emerged as a magnet for Caribbean musicians looking to expand their performing and recording horizons in the prewar years. In Harlem's dance halls and theater stages, and in midtown recording studios, early calypsonians and Trinidad dance bandleaders rubbed shoulders with native-born black Americans and native and foreign-born Latinos, absorbing new musical influences that would help shape the modern calypso style. Decades later, a similar process would unfold in Brooklyn studios, where elements of black American soul and funk would contribute to the emerging soca sound. New York's stature as a center of the entertainment and recording industries throughout much of the twentieth century set it apart from Toronto, and to a lesser extent from London, explaining in part why calypso (and later soca) assumed such a prominent position in Harlem and Brooklyn Carnivals.[49]

Beyond such comparative speculations, one thing we know for certain is that these Trinidad-inspired Carnivals formed a transnational network of calypsonians, musicians, steelband arrangers, masquerade designers, and avid fans who traversed the globe annually to perform, create, and play. The vitality of this overseas Carnival network underscores the critical role that diaspora has played in the process of cultural globalization. Caribbean communities in North America and Europe provided the fertile ground for the globalization of local cultural practices such as Trinidadian Carnival. Once arrived, Carnival served as a powerful symbol around which migrants could unite to celebrate a shared Caribbean identity and negotiate social and political relationships with their host society. In terms of globalization theory, the spread of overseas Carnivals challenges the adage that cultural production flows exclusively one way, "from the West to the rest," provoking the previously cited question by Nurse, "Who is globalizing whom?"[50] To address this query, we turn to the dance halls and streets of Harlem, where the first significant Trinidad-style Carnival outside the Caribbean was established.

Notes

1. A concise history of Trinidad's settlement is found in Errol Hill, *The Trinidad Carnival* (University of Texas Press, 1972; 2nd ed., New Beacon Books, 1997), pp. 6–15. A cultural history of Port of Spain is found in Stephen Stuempfle, *Port of Spain: The Construction of a Caribbean City, 1882–1962* (University of West Indies Press, 2018), pp. 10–15.

2. Hill, *Trinidad Carnival*, p. 21. Hill suggests that the transfer of Canboulay emancipation processions from August to the midnight Dimanche Gras opening of pre-Lenten Carnival took place as early as 1848. Hill, *Trinidad Carnival*, p. 30.

3. Useful studies of nineteenth- and early twentieth-century Trinidad Carnival include Andrew Pearse, "Carnival in Nineteenth Century Trinidad," *Caribbean Quarterly* 4, nos. 3–4 (March/June 1956): 175–193; Daniel Crowley, "The Traditional Masques of Carnival," *Caribbean Quarterly* 4, nos. 3–4 (March/June 1956): 194–223; Hill, *Trinidad Carnival*; John Cowley, *Carnival, Canboulay and Calypso: Traditions in the Making* (Cambridge University Press, 1996); and Hollis "Chalkdust" Liverpool, *Rituals of Power and Rebellion: The Carnival Tradition in Trinidad and Tobago* (Research Associates School Times, 2001).

4. Hollis Liverpool, "Origins of Rituals and Customs in the Trinidad Carnival: African or European?," *Drama Review* 42, no. 3 (Fall 1998): 37.

Liverpool lays out his critique of earlier Eurocentric interpretations of Trinidad Carnival in his "Preface," in *Rituals of Power and Rebellion*, pp. viii–xvii.

5. Richard Waterman, "African Influences on the Music of the Americas," in *Mother Wit from the Laughing Barrel: Readings in the Interpretation of African American Folklore*, edited by Alan Dundes (Prentice Hall, 1973), p. 85. Reprinted from Sol Tax, ed., *Acculturation in the Americas* (University of Chicago Press, 1952), pp. 207–218.

6. For further background on the process of musical creolization between African and European traditions in the Caribbean, see Peter Manuel, *Caribbean Currents: Caribbean Music from Rumba to Reggae* (Temple University Press, 1995), pp. 5–16. A thorough survey of creolized Afro-Euro vernacular music in the Caribbean is found in John Storm Roberts, *Black Music of Two Worlds*, 2nd ed. (Schirmer Books, 1997), pp. 101–156.

7. The term "calypso tent" dates back to the 1920s when temporary structures were erected from bamboo and coconut palms in the weeks before Port of Spain's Carnival. Their antecedents, Carnival band tents, housed masquerade bands along with the chantwells (accompanied by percussionists and string bands), who taught them songs for Carnival processions. Eventually, the temporary calypso tents were replaced by indoor venues, including theaters, auditoriums, and clubs. During a calypso tent show, multiple calypsonians would sing, one at a time, backed by a house band and a small chorus. An emcee introduced each singer to the audience. For the transformation of Carnival band tents into calypso tents, see Stuempfle, *Port of Spain*, pp. 205–208. For more on music in the tents, see Donald Hill, *Calypso Calaloo: Early Carnival Music in Trinidad* (University Press of Florida, 1993), pp. 64–85; and Cowley, *Carnival, Canboulay and Calypso*, pp. 134–227.

8. Among the best studies of the early history of calypso are Daniel Crowley, "Toward a Definition of Calypso (Part 1)," *Ethnomusicology* 3, no. 2 (May 1959): 55–66; Hill, *Trinidad Carnival*; Gordon Rohlehr, *Calypso and Society in Pre-Independence Trinidad* (Self Published, Port of Spain, Trinidad, 1990); Hill, *Calypso Calaloo*; and Jocelyn Guilbault, *Governing Sound: The Cultural Politics of Trinidad's Carnival Musics* (University of Chicago Press, 2007), pp. 21–38.

9. Gordon Rohlehr, *A Scuffling of Islands: Essays on Calypso* (Lexicon Trinidad Ltd., 2004), pp. 374–449.

10. The most complete account of the emergence of steelbands from drum and tamboo bamboo ensembles in Trinidad is found in Stephen Stuempfle, *The Steelband Movement: The Forging of a National Art in Trinidad and Tobago* (University of Pennsylvania Press, 1995), pp. 32–75.

11. Ibid., p. 44.

12. For a discussion of the emergence of complex Panorama arrangements and the responsible arrangers, see Shannon Dudley, *Music from Behind the Bridge: Steelband Spirit and Politics in Trinidad and Tobago* (Oxford University Press, 2008), 151–172.

13. Victor Turner, *From Ritual to Theatre* (New York: Performing Arts Journal Publications 1982), p. 48.

14. Thomas Turino, *Music as Social Life: The Politics of Participation* (University of Chicago Press, 2008), p. 43.

15. Ibid., p. 59.

16. Paul Gilroy, *The Black Atlantic: Modernity and Double Consciousness* (Harvard University Press, 1993), p. 200.

17. Turino, *Music as Social Life*, p. 26.

18. Ibid., p. 59.

19. The establishment and politics of Trinidad's National Calypso Competition is discussed in Guilbault, *Governing Sound*, pp. 70–74.

20. Dudley, *Music from Behind the Bridge*, p. 199. See Dudley's discussion of the rise of the Trinidad Panorama and its role in the transformation of steelband culture (pp. 137–150).

21. Earl Lovelace, "The Emancipation Jouvay Tradition and the Almost Loss of Pan," in *Carnival Culture in Action: The Trinidad Experience*, edited by Milla Cortez Riggio (Routledge, 2004), pp. 187–188.

22. See Donald Hill's discussion of the evolution of indoor tent calypso in relationship to outdoor *kalinda* and *lavways* in *Calypso Callallo*, pp. 5–6.

23. See Shannon Dudley's discussion of the musical gains and losses that Panorama has brought to the steelband movement in *Music from Behind the Bridge*, pp. 197–199.

24. Turino, *Music as Social Life*, pp. 26–27.

25. The history of pre–World War II calypso recordings is covered in Hill, *Calypso Callallo*, pp. 114–144.

26. Andrew Martin, *Steelpan Ambassadors: The US Navy Steel Band, 1957–1999* (University Press of Mississippi, 2017), p. 96.

27. Stuempfle, *Steelband Movement*, p. 169. See pp. 167–169 for a discussion of steelband recordings of the 1950s and 1960s. For a technical discussion of the problems inherent in recording steelbands, with their high shrill and low rumbling frequencies, see Martin, *Steelpan Ambassadors*, pp. 95–97.

28. For a discussion of clashes between Carnival revelers and the British authorities, see Pearse, "Carnival in Nineteenth Century Trinidad," pp. 187–189.

29. For a discussion of colonial officials and PMN leaders attempts to improve and control calypso, see Guilbault, *Governing Sound*, pp. 69–71.

30. Ibid., pp. 88–89.

31. Ibid., pp. 259–260.

32. For more on the violence surrounding the early steelbands and the complex relations between them and the authorities, see Stuempfle, *Steelband Movement*, pp. 60–68.

33. Ibid., pp. 116–124.

34. Dudley, *Music from Behind the Bridge*, pp. 137–150.

35. Stuempfle, *Steelband Movement*, p. 227.

36. Keith Nurse, "Globalization in Reverse: Diaspora and the Export of Trinidad Carnival," in *Carnival Culture in Action: The Trinidad Experience*, edited by Milla Cortez Riggio (Routledge, 2004), pp. 246–247.

37. For an overview of Trinidad-style Carnivals in the diaspora, see Frank Manning, "Overseas Caribbean Carnivals: The Art and Politics of a Transnational Celebration," *Plantation Society in the Americas* 3, no. 1 (1990): 47–62.

38. For a discussion of the spatial dimensions of Port of Spain's Carnival, see Stuempfle, *Port of Spain*, pp. 214–216.

39. Hill, *Trinidad Carnival* (1997), xxiii.

40. Manning, "Overseas Caribbean Carnivals," p. 58; Patricia Alleyne-Dettmers, "The Relocation of Trinidad Carnival in Notting Hill, London and the Politics of Diasporisation," in *Globalisation, Diaspora and Caribbean Popular Culture*, edited by Christine G.T. Ho and Keith Nurse (Ian Randle, 2005), p. 71.

41. Debates over which musics representing which cultures should be featured at the Notting Hill Carnival are reviewed in Tina Ramnarine, *Beautiful Cosmos: Performing and Belonging in the Caribbean Diaspora* (Pluto Press, 2007), pp. 185–190.

42. Alleyne-Dettmers, "Relocation of Trinidad Carnival," pp. 71–72.

43. Nurse, "Globalization in Reverse," p. 246.

44. Manning, "Overseas Caribbean Carnivals," p. 51.

45. Lyndon Phillip, "Reading Caribana 1997: Black Youth, Puff Daddy, Style and Diasporic Transformations," in *Trinidad Carnival: The Cultural Politics of a Transnational Festival*, edited by Garth Green and Philip Scher (Indiana University Press, 2007), pp. 111–118.

46. Nurse, "Globalization in Reverse," p. 246.

47. Ramnarine, *Beautiful Cosmos*, pp. 201–202.

48. Manning, "Overseas Caribbean Carnivals," pp. 50–58.

49. London did enjoy a robust calypso club and recording scene in the 1950s, thanks largely to the efforts of Lord Kitchener, who relocated there (and eventually to Manchester) between 1948 and 1962. Beginner, Invader, Lion, and other calypsonians followed Kitchener to the UK in the 1950s to perform and record. See Rohlehr, *Calypso and Society*, pp. 515–521. Impressive as the London 1950s calypso scene was, it could not rival that of New York in terms of overall scope and history.

50. Keith Nurse, "Globalization and the Trinidad Carnival: Diaspora, Hybridity, and Identity in Global Culture," *Cultural Studies* 13, no. 4 (1999): 683.

2

Harlem's Caribbean Dance Orchestras and Early Calypsonians

The British colonial government's decision to ban Trinidad's street Carnival during World War II did not dissuade Caribbean Harlemites from celebrating in their new home. Since the mid-1930s, the expatriate Trinidad bandleader Gerald Clark had been organizing dances to coincide with Carnival festivities back home. For the February 1942 celebration, Clark decided to move from Harlem's 138th Street Renaissance Casino to the larger Royal Windsor hall, centrally located on 66th Street, in order to accommodate the enormous crowd that was anticipated to attend the eighth annual event.[1] "[H]eretofore confined more or less to the local population of Harlem," the *New York Amsterdam News* reported, each year the dance was "attracting more and more Trinidad-enthused audiences from outside that sector who have been regaled by the native calypso music and dances which identify this event." Describing the dance as the "Mardi Gras of this Caribbean island," the preview promised "masks, costumes, painted bodies and all, and as such will be an authentic duplication of what goes on just at that time in the native land." Revelers would be treated to the sounds of Clark's Caribbean Serenaders and "native entertainers performing Rumbas, Congos, Spanish Valses and Pesos, and calypso contests."[2] A separate ad for the dance announced a "Battle of Calypsos" between the singers MacBeth the Great (Patrick MacDonald) and Wilmoth Houdini, as well as prize money for the most original and comical costumes.[3]

Clark's move from Harlem to the larger midtown venue was telling on several levels. On the one hand, it reflected the desires of New York's growing English-speaking Caribbean community for a more expansive Carnival celebration through an "authentic duplication" of Trinidadian music, dance, and masquerading. The move to the larger Royal Windsor venue was necessitated by community demand and foreshadowed the establishment, five years down the road, of an outdoor Carnival on a much grander scale. Clark's orchestra and his cadre of calypso singers, along with the soon-to-emerge Harlem steelbands, would play a vital role in these early New York Carnival celebrations.

On the other hand, the move to a centrally located midtown venue signaled Clark's desire to bring together the two main constituencies he had been courting in recent years: his native uptown Caribbean population, which was steeped in Carnival music, and the downtown, predominantly white, "Trinidad-enthused audiences from outside that sector," which had lately discovered calypso through Clark's recordings and highly publicized Greenwich Village club dates. Harlem's Carnival celebrations would remain primarily Afro-Caribbean events, but the dance orchestras, calypsonians, and steelband players who provided the music were constantly seeking to broaden their audiences by crossing over into new cultural arenas. Indeed, the rise of Harlem's Carnival parade coincided with an upsurge in interest in calypso music by non-Caribbean white and black Americans that culminated in the national "calypso craze" of the 1950s. As we will see, from the 1930s through the early 1960s, New York's Anglophile-Caribbean musicians and their promoters sought to foster several distinct market audiences, including the city's expanding Caribbean populace and their African American and Latino neighbors in Harlem; the downtown, non-Caribbean club and concertgoers; and Caribbean listeners back in the islands who might purchase their records.

In terms of broader cultural goals, Clark's midtown dances reflected the dual agencies that scholars have attributed to overseas Carnival activities: to tighten the bonds among Caribbean migrants through the celebration of shared Carnival cultural expressions, and to encourage cross-cultural dialogue that could foster resistance to or promote integration with their host society.[4] Regarding the latter, music and dance might build bridges between the recently arrived islanders and their African American neighbors in Harlem, while offering opportunities to connect with downtown progressive white audiences. Clark and his calypsonians moved fluidly between these worlds, both contesting and reinforcing conventional racial norms at a time when New York was struggling to come to grips with its increasingly diverse population stemming from waves of World War II internal migration and postwar relocation of Puerto Rican citizens and immigration from abroad. The story of Harlem Carnival and its music was destined to become part of the broader narrative of New York's rise to prominence as a global city and as a Caribbean crossroads in the second half of the twentieth century.

Using Clark's dance orchestra and calypsonians as points of departure, this chapter and the next aim to widen the parameters of Harlem Carnival by exploring new realms of cultural performance that have been underrepresented in previous scholarship. First, attention is turned to the host of Caribbean-themed dances and calypso performances that were popular in Harlem's clubs and dance halls from the mid-1930s through the 1950s, and to the calypso shows that proliferated in midtown concert halls and downtown clubs during this period. The following chapter will focus specifically on Clark's pre-Lenten Dame Lorraine Galas and the outdoor

Carnival parades that occupied the streets of Harlem every Labor Day from 1947 through the early 1960s.

Gerald Clark and the Early Dance Orchestras

Gerald Clark was not the first Trinidadian musician to perform Carnival music in New York. That honor would go to the bandleader and violinist George "Lovey" Bailey, who in 1912 brought his twelve-piece string orchestra to New York to tour and record for the Victor and Columbia record companies. The group, comprising string and wind instruments, played a variety of dance genres popular in the southern Caribbean and Latin America, including paseos (duple-meter instrumental arrangements of early calypso and related Carnival songs), vals (triple-meter waltzes), and tangos. Their style was heavily influenced by the string band tradition that had been imported into Trinidad from Venezuela and become popular around the Caribbean by the turn of the twentieth century. Melodic themes were generally played in unison on violin, flute, and clarinet, often followed by clarinet and flute counterpoint lines, all over a strumming rhythm section of guitars, cuatros, string bass, and piano. Lovey played for elite dances and Carnival masquerade balls in Trinidad, but little is known of his orchestra's activities in the United States before they returned home following their recording sessions.[5]

The classically trained pianist and bandleader Lionel Belasco (1882–1967) took a different path. He migrated from Port of Spain to New York in the 1910s and made the city his base of operations for the rest of his career. Belasco was a true transnational. The son of a Trinidadian Creole mother and a Sephardic Jewish father, he was born in Barbados, grew up in Trinidad and Venezuela, migrated to Harlem as an adult, and traveled regularly between New York, the Caribbean, and Europe as a professional musician. Belasco engaged in multiple musical activities. He performed as a soloist and cut piano rolls; accompanied the Guyanese vaudeville singer Phil Madison, concert vocalist Massie Patterson, and calypsonian Wilmoth Houdini; copyrighted dozens of calypso melodies; and directed numerous ensembles that recorded Caribbean- and Venezuelan-style dance music in the 1920s and early 1930s. He returned regularly to Trinidad during that period, where he served as a judge for Carnival events and picked up the latest songs, which he brought back to New York to rearrange and record. For more than a decade Belasco was most the influential proponent of Trinidadian music in the United States.[6]

Other New York–based Caribbean orchestras, most notably ensembles led by St. Vincent–born pianist Walter Merrick and Trinidadian violinist Cyril Monrose, played dance repertoires of paseos and vals in the 1920s.[7] The Victor Record Company, which made the first recordings of Merrick's and Monrose's groups, actively sought to expand its sales beyond the Caribbean to include the burgeoning US immigrant communities, as evidenced by their 1923 advertisement for Monrose's Orchestra and vocalist Phil Madison:

> The steady increase of the West Indian population along the eastern seaports of the United States has stimulated the interest for West Indian records issued by the Victor Company. Phil Madison, one of the favorite singers in the West Indies, is giving a few numbers to the accompaniment of the piano and ukulele and the Monrose's Orchestra appears with instrumental selections which are sure to be welcomed by West Indians in this country.[8]

In 1927 Belasco's orchestra backed the Trinidadian calypsonian Wilmoth Houdini on a track titled "Good-Night Ladies and Gentlemen." The guitarist for the session was Gerald Clark, a recently arrived Trinidad migrant who would form his own band, the Night Owls, in the early 1930s. The small ensemble played dance music similar to that of the Bailey, Belasco, and Merrick orchestras and accompanied calypsonians, mainly in recording sessions. In addition to himself on guitar, his studio groups included clarinet, violin, cuatro, string bass, and piano, as well as the occasional trumpet and banjo. Based on the recordings Clark made for Varsity (1931) and Bluebird (1933), the Night Owls' repertoire included rumbas, foxtrots, paseos, and waltzes. "Carmelita" (1933), for example, is a typical Caribbean instrumental dance waltz. Clark's arrangement foregrounds clarinet, violin, and trumpet harmonizing throughout an AA/BB/CC thematic structure and straightforward waltz meter.[9] "Cocotte Medley" (1933), a lilting, duple-meter dance paseo, opens with a bouncy clarinet-violin-trumpet theme over a syncopated habanera rhythm. Following a bridge that modulates to a new key and tune, the clarinet and trumpet alternate embellished themes followed by two final choruses of interweaving clarinet, trumpet, and violin lines.[10] Another dance paseo, "Susan Medley" (1933), features a minor-tinged, syncopated melodic line carried by the clarinet and a stop-time section with the clarinet, trumpet, and violin trading riffs with the piano and string bass. The two final choruses swing to a polyphonic mix of wailing clarinet, trumpet, and violin over a habanera bass line.[11]

Both paseos reveal Clark's familiarity with popular jazz and Tin Pan Alley styles of the day, along with his willingness to blend American musical idioms with his Caribbean dance rhythms. This was not surprising, for the backing arrangements Clark and his bandmates employed on Houdini's earlier recordings suggest they had absorbed the syncopated rhythms, polyphonic texture, and bluesy tonalities of early African American jazz. For example, the Night Owls' 1931 Brunswick recording "Stop Coming and Come" features clarinet and trumpet trading ornamented solos in between Houdini's verses, then weaving together on the final refrain over a chunking rhythm section of banjo, guitar, and string bass in the swinging style of a New Orleans jazz band.[12] At least one of the musicians on the recordings, the bassist Al Morgan, was identified as being from New Orleans. The jazz critic Eugene Williams commented that Clark's Night Owls "play with a spirit and swing which could serve a model for many American jazz bands."[13] Clark's Night Owls were not the first Caribbean band to employ jazz-influenced arrangements for their vocal accompaniments. Trinidad-born stage entertainer Sam Manning, whose repertoire ranged from calypsos to vaudeville songs and blues, recorded with small New Orleans–style jazz ensembles in the late 1920s and early 1930s.[14]

In 1934 Clark changed the group's name to the Caribbean Serenaders. He continued to record with Houdini and other calypsonians while expanding his small studio group for Caribbean dance dates. He soon landed a regular Sunday afternoon radio show on station WHN, bringing the sounds of Trinidadian Carnival music to New York's airways on a weekly basis. Clark would go on to become the top promoter of Caribbean dance and calypso in the 1930s and 1940s, producing dances, helping to arrange recordings for calypsonians and supplying their back-up band, and working as an agent for Decca Records.[15] Discographic research suggests that Clark and some iteration of his ensemble played for a majority of calypso recordings made in the United States before World War II.[16] He occasionally returned to Trinidad to seek out fresh calypso talent, and in 1934 he worked with the businessman Edward Sa Gomes, in conjunction with Decca and ARC records, to bring the calypsonians Atilla the Hun (Raymond Quevedo) and Roaring Lion (Rafael de Leon) to New York to perform and record.[17] In 1937 the *Trinidad Guardian* reported that Clark had returned home for a few months and would be featured in a series of shows.[18] While it is doubtful that he could have afforded to bring his entire ensemble to perform with him in Trinidad, one notice advertised Gerald Clark and his "Famous New York Orchestra" headlining a vaudeville show at Port of Spain's Empire Theater in mid-August of that year.[19]

Although no recordings of the larger dance ensemble are known to exist, Clark did extensive work with a five- to six-piece studio aggregation of the Serenaders. For the calypso singers the group provided light accompaniment. The clarinet, the violin, and an occasional trumpet contributed introductions, codas, and eight- or sixteen-bar thematic interludes in between the verses of the vocalist. The popular calypsos "Edward the VIII," sung by Caresser (1937, Decca Records), and "Walter Winchell," sung by the Duke of Iron (1939, Varsity Records), are exemplary.[20] The clarinet parts often featured embellishments of standard themes but generally stopped short of more complex melodic improvisation. However, a number of Clark's musicians were well versed in jazz techniques, particularly the Puerto Rican clarinetist Gregory Felix, whose vibrato and rhythmic sensibilities have been compared to those of iconic jazz clarinetist Sidney Bechet.[21]

Reviewing Clark's Varsity and Decca releases, Gama Gilbert of the *New York Times* noted that between vocals "the refrain is generally taken up by a solo instrument, which proceeds from a mere statement of the tune to ornamentation by trills and turns and finally variation on the harmony—call it swing if you like."[22] In live performance the soloist was no doubt given more freedom, as a *New York Sun* reviewer observed at a show at the Village Vanguard: "If you listen closely, you can hear a kind of swing improvisation on the tunes during the pauses of the singers, especially from the clarinet player, who is a kind of secondary soloist."[23] The *Baltimore Afro-American* reported, "It is in the singer's pauses that some rare swinging improvisations pour forth—the pianist and clarinetist are almost 'taken out of themselves' as they lend themselves to the gay abandon of this rhumba-like swing."[24] Although the clarinetist was not named in the review, it was most likely Felix, who played regularly with Clark at the Vanguard gigs in addition to leading his own ensemble, Felix and his Krazy Kats.

Nearly all the prewar calypso recordings were made in New York or by New York–based companies that sent recording teams to Trinidad. In New York studios the sounds of jazz, blues, ragtime, and Tin Pan Alley began to seep into the accompaniments of Clark's and Felix's orchestras, thereby reshaping the traditional calypso sound. These early New York recordings unquestionably contributed to the transition of calypso accompaniments from the older, Venezuelan string-band style to the modern jazz-inflected arrangements that featured more elaborate instrumental lines and gave prominence to reed and brass voicings.[25] When visiting calypsonians came to the city to record, Clark would arrange engagements that opened up new markets for the performers and their recordings. Such musical and economic connections between Trinidad and New York were vital to the development and growth of early calypso music. While certainly Trinidadian in origin, calypso's evolution in the prewar years was indelibly shaped in a transnational milieu.

Clark's larger Serenaders dance orchestra was reported to consist of eleven to twelve musicians plus a singer.[26] Based on the instrumentation of the small studio bands, we can surmise that the dance orchestra consisted of a basic rhythm section of guitar, cuatro, piano, string bass, and drums, as well as some combination of clarinets, violins, and trumpets. His uses of multiple brass and reeds in the dance band are uncertain, given the absence of large ensemble recordings and surviving scores. But we know that by the late 1930s Trinidad-based dance ensembles such as the Harmony Kings and Codallo's Top Hatters Orchestra were employing larger reed and brass sections, at times in simple call-and-response voicings, to emulate an American big band sound.[27] There is little reason to doubt that Clark and his Serenaders would have followed suit in live dance settings.

The Serenaders' repertoire was broad, including calypso-based paseos and vals and various Latin genres, as described by a 1934 *Variety* reporter who heard Clark's radio show: "[The Serenaders] specialize in the odd broken rhythms of Cuba and Latin countries. It's 100% rumba-tango-son-foxtrot-paseo stuff."[28] Those "odd broken rhythms" no doubt referred to the syncopated bass lines (most often some variation of a basic habanera rhythm) laid down by the string bass and the piano's left hand. These bass figures, when combined with the strumming guitar, right-hand piano ostinato patterns, and syncopated melodic lines on the clarinet and violin, created a lilting, buoyant pulse ideal for dancing. The lack of percussion—a hallmark of much Latin music—on any of Clark's recordings or club dates with his small groups is somewhat curious. Much of his work was accompanying calypsonians whose vocals required only elementary instrumental accompaniment, and financial concerns probably figured in his preference for smaller ensembles. The one live recording of a 1946 Town Hall concert provides our only hint at what his expanded dance ensemble might have sounded like. On the instrumental paseo "I'm a Better Woman Than You," two hand drums and prominent maracas create a thick rhythmic texture absent on the studio recordings but common to much Latin dance music.[29]

Regardless of the instrumentation, by all accounts the Serenaders were known for their Latin-tinged dance pieces in addition to their mainstay of calypsos. This was a prudent strategy, for as the 1930s unfolded, Latin music was becoming increasingly popular in Harlem dance halls. Orchestras led by the Afro-Cuban flutist Alberto Socarras and Puerto Rican trumpeter Augusto Coen played black American swing and a variety of Latin styles ranging from Cuban boleros, guararchas, and sones to Puerto Rican danzas and plenas. Many bands also included rumbas and tangos in their repertories.[30] Indeed the generic term "Latin" was somewhat amorphous at that time, often serving as a catch-all designation for any music from the Caribbean or South America. The culture critic Floyd Calvin, writing in the *Afro-American* in 1936, marveled at the cornucopia of musics played by Harlem's "Latins of color," including songs and dances from Cuba, Jamaica, the Virgin Islands, Trinidad, and the South American pampas (no doubt a reference to Argentina and Venezuela).[31]

Trinidadian migrants themselves were already familiar with tangos, rumbas, and other Latin dance styles that had become popular in Port of Spain and other Caribbean port cities. Sharing the Rockland Palace stage in Harlem in January 1935 with Fletcher Henderson's renowned swing orchestra, the Serenaders were billed as a Latin band known for "the tunes that radiate with 'a touch of sunny Spain'—'a glimpse of gay Madrid,' and the spices of the blue Caribbean."[32] *La Asociacion Venezolana Pro-Patria* hired "El Metro Gerald Clarke con sus Caribbean Serenaders" for "Una Noche de Carnival en Caracas" at the Hotel Seville on Madison Avenue and 29th Street.[33] Moreover, a number of Clark's regular band members were of Latin descent, including the clarinetist Gregory Felix from Puerto Rico, violinist Victor Pacheco from Cuba, and bass player Rogelio Garcia. Clark shrewdly advertised his group as the Caribbean Serenaders, not the Trinidadian Serenaders, and boasted a broad repertoire suitable for Harlem's diverse English- and Spanish-speaking black populace, nearly a quarter of whom were, by the 1920s, estimated to be Afro-Caribbean by birth or parentage.[34] From a broader global perspective, the Serenaders were typical of vernacular dance orchestras throughout the Spanish-, French-, and English-speaking Caribbean who mixed wide-ranging local styles—paseos, rumbas, sones, tangos, mentos, and so forth—with syncopated American jazz. In her study of Caribbean musical migration, Lara Putnam reminds us that these "sometimes-paid players and (their) dance-loving fans brought musical repertories with them as they traveled from island to island or shore to shore (including migrations north to New Orleans and Harlem)."[35]

Autoexoticizing at the Village Vanguard

Clark's career surged, and the trajectory of calypso in New York took an unexpected turn in 1939. After hearing a recording by the Caribbean Serenaders, Village Vanguard owner Max Gordon contacted Clark and booked him for his popular Greenwich Village café. Gordon had a long-standing interest in jazz and folk music and was one of the first promoters to introduce downtown audiences to noted black artists, ranging from jazz legends Sidney Bechet and Mary Lou Williams to blues icons Lead Belly and Josh White.[36] Clark opened in August of that year with a five-piece group backing two calypsonians and a floor show that featured a Caribbean dance review led by Billy "Calypso Kid" Matons.[37] Over the next two years, Clark's shows would feature the New York–based calypsonians Duke of Iron, MacBeth the Great, and Sir Lancelot, as well as the leading Trinidad-based singers Lord Invader and Caresser, who visited the city to record with him. Clark and his singers and dancers received rave reviews from the mainstream press and became a fixture at the Vanguard for several years, bringing calypso songs to young, po-litically sophisticated downtown audiences. According to New York *Sun* reporter Malcolm Johnson, the Vanguard crowd responded to the music's "romance, satire, naiveté, irony, man-of-the-street philosophy and humor, and pointed, discerning comment on current events and public figures."[38]

Clark's performances at the Vanguard were notably different from those in Harlem dance halls. In the latter, the Serenaders were a dance or-chestra that occasionally backed calypsonians. They played for Caribbean and black American audiences, boasting a broad repertoire that included Latin and American instrumental pieces as well as calypsos. But down-town they were a stage band for seated, predominantly white listeners, providing backup for calypsonians and Matons's dance review. Whether or not the calypsonians sang the same songs as they would for their up-town Caribbean audiences is uncertain, but calypsos with American themes ranging from President Roosevelt and Walter Winchell to Bing Crosby and J. Edgar Hoover were reported as favorites with the down-town crowd.[39] Ironically, it was the downtown club scene, with its pro-gressive white patrons, rather than the uptown dance halls frequented by Caribbean migrants, that afforded Clark's calypsonians their best op-portunity to showcase their vocal and poetic skills in an intimate setting reminiscent of the calypso tents of Port of Spain.[40] Singers and musicians moved comfortably between these downtown presentational and uptown participatory performance settings, modifying their shows to suit the needs of their varied audiences.

The attraction that Trinidadian calypso held for the white Village audiences underscores the complex and often contradictory cultural politics of social boundary crossing in the heterogeneous, modern metropolis. The fact that the calypsonians sang in English, albeit sometimes with a heavy island accent, made the music more accessible to North American audiences than similar song forms from Cuba, Puerto Rico, and other areas of Latin America. Moreover, the calypsonians' penchant for engaging in social commentary and political satire was no doubt appealing to left-leaning listeners. But there were other factors. Calypso's allure to non-Caribbean spectators was, in part, an extension of a white fascination with early jazz, classic blues, Latin dance styles, and other related genres of black urban music that had been percolating since the 1920s. The folk music revival, inaugurated by Lead Belly's arrival in New York in 1935, spurred further curiosity about African American roots music.

While many whites experienced a genuine aesthetic connection to such vernacular styles—a number became active performers of jazz, blues, and so forth—there is little doubt that their propensity to exoticize black artists and romanticize their culture was part of the equation. During the 1920s, "nightly thousands of white visitors . . . made their way to Harlem," recounted Jervis Anderson. Based on his reading of white newspaper and literary accounts of the scene, Anderson surmised, "There they enjoyed its 'hot' and 'barbaric' jazz, the risqué lyrics and 'junglelike' dancing of its cabaret floor shows, and its other 'wicked' delights."[41] "In Jazz Age New York," theorized Fiona I. B. Ngô, "exotic tropes of empire had captured the imaginations of the city denizens." Regarding Caribbean and the South Seas cultures, "[n]ightclubs featured performances and décor inspired by idyllic dreams of island paradises," thereby serving as symbolic extensions of colonial subjectivity in the domestic realm.[42] During the late 1930s, John Lomax promoted Lead Belly to white urban audiences as an authentic folk primitive who was "sensual as a goat" and who sang "raw folk songs." A publicity picture of the singer in overalls, perched on cotton sacks, was used to emphasize his rural roots.[43]

The above-cited *Sun* review that characterized calypso as "naïve" hints at the patronizing descriptive language that was common in mainstream press accounts of the music. Richard Manson of the *New York Post* commented on the "charming and wacky" accents of the Vanguard Calypsonians, adding that their lyrics "are simple enough and the emotions expressed are as elementary as the facts of life."[44] More explicit was the aforementioned *Times* review of Clark's calypso recordings, where Gilbert characterized the music and lyrics as "childishly naïve" and haughtily suggested that the singers' "dislocation of accents, together with the grammatical primitiveness and the voices innocent of cultivation, make a combination that is often hilarious."[45] Another *Times* reviewer, Meyer Berger, offered the following description of a performance by MacBeth at a 1940 Vanguard show:

A saddle-colored little Negro moved out of the dark beyond the orange spot. He wore rose-colored silk zouave pantaloons, black silk blouse, green-striped turban with a tuft of rose feathers. . . . The orchestra lightly sketched in cut-time music—thumping, voo-doo stuff. The little Negro lifted the gourds. He beat out the time with them, closed his eyes. He jerked at the knees and his head rolled the rhythm. His voice was nasal and thin.[46]

Portraying MacBeth as diminutive, flamboyantly effeminate, naturally rhythmic, and prone to "voo-doo" possession underscored a primitive otherness that clearly held appeal for Berger and, presumably, his fellow club-goers and sophisticated readers. His remarks reflect a broader set of cultural assumptions that had gained credence at the time. During the interwar years the cult of the primitive had emerged as a vital component of modernism, with disturbing implications, as Ngô has observed: "Primitivism produced a discourse about the racial other through a double bind of idealization and denigration. In either case the racial other must stay in its place."[47]

Clark's staged Vanguard shows for white audiences were completely detached from street Carnival or his pre-Lenten Dame Lorraine celebrations and were no doubt consumed, at least in part, as exotic spectacle. This raises the troubling specter that such performances simply validated essentialist stereotypes and cast dark-skinned Caribbean islanders as the racial Other. While acknowledging these concerns, to dismiss such biracial encounters as inherently disingenuous and exploitative elides the complex and often ambiguous nature of cultural exchange in the arena of music and dance. MacBeth's attire and behavior exemplified trends to market Caribbean Carnival to North American tourists and club patrons as a grand spectacle of colorful masquerading, rhythmic music, and erotic dancing—the great tropical bacchanal fraught with the temptation and fantasies of the unknown. Calypsonians and their promoters understood this, with the former often willing to dress in stereotypic tropical regalia and engage in suggestive stage theatrics to meet audience expectations and garner more generous wages and tips. Indeed, this sort of self-conscious autoexoticizing marked many forms of performance aimed at tourists throughout the Caribbean and in the diaspora. In such instances, minority cultural actors sought to reappropriate exotic stereotypes, thereby creating situations in which "the exoticism is taken over by the exoticized other, reproduced, and employed for the people of that other and to their own benefit."[48]

At the Vanguard such autoexoticizing was apparently at play, as MacBeth and other calypsonians sought control over the process of cultural representation and aimed to turn it to their own advantage. Personal agency was a factor—while MacBeth chose to dress in garish tropical garb, Clark and his musicians, as well as the calypsonian Sir Lancelot, presented themselves as formal artists attired in a tuxedo and white dinner jackets (see Figure 2.1). The Vanguard's audiences were left to

Figure 2.1. Gerald Clark Orchestra, circa 1940 (MacBeth on far left, Lancelot in the middle in a tuxedo, Clark on far right with a aguitar) (courtesy of Ray Funk).

ponder a conundrum: Were they viewing wild exotics, costumed professional entertainers, or both?

Despite the obvious unequal power dynamic between black artists and white promoters, Clark's and Gordon's Vanguard shows did provide a space for bicultural social interaction, while also affording at least some income and exposure for musicians and singers with limited employment options. The black press measured Clark's downtown success as cultural validation across the divides of race and class, boasting that thanks to his prestigious Village Vanguard appearances, "the first families of Fifth and Park Avenues rave about calypso tunes."[49] Clark was clearly proud of his Vanguard performances, devoting more than two-thirds of his personal scrapbook collection to clippings of his downtown shows.[50] He and his calypsonians saw themselves first and foremost as professional stage entertainers who needed to open up new markets for their wares. Serving as cultural ambassadors in a segregated society and an entertainment world still littered with the remnants of minstrelsy was a tricky business that yielded mixed results at best. Their initial crossover forays foreshadowed the conundrum that future Caribbean musicians would face—how to broaden their markets in order to earn a viable living while maintaining artistic integrity and allegiance to heritage. Equally challenging was trying to accomplish such economic and artistic ends without perpetuating exotic and racialized stereotypes.

Taking a broader view, we can ask what, if any, challenge New York's Carnival dance orchestras and calypsonians presented to conventional Western music sensibilities and social order during the period leading up to decolonization in the Caribbean and Africa. Conversely, we might question to what extent they supported colonial musical norms and, by extension, the larger hegemony of the colonial project under which Clark and the early calypsonians had grown up.[51] The answers to these questions are not straightforward, for, as Stuart Hall has noted, hegemony is often incomplete and contested in the arena of popular culture.[52] On the one hand, the embrace of Western fixed-pitch instruments and thematic and verse/chorus closed forms—initially in Trinidad and around the Caribbean, then later in Harlem—suggested a capitulation to colonial standards of musical propriety. Moreover, the growth in popularity of Carnival music among New York's white audiences was in part anchored to a logic of domestic imperialism. That is, cosmopolitan club-goers presumed a priori that the recently arrived natives from the tropical hinterlands could provide them with exotic musical entertainment. Yet those same natives had to be controlled and contained as they had been under colonial rule, due in part to what the *Times* characterized as their "primitiveness" and "innocence of cultivation"—ironically the very features of their music that downtown listeners found so alluring.[53]

On the other hand, the emphasis on "broken" (syncopated) rhythms, rough instrumental and vocal timbres, and aural arrangements marked by flights of improvisation produced sounds that defied the conventions of the European military and marching bands from which the dance ensembles had evolved. Panning out to a wider global and deeper historical perspective, we now recognize that the groups led by Belasco, Merrick, Clark, Felix, and the New York calypsonians belonged to a large cohort of vernacular dance bands and songsters whose music was captured on disc in port cities around the world soon after the advent of electronic recordings in the mid-1920s. As Michael Denning has argued, the "noisy" sounds of these ensembles circulated the globe on shellac records, challenging "not only the musical codes of empire and racial supremacy, but also the improving and uplifting ideologies of many colonial elites." Denning viewed these groups as part of a far-reaching cultural revolution between the world wars involving native and hybrid forms of working-class music-making that portended a "decolonization of the ear" around the world, eventually coming "to figure the utopian promise of decolonization itself."[54] The 1927 New York recordings by Houdini and Clark, along with the 1934 recordings by Atilla the Hun and Clark, were among the musical examples Denning cited.[55] Atilla traveled sporadically to New York to record, while Houdini was one of a cadre of Trinidad singers to settle there and the first to establish a beachhead for calypso in Harlem.

The New York Calypsonians

By 1941 Clark was receiving accolades from the *Amsterdam News* as the "orchestra leader who has done more than any other man to popularize calypso music." The article announced with some pomp that four "outstanding exponents" of calypso were currently residing in New York: Houdini (Frederick Wilmoth Hendricks), the Duke of Iron (Cecil Anderson), MacBeth the Great (Patrick MacDonald), and Sir Lancelot (Lancelot Pinard).[56] Of these, Wilmoth Houdini (1895–1977) was the most well known. Born in Trinidad, he played in a Port of Spain Carnival mas band and sang in the city's calypso tents as a young man before taking a job as a seaman and eventually migrating to New York. There he made his first recordings in 1927 with a band that included Lionel Belasco and Gerald Clark. Over the next decade he established himself as Harlem's leading calypsonian, playing at parties and dances, and recording more than a hundred sides with bands led by Clark and Felix in addition to his own ensemble.[57] A gifted wordsmith, Houdini tackled complex issues in songs such as "African Love Call" (1934), in which he expressed his gratitude toward the United States while pledging allegiance to Marcus Garvey's philosophy of Pan-Africanism.[58]

Like Clark and Belasco, Houdini returned to Trinidad occasionally in search of new material and to "renew me inspiration" as he told the *New Yorker* writer Joseph Mitchell in 1939.[59] In 1939 and 1940, Decca Records released album collections of his songs that featured local New York topics such as Roosevelt's visit to the 1939 World's Fair and a celebration of Harlem's nightlife. The album *Harlem Seen through Calypso Eyes* (1940) included "Good Old Harlem Town," a song chronicling a late-night romp through the neighborhood's hottest night spots, including the Golden Gate Ballroom, the Savoy, and Smalls Paradise. In "Harlem Night Life," Houdini described a boisterous gathering where partygoers danced to the latest rumba and boogie rhythms while enjoying southern-style pigs' feet and chitlins. But the revelers failed to sing, he lamented, any Caribbean songs like "Dingolay" or "Glory Day." Houdini added portions of both traditional songs in between his colorful accounts of the party, thereby acknowledging and mediating the tensions between Harlem's African American and Caribbean residents.[60]

Following the immensely successful Ella Fitzgerald and Louis Armstrong cover of his song "He Had It Coming" ("Stone Cold Dead in the Market") in 1945, Houdini enjoyed a flash of notoriety that led to appearances in the midtown venues Carnegie Hall and Town Hall in 1946 and 1947, and to his own production of a Carnival extravaganza in the Golden Gate Ballroom in February 1947. He disappeared from the scene by the late 1940s, supplanted by a new generation of modern singers. Houdini's contributions to the New York calypso scene were immense, leading the calypso historian Donald Hill to dub him "the first true calypsonian to record extensively and popularize the genre outside Trinidad."[61]

While Houdini could boast genuine roots in Port of Spain's calypso tents, a number of Clark's Vanguard calypsonians began their singing careers in New York and had little direct contact with Trinidad Carnival. Cecil Anderson (1906–1968), with the stage sobriquet the "Duke of Iron," was born in Trinidad and migrated to New York with his family in 1923. He began singing in the 1930s with his own small band around Harlem and made several recordings with Gregory Felix's Krazy Kats and Clark's Caribbean Serenaders in the late 1930s. Then, in 1939, he joined Clark's Village Vanguard calypso review. He would go on to appear in calypso shows at Carnegie Hall, Town Hall, and the Brooklyn Academy of Music, and occasionally at folk festivals and on Oscar Brand's folk music radio show.[62] Like Houdini, Anderson began to write and sing calypsos that would appeal to American audiences. "Walter Winchell" (1939) was a satirical poke at America's most famous gossip columnist of the era. "USA" (1939) sounded a tribute to his new home in America, boasting the patriotic introductory verse, "I am happy just to be / In this sweet land of liberty," and a chorus proclaiming, "Now where can you roam when you ain't got a home? / USA / Oh where can you flee to a land that is free? / USA."[63] In 1945 he released "Calypso Invasion," a song recounting in no modest terms his own success in New York, while warning other calypsonians to consult with him regarding a "tough situation" or risk "ruination."[64]

The Trinidadian-born Lancelot Pinard (1902–2001) arrived in New York sometime in the 1920s with plans to study medicine, but he pivoted to a career in music after hearing the renowned African American concert singer Roland Hayes. He had never sung calypso as a youngster, instead taking formal voice lessons at his exclusive parochial school in Cumuto. Pinard sang in a clear, high tenor voice that so impressed Gerald Clark that he invited him to consider trying his hand at calypso singing. Pinard agreed, making his debut as a calypsonian in 1940 at Clark's Village Vanguard show, and eventually recording a number of songs with the Caribbean Serenaders on the Varsity and Keynote labels. He worked in and out of New York throughout the 1940s, playing for Harlem and downtown audiences as a featured singer in Clark's orchestra while occasionally writing New York–themed calypsos such as "A Walk in Central Park." During this time he also became involved in New York's folk music revival, joining Pete Seeger's left-leaning People's Songs organization and appearing with Clark at their benefit concerts. Proclaiming camaraderie with Seeger's folk-singing activists, in 1948 Pinard contributed a letter to the People's Songs Bulletin in which he pronounced, "Calypso Singers are true people's artists, and calypsos, like people's songs, come straight from the heart of the people."[65] He supported the 1948 Henry Wallace presidential campaign, having previously composed a calypso rendition of the then vice president's famous 1942 "Century of the Common Man" speech and recording it with Clark's Serenaders.[66] Pinard's precise vocal articulation and clean timbre—his ability to "enunciate each word clearly and distinctly," as one reviser observed—made him a favorite with non-Caribbean listeners.[67] He went on to enjoy a lucrative career in radio, film, and television, eventually settling in California.[68]

While Sir Lancelot traversed the United States and Europe in the years after he arrived in New York, Patrick "MacBeth the Great" MacDonald (1905–1957) stayed closer to home, establishing himself as one of Harlem's most popular calypso singers and bandleaders in the 1940s and 1950s. He arrived from Trinidad in 1928 and began his career as a calypso singer in the mid-1930s, eventually joining Clark's Village Vanguard show in 1940. According to a reporter from the *Afro-American*, MacBeth's gaudy dress and stage theatrics "[stole] the show," providing a sharp counterpoint to Sir Lancelot, who dressed immaculately in a white dinner jacket and spoke in a "British clipped manner."[69] MacBeth recorded for Varsity Records with Clark and became his favored vocalist at Harlem dances and midtown concerts until he split off and formed his own dance orchestra in 1947. MacBeth the Great and His Creole Rhythm Boys, as he often billed his band, were in strong demand for Harlem's Caribbean dances and boat rides and would become a fixture in the Seventh Avenue Carnival parade.[70]

On December 21, 1946, People's Songs staged a well-publicized concert titled "Calypso at Midnight" at Town Hall in midtown. Fortunately, the concert was recorded, providing an early sonic record of a live New York calypso performance. The program featured Gerald Clark's ensemble backing calypsonians MacBeth and the Duke of Iron, along with another recently arrived Trinidadian, Rupert "Lord Invader" Grant (1914–1961). Clark's usual five-piece clarinet/violin/guitar/string bass/piano band was expanded for the show to include two drums, hand percussion, and occasionally a cuatro played by Duke of Iron. The evening was hosted by the folk music impresario and scholar Alan Lomax, who offered lengthy introductions to each piece and encouraged the singers to talk about their songs. The program included classics such as "Calypso Invasion" sung by Duke of Iron, "Stone Cold Dead in the Market" sung by MacBeth, and "Rum and Coca-Cola" sung by Invader. A staged calypso drama, composed and produced by Invader, featured the three costumed calypsonians as a native Trinidadian man (Invader), an American GI (Duke), and a Trinidadian woman (MacBeth in drag). In an attempt to bring a deeper cultural dimension to the program by demonstrating the precursors of calypso, the two drummers staged a stick fight, while Invader chanted a call-and-response *lavway* that might have accompanied such a competition in Trinidad. The three calypsonians also came together to re-create a traditional "Calypso War" in which they exchanged extemporaneous verses of insult. The concert ended with Invader singing "God Made Us All," a plea for racial justice and an end to colonial rule.[71]

People's Songs' sponsorship of "Calypso at Midnight" and Lomax's didactic introductions positioned calypso as a genre of local "people's" folk music that fit into a broader discourse of music, culture, and political struggle popular in New York's leftist folk music circles at the time. It was no coincidence that People's Songs' founder and popular folk artist Pete Seeger had been singing and promoting calypsos since the early 1940s, no doubt drawn to the music's tradition of social satire and protest.[72] He occasionally played with Invader and can be heard accompanying him on "God Made Us All" at a union hootenanny that was recorded earlier in 1946.[73] Clark and the calypsonians were generally sympathetic to such progressive causes, but they had additional professional motivations for participating. The "Calypso at Midnight" and similar midtown shows provided exposure to another new American audience who, perhaps more than the downtown club-goers, appreciated their music from a deeper cultural perspective and might support them through the purchase of future concert tickets and recordings.

Unlike the other New York expatriate singers, save Houdini, Grant arrived with bona-fide calypso credentials, having cut his teeth singing in Carnival tents and contests in Port of Spain. When he first sailed to New York in the spring of 1941 he had already made a series of popular recordings with RCA Blue Bird and Decca companies during their sojourns in Trinidad in the late 1930s. Grant returned to Trinidad after a Decca recording session with Clark's orchestra, but he came back to New York in 1945 to litigate a lawsuit over alleged plagiarism of his song "Rum and Coca-Cola," which had become a huge hit for the Andrews Sisters following its release by Decca in 1945. Grant remained in New York for several years, singing regularly with Clark's and Felix's orchestras at uptown venues such as the Golden Gate Ballroom, the Park Palace Ballroom, and the Calypso Club Ballroom. In 1946 Grant began an association with Moe Asch and Disc Records (the forerunner to Folkways Records), which resulted in three albums that brought him to the attention of People's Songs and the New York folk music scene. He recorded several New York–themed songs for Asch, including "New York Subway," a humorous account of his attempts at navigating the city's perplexing transit system during his initial 1941 visit: "When I first landed in the USA / Listen how I got lost on the Subway / I had a date with a chick, and I went to Brooklyn / But I couldn't find my way back home the following morning." After receiving confusing instructions about the uptown train from a policeman, Grant vents his frustrations at the cabs "passing you empty and yet they won't stop," a subtle reference to the racial profiling that black New Yorkers regularly experienced. The song's Brooklyn setting evidences the growing Caribbean population in the borough that would eventually supplant Harlem as the Caribbean center of New York.[74] In April 1948 Grant recorded another New York–themed calypso, "Labor Day," a detailed chronicle of Harlem's first street Carnival. Following the successful adjudication of his "Rum and Coca-Cola" lawsuit in the late 1940s, Grant returned to Trinidad, where he remained for five years before journeying to England and finally back to New York in 1959. He continued to record for Asch's Folkways records up until his death in 1961.[75]

By the early postwar years, calypso had become an integral component of New York City's diverse popular music landscape. Anchored in Harlem dance halls and clubs frequented by Caribbean migrants, the singers and orchestras spread south to midtown concert halls and downtown clubs,

Figure 2.2. Wilmoth Houdini, Duke of Iron, and Lord Invader, Renaissance Ballroom, Manhattan, July 1947. Photo by William Gottlieb (courtesy of the Library of Congress).

where they were enthusiastically received by the hip Village set and folk music enthusiasts. They crossed boundaries, serving simultaneously as popular entertainers and supposed bearers of "authentic" traditions, reminding Caribbean migrants of their shared heritage while introducing their culture to a broader set of New York music aficionados. As cultural actors, New York's calypsonians assumed different positions with respect to their various audiences. Most Greenwich Village listeners viewed calypsonians as popular entertainers whose music they vaguely associated with exotic island culture. To Lomax's and Seeger's urban folkies, they were traditional performers whose songs expressed the struggles and delights of some broadly imagined community of common folk. Within Harlem's Caribbean diasporic community, the calypsonians were valorized as artists who gave voice to native culture. Even Anderson, Pinard, and MacBeth, who were not practiced calypso tent performers, understood their dual roles as professional singers and tradition-bearers who carried the cultural freight that could, for a price, ease the tensions of their homesick brothers and sisters.

In their capacity as community artists and purveyors of Caribbean culture, the orchestras led by Clark, Felix, and MacBeth, along with the cadre of New York calypsonians, performed year-round for dances and fetes in Harlem. They played events, sometimes but not always identified as Caribbean gatherings, sponsored by social and athletic clubs, churches, unions, and various community organizations. The *New Yorker* journalist Joseph Mitchell's 1939 account of a dance sponsored by an organization called the Trinidad Carnival Committee offers a detailed chronicle of such a performance at a modest-sized Harlem venue. The "picnic," as Mitchell claimed such events were commonly referred to by their "the homesick West Indian" organizers, took place on the third floor of "a seedy building" on Lenox Avenue, just below 116th Street. Music was provided by the Krazy Kats, one of the "two good hot West Indian Bands" Mitchell identified in Harlem at the time (the other being the Caribbean Serenaders). The orchestra was led by the clarinetist Gregory Felix and included a pianist, a drummer, a violinist, and Wilmoth Houdini singing and playing maracas and bottle. Mitchell went on to report on the event:

Then, with no preliminaries at all she (pianist Gale Wilhelmina) and the others took their places and began playing a rumba. Almost immediately, as if by signal, people started coming up the stairs in droves. Soon there were more than two hundred Negroes in the little hall.

Following several more instrumental pieces, again identified only as "rumbas" by Mitchell, Houdini joined the group:

He went inside the band enclosure, stood up on a chair, and yelled, "Now then me lads!" The band livened up when he began shaking the maracas. Presently the hall was seething with Lindy-hop, Susy-Q, and shim-sham-shimmy dancers, and Houdini stuffed the maracas in the pockets of his jacket and picked up a megaphone. The dancers seemed to pay no attention as he sang, but the old women sitting stiffly on the slat-backs along the wall listened attentively with smiles on their faces.

After grabbing a drink while the band played yet another rumba, Houdini was back to sing the popular calypso "Johnny Take My Wife":

Houdini returned to the enclosure and got up on his chair. He began a rhythmic, tantalizing beat on the bottle and the spoon. Soon he was making more noise than the other musicians. After a while he abruptly began to sing.

The evening progressed with Houdini interspersing his songs between instrumental numbers. When he wasn't singing he drank with patrons and helped to distribute plates of chicken and rice pelau and meat patties. The latter, he claimed, were of his own making.[76]

Houdini's picnic was not billed as a Carnival or masquerade dance, but the event, as described by Mitchell, was unmistakably Caribbean, with Felix's dance-inducing rumbas, Houdini's traditional calypso songs, and distinctly Trinidadian cuisine as the main attractions. These sorts of small dances and fetes were clearly more informal than Clark's elaborate Dame Lorraine Galas, attracting several hundred rather than several thousand patrons. The "star" (and probable producer) of the show, Houdini, sang through a megaphone (rather than a microphone and loudspeakers) while perched on a makeshift chair/stage, and then served the food that he had helped cook. The gathering revealed, at least from Mitchell's perspective, something of a generational divide. Apparently the younger clientele were more interested in dancing than in heeding the lyrics of Houdini's calypso songs, while the older women, sitting on the sidelines, "listened [to him] attentively." But this situation demonstrated a broader challenge for Houdini and other New York calypsonians as well as their musicians— calypso music was inherently a vocal genre, but it had to be danceable in the club and hall settings where it was most often performed in Harlem.

Mitchell did not specify whether the shimmy-shaking "Negro" dancers were all of Caribbean ancestry, or whether the crowd included some native-born African Americans. In any case many of the young dancers, Caribbean and otherwise, were quite familiar with the latest urban black dance styles. Nor did they hesitate to cut a few steps, even if the orchestra was playing Caribbean rumba or calypso pieces. The allure of contemporary African American dancing was powerful enough to penetrate even the most traditional Caribbean celebrations, as a description of dancers at a Dame Lorraine Gala a decade later confirmed: "Some of the younger folk at the Carnival intermittently burst out with hep versions of the Shag, Big Apple, Lindy or Bob Hop in spite of the calypso tempos of Gerald Clark's band."[77] Evidently a variety of traditional Caribbean and African American dances co-existed on Harlem dance floors at this time, with younger Caribbean migrants eager to embrace the latest black fashions and perform them in their own cultural spaces. On the flipside, many of these island revelers did not limit themselves to Caribbean-themed events, and regularly participated in the neighborhood's broader nightlife offerings. As Putman has suggested, "the dancing masses of Caribbean origin had a major impact on the swing music of Harlem."[78] The proliferation of Caribbean dances such as Houdini's "picnic" show reveals that by the early postwar years, Carnival music and dance had become thoroughly interwoven into the cultural fabric of black Harlem.

In February 1947, Houdini, under the auspices of the Calypso Musical Enterprises, Ltd., organized an event he billed as a "Traditional and

Colorful Afro-West Indian Shango Carnival and Dance." Scheduled to coincide roughly with the Trinidadian pre-Lenten festival, the program featured a "conclave of calypso champions" including Houdini, the Duke of Iron, MacBeth, Lancelot, Invader, Lady Trinidad, and Queen Calypso. Over $1,200 in prize money would be awarded to the best masquerades and individual costumes.[79] "Houdini was convinced that people could find a virtual transplanting of one of the famous tent carnivals, with all the colorful excitement, to a New York locale," commented Joe Bostic in the *Amsterdam News*.[80] Houdini's Shango and Dance extravaganza was actually the latest in a string of annual pre-Lenten Carnival dance/masquerades that had been held regularly in New York for more than a decade. Yet demand for an outdoor fete similar to Trinidad's vaunted three-day Carnival had been brewing for a number of years, and finally that summer the celebration would empty out of the dance halls and into the streets of Harlem. When it finally happened, Houdini and the other New York calypsonians, Clark and his dance orchestra, and the recently arrived steel pan men were there to provide the music.

Notes

1. "Dame Lorraine and Carnival Dance Held at Royal Windsor," *New York Age*, 21 February 1942.
2. "Calypso Carnival Is Slated for Royal Windsor Feb. 15," *New York Amsterdam News*, 31 January 1942. See also "Trinidad Steps into Picture at Dame Lorraine Fete," *New York Amsterdam News*, 14 February 1942.
3. Display ad, *New York Amsterdam News*, 31 January 1942.
4. Keith Nurse, "Globalization and Trinidadian Carnival: Diaspora, Hybridity, and Identity in Global Culture," *Cultural Studies* 13, no. 4 (1999): 680.
5. By the mid-nineteenth century, string/woodwind bands were popular at elite dances, Christmas celebrations, and Carnival balls in Trinidad. The violin, guitar, and cuatro may have been imported by Venezuelan migrants. The band Lovey brought to record in New York consisted of flute, clarinet, violins, piano, guitars, cuatros, mandolin, and string bass. See liner notes by Steve Shapiro for *Lovey's Original Trinidad String Band* (Bear Family Records, BCD 16057 AH, 2012).
6. Lionel Belasco's biography is drawn from Donald Hill, *Calypso Calaloo: Early Carnival Music in Trinidad* (University Press of Florida, 1993), pp. 120–125; and liner notes by Donald Hill for *Lionel Belasco: Good Night Ladies and Gents* (Rounder CD 1138, 1999).
7. Background on Walter Merrick is found in Hill, *Calypso Calaloo*, p. 122. Merrick's and Monrose's recordings are discussed on pp. 140–141.
8. The 1923 Victor announcement appears in John Cowley, "West Indian Blues: An Historical Overview 1920s–1930s," in *Nobody Knows Where the Blues Come From*, edited by Robert Springer (University Press of Mississippi, 2006), pp. 187–263. PDF at http://sas-space.sas.ac.uk/3080/1/Cowley_WIBtext.pdf (accessed 18 August 2016), p. 4.
9. The 1933 recording of "Carmelita" by Gerald Clark and his Night Owls can be heard on YouTube, at https://www.youtube.com/watch?v=6QOjISVvcDg.

10. "Cocotte Medley—Paseo," recorded 19 August 1933, NYC, by Gerald Clark and his Night Owls (Bluebird B-4909). Recording courtesy of collection of Richard Noblett.

11. "Susan Medley—Paseo." Recorded 19 August 1933, NYC, by Gerald Clark and his Night Owls (Bluebird B-4910). Recording courtesy of collection of Richard Noblett.

12. The 1931 recording of "Stop Coming and Come" by Wilmoth Houdini and Gerald Clark and his Night Owls can be heard on YouTube, at https://www.youtube.com/watch?v=SuX4xLVa_rI.

13. Eugene Williams, "Notes" to *Songs of Trinidad: Calypso Classics Composed and Sung by Wilmoth Houdini with Gerald Clark's Night Owls* (Brunswick Collectors' Series Album No. B-1023, 1946). This four-record set was a re-release of the original 1931 Brunswick recordings—including "Stop Coming and Come"—by Houdini backed by Clark's Night Owls. In addition to New Orleans native Al Morgan on bass, the other musicians on the recordings were identified as West Indian. They included Walter Bennett on cornet, Walter Edwards on clarinet and saxophone, Berry Barrow on piano, Joshy Paris on guitar, and Charlie Vincento on banjo and cuatro. Clark was identified as the band director.

14. Listen, for example, to the bluesy, New Orleans–style accompaniment to Sam Manning's "Back to My West Indian Home" (Colombia Records, 1930), at https://www.youtube.com/watch?v=idvER4ZiS1c. Manning was considered more of a vaudeville/blues singer than a calypsonian, although he made a number of calypso recordings between 1923 and 1930 in New York. His songs and instrumental accompaniments were an innovative blend of Afro-Caribbean and black American influences, and he enjoyed considerable popularity among Caribbean and native audiences. See Hill, *Calypso Calaloo*, pp. 123–125; and Cowley, "West Indian Blues," PDF, pp. 8–9.

15. Background on Gerald Clark and his activities in New York is found in Hill, *Calypso Calaloo*, pp. 159–166; and Donald Hill, "I am Happy in This Sweet Land of Liberty, the New York Calypso Craze of the 1930s and 1940s," in *Island Sounds in the Global City: Caribbean Popular Music in New York*, edited by Ray Allen and Lois Wilcken (University of Illinois Press, 1998), pp. 79–83.

16. *Calypso Craze, 1956–1957 and Beyond*, CD/DVD set and booklet, edited by Ray Funk and Michael Eldridge (Bear Family Records, 2014), p. 9.

17. Hill, *Calypso Calaloo*, p. 127.

18. Clipping of *Trinidad Guardian* article from Gerald Clark scrapbook, circa August 1937.

19. Advertisement from *Trinidad Guardian* for Empire Theater Vaudeville Show from Gerald Clark scrapbook, circa August 1937.

20. The 1937 recording of "Edward the VIII" by Caresser can be heard on YouTube, at https://www.youtube.com/watch?v=fN0ZYIyKDJY. The1939 recording of "Walter Winchell" by the Duke of Iron and Gerald Clark's Caribbean Serenaders can be heard on YouTube, at https://www.youtube.com/watch?v=ftdqIsHhpKI.

21. Norman Weinstein noted that Gregory Felix's "broad vibrato and sense of swing evoke Sidney Bechet," in "Tropical Punch: Rounder's *Calypso After Midnight*," *Boston Phoenix*, 27 January–3 February 2000; available online at http://www.bostonphoenix.com/archive/music/00/01/27/CALYPSO.html.

22. Gama Gilbert, "Records: Calypso," *New York Times*, 7 April 1940.

23. Malcolm Johnson, "More about Gerald Clark's Calypso Artists," *New York Sun*, 7 May 1940.

24. "New Kind of Singing: Calypso Has Four Parts," *Baltimore Afro-American*, 22 June 1940.

25. Tracing the jazz influences in the calypso arrangements of the 1920s and 1930s warrants further investigation. There is evidence that prior to Clark's and Houdini's jazz-influenced New York recordings, dance orchestras in Trinidad were familiar with "jazz" music. Gordon Rohlehr cites Trinidad newspaper reports that by the early 1920s some Port of Spain dance hall bands had "abandoned the Quadrille to play Jazz," and that during Carnival, "several orchestral bands [were] parading the streets and fending the latest in jazz music." Gordan Rohlehr, *Calypso and Society in Pre-Independence Trinidad* (self-published, Port of Spain, 1990), pp. 41, 117. While the newspaper's use of the term "jazz" in the early 1920s may well have referred to syncopated dance music and ensemble-ragtime rather than Armstrong-style early jazz arrangements built around improvised soloing, the Trinidad bands were clearly aware of American popular trends of the time. This suggests that the eventual move toward more sophisticated instrumental themes and the prominence of brass and reed instruments for calypso accompaniment may have come directly from Trinidad-based ensembles—who no doubt listened to early black American jazz and ragtime recordings and had access to American songbooks and music scores—as well as from Clark and his New York musicians. Rohlehr and other critics were not pleased with the replacement of old-time Quadrille-style calypso accompaniments by jazz-influenced arrangements. He charged that "[a] jazz straight jacket was forcibly imposed on the fluid prosody of Calypso," whose original rhythmic structures drew not from American popular styles, but from "Latin style syncopation and roots in calinda, bel air, and bamboula [traditional Caribbean folk styles]." Gordan Rohlehr, *A Scuffling of Islands: Essays on Calypso* (Lexicon Trinidad LTD, 2004), p. 378.

26. The *New York Age* (8 July 1950) reported that Clark's Caribbean Serenaders consisted of eleven instrumentalists and a vocalist. The *Trinidad Guardian* (24 February 1957) noted that Clark employed a twelve-piece orchestra for dancing and a five-piece unit for accompanying calypso singers.

27. Recordings of the Harmony Kings and Codallo's Top Hatters Orchestra dance tunes, as well as various calypso-backing ensembles using multipart brass and reed arrangements that were made between 1938 and 1940 in Trinidad, can be heard on *West Indian Rhythm* (Bear Family Records BCD 16623 JM, 2006).

28. "Caribbean Serenaders," *Variety*, 13 February 1934.

29. A recording of "I'm a Better Woman Than You" by Gerald Clark can be found on *Calypso After Midnight* (Rounder 11661-1841-2, 1999).

30. The dance orchestras of Alberto Socarras and Augusto Coen are discussed in Ruth Glasser, *My Music Is My Flag: Puerto Rican Musicians and Their New York Communities* (University of California Press, 1995), pp. 79–83. For more on popular Latin song and dance styles in New York City, see John Storm Roberts, *The Latin Tinge: The Impact of Latin American Music on the United States* (Oxford University Press, 1979). See especially chapter 3 on tango, chapter 4 on rumba, and chapter 5 on Afro-Cuban jazz.

31. Floyd Calvin, "Harlem Gets Color from 'Latin Quarter,'" *Baltimore Afro-American*, 8 February 1936.

32. Unidentified ad, 1935, in Gerald Clark's Scrapbook, page 6, courtesy of Donald Hill.

33. Unidentified ad, circa mid-1930s, in Gerald Clark's Scrapbook, page 3, courtesy of Donald Hill.

34. Gilbert Osofsky, *Harlem, the Making of a Ghetto*, 2nd ed. (Harper Torchbook, 1971), p. 131. Nancy Foner reports that by 1920, foreign-born Afro-Caribbean people made up, approximately a quarter of New York's black population, and by 1930 nearly a fifth. Nancy Foner, ed., *Islands in the City: West Indian Migration to New York* (University of California Press, 2001), p. 4.

35. Lara Putnam, *Radical Moves: Caribbean Migrants and the Politics of Race in the Jazz Age* (University of North Carolina Press, 2013), p. 157.

36. For more on Lead Belly and Josh White playing at the Village Vanguard, see Elijah Wald, *Josh White: Society Blues* (Routledge, 2002), pp. 91–92. See also Max Gordon's memoir, *Live at the Village Vanguard* (Da Capo Press, 1980).

37. Gerald Clark's appearances at the Village Vanguard are well described in Hill, *Calypso Calaloo*, pp. 159–163; and in Hill, "I Am Happy in This Sweet Land of Liberty," pp. 79–83.

38. Malcom Johnson, "Gerald Clark and His Calypso Artists at the Village Vanguard," *New York Sun*, 5 April 1940.

39. See Hill, "I Am Happy in This Sweet Land of Liberty," pp. 79–83.

40. For more on Trinidad's early calypso tents, see Hill, *Calypso Calaloo*, pp. 64–80. The Village Vanguard shows resembled Trinidad calypso tents in their presentation of multiple calypsonians in a small venue where most of the audience was listening, not dancing. There were, however, important differences. The tents in Trinidad during the 1920s and 1930s were annual gatherings where dozens of calypsonians competed with their latest songs for local audiences. This changed drastically during World War II and in the postwar years, "as singers catered to the tastes of GIs and tourists who come in great numbers after the war" (pp. 82–83).

41. Jervis Anderson, *This Was Harlem: 1900–1950* (Farrar, Straus and Giroux, 1981), p. 139.

42. Fiona I. B. Ngô, *Imperial Blues: Geographies of Race and Sex in Jazz Age New York* (Duke University Press, 2014), p. 1.

43. See Benjamin Filene's insightful discussion of Lomax's promotion of Lead Belly in *Romancing the Folk: Public Memory and American Roots Music* (University of North Carolina Press, 2000), pp. 59–64.

44. Richard Manson, "Calypso Ballads Unique Fare at Village Vanguard," *New York Post*, 2 September 1939.

45. Gilbert, "Records: Calypso."

46. Meyer Berger, "About the Town," *New York Times*, 11 March 1940.

47. Ngô, *Imperial Blues*, p. 16.

48. Xiaofan Amy Li, "Introduction: From Exotic to the Autoexotic," *PMLA* 132, no. 2 (March 2017): 393.

49. "Calypso, the Unique Music of Trinidad, Has Its 4 Outstanding Exponents Here," *New York Amsterdam News*, 29 March 1941.

50. Gerald Clark's scrapbook is from Don Hill's personal collection.

51. The issue of colonial hegemony is germane to the discussion of New York Caribbean music during the 1930s and 1940s. All the Harlem Caribbean dance orchestra musicians and singers grew up under British colonial rule, for Trinidad at the time was a British colony, and would

remain so until 1962. During World War II the United States, with the blessing of the United Kingdom, set up military bases in Trinidad, thereby extending its own "unofficial" colonial political and economic influence over the island.

52. Stuart Hall, "Notes on Deconstructing the Popular," in *People's History and Socialist Theory*, edited by Raphael Samuel (Routledge, 1981), pp. 227–240.

53. Ngô argues that between the world wars, New York clubs and dance halls offered "contact zones" where native blacks and whites could commingle with foreign-born migrants. Such multiracial spaces, informed by imperial logic, offered opportunities both to challenge and preserve existing racial and gender norms. See Ngô, *Imperial Blues*, pp. 33–38.

54. Michael Denning, *Noise Uprising: The Audiopolitics of a World Musical Revolution* (Verso Press, 2015), p. 140.

55. Ibid., p. 23.

56. "Calypso, the Unique Music of Trinidad," *New York Amsterdam News*, 29 March 1941.

57. Background on Wilmoth Houdini is found in Hill, *Calypso Calaloo*, pp. 176–181.

58. The 1934 recording of Wilmoth Houdini's "African Love Call" can be heard on YouTube, at https://www.youtube.com/watch?v=CmUDpLFtgO0.

59. Joseph Mitchell, "Houdini's Picnic," *New Yorker*, 6 May 1939, pp. 61–71. Cited from reprint of the article in Joseph Mitchell, *Up in the Old Hotel* (Vintage Books, 1993), p. 260.

60. "Good Old Harlem Town" (Decca 18101, 1940); "Harlem Night Life" (Decca 18102, 1940). Both recordings are found on the 1940 Decca 78 album *Harlem Seen through Calypso Eyes* by Wilmoth Houdini.

61. Hill, *Calypso Calaloo*, p. 181.

62. Background on the Duke of Iron is found in *Calypso Craze*, edited by Funk and Eldridge, pp. 10–14.

63. The 1939 recording of "USA" by the Duke of Iron and Gerald Clark and Caribbean Serenaders can be heard on YouTube, at https://www.youtube.com/watch?v=I1GOEdLgDaw.

64. The 1939 recording of "Calypso Invasion" by the Duke of Iron and Gerald Clark and Caribbean Serenaders can be heard on YouTube, at https://www.youtube.com/watch?v=Nhuct_xVVS4.

65. Cited in Peter Goldsmith, *Making People's Music: Moe Asch and Folkways Records* (Smithsonian Institution Press, 1998), p. 178.

66. The 1942 recording of "The Century of the Common Man" by Sir Lancelot and Gerald Clark's Orchestra can be heard on YouTube, at https://www.youtube.com/watch?v=C4KKpz93j10.

67. Johnson, "Gerald Clark and His Calypso Artists."

68. Background on Lancelot Pinard is found in "Lancelot Pinard; Musician Brought Calypso to U.S.," *Los Angeles Times*, 18 March 2001; and *Calypso Craze*, edited by Funk and Eldridge, pp. 15–16.

69. "New Kind of Singing," *Baltimore Afro-American*, 22 June 1940.

70. Background on Patrick MacDonald is found in "MacBeth the Great, Calypso Singer Dies," *New York Amsterdam News*, 2 February 1957; and *Calypso Craze*, edited by Funk and Eldridge, p. 17.

71. The 1946 "Calypso at Midnight" show was recorded and is available on two CDs: *Calypso at Midnight* (Rounder 11661-1840-2, 1999) and *Calypso after Midnight* (Rounder 11661-1841-2, 1999), both with extensive booklet notes by Steve Shapiro, Don Hill, and John Cowley.

72. Andrew Martin notes that Seeger began singing calypsos while he was in the US Army in 1942, and included the calypsos "Mary Anne" and "New York Subway" in the repertoire of his folk group the Weavers in the early 1950s. During a 1956 visit to Trinidad, Seeger became enamored with the steel pan and helped promote the instrument in the United States. He arranged for Kim Loy Wong and his steelband to come to New York to record for Folkways Records, wrote a manual on how to play the steel pan, and produced the seventeen-minute film *Music from Oil Drums*. See Andrew Martin, "A Voice of Steel through the Iron Curtain: Pete Seeger's Contributions to the Development of Steel Band in the United States," *American Music* 29, no. 3 (Fall 2011): 353–380.

73. Invader's 9 May 1946 recording of "God Made Us All," with Pete Seeger on banjo, can be heard on *Lord Invader: Calypso in New York* (Smithsonian Folkways CD 40454, 2000).

74. The 1946 recording of "New York Subway" by Lord Invader with Felix and his Internationals can be heard on the above cited *Lord Invader: Calypso in New York City*, or on YouTube, at https://www.youtube.com/watch?v=XqTPZfM3Wpk.

75. Background on Rupert Grant, Lord Invader, is found in John Cowley, *Lord Invader: Calypso in New York City* (liner notes to Smithsonian Folkways CD 40454, 2000).

76. Descriptions and quotes of the 1939 dance taken from Joseph Mitchell, "Houdini's Picnic," *New Yorker*, 6 May 1939, pp. 161–171. Cited from reprint of the article in Mitchel, *Up in the Old Hotel*, pp. 253–266.

77. "Dancing in the Aisles" photo caption, *New York Amsterdam News*, 5 March 1949.

78. Putnam, *Radical Moves*, p., 157.

79. Display ad, *New York Amsterdam News*, 25 January 1947.

80. Joe Bostic, "Houdini, King of Calypso, at Gate, Feb. 2nd," *New York Amsterdam News*, 1 February 1947.

3

Harlem Carnival
Dame Lorraine Dances and the Seventh Avenue Street Parade

No one can identify with certainty the first homesick Trinidadian to play mas in New York. But Rufus Gorin (1909–1983) was unquestionably one of the earliest. Shortly after arriving in the United States, he was reported dressing in a bat costume in the hall of his apartment house during the 1928 Carnival season. Gorin had grown up playing mas in his Port of Spain neighborhood, and the bat was a character in his mother's dragon band.[1] At that time there were no organized Carnival festivities in New York, but by the late 1920s, groups of Caribbean migrants were evidently running small private dances and parties in the weeks leading up to Ash Wednesday. These noisy celebrations occasionally drew the ire of the local authorities. According to one account, "the first maskers trouping from door to door at Carnival time were ordered off the streets by rough policeman," an indication, noted the reporter, of the "intolerance exhibited toward West Indians during the early waves of West Indian immigration."[2] Clashes between Carnival revelers were common in Trinidad, and the incident was a harbinger of confrontations to come in Harlem and Brooklyn.

Indoor masquerading parties spilling into the streets during this time were a reminder that Carnival was by nature a communal, outdoor event. Gorin recalled that in 1934 or 1935, another Trinidadian, Jessie Waddell Crompton, attempted to stage a small street Carnival in Harlem.[3] Her initial efforts were unsuccessful, and it would be a decade before she was able to acquire a permit to stage a full-fledged Carnival parade on Seventh Avenue. Meanwhile, more organized pre-Lenten Carnival dances began to proliferate.

Gerald Clark's Dame Lorraine Carnival Dances

The first large-scale Carnival dances were those produced by the bandleader Gerald Clark. By the mid-1930s Clark's star was on the rise, thanks to his radio appearances and his dance orchestra's numerous performances for social clubs and fraternal groups at Harlem's grand ballrooms, including the Lido (146th Street and Seventh Avenue), the Renaissance Casino (138th Street and Seventh Avenue), the Rockland Palace (155th Street and Eighth Avenue), and the Park Place Ballroom (West 110th Street and Fifth Avenue). There is no record of a specific Carnival dance in 1934, but tropical themes were in abundance. Clark and his Caribbean Serenaders played for what was billed as a "Dance of the South Sea Isles," which promised a "tropical extravaganza" for those attending the mid-September event at the Lido Ballroom.[4] An October dance sponsored by the Mercury Athletic Club at the Renaissance was advertised as "Caribbean Nights" and featured a "clash" between Clark's Caribbean Serenaders and the house orchestra led by the Panamanian-born violinist Vernon Andrade.[5] The latter, of Jamaican parentage, directed the Renaissance orchestra that purportedly consisted of half "West Indian" players.[6]

Clark's first pre-Lent Carnival dance was staged at the Lido Ballroom on 2 February 1935. Produced by Mrs. Rhoda Weeks and featuring Clark's ensemble, the Harlem club was "transformed into a masquerade day in Trinidad," reported the *New York Amsterdam News*.[7] The event was evidently so successful that Clark's Serenaders and Andrade's orchestra squared off again in early March at the Renaissance for a "Fiesta" night that would evoke "the gay Carnival spirit."[8] The Renaissance, known for hosting events sponsored by Caribbean benevolent societies, civic associations, and political reform groups, would become Clark's favored venue for his annual Carnival dances, which he staged for nearly two decades. In 1937 Clark predicted his dance would "out-Carnival the traditional Trinidad Carnival itself," with a "colorful Carnival day scene" and a "Chantwell competition with Wilmoth Houdini."[9] The following year there is no record of an event at the Renaissance, but a "Carnival Review" was to take place at the Park Palace Ballroom, with music by the Royal Trinidadians, including two of Clark's regular players, Victor Pacheco and Gregory Felix. Whether Clark was part of the orchestra is not known, but the evening was advertised to include the calypsonian Houdini leading a "review demonstration in the disguise of a dragon beast, Zaniemo."[10]

By 1939 Clark was billing his event as the "Gala Dame Lorraine," a reference to an early nineteenth-century female Carnival character who was always elegantly dressed, exaggeratedly voluptuous, and famous for parodying Trinidad's aristocratic French planters. The Dame herself was often played by male cross-dressing masqueraders. The 1939 affair featured the Caribbean Serenaders playing "sensational Rhumbas, Spanish Valse, Paseos and all the latest hits," the latter presumably calypsos sung by Houdini. The program promised to appeal to both Latin and island sensibilities, offering guests "a glimpse of gay Madrid and the spices of the blue Caribbean."[11] Lest readers doubt the ceremonial nature of the annual Carnival gatherings, a 1941 account in the *New York Sun* announced, "Natives of Trinidad Living Here Dance and Sing in Pre-Christian Saturnalia." A diverse audience numbering in the thousands was reported in attendance: "The celebration was not confined to former residents of the West Indies, though they predominated. It was evident from the size of the crowd that many other Harlemites had come along, though there is a large colony of West Indians in that community. It is the seventh year that the fete has been observed and Mr. Clark predicted that if interest continued to grow, a larger auditorium would have to be obtained to hail the arrival of the next Lenten season."[12]

The following year Clark did move his dance to the larger Royal Windsor venue in midtown. A reporter from the *New York Age* pronounced the 1942 dance to be a tremendous success, where "Harlemites and Broadway celebrities found joy in socializing with one another."[13] But Clark's vision of an annual integrated midtown celebration did not materialize, and he found his Gala Dame Lorraine back in Harlem's Renaissance the following year. The *Amsterdam News* reporter Bill Chase attended what he described as a "colorful event" with a capacity crowd. He was particularly taken by the array of mas characters: "The costumes worn by the prize winners including the Clowns (Darling Club S.C.), the Indians, Red Riding Hood, the Coolie Woman, half man and bride, the donkey lady, the Martinique etc., were costly and colorful—but the prize money was good too."[14]

Chase's attention to the costumes underscores the importance of masquerading at the Dame Lorraine Galas that Clark billed as "stupendous spectacle[s] of Carnival Bands in competition."[15] These were more than conventional masquerade balls where attendees dressed in individual costumes. In true Carnival spirit, mas bands of up to twenty members came clad in themed costumes to compete for prize money. *Amsterdam News* photo spreads from the late 1940s and early 1950s featured photographs of prize-winning bands decked out as Coty Dancing Girls, Bejan Gals, Balinese Ballerinas, Pirates, Juju Warriors, and Bat Men and Creole Bells. Individuals dressed as bats, jamet-men, and an African chief wearing intricate wire and screen headgear competed for the most original costume prize.[16]

These costume competitions involved a "Dame Lorraine Call," during which individuals and mas bands would take turns dancing through the hall and presenting themselves to a group of judges. An account of one Rockland Palace event reported that "during the [masquerade] contest the dance floor was cleared and those taking part in the affair danced around for the benefit of the thousands that crowded both the main floor and the balcony to look on, and the dancing was done to Virgin Island and West Indian music, played by Gerald Clark and his Caribbean Orchestra."[17] At another Rockland Palace gathering, "music by the MacBeth Creole Rhythm Boys started off the procession of costumed bands and individual clubs which competed for cash prizes."[18] A band of Balinese Ballerinas "captured first prize as a group for their unusual costumes and performance" at a 1950 affair.[19] The Dame Lorraine Call at an early Renaissance Casino show was preceded by a series of recitations (in *patois* dialogue) by masqueraders that "reeked with the same bawdy humor which marked the Elizabethan era." The densely packed dance floor was eventually taken over by "a collection of bats and vampires. It was this last group, rushing onto the floor, screeching and waving their wings, who cleared sufficient space for the rest of the maskers to present tableaux [to the judges]." The band of bats and vampires was, however, penalized, because they "persisted in dancing all the time" rather than assuming the required final pose in front of the judges. They were demoted to third-place, running behind the winning group of mermaids and a second-place band depicting Cleopatra and her attendants.[20] Costumed mas bands would eventually appear and compete in the Carnival dances that were held in conjunction with the Labor Day Carnival parade (discussed below). "A highpoint of the dance was the floor show staged shortly after midnight. Featured in the show were a number of islanders in native costumes and the various bands that were scheduled for the parade."[21] The performance of mas through the processing and dancing of costumes, a hallmark of Trinidad street Carnival, was a major attraction of the Dame Lorraine Galas and key to the events functioning as self-conscious cultural display and ritual.

A rival dance, billed as a "Grand Calypso Party," was held at 650 Lenox Avenue in March 1943. Gregory Felix and his Orchestra with MacBeth, along with calypso singer La Belle Rosette, were the featured performers. "Dress and disguise will be optional," ran the announcement, and "a true carnival night in Trinidad is promised."[22] Clark continued at the Renaissance for the next three years, fending off competition by advertising the event as "The One, the Only, the Original Gala Dame Lorrain and Carnival Dance."[23]

In 1947 Houdini sought to upstage Clark by producing his own Carnival dance at the Golden Gate Ballroom on 2 February. Not to be denied, Clark presented "Calypso Season in Trinidad: A Grand Concert and Dance" on 19 January at the Club Sudan (142nd Street and Lenox Avenue) with the Serenaders and Invader, MacBeth, and the Duke of Iron.[24] Apparently, demand for Carnival celebrations was high enough that year to support major events within two weeks of each other. Clark's pre-Lenten Dame Lorraine dances and their attending masquerade competitions continued into the 1950s. The dances had grown so popular that in 1951 there were three competing events sponsored by Clark at the Rockland Ballroom, Duke of Iron at the St. Nicholas Arena (66th Street and Columbus Avenue), and MacBeth at the Park Palace. An *Amsterdam News* observer opined that the crowds of costumed dancers were "home again—for a few hours—for a few days—home in Trinidad at Carnival time when the island rocks under the rhythm of dancing feet."[25]

The continued success of Clark's Dame Lorraine and the rival Carnival dances confirmed that by the early postwar years, members of New York's Caribbean migrant communities were eager to support annual Carnival celebrations that combined three essential components of Trinidadian Carnival: dance orchestras, calypso song battles, and masquerade contests. They aimed to not only "evoke the spirit of Carnival," but also to literally experience a sense of being "home again." They sought to "transform" their Harlem dance halls into authentic Trinidad masquerades and to "transplant" famous Carnival tents to Seventh Avenue to re-create "a true Carnival night in Trinidad." Immersing themselves in deep cultural expressions, they danced to familiar paseos, sang along to popular calypsos, and played mas as traditional Carnival characters. In doing so they came together as active participants, not passive bystanders, in the process of cultural production, validation, and identity-formation. Their engagement in performance countered geographic dislocation by blurring the boundaries separating their new and native homelands.

Harlem's Seventh Avenue Carnival Parade

As World War II drew to a close, demand for Carnival activities was on the rise as New York's Caribbean community experienced a slight uptick in immigration.[26] The resumption of Trinidad's own pre-Lenten Carnival in 1946, following a four-year hiatus due to the war, no doubt energized New York's migrants to devise a plan for moving their own celebration from the dance halls to the streets of Harlem. The desire for an outdoor Carnival event finally materialized in 1947 when Jessie Waddell Crompton, working under the auspices of the Trinidad Pageant Carnival Committee, acquired a permit to stage an outdoor Carnival parade up Harlem's Seventh Avenue.[27] Evidently the event was originally conceived of as a "Trinidad Day" celebration, but according to a press account in Jamaica's *Daily Gleaner*, pressure from various local Caribbean civic organizations and businesses led Waddell Crompton to move ahead under the broader banner of "West Indian Day" in order to "galvanize morale" among Harlem's diverse English-speaking island populations.[28] In deference to New York winters, Waddell Crompton and her committee decided to move the event from its traditional pre-Lenten date in February or March to the late-summer Labor Day holiday. Little is known about Waddell Crompton other than that she came to New York in the 1920s from Trinidad and was well enough connected in Harlem circles to form a cultural organization and acquire a city parade permit. She surely understood the potential power that public cultural display might hold for Caribbean migrants in a neighborhood famous for its military, fraternal, and United Negro Improvement Association parades.[29]

American parades were, as the historian and folklorist Susan Davis has aptly noted, "dramatic representations" and "political acts" serving "as tools for building, maintaining, and confronting power relations." On the one hand, they functioned as events advocating for cultural respectability; on the other hand, they could challenge and satirize the powers-that-be through disorder and burlesque.[30] Harlem's Carnival parade would do both. From the beginning, Waddell Crompton envisioned an outdoor Carnival parade as more than a huge fete for homesick Trinidadians. Her goal, as reported by the local Harlem papers, was to "promote a closer relationship in New York between citizens of West Indian ancestry and native Americans. It was the belief of [Waddell Crompton and the other] founders that a greater understanding of the cultural backgrounds of the two peoples would strengthen the bonds of friendship and respect between them."[31] Fostering dignity and understanding through the public sharing of diverse cultural expressions would, decades later, become one of the central mantras of Brooklyn Carnival, fitting neatly into the politics of urban multiculturalism that would take hold in the post–civil rights era. In the early postwar years, Waddell Crompton's project was ahead of its time.

Harlem's first Carnival parade took place around 3 o'clock on Labor Day Monday, 1 September 1947. The procession began at Fifth Avenue and 110th Street, turned north up Seventh Avenue and proceeded to 142nd Street, and terminated near the Golden Gate Ballroom, where a Carnival dance took place until midnight. The *New York Age* trumpeted, "50,000 Harlemites Watch First Annual Trinidad Carnival and Parade." The event bore similarities to conventional American civic parades, featuring "a cavalcade of floats, decorated trucks, cars, and horse-drawn vehicles," with contingents representing Caribbean businesses, civic leaders, and students. What distinguished Waddell Crompton's pageant were the groups of costumed bands that sought to "bring to view Trinidad's traditional festival-Carnival." Mas bands themed as followers of Christopher Columbus and Mahatma Gandhi, along with characters depicting bats, clowns, cats, dude ranchers, and a variety of fancy "make believe" costumes were reported. As in Trinidad, these bands proceeded through the streets to the sounds of "original calypso orchestras that furnished music throughout the parade."[32] The orchestras were not identified, but there can be little doubt that one was led by Gerald Clark. A second dance, billed as a "Calypso Carnival," was advertised to take place at the Calypso Club (139th Street and Seventh Avenue) that evening following the parade. "Floats, Costumed Dancers and the World's Greatest Calypso Singers" were promised.[33]

Ramona Lowe, a reporter for the *Jamaican Daily Gleaner*, was on hand and offered a fuller account of the parade's music and costuming. The aforementioned New York calypsonians were prominent. Lord Invader was spotted atop "the Calypso Club float," while the Duke of Iron, leading his "dancing band," was "improvising an appropriate calypso called 'Clear de Road' as the eager onlookers closed in on the parade." MacBeth the Great "rode with his family group atop a float advertising his mother's West Indian cooking." Lowe also identified several "steel bands, with their members blowing on old iron pipes, drumming on empty oil cans, kitchen utensils, or whatever came to hand." These were no doubt early iterations of steel/percussion bands, perhaps the first to appear in a Harlem public event: "[they] were novel to most of the spectators, but West Indians on the sidelines caught up the rhythms in sinuous body movements." Numerous mas bands were reported, including groups of Blue Devils, Red Devils, Parisian Dandies, Red Indians, Dude Ranchers on horseback, and Buccaneers of the Spanish Main. MacBeth's dance orchestra, which included the Cuban violinist Victor Pacheco and clarinetist Gregory Felix, performed at the evening dance at the Golden Gate ballroom.[34]

Another intriguing description of the first Harlem parade and its music comes from a "sung newspaper" source—a calypso composed by Lord Invader sometime between the 1947 Labor Day Carnival celebration and the following April, when he recorded the song "Labor Day." Invader recounts a lively scene: "Seventh Avenue was jumpin' / Everybody was shakin'. . . . From A-Hundred-Ten to One-Forty-Second / We had bands of all descriptions / I am not only speaking of West Indians / Ninety Percent was Americans / They Love Carnival / That is why they join the Bacchanal." Invader's demographic observation confirms that many of Harlem's African American residents were eager to join in the parade along with their Caribbean neighbors. He went on to call out the other calypsonians that were there: "MacBeth the Great and Houdini / They all joined the festivity / Also the Duke of Iron / He was Leading a Band."[35] Invader's account confirms Lowe's report that he, Duke, and MacBeth appeared at the initial Harlem parade. Houdini was there as well, as evidenced by a photograph appearing in the *Chicago Defender* that captures him perched on what looks like the roof of a car, decked out in a cape and calypso crown and beating out a rhythm on a glass bottle.[36]

Subsequent local press accounts affirmed that orchestras and calypso singers were a vital component of the Seventh Avenue parade. An *Amsterdam News* photo spread of the 1951 street Carnival includes a dramatic image of MacBeth, guitar in hand, perched on a long, festively decorated float, with his orchestra of approximately ten reeds, brass, and percussionists behind him. A single microphone on a stand and a round speaker placed prominently in front of the band suggests that a simple sound system, no doubt battery-powered, provided light amplification for the singer. The float is being towed up Seventh Avenue, where it passed a reviewing stand in front of the Calypso Club.[37] MacBeth was the most regular participant in the parade, according to press coverage, appearing with his band on a float from the initial 1947 parade until his death in 1957. In 1950 his orchestra and Gerald Clark's band treated celebrities in the reviewing stand to "a maze of West Indian rhythms."[38] Fats Greene, who took over MacBeth's band in 1957, appeared at the parade in 1958 along with a second float-mounted orchestra led by the Brooklyn bandleader Daphne Weeks.[39] The Greene and Weeks orchestras would again participate in the 1959 parade, squaring off in "A Battle of Music: American-Calypso" at the Renaissance Ballroom.[40]

With Clark cutting back on his musical activities and the passing of MacBeth in 1957, Greene and Weeks emerged as the two most popular Caribbean dance orchestra leaders for Harlem Carnival-related events. The Panamanian-born saxophonist and clarinetist Claude "Fats" Greene (1913–1968) migrated to New York as a young man and established himself as a musician and arranger. Throughout the 1950s he was second-leader of MacBeth's Creole Rhythm Boys and the Vernon Andrade Orchestra before taking over the directorship of MacBeth's band in 1957 and changing the name to the Fats Greene Orchestra.[41] He would make a number of recordings with the band, often backing calypso singers, and in 1966 he scored a minor hit with the tune "'Fats' Shake 'M' Up" (discussed in chapter 6). The bassist Don Byron Sr., who joined Greene's band around 1957, recalled that they played American popular standards, waltzes, and Latin mambos and rumbas, but they were primarily known for their instrumental calypsos and for backing calypsonians. Greene arranged the tunes, everyone read charts, and occasionally Prichard Chessman and Greene took jazzy solos on tenor sax and clarinet, respectively. They played at dances all over Harlem and eventually in Brooklyn, and always for Labor Day Carnival, as Byron described:

> Yes, Labor Day was a time when lots of people would go to the parade on Seventh Avenue. There would be [masquerade] bands and costumes and calypso melodies that most people knew. MacBeth and the Duke of Iron would sing. We would be on a float, like an open truck fixed up to look like a float. We had the whole band, including the trap drums and horns and Al Thomas [who had replaced MacBeth] singing. There would be groups of people, in front and in back of the float, marching and dancing along to the music. We used to go into the Armory at 148th Street and Fifth Avenue—that was the end of the parade where people wearing costumes would go.[42]

Daphne Weeks (1913–2004), a native of Port of Spain, grew up in a family of women pianists and led her own small dance ensemble before she relocated to New York in 1947. She began playing as a solo pianist in Harlem and Brooklyn and eventually, with advice from Gerald Clark, formed her own orchestra in the late 1940s. Like many of Harlem's Caribbean bands, her twelve-piece ensemble boasted an international lineup, with players from Trinidad, Guyana, St. Thomas, Cuba, Costa Rica, and the United States. Her repertoire included jazz and American standards, but calypso (and later reggae) was the band's forte as they played for Caribbean clubs, fraternal organizations, and Carnival dances throughout the late 1950s into the 1970s. Weeks, unique in her status as a female Caribbean orchestra leader, followed the migration from Harlem to Brooklyn, where she played for the borough's first Carnival dances and became a mainstay in the community.[43]

While most newspaper coverage concentrated on the "galaxy of colorful costumes," calypso music was mentioned every year, suggesting that the orchestras provided an essential component for parade participants and observers alike. In addition, the orchestras and their singers were always featured at the after-parade ballroom galas, where they played dance music and accompanied the stage shows that featured the winning parade costumes. Increasingly the outdoor parade and dances were folded together as one Carnival festival. The 1951 Carnival celebration was billed as a three-day affair, with dances at the Rockland Ballroom bookending the Labor Day parade.[44] The 1953 Carnival included Friday, Saturday, and Sunday evening dances at the Park Palace and a Monday "monster Harlem Mardi Gras parade" to be followed by a final dance at the Renaissance Casino.[45]

Calypso orchestras fronted by a singer were not the only music heard on Seventh Avenue. More conventional marching bands, such as the St. Police Athletic League Drum and Bugle Corp. and the St. Martins Cadets were regular features, although at least one observer claimed the crowd paid little attention to them.[46] Smaller groups of musicians were also prominent. A trio consisting of a piano, saxophone, and maracas, presumably on some sort of truck, was pictured at the 1948 parade. That same year a mas band was accompanied by two marching saxophonists and a clarinet.[47] Descriptions of dancing mas bands suggest they often provided their own rhythmic accompaniment, with members playing drums, maracas, cowbells, spoon and bottle, and other hand percussion instruments. Bystanders reported "costumed bands beating out calypso rhythms," "hundreds of calypso and mambo dancers hopp[ing] to the rhythms of twenty small bands," and "an assortment of beaters, flailing manfully at everything from bongo drums to empty Pepsi-Cola bottles."[48]

A series of rooftop photographs of the 1949 parade, taken by the Harlem Renaissance critic Carl Van Vechten, provide an inventory of musical offerings. One shot depicts a conventional marching band consisting of drummers and glockenspiel players dressed in military outfits fronted by a half-dozen baton-twirling majorettes. The audience presses in but remains behind police barricades on the sidewalk. At the center of a second photograph are five musicians, three with guitars and two with maracas, leading a group of approximately twenty women dressed in long, flowing skirts and head scarves. The former were apparently calypso singers, the latter a small mas band. While no orchestra is seen in the photograph, the back of an empty float is visible just in front of the five musicians, suggesting they may have jumped down from their mobile perch to join the masqueraders on the street (see Figure 3.1). A third photograph focuses on a procession led by a small group of musicians dressed as Frenchmen (wearing matching French-style dark berets, horizontal-striped shirts, and black slacks). Three beat single steel pans held in place by straps that loop around their necks (known as pan-around-the-neck), three play conical skin drums strapped over their shoulders, and several shake maracas. Four animated dancers, also dressed in Frenchmen outfits, proceed in front of the musicians. Just behind them is a mas/percussion band of ten individuals dressed in what appear to be pirate outfits, playing maracas and a gourd shaker. The controlled structure of the parade appears to have broken down, as several dozen noncostumed parade spectators had crossed the police barricade into the street to join the mas band and steel pan players (see Figure 3.2).[49]

Figure 3.1. Unknown calypsonians on Seventh Avenue, Harlem Carnival, 1949. Photo by Carl Van Vechten © Van Vechten Trust (courtesy of the Museum of the City of New York and the Carl Van Vechten Trust).

Figure 3.2. Unknown steelband on Seventh Avenue, Harlem Carnival, 1949. Photo by Carl Van Vechten © Van Vechten Trust (courtesy of the Museum of the City of New York and the Carl Van Vechten Trust).

Enter the Steelbands

Lowe's 1947 reference to steelbands "drumming on empty oil cans," along with Van Vechten's 1949 photographs, reveals that steel drums were present at the early Harlem parades, foreshadowing the essential role the instrument would come to play in New York's Carnival soundscape. By the early postwar years, ensembles playing multi-pitched, melody-producing steel drums had become vital components of Trinidad's Carnival celebration. At that time, however, steelbands were a new and relatively unfamiliar phenomenon for many of Harlem's Caribbean migrants. The earliest press report of a named steelband was an announcement in the *Amsterdam News* that "Rudy King and his sensational Steel Band" would perform at the 1949 parade. Perhaps King is one of the three pianists seen in the Van Vechten photograph, although this is difficult to confirm. The article provides a brief explanation of the "recent Trinidad innovation" of employing instruments fashioned from discarded gasoline drums.[50] Instruments resembling steel drums were heard on Seventh Avenue during the 1950 parade: "An additional musical treat this year was the appearance of a youthful Kettle Drum band. The odd tones of those metal instruments blended heartily with the more orthodox instruments of their Americanized brothers."[51] The reporter was clearly fascinated with the new instruments, presumably some form of early steel drums, while struggling with what to make of its "odd tones" and how they might stack up to conventional Western instruments. In 1955 a *New Yorker* reporter observed "a raffish-looking steelband, miraculously producing solid music from old oil drums."[52] In 1957 an outfit called Nobles Steel Band added "a tropic tinge with the rhythm beats from their rose-red steel drums" to the Carnival dance at the Rockland Casino.[53] The following year the *Amsterdam News* listed three steelbands on the parade route: Serenaders in Steel, Cecil Monique's Steel Band, and Carlos Caldera's Steel Band.[54] A 1959 account of the parade noted that sidewalk spectators "joined the march after succumbing to the irresistible calypso tempo of the steel bands," in a scene reminiscent of Van Vechten's photograph from a decade earlier.[55]

Little was written about these early steelbands, and they were rarely recorded. Recollections of two early bandleaders, Rudolph "Rudy" King and Reynolds "Caldera" Carabello, and pan man Carlton Munroe, provide historical context. Rudy King (1931–2004), considered by many to be New York's premiere steel pan pioneer, migrated to Brooklyn in 1949. As a teenager in Port of Spain he had played with Trinidad's Eastside Kids Steel Orchestra and learned to build and tune steel pans. When he arrived in New York he was knowledgeable about the latest innovations in both playing and tuning techniques at a time when the steelbands were in their infancy. He was soon building pans from old oil drums in an alley next to his aunt's apartment in Brooklyn. Within a year he had moved to Harlem, where he formed a small group of six players he dubbed the "Trinidad Steelband" to assure potential fans of the band's authentic Caribbean roots. At first each member played a single pan strapped around his or her neck, but as the group progressed they began to employ multiple pans mounted on stands. King recalled that his early band consisted of a twelve-note lead tenor pan, a ten-note second pan, a seven-note guitar pan, a four-note bass pan, a two-note dudup, and one or more percussionists.[56]

Carlton Munroe (b. 1934), who as a teenager played with King in the early 1950s, recollected a similar configuration of four pan players: King and himself playing tenor pans along with a second tenor and a guitar pan. Percussion was provided by maracas, iron, and sometimes bongos and bottle and spoon. King built all the pans and arranged the group's songs, which Munroe remembered as consisting of popular calypsos such as "Maryanne" and "Brown Skin Girl," along with American pop standards such as "Cheek to Cheek" arranged with a calypso beat. The group played at Caribbean fetes and dances, including Carnival-related affairs at Park Palace and Rockland Palace, where they appeared alongside orchestras led by Clark, MacBeth, and Daphne Weeks.[57] According to Munroe, King brought his first small group out for the Seventh Avenue Carnival sometime around 1950 or 1951.[58] The crowd was enthused at the sight and sound of the new instruments:

> Those who like the music are jumping up and dancing and having a good time. Some get involved, maybe with a bottle and spoon for some background. Some would stand on the side, some would follow us. . . . At points people crowded in around us. This was a new thing for them—back then some of them had never seen steelband before. And they wanted to get close and look at the drum—even wanted to touch it, you know. That was new. . . . We had three or four songs, and we played them over and over. OK, "Brown Skin Girl," over and over, there was no deep arrangement."[59]

Munroe confirmed that King's early band would have lacked the melodic range and sectional complexity of modern steel orchestras, but was well suited for street Carnival, where a strong rhythmic groove was paramount. Structurally, tunes consisted of a simple repeated melodic line or perhaps an elementary verse/chorus form: "There were no change of keys, no big [theme] changes. It was strictly by how the song went—the verse and chorus, over and over. Back then we didn't have enough notes to do it any other way."[60] A 1960 recording that King made for Elektra Records affirms Munroe's basic assessment of the music—the tunes were arranged in relatively simple verse/chorus form. Two or three tenor pans play the lead melody in unison, a second tenor and guitar pan play an elementary countermelody or strum chords, and a set of bass pans lays down a low melodic line (the bass pans had replaced the two-note dudup from King's earlier instrumental configuration). Maracas and iron provide light percussion and a lilting rhythm.[61] These simple ("no deep") arrangements designed for street Carnival stood in contrast to the complex, multi-themed arrangements that would soon become the hallmark of Panorama tunes.

King recalled that it was sometime in the mid-1950s that he brought a larger ensemble to the Harlem Carnival parade (perhaps the "raffish-looking" steelband cited in the 1955 *New Yorker* article), wearing T-shirts with "Trinidad Steelband" emblazoned on the front (see Figure 3.3). The group of approximately twenty players, each wielding a pan-around-the-neck, was well received, and they returned in subsequent years.[62] King remembered that by the late 1950s, other groups were joining his Trinidad Steel Band on the streets for Harlem Carnival. These included Lawrence "Pops" McCarthy's Harlem All Stars (sometimes known as the Tropitones), Brooklyn-based Caldera's Moderneers (probably referred to as Carlos Caldera's Steel Band in the 1958 *Amsterdam News* piece), and Brooklyn-based Conrad Mauge's Trinidad Serenaders (probably referred to as the "Serenaders in Steel" cited above). Reynolds "Caldera" Caraballo (b. 1931) grew up in King's neighborhood in Port of Spain and came to Brooklyn in 1956. A talented pan player and arranger, he was immediately

Figure 3.3. Rudy King and his Trinidad Steelband, Seventh Avenue, Harlem Carnival, 1958 (courtesy of Rudy King).

recruited into King's band, where he stayed until 1958, when he left to form his own steel orchestra, the Moderneers.[63] He and King claimed that their early steelbands were not officially affiliated with any masquerade bands, nor were they formally invited to play by the parade organizers. "We just showed up," recalled King, "in the spirit of Carnival." Caraballo surmised that the parade officials were concerned that steelbands might disrupt an otherwise orderly event: "You see this was a real parade [unlike Carnival in Trinidad] that was trying to start at point A and end at point B," he recalled, "and the steelbands could slow everything down, with all the people coming out on the street and dancing around us. So they kept us in the rear."[64]

Neither King nor Caraballo restricted their playing to the Caribbean community. After joining the musicians union in 1951, King was able to acquire well-paying engagements at midtown and downtown venues, including Circle in the Square, Café Wah?, and the Village Gate.[65] Art D'Lugoff, owner of the Gate, booked him into a Carnegie Hall "Steelband Clash" that he organized in 1958 and would serve as King's unofficial manager for a number of years. King played several stints at Chicago's Blue Angel Club and toured the East Coast with a small group that he sometimes fronted as a vocalist. Caraballo performed as one of three pan players in the short-lived Broadway show *House of Flowers* by Truman Capote and Harold Arlen, and toured with Harry Belafonte for a short period in the early 1960s. His Moderneers played at the Village Gate and other downtown clubs as well as at private suburban parties and country clubs. These later opportunities increased in the early 1960s thanks to Belafonte's best-selling recordings, which introduced wider American audiences to stylized versions of calypsos and Caribbean folk songs. When performing for white audiences, King's and Caraballo's bands played mostly Belafonte hits, including "Mary Anne," "Jamaica Farewell," and "Matilda," as well as calypso-tinged arrangements of American popular and jazz standards. Catering to popular images of Caribbean entertainers, they autoexoticized by donning colorful matching outfits, sporting straw hats, and including a floor show featuring a sensual limbo dance. However, they maintained a separate repertoire, consisting primarily of the latest calypsos from Trinidad, for Caribbean dances and Labor Day street Carnival.[66]

In many ways King's and Caraballo's varied musical experiences mirrored those of the New York's expatriate calypsonians. Perceived as authentic exponents of the new steelband music, they moved comfortably across the boundaries of New York's diverse cultural landscape, entertaining Caribbean and American audiences, as opportunities arose. They served simultaneously as community tradition-bearers and popular entertainers, at times collapsing distinctions between the two.

Caraballo's concerns over the steelband's potential to disrupt the Harlem parade were well founded. Harlem's street Carnival had always vacillated between a conventional American civic parade, replete with marching bands, festive floats, beauty queens, business and political leaders, and community organizations, and the chaos of Trinidadian street Carnival.

A rooftop photograph of the 1950 parade that appeared in the *Amsterdam News* pictures an orderly procession of floats and dignitary-bearing automobiles, with spectators confined to the sidewalks behind the police barriers that lined Seventh Avenue.[67] But as the decade wore on and the crowds swelled to 150,000 spectators and 5,000 marchers, that order tended to break down, especially when the mas and steelbands appeared.[68] "From time to time," stated an observer at the 1955 parade, "a knot of onlookers, carried away by a particularly provocative beat, would burst in to the street to become impromptu marchers themselves." That proactive beat was furnished by a steelband and the aforementioned "beaters" of drums and bottles.[69] "Spectators Join Calypso Parade: March by 5,000 becomes a Carnival for 120,000 on Upper Seventh Avenue," ran a headline in the *New York Times* describing the 1959 event. "The wonder of the parade, however, was that it rapidly became an audience-participation affair," noted reporter Michael James. He went on to explain:

Once it got properly started there was no way of distinguishing the official parade from the spectators who had joined the march after succumbing to the irresistible calypso tempo of the steel bands. . . . There was no form to the march. It was led off by a steel band. Other steel bands marched at intervals in the parade, which took about an hour to pass the reviewing stand. Much of the group fell in behind the first group of young men and women in Caribbean costumes banging on converted oil drums. . . . When the last of the calypso ensembles had passed, the great majority of the audience was in the street. Dancing to the general enjoiner to "shake it man, shake it."[70]

Returning to Thomas Turino's model, what began as a "presentational" performance of musical ensembles and masqueraders parading for spectators behind police barricades evolved (or devolved, from the organizer's perspective) into a "participatory" celebration as those spectators took to the street and became performers themselves.[71] When the anarchy of street Carnival trumped the orderly parade, it was often steelbands, with their "irresistible tempos," at the center of the action, tempting bystanders to "shake it man" and join the dancing throng.

Growing concerns over crowd size and order prompted West Indies Day Association president Evans Butcher, who had taken over the position from Jessie Waddell Crompton, to issue a public notice for participants (especially groups) to send him postal cards requesting permission to participate in the 1959 parade. Instructions on "direction and location" would be issued to accommodate the expected "large increase in attendance in the parade." Butcher followed up his call for order with a plea for pan-Caribbean unity, asking "West Indians from all the various Islands to attend." "Please do not stand on the side lines as a looker-on and linger," he implored. "Come out and help us to make this a National Day. Something to be proud of, admired and respected. Make it a tradition."[72] His reference to a "National Day" moved the discourse from the local to the international, no doubt resonating with many members of Harlem's Caribbean populace, whose native homelands were, at that point in history, embroiled in struggles to gain independence from Great Britain.

More serious than disorderly and overzealous revelers were increased fears of violence as Carnival entered into the turbulent decade of the 1960s. On 9 September 1961, Harlemites awoke to the *Amsterdam News*'s sensationalist banner headline: "West Indian Parade Ends in Riot." What was initially described as "a bottle throwing escapade" turned into a serious brawl that resulted in the injury of ten policemen and two civilians. Steel pan players were in the center of the melee, as a photographer situated near the back of the parade reported to the paper:

In front of us was a steel band. At 141st Street and Seventh Avenue a spectator grabbed one of the drums. The drummer and spectator tugged back and forth. The drummer succeeded in freeing the drum from the spectator and crashed it over his head. Another drummer banged another man, apparently with the first spectator, over the head and a fight started. Police tried to stop the fight but bottles and bricks came from all directions and reinforcements were called.[73]

This sort of account reflects the conundrum that steelbands had been facing in Trinidad for decades. On the one hand, their music was necessary to unleash the deepest celebratory spirit of street Carnival by fostering a sense of oneness among musicians, masqueraders, and onlookers turned dancing participants. On the other hand, their propensity to bog down the processional, coupled with their reputation as violence-prone "badjohns" and "robustmen," as they were disparagingly called back home, often put them at odds with the parade organizers and police whose job it was to maintain order.[74] The Harlem organizers evidently tolerated the steelbands as something of a necessary evil because they wanted to showcase what they perceived to be authentic Trinidad Carnival culture. But tensions between steelbands and parade organizers would only intensify when Labor Day Carnival moved to Brooklyn.

Evans Butcher declared that the "ruffians" who instigated the violence at the 1961 parade "were definitely not West Indians." His remarks revealed a breach between the Caribbean and native black Carnival-goers, implying that the latter were responsible for the trouble. "Everyone knows that West Indians do not carry knives or implements for committing crimes," he angrily proclaimed. Butcher reiterated that "the parade has now become an institution and the West Indian Community will not permit hooligans to stop it. We are already planning for next year."[75] Unfortunately for Harlem's Caribbean community, Butcher's bold assertion turned out to be a hollow one. On 4 September 1962, the *New York Herald Tribune* reported, under the heading "No Calypso Parade," that the "riotous affair" had "got out of hand last year. Nine policemen were injured with whiskey bottles and other objects when they attempted to keep onlookers separated from the brightly costumed young girls dancing to the steel drum bands. When the parade organizers asked for the usual permit this year, on Saturday, police told them drily they were 'too late.'"[76] Following this note, all press accounts of the Carnival parade ceased. Apparently the 1961 incident proved to be too much for the authorities, who were, against the backdrop of the burgeoning civil rights movement, becoming increasingly wary of large gatherings of black people. After fourteen years, the Harlem celebration had come to an end.[77]

Performing Cultural Identity in the Diaspora

The Harlem Carnival parades, along with Clark's early Dame Lorraine dances, were the earliest demonstrations of cultural performance creating focal points for Caribbean community and identity in the diaspora. In these public settings, the singing, dancing, and masquerading migrants came together to celebrate their shared culture. Serving as a temporary antidote for the distress of cultural and geographic dislocation, such participatory performances satisfied nostalgic yearnings for home by transporting Carnival celebrants back to the islands, at least for an afternoon or an evening. There was, however, an important caveat: all Caribbean people were welcomed to participate, but only on Trinidadian terms. That is, Harlem jumped up to a Trinidad-style Carnival, anchored in the essential cultural forms of Trinidadian calypso, steelband, and masquerading. The Carnival organizers, the bandleaders (save Puerto Rican native Gregory Felix), the New York calypsonians, and the early pan players were all born or reared in Trinidad. The question of how to position the event as a pan-Caribbean festival, one that would attract the increasing numbers of Jamaicans, Barbadians, Guyanese, Grenadians, and other English-speaking Caribbean migrants who were streaming into central Brooklyn by the late 1960s, would prove a persistent challenge for Brooklyn's Trinidadian Carnival organizers.

Harlem Carnival also set a precedent for the cultural discourse among New York's Caribbean migrants and their various urban neighbors. Parade organizers Waddell Crompton and Butcher believed that a properly promoted, highly visible Carnival festival could serve to "strengthen the bonds of friendship and respect" between Caribbean migrants and their black and white American neighbors. In doing so the Harlem sponsors initiated a strategy grounded in the practice of cultural pluralism that their Brooklyn counterparts would soon embrace. Assessing success in this arena is difficult, but Invader's observations on the diverse nature of the crowd at the initial parade and accounts of mixed Caribbean/African American audiences at Clark's Dame Lorraine dances suggest that significant numbers of Harlem's African American populace were involved in Caribbean Carnival, either as participants or spectators. Reports that calypso rhythms, Latin rumbas, and Lindy Hop steps comfortably commingled on the dance floors of Dame Lorraine Galas offer further evidence of cultural interchange between island and native black New Yorkers. A shared African heritage of song and dance styles no doubt facilitated such interaction, and we can assume that a degree of respect and camaraderie would have been fostered. Participatory musical performance on the streets and in dance halls was a potential connecting force for the diverse peoples of the black Atlantic who now claimed Harlem as their home.

Carnival celebration and its attendant calypso scene also provided a space for cultural contact and dialogue between Harlem's Caribbean community and downtown white audiences. The situation, however, was complicated, with music both contesting and reinforcing conventional racial norms. Clark and the New York Calypsonians certainly found receptive listeners for their music at the Village clubs and midtown concert halls in the 1940s, although they were no doubt viewed as purveyors of cultural spectacle as much as practitioners of serious art. And there is scarce evidence that white fans journeyed uptown with any regularity to take part in his Dame Lorraine dances or the Harlem parade. Coverage of the parade by the *Times* and the *New Yorker* did bring wider visibility to the event, but neither shied away from racially essentialized language and overtly sexual imagery. A "full-throated and uninhibited crowd," "undulating girls unfathomably decked out in butterfly costumes," "a raffish-looking steelband," and "beaters flailing manfully" were among the titillating descriptions of characters appearing in the *New Yorker*'s 1955 account of Harlem's "Mardi Gras."[78] The line between the validating cultural expression and perpetuating racial stereotypes was thin and often blurry.

The Calypso Craze—Cultural Exposure and Appropriation

The commercial "calypso craze" that swept the United States in the 1950s was yet another arena of cross-cultural contact that presented New York's Caribbean community and its Carnival musicians with both opportunities and dilemmas. National interest in calypso rose with the 1945 success of the Andrews Sisters' cover of Invader's "Rum and Coca-Cola," reached its zenith with the release of Harry Belafonte's 1956 *Calypso* LP on RCA, and quickly subsided by decade's end with the advent of the commercial folk music revival and the rejuvenation of rock and roll in the early 1960s.[79] Although the commercial popularization of calypso roughly mirrored the rise and fall of Harlem Carnival, they have been generally viewed as independent movements. The calypso craze, as Andrew Martin has argued, was grounded in the exoticized "difference" that white patrons ascribed to Carnival music. This was in contrast to a deep sense of cultural "sameness" that allowed Harlem's Caribbean community to embrace the music and celebration as shared cultural heritage.[80] The result, according to Martin, was a "filtered version of calypso music and culture in the United States—one that is saturated with postwar American hegemonic visions of island bliss and happiness," and one representing a "starkly different reality from the genre's Trinidadian roots."[81]

Despite these divergent paths, the commercial craze did have some, albeit indirect, effects on Harlem Carnival and its musicians. By the mid-1950s a growing national interest in calypso no doubt prompted initial coverage of the Harlem street Carnival by the mainstream white press, particularly the *Times* and the *New Yorker*. While such media coverage sometimes slipped into sensationalism, it did bring national notoriety and a degree of cultural prestige to the event. The New York Calypsonians Duke of Iron, Sir Lancelot, and Lord Invader benefited indirectly from the overall surge in national popularity of calypso with increased club dates and touring opportunities, as did the small steelbands led by King, Caraballo, and Mauge. The fact that Elektra Records was willing to take a chance and record King's relatively unknown Original Trinidad Steel Band in 1960 was no doubt an attempt to capitalize on the brief national popularity of calypso.[82]

While these local calypsonians and pan players welcomed the sudden attention to their craft and appreciated the slight increase in demand for their music, they were frustrated that in the long run their careers benefited only marginally. None of the New York–based Carnival musicians had hit recordings or gained national acclaim.[83] Those rewards would fall to Belafonte and a host of non-Caribbean folk and pop singers, ranging from the Tarriers and the Kingston Trio to the Mills Brothers, Rosemary Clooney, and Nat King Cole. Such developments prompted several black critics to express broader reservations. "Once again Tin Pan Alley has raided Harlem," warned Alvin White of the *Afro-American*. "Calypso evenings at Carnegie Hall are lining the pockets of promoters while the performers get peanuts. Colored singers not only have to compete with each other, now they are threatened with the wholesale invasion of calypso by white singers and orchestras."[84] The Trinidadian actor, dancer, and choreographer Geoffrey Holder voiced his displeasure with Belafonte and the other interlopers for what he viewed as their misrepresentation of his country's native art form. They did not sing "true calypso," but rather "Manhattan calypsos," a style he identified as "an American version of West Indian melodies and lyrics." A Manhattan calypso, Holder charged, was "slicked up, prettied up, and sophisticated up. It is not spontaneous, it is calculated." It had little in common with genuine Trinidad calypso songs, which, he lamented, were not accessible to the broader American public because they were "too foreign, too unfamiliar."[85]

Comparing Harlem's prewar calypsos with the 1950s commercial Manhattan calypsos is instructive in underscoring the complex and sometimes contradictory dimensions of musical hybridity as it unfolded in the diaspora. The former melded the original Trinidad calypso with elements of American jazz, blues, and Tin Pan Alley, while the latter adapted idioms from folk and pop music styles. Such creolized forms could potentially open up spaces for cross-cultural dialogue, but the results were often unpredictable and uneven. In the case of Harlem calypso, where a high degree of control was maintained by the Caribbean musicians, the outcome was a robust mix that was artistically transformative and culturally empowering. But when artistic control was wrested from the originators, and the performers were by and large cultural outsiders, the result was the short-lived, aesthetically vacuous, and financially exploitive music of the calypso craze. Harlem calypsos, performed in community settings for migrant audiences, were strong markers of cultural affirmation, while the popular Manhattan calypsos that reached broader biracial audiences clearly bowed to bottom-line corporate interests.

Yet celebrating Harlem calypso for its cultural authenticity and empowering sensibilities, while dismissing Manhattan calypsos as overly commercialized and exploitive pap, is too reductive. Harlem calypsos played a role in exoticized downtown shows for white audiences, and Manhattan calypsos did introduce Trinidad and its music—albeit a watered-down version of that music—to a wider international audience to the benefit of a few Caribbean artists. As Jan Nederveen Pieterse has theorized, hybridity problematizes cultural boundaries, those metaphorical delineations that supposedly define and separate groups of people.[86] The musical hybridization that produced calypso in New York more often than not resulted in porous, messy boundaries that affirmed and challenged social norms and cultural hierarchies.

Additional tropes of tropical exoticism and racial primitivism wound their way through the popular presentation of Carnival music throughout the 1950s. The calypso clubs that proliferated in New York and other American cities during the period "created an imaginary Caribbean atmosphere with fishnets, palm frond and other trappings. Performers often wore straw hats and striped floral outfits unlike the dress suits worn by calypsonians in Trinidad." In these venues, American audiences were particularly appreciative of "risqué lyrics, limbo dancing, and steel pans."[87] Reviewing the 1954 Caribbean-themed Broadway production *House of Flowers* by Truman Capote and Harold Arlen, *Times* critic Brooks Atkinson offered the following description of the dancing and music: "Tall and short Negroes, adults and youngsters, torrid maidens in flashy costumes and bare-chested bucks break out into a number of wild, grotesque, animalistic dances. And a steel band provides a haunting accompaniment."[88]

Whatever opportunities the commercial craze offered for increased Caribbean cultural exposure and financial gain were tempered with questions of artistic misrepresentation, cultural appropriation, and racial stereotyping. There is little to suggest that the short-lived national enthusiasm for all things calypso did much to promote Waddell Crompton's vision of "strengthen[ing] the bonds of friendship and respect" between Caribbean Harlem and mainstream white America.

Nascent Transnationalism and the Move to Brooklyn

The termination of Harlem's Labor Day parade did not signal the demise of Caribbean Carnival music in New York. Coming on the eve of significant changes in US immigration law that would ignite a new wave of migration, Harlem's loss would soon become Brooklyn's gain, as the borough emerged as the undisputed center of Afro-Caribbean New York by the late 1960s. The upsurge in migration would usher in a new generation of calypsonians, band musicians and arrangers, and pan players who would help shape a more elaborate Labor Day Carnival and feed a burgeoning Caribbean music scene.

Harlem's relatively short-lived Carnival set in place the basic model for the soon-to-be-realized Brooklyn celebration, while also serving as a harbinger of challenges to come. In terms of structure, a large and public outdoor gathering—situated somewhere between a conventional parade and the chaotic street Carnival procession—was established as the centerpiece of the festivities. This paradoxical relationship between parade and street Carnival would continue to plague organizers and participants—particularly the steel and mas bands—as the Brooklyn event took shape. The afternoon parade had been extended to a weekend of events that would feature instrumental orchestras, calypsonians, steelbands, and staged performances by dancers and masqueraders. While the dance orchestras and steelbands maintained a staple of Latin-style rumbas, waltzes, and American popular tunes in their repertoires, Trinidad calypso music, either sung or instrumental, emerged as the defining cultural expression for all Carnival-related events.

Harlem Carnival foreshadowed the transnational flow of cultural actors and expressive forms that would become a hallmark of its Brooklyn progeny. The Harlem Labor Day parade and attendant Carnival dances were built around styles of music, dance, and masquerading imported by Trinidadian émigrés. Connections to home were maintained and refreshed through visiting calypsonians who journeyed north to perform and record in New York studios. Indeed, it was these recordings—made in New York or at portable operations set up in Trinidad by American record companies, and marketed throughout the islands and North America—that allowed Harlem's singers, musicians, and fans to stay current with the latest Trinidad Carnival music. Easy-to-circulate commercial recordings became the lifeblood of transitional Carnival music from the late 1920s well into the 1950s.

Lionel Belasco traveled back and forth to Trinidad in the 1920s and 1930s in search of new material, as did Gerald Clark and Houdini, at least in the early years of their careers. By the time of the first outdoor Harlem Carnival, these musicians had cut back on their travels to Trinidad.[89] New York's calypsonians, with the exception of Lord Invader, developed their careers independently from the Trinidad Carnival tents, and there is no indication that King or the other influential Harlem pan players traveled home with any regularity to reconnect with the Trinidad steelbands during the 1950s. The paucity and high costs of air travel between New York and Trinidad at that time were no doubt prohibitive. Apparently, the orchestra musicians, calypsonians, and pan players found enough work between Harlem's Caribbean migrants and the city's white audiences to maintain their careers (which could be augmented with day jobs when necessary) without routine and expensive travel back to the Caribbean. Likewise, they formed a pool of local talent from which the Harlem parade organizers and dance hall promoters could draw. This abundance of musicians, coupled with the relatively small scope of Harlem Carnival, negated the necessity to regularly import performers from Trinidad and kept the annual event somewhat insular.

By contrast, the organizers of Brooklyn Carnival would regularly bring in popular calypsonians, and occasionally steelbands, from Trinidad and other islands to headline their larger events. As additional overseas Carnivals were established in London and Toronto in the late 1960s and affordable air travel became more available, a network of singers, musicians, costume-makers, and diehard fans would soon circulate the globe, reconnecting diasporic communities with their Trinidad homeland and reinvigorating their local Carnival celebrations. The transnational dimensions of New York Carnival, initially established in Harlem, would expand dramatically when the celebration moved across the East River to central Brooklyn.

Notes

1. Donald Hill, "A History of West Indian Carnival in New York to 1978," *New York Folklore Quarterly* 20, nos. 1–2 (1994): 48.

2. Ramona Lowe, "New York Celebrates West Indian Day," *Daily Gleaner*, 23 September 1947. Lowe's report of the rough treatment early Carnival masqueraders suffered at the hands of local police is drawn from a souvenir journal distributed by the 1947 parade organizers that referred back to the earliest Harlem Carnival parties in the late 1920s.

3. Hill, "History of West Indian Carnival," p. 49. Reports of early outdoor Carnival activity in Harlem are thin; Hill's citing of Gorin's recollections come from an interview anthropology student Robert Abrahams conducted with Gorin in 1977.

4. "X Club Presenting Caribbean Serenaders," *New York Age*, 8 September 1934.

5. "Mercury Athletic Club," *New York Age*, 20 October 1934.

6. Vernon Andrade was known primarily as a jazz musician, but his orchestra played various Latin styles as well as American jazz and standard dance music. His contributions at the Renaissance Casino in the 1930s are discussed in Lara Putnam, *Radical Moves: Caribbean Migrants and the Politics of Race in the Jazz Age* (University of North Carolina Press, 2013), pp. 161–163.

7. "Holds Carnival," *New York Amsterdam News*, 9 February 1935.

8. "Istmica Plans Near Completion for 'Fiesta,'" *New York Age*, 23 February 1935.

9. "Carnival Time," *New York Amsterdam News*, 16 January 1937.

10. "Carnival Revue," *New York Amsterdam News*, 22 January 1938.

11. "Gerald Clark Featuring Gala Dame Lorraine," *New York Age*, 18 February 1939.

12. "Masked Revels Divert Harlem—Natives of Trinidad Living Here Dance and Sing in Pre-Christian Saturnalia," *New York Sun*, 26 February 1941.

13. "Dame Lorraine and Carnival Dance Held at Royal Windsor," *New York Age*, 21 February 1942.

14. Bill Chase, "This and That," *Amsterdam News*, 13 March 1943.

15. See display ad, "Gerald Clark Presents the One, the Only, the Original Gala Dance Lorraine and Tenth Annual Carnival Dance," *Amsterdam News*, 12 February 1944.

16. See photo spreads in "Gay Dame Lorraine Carnival Ends Pre-Lent Season," *New York Amsterdam News*, 5 March 1949; "The Dame Lorraine Carnival Shows the Best in Costume," *New York Amsterdam News*, 25 February 1950; and "Mardi Gras Comes North," *New York Amsterdam News*, 17 February 1951.

17. "Carnival Dance Benefits Hospital," *Philadelphia Tribune*, 17 January 1950.

18. "Trinidad-American Club Stages Carnival Dance," *New York Age*, 2 February 1957.

19. "Dame Lorraine Carnival Shows the Best in Costume."

20. "Masked Revels Divert Harlem Natives of Trinidad."

21. "Mardi Gras Dancers Fill Renaissance," *New York Amsterdam News*, 6 September 1952.

22. "Socially Speaking," *New York Amsterdam News*, 6 March 1943.

23. Display ads in the *New York Amsterdam News* on 12 February 1944, 3 February 1945, and 2 March 1946.

24. Display ad, *New York Amsterdam News*, 11 January 1947.

25. "Mardi Gras Comes North," *New York Amsterdam News*, 17 February 1951. See also "Gay Dame Lorraine Carnival Ends Pre-Lent Season" and "Dame Lorraine Carnival Shows the Best in Costumes."

26. Caribbean in-migration to the United States virtually ceased during the Depression, but with the end of World War II the numbers began to rise slowly, up until 1952, when the McCarran-Walter Act placed new restrictions of the use of quotas for British and other colonial subjects. Although the numbers were small throughout the rest of the 1950s, most of the Caribbean Anglophile immigrants entering the United States settled in New York City. The number of foreign-born blacks in the United States, approximately half of whom lived in New York City, increased from 83,941 to 113,842 between 1940 and 1950, and grew to 123,322 by 1960. See Philip Kasinitz, *Caribbean New York: Black Immigrants and the Politics of Race* (Cornell University Press, 1992), pp. 24–26.

27. "50,000 Harlemites Watch First Annual Trinidad Carnival and Parade; Dance at Golden Gate," *New York Age*, 6 September 1947.

28. Lowe, "New York Celebrates West Indian Day."

29. See Stephen Robertson, "Parades in 1920s Harlem," Digital Harlem Blog, 1 February 2011, https://digitalharlemblog.wordpress.com/2011/02/01/parades-in-1920s-harlem/.

30. Susan Davis, *Parades and Power: Street Theatre in Nineteenth-Century Philadelphia* (University of California Press, 1986), pp. 5, 159–166.

31. "Celebrations Mark WI Rating in Community: Three Days of Merrymaking Highlight Various Cultures," *New York Amsterdam News*, 8 September 1951.

32. "50,000 Harlemites Watch First Annual Trinidad Carnival and Parade."

33. Display ad, *New York Amsterdam News*, 30 August 1947.

34. Lowe, "New York Celebrates West Indian Day."

35. The 1948 recording "Labor Day" by Lord Invader is found on *Lord Invader: Calypso in New York* (Smithsonian Folkways SFW CD 40454, 2000). Although the song was not released by Folkways Records until the 1950s, liner notes compiler John Cowley claims a 9 April 1948 contract between Invader and Folkways dates the piece. Crowley also notes that Invader's chorus is based on a 1946 Lord Kitchener calypso, "Jump in the Line and Wag Your Body on Time."

36. Photograph display, *Chicago Defender*, 13 September 1947.

37. MacBeth's Orchestra is pictured under the banner "Harlem Turns Out for Annual West Indies Day," *New York Amsterdam News*, 8 September 1951. The 139th Street parade reviewing stand is mentioned in "Celebrating West Indies Day," *New York Amsterdam News*, 1 September 1951.

38. "WI Parade Short but Successful," *New York Age*, 9 September 1950.

39. "165,000 Watch Indies Day Parade," *New York Age*, 6 September 1958.

40. West Indian Day Association flyer for 7 September 1959 Carnival events, courtesy of Don Hill. The Greene-Weeks "battle" was also announced in the *New York Age* (12 September 1959).

41. "Claude 'Fats' Greene Inherits MacBeth the Great's Baton," *New York Age*, 18 May 1957; "Fats Greene Buried in Flushing," *New York Amsterdam News*, 20 January 1968.

42. Don Byran Sr., interview with author and Ray Funk, 7 September 2014.

43. Daphne Weeks, interview with Don Hill, 26 March, 1976, Brooklyn, NY; interview with Bob Abrahams, 13 June 1977. Interview transcripts courtesy of Don Hill.

44. "West Indian Carnival Spirit Lasted 3 Days," *New York Amsterdam News*, 8 September 1951.

45. "Mardi Gras Set for Sept. 4-5-6," *New York Amsterdam News*, 5 September 1953.

46. Michael James, "Spectators Join Calypso Parade: March by 5,000 Becomes a Carnival for 120,000 on Upper Seventh Avenue," *New York Times*, 8 September 1959. Conventional marching bands are noted in "165,000 Watch Indies Day Parade."

47. "West Indians Hold Spectacular Labor Day Parade," *New York Amsterdam News*, 11 September 1948.

48. "West Indian Carnival Spirit Lasted 3 Days," *New York Amsterdam News*, 8 September 1951; "Two Thousand Join Parade of West Indians," *New York Times*, 7 September 1954; "Talk of the Town: Mardi Gras," *New Yorker*, 17 September 1955.

49. All three Carl Van Vechten photographs of the 1949 Harlem Carnival parade can be viewed at the City Museum of New York's website, http://collections.mcny.org/C.aspx?VP3=SearchResult_VPage&VBID=24UP1GYTAHGE&SMLS=1.

50. "Diplomat, O'Dwyer to Witness West Indians Parade Saturday," *New York Amsterdam News*, 3 September 1949. Dating the first appearance of Rudy King and his steelband in the Harlem parade is difficult.

While the *New York Amsterdam News* previously announced that King and his steelband were to appear in that year's event, there is reason to question the accuracy of this report. According to King, he did not arrive in New York until 1949, making it questionable whether or not he could have assembled an entire steelband for the 1949 Carnival so quickly. Evidence from bandmate Carlton Munroe (see below) suggests that King first brought a small steelband out for the Harlem parade in the early 1950s.

51. "WI Parade Short but Successful."

52. "The Talk of the Town: Mardi Gras."

53. "Trinidad American Club Stages Carnival Dance," *New York Age*, 2 February 1957.

54. "165,000 Watch Indies Labor Day Parade."

55. James, "Spectators Join Calypso Parade."

56. Information on Rudy King is drawn from an interview with the author and Leslie Slater, 25 October 1995, Brooklyn, NY.

57. Carlton Munroe, interview with author, 8 August 2016, Brooklyn. An 11 December 1954 "Community" notice in the *New York Age* announced a dance at the Rockland Palace featuring music by Gerald Clark's Caribbean Serenaders and Rudolph King's Trinidad Steel Band.

58. Munroe could not identify the exact year of the King band's first appearance in Harlem Carnival, but it had to be sometime between his first meeting King around 1950 and his induction into the Armed Services in December 1953. He recalled performing with King at the Harlem parade two or three times during that period. Munroe, interview, 8 August 2016.

59. Ibid.

60. Ibid.

61. *The Original Trinidad Steel Band* (Elektra Records EKL-139, 1960). Listen, for example, to "Steel Meringue," available on YouTube, at https://www.youtube.com/watch?v=65jXvvDzXVY.

62. King, interview, 25 October 1995.

63. Information on Reynolds "Caldera" Caraballo is drawn from an interview with the author, 9 June 1996, Brooklyn, NY.

64. Ibid.

65. Rudy King was the first steel pan player to join the American Federation of Musicians Local 802. Carlton Munroe claimed that King had to fight, and eventually prevailed, to have the steel pan recognized as a bona-fide musical instrument. Munroe, interview with author, 8 August 2016.

66. For further discussion of the repertories and performance settings of New York City's early steelbands, based on interviews with Rudy King, Reynolds Caldera Caraballo, and Conrad Mauge, see Ray Allen and Les Slater, "Steel Pan Grows in Brooklyn: Trinidad Music and Cultural Identity," in *Island Sounds in the Global City: Caribbean Popular Music and Identity in New York*, edited by Ray Allen and Lois Wilcken (University of Illinois Press, 1998), pp. 119–122.

67. See photograph spread under "West Indies Day Parade Replete with Fun, Girls, Best Ever," *New York Amsterdam News*, 9 September 1950.

68. Crowd estimates of Carnival participants and observers tended to vary and may have been exaggerated. The initial 1947 parade crowd was estimated at 50,000 (*New York Age*, 6 September 1947). A preview of the 1950 parade predicted a turnout of a million and a half spectators, but was revised to a more reasonable 100,000 the following week (*New York Age*, 2 September 1950 and 9 September 1950). Subsequent estimates

were as high as 150,000 (*New York Amsterdam News*, 8 September 1951), 150,000 (*New York Times*, 7 September 1954), and 165,000 (*New York Age*, 6 September 1958).

69. "Talk of the Town: Mardi Gras."

70. James, "Spectators Join Calypso Parade."

71. Thomas Turino, *Music as Social Life: The Politics of Participation* (University of Chicago Press, 2008), p. 26.

72. West Indian Day Association flyer for 7 September 1959 Carnival events, courtesy of Don Hill.

73. "West Indian Parade Ends in Riot," *New York Amsterdam News*, 9 September 1961.

74. Steelband violence was a contentious issue during the postwar Carnival celebrations in Trinidad. According to folklorist Stephen Stuempfle, members of the middle and upper class came to view "the steelband movement as a threat to the social order. The violence and chaos of the steelbands could be easily associated with demonstrations, riots, and general social unrest that had become so prevalent." See Stephen Stuempfle, *The Steelband Movement: The Forging of a National Art in Trinidad and Tobago* (University of Pennsylvania Press, 1995), p. 62.

75. "Hooligans Disrupt Parade: Blame Non-West Indians for Clashes on Labor Day," *Pittsburgh Courier*, 16 September 1961.

76. "The Holiday Parade on E. 108th Street," *Herald Tribune*, 4 September 1962.

77. There has been some confusion in the scholarly literature regarding the date of the last Harlem Carnival parade. In 1979 Donald Hill and Robert Abramson stated that the Harlem Carnival lasted until 1964, when "a small riot disrupted the parade." See "West Indian Carnival in Brooklyn," *Natural History: Incorporating Nature Magazine* 88, no. 7 (August–September 1979): 83. Hill repeated this narrative in 1994, noting that the 1964 Carnival parade was "halted by 'hoodlums,'" as Carnival participants described them, who pelted the masqueraders with bottles and rocks. Mr. Gorin's parade permit was lost and he moved to Brooklyn." See Hill, "History of West Indian Carnival," p. 49. The 1964 date has threaded through the secondary scholarship on Brooklyn Carnival, including my own previous writings. However, the above-cited *Herald Tribune* article confirms that there was no Harlem parade in 1962, and the absence of any mention of the event in the *Amsterdam News* from 1962 on strongly suggests that 1961 was the last time the official Carnival Labor Day celebration was held on Seventh Avenue. It may be that Hill and Abramson, and their main informant, Rufus Gorin, were conflating the 1961 Carnival disturbance with the unrelated Harlem riots of the summer of 1964, which received a good deal of media attention. Hence the inaccurate 1964 date.

78. "Talk of the Town: Mardi Gras."

79. For more on the calypso craze, see Ray Funk and Donald Hill, "Will Calypso Doom Rock 'n' Roll?: The U.S. Calypso Craze of 1957," in *Trinidad Carnival: The Cultural Politics of a Transnational Festival*, edited by Garth Green and Philip Scher (Indiana University Press, 2003), pp. 178–197; and *Calypso Craze, 1956–1957 and Beyond*, CD/DVD set and booklet, edited by Ray Funk and Michael Eldridge (Bear Family Records, 2014).

80. Andrew Martin, "Pan-America: Calypso, Exotica, and the Development of Steel Pan in the United States" (PhD diss., University of Minnesota, 2011), p. 30.

81. Andrew Martin, *Steelpan Ambassadors: The US Navy Steel Band, 1957–1999* (University Press of Mississippi, 2017), p. 9.

82. Rudy King's 1960 LP *The Original Trinidad Steel Band* (Elektra Records) included a potpourri of instrumental pieces that were labeled calypsos, meringues, and mambos. In addition, the album featured a number of American pop tunes, including "Cheek to Cheek," "Autumn Leaves," "Begin the Beguine," and "Sweet and Gentle." The inclusion of these American standards, arranged with light calypso rhythms, suggests that the audience for the recording comprised, at least in part, middle-class whites who were familiar with popular Belafonte-style calypsos.

83. The Mighty Sparrow and Lord Melody were two influential Trinidadian calypsonians whose careers benefited tangentially from the commercial calypso craze, at least in its aftermath. Both singers made recordings for the American independent label Cook and for RCA Records—Sparrow's Cook releases were between 1958 and 1960, and his RCA releases between 1960 and 1963; Melody's Cook releases were between 1957 and 1962, and his RCA releases between 1959 and 1963. Both eventually relocated in New York in the 1960s where they performed for Caribbean and white audiences. Melody worked for Harry Belafonte, and Sparrow used the city as a base for international touring.

84. Alvin White, "Calypso Is the Things," *Baltimore Afro American*, 23 February 1957.

85. Geoffrey Holder, "The Fad from Trinidad," *New York Times Magazine*, 21 April 1957. It should be noted that Belafonte was born in New York of Jamaican parentage, but had little direct experience with Trinidadian-style calypso (Jamaica, at that time, had no Carnival tradition, and calypso was the providence of Trinidad and the adjacent Lesser Antilles). Belafonte, dubbed "The Reluctant King of Calypso," was not considered a genuine calypsonian by most Trinidadians. He saw himself as more of a folksinger than a calypsonian. See Funk and Hill, "Will Calypso Doom Rock 'n' Roll," 182–189; and Funk and Eldridge, *Calypso Craze*, pp. 42–43.

86. Jan Nederveen Pieterse, *Globalization and Culture: Global Melange* (Rowan & Littlefield, 2015), p. 101.

87. Ray Funk and Stephen Stuempfle, "Calypso: World Music," exhibition at the Historical Museum of South Florida, 2007. Quoted in Martin, *Pan-America*, p. 49.

88. Brooks Atkinson, "Theatre: Truman Capote's Musical," *New York Times*, 31 December 1954.

89. In 1957 Gerald Clark told the *Trinidad Guardian* that he had returned to the island to observe Carnival for the first time in twenty-eight years, dating his previous visit to 1929 (*Trinidad Guardian*, 24 February 1957). This does not coincide with a clipping of a *Trinidad Guardian* article from the Gerald Clark scrapbook that chronicles his 1937 visit to Trinidad. There is no evidence that Clark visited Trinidad between 1937 and 1957.

4

Carnival Comes to Brooklyn

On Labor Day 1966, a young Trinidadian named Winston Munroe (b. 1945) landed at New York City's Kennedy Airport. Like many ambitious Caribbean migrants, Munroe came to the United States with dreams of pursuing an education and establishing a professional business career. But he was also a talented steel pan player, a veteran of the Starlighters and Silhouettes steelbands in Trinidad. He knew that Harlem's celebrated Labor Day Carnival parade had been shut down several years earlier, but rumor had it that some sort of activity was resurfacing in Brooklyn. Those reports, Munroe recalled, were quickly confirmed:

> When I arrived at the airport I was met by a cousin of mine, and he took me directly to the Labor Day Carnival in Brooklyn, which was on St. John's Place, in Crown Heights, at the time. One of the guys had a tenor pan, and I started playing on it. We played Sparrow's "Patsy." It wasn't exactly a band, just a group of guys with one tenor pan, a couple of irons, and a conga drum. . . . And it wasn't like a real parade, we just had two blocks. We moved back and forth down these blocks—I think it was on St. John's around Classon and Washington Avenues—there was an Armory around there. People had J'Ouvert costumes, simple stuff, no fancy costumes. The music was just us on the truck and some other people playing percussion, like a rhythm band.[1]

Munroe's story offers testimony that the closing down of Harlem Carnival in 1961 did not lead to the cessation of Carnival activity in New York. Within a few years of his arrival, the informal Crown Heights street processions and block parties he described would morph into a three-day official Carnival event that included an enormous Eastern Parkway parade and attendant stage shows at the Brooklyn Museum and other nearby venues. In 1972 an annual Panorama contest was established as part of the Labor Day festivities. During the ensuing years, Brooklyn's

Labor Day Carnival would expand into the borough's premiere cultural event, attracting millions of viewers and providing a nurturing environment for the growth of steelband and calypso, as well as the emerging soca style. Carnival music, as this and the next chapter will explore, lay at the heart of the celebration.

The migration of Carnival and its music to Brooklyn was no accident. Concurrent with the demise of its Carnival celebration, Harlem's position as the center of New York's Anglophone Caribbean community was beginning to diminish as residents and new migrants increasingly spread out to Brooklyn, Queens, and the South Bronx. The 1965 Hart-Celler Immigration Reform Act, passed the year before Munroe's arrival in Brooklyn, proved pivotal in terms of realigning the city's Caribbean population. The new law abolished the old national quota system that favored northern Europeans and opened the door for increased in-migration from the Caribbean, Latin America, and Asia. The result was a boon for emigration from Jamaica, Trinidad, Haiti, Barbados, Grenada, coastal Guyana, and other small Caribbean islands to New York, which saw its non-Hispanic Caribbean population increase more than five-fold between 1965 and 1980, swelling to nearly 300,000 according to the 1980 census.[2] The central Brooklyn neighborhoods of Crown Heights, Prospect Heights, Bedford Stuyvesant, and East Flatbush received the lion's share of this new wave of island migrants. Improvements in transportation and mass communication allowed them to maintain closer ties with their home countries than had their predecessors, permitting those from Trinidad to keep up with the latest developments in Carnival masquerading, calypso, and steelband. By the late 1960s the stage was set for the re-emergence of Carnival on a scale not seen in Harlem.

Neighborhood Carnival in Crown Heights

When the mas bandleader Rufus Gorin relocated from Harlem to Brooklyn around 1960 he was determined to establish a Labor Day Carnival celebration in his Crown Heights neighborhood. In an open letter to masqueraders and musicians issued in August 1961, Gorin announced "The Parisian Dandies 2nd Annual Parade and Dance in Brooklyn on Labor Day, September 4, 1961." Gorin's invitation read, "Half of the fun depends upon the original ideas formulated by the music of which you are a major part. Therefore, we seek assistance from you and many other bandleaders by participating in this parade." The invitation gave Gorin's Lefferts Place address in Crown Heights, the presumed location of the event.[3] There are few other written accounts of these early gatherings, but recollections suggest that Gorin's initial efforts resulted in a series of informal block parties and spontaneous costumed parades in Crown Heights and Bedford Stuyvesant over Labor Day weekend. The impromptu St. John's Place parade described by Winston Munroe was typical, with revelers sporting simple, J'Ouvert costumes jumping up to a hastily assembled pan-and-rhythm band. More organized steelbands were often part of the mix at block parties, recalled steelband man Clyde Henry:

> Back then [mid-1960s] a very outstanding mas man named Rufus Gorin used to organize block parties. As a matter of fact there was an Armory up around Dean Street, and we used to play around that area there. And there were certain areas in the community where the residents would get together and have block parties, and they would request a steelband to come and play. See there was no Panorama at that time, so many of the steelbands, smaller groups, would just get together and play mostly in the summertime at these block parties. We played mostly Caribbean music, calypsos and a little Latin, and maybe one or two American songs set to a calypso beat.[4]

Gorin's early gatherings, however, resulted in his arrest for allegedly playing Carnival without a permit when police decided one of his street fetes was getting too disorderly. At his hearing, the judge suggested that Gorin form an official organization and apply for a permit for his Carnival parade. He did just that, and in November 1966 New York State granted him a certificate of incorporation for the United West Indian Day Development Association (UWIDDA). The following year Gorin, under the auspices of the UWIDDA, applied for and was granted a permit to hold a parade in his Crown Heights neighborhood.[5] On Labor Day 1967, Carnival officially came to Brooklyn.

But Gorin was an artist, not an organizer. With no institutional structure, he quickly grew frustrated at the bureaucracy involved in staging a Carnival event, and sometime in the late 1960s he ceded leadership of the organization to a younger colleague and fellow Trinidadian, Carlos Lezama (1923–2007), a New York City transit worker. Lezama, who possessed strong organizational and political skills, would be elected chairman of the organization, which was named the West Indian American Day Association (WIADA) around 1971, and the West Indian American Day Carnival Association (WIADCA) in 1974.[6]

Lezama continued to oversee neighborhood parades during the later 1960s. Minutes from the 2 June 1967 UWIDDA meetings report that the post office on St. John's Place, between Troy and Albany, was a possible site for the parade reviewing stands. It was also decided that the orchestra's run by Syd Joe and Daphne Weeks, along with Gabriel's Steelband, would play for the association's two Labor Day dances at an undisclosed location.[7] The parades were apparently modest affairs, based on the Harlem model of mas costumes, steelbands, and a calypsonian on a truck backed by a lightly amplified ensemble. One participant recalled that in 1967 a group of several thousand gathered around the intersection of Ralph Avenue and St. John's Place in Crown Heights and paraded west (presumably down St. Johns Place), terminating around Washington Avenue. Leading the parade, which included six bands (not specified as mas or steelbands), was a truck carrying Syd Joe's Orchestra and the calypsonian Mighty Sparrow.[8] Others recall masqueraders and steelbands, including Caldera Caraballo's Moderneers, Rudy King's Tropicans, and Pops McCarthy's Harlem All Stars, processing down various routes in Crown Heights, culminating in dances at the Dean Street/Crown Heights Armory (between Washington and Grand Avenues), where music was provided by an orchestra, most likely Syd Joe and his Caribbean All Stars and a steelband.[9]

The mid-1960s Brooklyn block parties and Carnival parades garnered no press coverage, but within the Caribbean community the activity caught the attention of the Mighty Sparrow (Slinger Francisco, b. 1935). Sparrow rose to fame following a series of Calypso Monarch and Road March victories in the late 1950s and 1960s, and by decade's end was challenging Lord Kitchener as Trinidad's most popular calypsonian.[10] In 1969, two years after his impromptu appearance in the 1967 St. Johns Place procession, but two years before WIADCA's first high-profile Carnival on Eastern Parkway, Sparrow chronicled the Crown Heights scene in a calypso appropriately titled "Mas in Brooklyn." The song opens: "Let me tell you something/about Labor Day in Brooklyn." "Mas in Brooklyn" proved to be prophetic, for in 1969, with Brooklyn's Carnival still in its infancy, Sparrow recognized that the borough's diverse island participants were ready to proclaim "Brooklyn Is Me Home." In the final verse he celebrated the unity of the borough's Caribbean migrants from Trinidad, Barbados, Grenada, and Jamaica, declaring "New York equalize you!"[11] The theme of Caribbean unity would soon be seized upon by Lezama and WIADCA as a central trope of Brooklyn Carnival, although Sparrow's "toute monde" vision was in reality a contested ideal.

At some point in the late 1960s, more organized parades took place on the west side of Prospect Park. Wilfred Thomas, who migrated from Trinidad in 1968 and would become the General Secretary for WIADA in 1971, recalled that the 1968 Labor Day parade proceeded from Grand Army Plaza south down Prospect Park West to Bartel Pritchard Square, a route adjacent to the predominantly white neighborhood of Park Slope. Similar parades, he believed, were held in 1969 and 1970. According to Thomas, the latter affair included a good deal of music, leading some "white folks" who lived near the park to complain that the Caribbean revelers were "disturbing the peace with the loudspeakers and calypso music and (steel) drums."[12] In 1970 the Prospect Park West Carnival parade received mentioned in the *Antillean Caribbean Echo*, whose editor was disappointed that the procession was not allowed to use the park's interior roadway.[13] The following week the *Echo* reported that an "estimated 35,000 spectators, mainly of West Indian origin and descent with their American friends attend the celebration." Seven masquerade bands competed, and Gorin's "Glory of the Aztec Indians" mas was awarded the $500 first prize. Following the parade and mas competition, spectators milled around the park listening to the eight steelbands that reportedly participated.[14] Winston Munroe, who played with one of those groups, recalled that in addition to the steelbands, the Daphne Weeks Orchestra processed down Prospect Park West atop a flatbed truck, reminiscent of the Harlem Carnival.[15]

Carnival Comes to Eastern Parkway

Lezama and WIADCA were finally able to obtain a permit to hold a parade on Eastern Parkway in time for the 1971 Labor Day Carnival.[16] The 29 August editions of both the *Echo* and the *New York Amsterdam News* previewed the event, the former with a headline reading "Brooklyn Mas: Eastern Parkway to Close for Monday 'Jump Up.'"[17] The latter announced that the parade would assemble at Grand Army Plaza on Labor Day morning and proceed (east) down Eastern Parkway to Lincoln Terrace Park at Rochester Avenue. The *Echo* predicted that "twelve bands of masqueraders, accompanied by floats and steel and wind orchestras" would participate.

Following the event, the *Echo* estimated the Carnival crowd at 400,000, and the *Amsterdam News* simply reported that "thousands" paraded on the Parkway.[18] While these numbers are difficult to verify and the former was probably an exaggeration, WIADCA's publicity had clearly generated a larger audience than anything seen in Brooklyn to date. Although there was no mention of steelbands by the press, nine mas bands were reported to participate, in addition to Moko Jumbie stilt walkers from the Virgin Islands and half a dozen floats, including those sponsored by NYC Model Cities, the British Honduras Association, and the Carnival Queens contingency. "In true Carnival fashion," the *Echo* recounted, the entire scene was somewhat chaotic: "Some of the thousands who lined the streets could not resist the temptation to join in the revelry, thus it was that several small bands of masqueraders found themselves squelched in the midst of hundreds of revelers who joined them for the jump-up."[19] In the early parades, spectators were apparently free to join in the fray of mas and steelbands on the Parkway.

The Eastern Parkway parade was not the only event sponsored by WIADCA over the 1971 Labor Day weekend. In order to further coordinate Carnival festivities, the association organized a Community Fair with crafts, theater, and steelbands on Saturday and Sunday afternoons at Lincoln Terrace Park, and a Sunday night Dimanche Gras dance and stage show on the grounds behind the Brooklyn Museum. The Trinidadian calypso stars Mighty Sparrow and Lord Melody, both of whom had relocated to New York, headlined the latter. Also included on stage were the Honduras Dance Company, a Virgin Islands Revue, two Brooklyn steelbands— Cliff Alexis's Trinidad Troubadours and the Sunlander Steelband—and appearances by the Carnival Queens. Music for the dance was provided by Daphne Weekes and her Orchestra. These evening stage shows, always taking place behind the Brooklyn Museum on Labor Day weekend prior to the big Monday parade, would become essential components of the festivities, providing WIADCA with an opportunity to showcase their

Carnival music, dance, and costuming away from the chaos of the street in a more formal, sit-down setting.

A twenty-page Carnival program booklet, published by WIADCA listed the above events along with greetings from New York State governor Nelson Rockefeller, New York City mayor John Lindsay, Congresswoman Shirley Chisholm, and Brooklyn borough president Sebastian Leone. The latter touted the event as "West Indian-American Weekend" in an official Borough of Brooklyn Proclamation. Lezama's connections had paid off, and he had clearly succeeded in making the local political powers take notice of his event and the broader Caribbean-American community. He laid out his agenda in his "Chairman's Message" without explicitly mentioning Carnival, but rather adopting the lofty rhetoric of heritage and multiculturalism. Caribbean New Yorkers, he declared, while separated from the "lands of our birth," have "stoutly refused to remove ourselves from the rich culture that has been our heritage." Rallying around that culture, he stated, would be "our most effective tool in our continuing efforts to carve a true identity in the great melting pot in which we find ourselves."[20] In subsequent journal statements, Lezama would elaborate on how the Carnival celebration was part of a larger strategy of Caribbean unity, stating "through this cultural endeavor [Carnival] we attempt to play our part in uniting the peoples of the Caribbean here and at home. It is only when West Indians are 'One People' culturally that political and economic integration and national identity may become feasible."[21] By avoiding any mention of Trinidad, whose Carnival was clearly the prototype for the event produced by an organization made up primarily of Trinidadian expatriates, Lezama underscored that the Labor Day celebration was for all Caribbean New Yorkers, regardless of their island affiliation. "One People," a vision outlined in Sparrow's earlier calypso "Mas in Brooklyn," would become WIADCA's mantra.

Lezama's message was well timed. Although the former Caribbean colonies had failed to unite under the West Indies Federation a decade earlier, a new awareness of a shared history and heritage had infused the Caribbean cultural zeitgeist in the 1960s as Trinidad, Jamaica, Barbados, and Guyana gained their independence from Great Britain (the other islands would follow in the 1970s and early 1980s). The United States civil rights and Black Power movements of the 1960s increased consciousness of African roots among all black peoples, and the 1976 Bicentennial celebrated America's unity in diversity. Uniting and mobilizing new immigrants under the guise of culture was an effective strategy for negotiating the complex matrix of New York City's ethnic politics in the 1970s.

Labor Day Carnival grew larger in 1972. The parade route was reversed to its present-day direction, beginning around Utica Avenue and proceeding west on Eastern Parkway up to the Brooklyn Museum and Grand Army Plaza. Henrietta Johnson Burroughs of the *Amsterdam News* reported a turnout of 80,000 participants, including "5,000 marchers resplendent in a colorful array of glitter feathers and velvets and swaying to the melodies of 18 steel bands," who "snaked their way several miles from Utica Avenue down Eastern Parkway to Prospect Park."[22] Burroughs was impressed with the turnout and breadth of the event, although her suggestion that the parade was larger than anything comparable in the West Indies and her reporting of eighteen steelbands were no doubt exaggerations. Burroughs also noted the organizer's disappointment at the dearth of mainstream-media coverage and the city's failure to provide adequate help with security and cleanup. She attributed these problems to racial bias, a charge that would continue to resurface in future years. The diversity of the parade was observed by Napier Pillai, who reported to readers of the *Overseas Express* back in Trinidad that the event was not strictly a "Trinidadian fete," as "there was a definite Latin sound in a number of the bands, and our black brothers from Panama, Puerto Rico, and Haiti were all there, dancing in the street."[23] Brooklyn's first Panorama was added to the Brooklyn Museum concert lineup that year. The annual steelband competition would eventually become a key component of the Labor Day weekend festivities, as will be discussed in the following chapter.

WIADCA's Carnival Fights to Expand

In August 1973, Horace Morancie, the powerful head of the New York Model Cities Program and a rival of Lezama, decided to stage an alternative Carnival celebration at Medgar Evers College, which was located only a few blocks from the Brooklyn Museum. Enlisting the help of Clyde Henry and pan-man-turned-journalist Leslie Slater, Morancie formed the Labor Day Caribbean Carnival Committee (LDCCC) and set about to produce the "1973 Caribbean Festival," a series of six outdoor shows over a two-week span. The first weekend, 24–26 August, promised to feature steelband, calypso, and reggae preliminary contests, as well as a Miss Carnival competition. The following weekend's presentations, which would be in direct competition with WIADCA's Labor Day Brooklyn Museum events, included the finalists for the three music categories as well as a Caribbean Showcase presentation featuring folkloric groups representing the traditions of Trinidad, Jamaica, Haiti, Panama, and the Virgin Islands.[24]

A correspondent from the *Amsterdam News* covered the first weekend and reported an enthusiastic response by a crowd of 2,500 to the opening night program, which included an impromptu appearance by Lord Kitchener, the venerated Trinidadian calypsonian who had won the 1973 Trinidad Carnival Road March competition, backed by the Syd Joe Orchestra.[25] This was no doubt much to the chagrin of Lezama and WIADCA, who had booked Kitchener, along with Sparrow and Singing Francine, to perform the next weekend at their Labor Day events behind the Brooklyn Museum.[26] However, there is no record of any calypso or reggae contest winners, and the Panorama was by all accounts an informal affair with no prize money.

Competition from the Medgar Evers event, as well as a "Carnival Extravaganza" held at the Manhattan Center on Saturday evening of Labor Day weekend, no doubt hurt attendance at WIADCA's Brooklyn Museum concerts.[27] But WIADCA's 1973 Labor Day parade was by all accounts a success, receiving unprecedented media attention, including for the first-time coverage from the major white papers. In a banner headline, the *Amsterdam News* trumpeted "It Looked Like All the World Was West Indian!" and touted the diversity of the event with the subtitle "Unity Is Theme as Many Groups March Together."[28] Reporter J. Zamgba Browne noted that congresswoman and grand marshall Shirley Chisholm marched with various dignitaries, and reported a crowd of over 800,000 spectators. Knolly Moses of the *Echo* estimated the crowd at one-and-a-half million, noting that many of the mas bands never completed the route to the reviewing stands in front of the Brooklyn Museum due to a bottle-neck at Rodgers Avenue.[29]

The following week another *Echo* reporter, Dalton James, described a similar scene, noting the "cacophony of noise" that occurred when the steel and brass bands were wedged together on the Parkway. James highlighted the Tropicans and the Pan Masters as two of the top steelbands, noting that the former included players once associated with Trinidad's prestigious Invaders, Starlift, and Desperadoes steelbands. Pan arranger La Barrie was reported to be investigating the possibility of taking his Pan Masters to Trinidad to compete in the following year's Panorama.[30]

The most gratifying coverage of the 1973 parade for WIADCA came from Judith Cummings's enthusiastic piece in the *New York Times*. She described a festive scene with a "parade of more than 20 Caribbean steel bands and dancing bands," estimating the crowd to be upward of 600,000. Cummings closed on a provocative note, quoting Congresswoman Chisholm as stating her desire to "eventually have our parade moved to Fifth Avenue, like all the other grand parades, specifically St. Patrick's Day and Columbus Day. We deserve as big a celebration as the other ethnic groups."[31] This issue would be a flashpoint of controversy between various politicians, community leaders, and WIADCA. The parade also drew a full-page spread in the *Sunday News*, where Jean Perry, who estimated the crowd size at 400,000, praised Lezama and his organization for producing such an extravagant event with a skeleton crew of volunteers and minimal government or private sponsorship.[32]

Despite the success of the 1973 parade, the following year Lezama and WIADCA again had to fight for control of Brooklyn Carnival. Over the summer of 1974 a splinter group, supposedly representing the majority of steelband players and masqueraders under the auspices of the New York Caribbean Carnival Council (NYCCC), was reported to be vying for control of the event.[33] Venting dissatisfaction with WIADCA's overall disorganization and lack of financial support for the steel and mas bands, the group had applied for a permit to move the Labor Day Carnival parade to Fifth Avenue in Manhattan in order to "reap the benefits of media coverage, business sponsorship of the bands, and greater police control of crowds that hamper the visibility of the costumes."[34] Clyde Henry, who identified himself as a member of NYCCC, told the *Amsterdam News*, "It takes more than $4,000 to put a steelband on the street. . . . We think that the contribution being made by the artists rates some kind of meaningful outside support and we think there is a much better chance of such support coming from Manhattan."[35] The *Amsterdam News* published a response from WIADCA that dismissed NYCCC's complaints and reasserted its right, as the founder of Brooklyn Carnival, to be the sole proprietor of the event.[36] In the end, Lezama and WIADCA prevailed and NYCCC was denied a permit for Fifth Ave.

The 1974 Carnival parade was touted as another success for WIADCA. An *Amsterdam News* headline announced, "One Million Participate in West Indian Parade," and the article included two full pages of pictures. The piece noted the participatory nature of the event, observing, "There is no real dichotomy between the parade celebrant and spectator. The spectator is at times celebrant; the celebrant spectator." Stressing a theme that was becoming a pattern in the black press, the article couched the event as an example of Caribbean unity in diversity, lauding "a togetherness that brought revelers from Trinidad and Jamaica, Haiti and Panama, St. Vincent, Grenada, Barbados, Dominica, and even Costa Rica to dance to each other's music and eat from each other's pots."[37] The description of "beautifully played calypso and reggae tunes on steel drums and various brass instruments" implied that even the Jamaicans and Trinidadians, traditional rivals in New York, were playing in harmony on Labor Day. How much reggae would have been played by steelbands on the road is uncertain, but its presence was certainly felt from sidewalk sound systems that competed with the steelbands playing calypso on the Parkway.[38] Grace Lichtenstein of the *Times* reported half a million in attendance, and quoted a policeman as describing the event as "a moving block party." In an about-face from her previous year's comments, Congresswoman Chisholm now voiced her support for keeping the parade in Brooklyn rather than moving it to Manhattan.[39]

Calypso and Dimanche Gras at the Brooklyn Museum

WIADCA's 1974 Dimanche Gras show featured performances by Trinidad's top three calypsonians—Sparrow, who had won that year's Trinidad Calypso Monarch competition; Shadow, whose calypso "Bass Man" had won the Trinidad Road March; and Kitchener, whose tune "Jericho," performed by the Harmonites, had won the Port of Spain Panorama competition. WIADCA could afford these top acts, recalled their public-relations manager Herman Hall, because the Trinidad government would help subsidize the costs of bringing the annual Calypso Monarch and Road March winners to New York as a way of boosting tourism.[40] Brooklyn's Caribbean community was directly tethered back home thanks to these musical ambassadors, one of whom, Sparrow, had been living in and working out of New York for more than a decade. Riding on the coat-tails of Belafonte's success, Sparrow began visiting in the city in the late 1950s to perform and eventually record. Sometime in the early 1960s he moved to New York, taking up residency initially on Rockaway Parkway in Brooklyn and later in Jamaica Hills, Queens. While he moved his family and business operations to New York, he retained a home in Diego Martin, maintained dual Trinidad-US citizenship, and remained active in Trinidad Carnival in between international tours. "I lived on a plane you could say," he recollected years later, "going from Trinidad to South America and back to Canada and then back to New York. We were moving all the time."[41] According to Gordon Rohlehr, Sparrow had become "a transnational mind caught between two worlds," a tension the singer ruminated on in his 1962 calypso "Sparrow Come Back." He began the song "Ah know ah have my fans in please / here in the West Indies," then reminded himself "But in New York people spending money / to promote me in Carnegie." Finally, in frustration he confessed "Ah don't know what the heck to do."[42] Sparrow was the first of the post-independence calypsonians to establish himself in New York while retaining a solid presence (and part-time residency) in Trinidad. Other singers, arrangers, and record producers would follow in the 1970s.

WIADCA's early 1970s Dimanche Gras shows were neither the first nor the only large-scale presentations of Sparrow and other leading Trinidadian calypsonians in New York. The city's Caribbean community had been treated to singers of notoriety since the inauguration of the annual Madison Square Garden Calypso Festival in 1969. Produced by Ed Harris and headlined by Sparrow, the initial event was spread over three days in late July and included performances by Calypso Rose, Lord Bitterbush, and the Pan Am North Stars steelband, the latter brought in from Trinidad exclusively for the show.[43] In 1970 and 1971, Lord Kitchener was added to the program, leading him to pen the calypso "Mas in Madison Square Garden."[44] The song verses take the form of instructional vignettes on how to play mas and correctly execute Carnival dance moves, while the chorus encourages all to "Have a good time / a gay time / a crazy time in Manhattan / It's mas in Madison Square Garden." Though seemingly aimed at tourists and Carnival neophytes in need of dance advice, the song proved tremendously popular among Caribbean audiences in New York and Trinidad, winning the 1971 Trinidad Road March and underscoring the symbolic import of the prestigious Garden event for expatriate Trinidadians and those back home.[45]

Around 1976 the Calypso Festival, still headlined by Sparrow, was moved to May and became billed as a Mother's Day Show. Eventually, perhaps motivated more by profit than the cultural politics that drove WIADCA's programming decisions, the Garden producers aimed to reach a broader Caribbean audience by including Arrow (Montserrat), Swallow (Antigua), Tony Gazette (Barbados), John Holt and the Wild Bunch (Jamaica), and Tabou Combo (Haiti) on the program.[46] The Garden Mother's Day show continued as a popular annual event and eventually moved to Brooklyn in the late 1980s.

Meanwhile, for the first time, WIADCA sponsored another popular component of Trinidad Carnival, a calypso competition, but one specifically for singers based in the United States. According to their 1975 Carnival program booklet, the 1974 "U.S. Calypso" contest was won by Lord Baker. The 1975 booklet also included a picture of the semifinalists who were scheduled to compete for the 1975 title. Lord Melody, Lord Bitterbush, Prince Galloway, Nap Hepburn, Lord Robin, and Lord Smithie had been chosen by a panel of judges from a field of sixteen calypsonians who competed at the Bellrose Ballroom on 23 August.[47] Of these contestants, Melody was the most well known, having won the Trinidad Monarch contest in 1954 and eventually relocated in New York in the late 1960s to write and tour with Harry Belafonte.[48] The others were lesser-known singers who had moved to New York, New Jersey (Galloway), or Washington, DC (Baker), where they continued to occasionally perform while working day jobs.

Next to Melody, Randolph "Count Robin" Hilaire (b. 1940) was probably the most successful of the New York–based calypso contestants. In 1976 he recorded a minor hit with "Sparrow Behave Yourself" for the Brooklyn-based Straker's Records label, and over the next decade he came out with several dozen additional sides for Straker's and Charlie's Records. In addition to his singing career and previously mentioned work with the Sonatas Steelband, Robin helped organize numerous successful Calypso shows in Brooklyn. But all of this activity did not bring in ample income, so he took a day job as a steamfitter with Union Local 638. This arrangement provided him with a steady salary and allowed him to go back to Trinidad for several months during the Carnival season to sing in the calypso tents and record. Robin exemplified the semi-professional transnational musician, a Trinidadian expatriate who resided in Brooklyn but maintained strong ties with his homeland.[49]

Robin won the 1975 US Calypso Competition, with Nap Hepburn and Lord Melody as runners-up.[50] One of the performers that year was Edward "Prince" Galloway (b. 1937), a native of St. Croix, Virgin Islands, who came to New York in 1953 as a teenager to live with his father in the Bronx. After a two-year stint in the US Army he came back to the Bronx, took a job as a hospital worker, and around 1957 began singing in the chorus of Lord Invader's group, which performed at clubs and dances. He eventually ventured off on his own, singing calypso in front of Manhattan-based orchestras led by Milo Francis, Fats Greene, Burt Samuel, and Claude Brewster. He moved to Brooklyn and then Jersey City in the early 1960s, and then back to the Virgin Islands in 1966. Around 1975 he returned to the United States, residing in Jersey City, where he continued to sing while studying refrigeration repair. In 1978 he moved once more to the Virgin Islands, where he would maintain his permanent residence and become more involved in that island's calypso scene. Galloway was a transnational

migrant for over two decades, establishing himself as minor calypsonian performer who recorded and performed in New York and the Virgin
Islands.[51]

One of the calypsos Galloway sang from the stage of the 1975 competition was an original song titled "Labor Day." The lyric celebrated
the throng of Eastern Parkway revelers, including "West Indians" and
"Yankees," who together "jump, bump, and break away," "smoking
ganga and drinking rum." He called out several of the favorite brass
orchestras, Milo and the Kings, Ron Berridge, and his accompanist
at the show, the Syd Joe Orchestra. Then Galloway proclaimed "No
Discrimination / All West Indians as one / And it's a bacchanal / Known
as West Indian Carnival."[52]

Like Sparrow's "Mas in Brooklyn," Galloway's "Labor Day" was a call
for unity and equality among all of Brooklyn's Caribbean peoples, regardless of their island affiliation. While this was certainly the intention
of WIADCA's "One People" philosophy, the reality was not so clear-cut
for a Virgin Islands singer like Galloway, who felt discriminated against
in the calypso competition. In reflecting on the song nearly forty years
later, he claimed that breaking into the Brooklyn Carnival scene was not
easy for non-Trinidadian singers such as himself, faulting WIADCA for
its clannishness and, from his perspective as an outsider, its insistence
that Carnival be structured as strictly a "Trinidad thing."[53]

In 1976 a third calypso contest was held, at which first place went
to Lord Crusader and second place to Robin, but there is no evidence
of any contests thereafter.[54] Hall attributes this to the lack of interest
in the local singers coupled with the difficulty in raising funds for ade-
quate prize money. If patrons were going to pay a hefty fee to come to the
WIADCA Labor Day shows they wanted to see the stars from Trinidad.
And the calypsonians Sparrow, Melody, Rose, Nelson, and Duke, who had
all relocated to New York by the 1970s, considered themselves too well
known internationally to sing in local contests. If they were to set foot on
the WIADCA Labor Day stage, they expected to be paid as headliners—and
they were.[55]

The 1975 WIADCA Labor Day shows featured yet another new
component—a reggae song competition. The impetus for its inclusion
was to bring more Jamaicans into Brooklyn Carnival—not an easy task,
given the old rivalries between Jamaicans and Trinidadians. The situation was even more difficult, since Carnival was a Trinidadian, not a
Jamaican, tradition, and WIADCA, the organizer of the event, was run
almost exclusively by Trinidadians.[56] But Lezama needed the Jamaicans,
who represented the largest contingency of Brooklyn's Caribbean community, and reggae seemed like the best way to involve them.[57]

Buoyed by the success of the international star Bob Marley in the
early 1970s, reggae had become popular among younger Caribbean
listeners, as well as among white North American and British fans, who
responded to the music's emphasis on heavy electric guitars, throbbing

bass, and messianic, ganga-inspired lyrics. But reggae exposed musical and cultural rifts that were island-specific and generational. The older Trinidadians who controlled Brooklyn Carnival preferred the lighter, lilting rhythms and satirical lyrics of calypso and were put off by the drug-tinged Rastafarian youth culture associated with reggae. Out on the street, the sonic rivalry became painfully palpable. During Labor Day Carnival, Don Hill reported hearing reggae recordings being blasted on sidewalk sound systems and side streets on the periphery of the parade, while calypso was being played by steel and brass bands on trucks that processed down the Parkway as part of the parade.[58] The *Amsterdam News* recounted a similar situation, observing, "On the sidewalks the pulsating sounds of reggae rockers blast from 1,000-watt speakers."[59] Jennifer Dunning of the *Times* tried to put a positive spin on the situation, noting that "the music of steel bands clashed happily with reggae played on sidewalk sound systems."[60] But the older WIADCA board members were anything but happy.

Lezama and Hall, on the recommendation of the WLIB disc jockey Ken Williams, finally decided to hold a New York Reggae Contest as part of the Carnival, but to avoid opposition from other WIADCA members the preliminary rounds were quietly held in venues outside of Brooklyn. In order not to overwhelm the program, only the first-place winners performed as part of the 1975, 1976, and 1977 WIADCA Dimanche Gras shows. "The old guys in the Carnival Association (WIACDA) didn't like it at all, and this one fellow on the executive board, he actually slapped me across the face for bringing reggae music into the Carnival!" recollected Hall. The WIADCA-sponsored Reggae Song Contests were not successful and were discontinued after several years as more professional reggae acts were added to the WIADCA Brooklyn Museum evening programs. Finally, in 1983, a separate Thursday night reggae show headlined by the Jamaican band Chalice was staged as part of the official Carnival festivities. But according to Hill and Hall, the Jamaican relationship with WIADCA remained uneasy, and eventually they sponsored their own Jamaican Beauty Queen and Reggae Contests apart from WIADCA and the Brooklyn Museum shows.[61]

In addition to the Reggae Song Contest, WIADCA continued to reach out to other island groups in hopes of encouraging expansion and diversity of participation. In 1975 they titled their Saturday Brooklyn Museum evening show "Night in the Caribbean," a program that showcased calypso and reggae, as well as Haitian, Costa Rican, and Trinidad and Tobago dance troupes. The following year "Caribbean Night" was moved to Friday evening and included dance groups from Jamaica, Haiti, Grenada, and Costa Rica.[62] The inclusion of these dance ensembles was aimed at stressing the diverse nature of Brooklyn's Caribbean communities while underscoring the common Afro-Caribbean folkloric drumming and dancing traditions they shared. Lezama hoped that official recognition of these non-Trinidadian groups would bring members of their communities into the Carnival fold.

From Calypso to Soca

As the 1970s wound down, new trends in technology and popular music tastes would signal dramatic changes for pan players and their followers. Steelbands had been the primary source of music for the initial Eastern Parkway parades. But in its preview to the 1978 Labor Day Carnival, the *New York Daily Challenge* reported tensions between Brooklyn's steel and mas bandleaders over the latter's decision to use amplified brass bands and deejays on sound trucks, rather than steelbands, to accompany them at the upcoming Eastern Parkway masquerade. The high cost of employing a steelband and the congestion the music ensembles brought to the Parkway were offered as explanations. While the mas bandleaders scoffed at accusations that they were consciously "boycotting" the local steelbands, the *Daily Challenge* reported that no major masquerade group was planning to hire a steelband that year. Clearly concerned about this new development, the paper's editors titled the piece "A Call for Unity among Carnival Artists" and proclaimed "both pan and mas are indispensable" to a successful Carnival.[63] But mirroring trends in Trinidad, Brooklyn's mas bands began gravitating away from steelbands toward deejays, whose modern sound equipment could produce a louder, bass-heavy sound that was ideal for dancing in a large, outdoor areas, where the lighter sonorities of a steelband would rapidly dissipate.

The music being played by deejays and the amplified bands was also changing at this time. By the mid-1970s a new style, called soca (soul/calypso), was challenging calypso as Trinidad's national popular music. Soca was a fusion of traditional calypso with African American soul, R&B, and disco music, emerging as a distinctive new style characterized by heavy bass lines, mechanical drums, buzzing synthesizer runs, and party-centered lyrics. Like Jamaican reggae, soca's mix was ideally suited for the high-volume, bass-throbbing sound systems that could be assembled in a stationary position for fetes, clubs, or sidewalk gatherings, or loaded on a large flatbed truck and paraded down Eastern Parkway (see Figure 4.1). The Brooklyn steelbands simply could not compete with the sound system-driven deejays and amplified soca bands at fetes or on the streets, and they redirected their attention toward preparations for the Panorama competition that would become the main stage for their public performances.

While the steelbands struggled to carve out their niche in Labor Day Carnival, calypso remained and soca became an essential component of the celebration. After 1976 WIADCA ceased sponsoring a US Calypso competition, but they continued to feature top calypso and soca acts at their Brooklyn Museum concerts. In addition to the iconic Trinidad stars Sparrow, Kitchener, and Shadow, who headlined the programs in the early 1970s shows, a cadre of Trinidad expatriates who had relocated in New York, including Calypso Rose, Singing Francine, Lord Nelson, and Mighty Duke, became mainstays in the mid-1970s. In an effort to reach out to other islands, WIADCA added Arrow (from

Figure 4.1. Sound truck on Eastern Parkway, 1982. Photo by Martha Cooper (courtesy of City Lore).

Figure 4.2. Calypso Rose on Eastern Parkway, circa 1982. Photo by Kevin Burke.

Monserrat), Swallow (from Antigua), and Short Shirt (from Antigua) to its roster of headliners in the late 1970s.[64] In addition, Sparrow, Rose, and other calypsonians occasionally appeared on floats during the Eastern Parkway parade.

The Brooklyn Museum concerts were not the only calypso shows in town. Sparrow's annual Madison Square Garden Festivals that began in 1969 came to mark the opening of a summer-long season of calypso activities that would culminate with Labor Day Carnival. Calypso singers from Trinidad and other islands would travel to New York to perform and record, and the city's own singers would find increased work at dances, fetes, concerts, and boat rides. Indoor venues known as calypso tents, similar to their Trinidad prototypes, were staged during the weeks prior to Labor Day when interest peaked. One of the first successful tents was the Tropical Cove, organized by Count Robin in the early 1970s in an upstairs club located on the corner of Fulton Street and Franklin Avenue. Robin recruited mostly local singers, including Nat Hepburn, Conqueror, Bitterbush, and Lord Smithie, and ran nightly shows during the week leading up to Labor Day Carnival. Robin also helped with shows at the Albemarle Theatre in the later 1970s, where he sang with Calypso Rose and the Mighty Duke. But his most successful efforts were the calypso tents he put together for the Rainbow Terrace, as described in the introduction of this work (see Figure I.1). Owned by the Caribbean businessman Frank Smith, the Terrace was a popular club located on Nostrand Avenue near Herkimer Street in Crown Heights. Using his contacts from Trinidad, where he helped run Shadow's tent, Robin assembled a group of top calypsonians and convinced BWIA Airlines to donate free tickets to bring them to New York, where Smith and Rawlston Charles would arrange housing. Beginning in 1980 and running for five or six years, the Terrace staged a Carnival tent that featured Sparrow, Shadow, Super Blue, Cro Cro, Funny, and Gypsy, with the Boyie Lewis Orchestra serving as the house brass band.[65]

In 1982 another entrepreneurial calypsonian, Hawthorne "King Wellington" Quashie, helped the record producer Michael Gould organize a rival tent at B's Calypso Castle, around the corner on Fulton Street and Bedford Avenue. Peter Noel of the *Amsterdam News* reported that the opening night was a spectacular success, featuring the Trinidadian comedian and emcee Bill Troutman and performances by Nelson, Duke, Explainer, Blue Boy, Swallow, and Wellington. During the week leading up to Labor Day, the two tents would have clashes, featuring music on alternating nights.[66]

Sometime in the mid-1970s, the record producer Rawlston Charles decided to plug into the Brooklyn Carnival festivities by sponsoring a Labor Day Saturday block party. Working independently from Lezama's organization, he began by setting up a small stage on the sidewalk in front of his store on the Saturday afternoon before Labor Day Carnival. The event eventually grew into a full-blown block party, requiring him to acquire a permit to close off several blocks on Fulton Street between Nostrand and Bedford Avenues. Charles would provide free food and drink, a stage, and a brass band. Invitations went out to any calypsonians in town to stop by for an impromptu appearance, and over the years such luminaries as Sparrow, Shadow, Rose, David Rudder, and members of Charlie's Roots showed up. Frank Manning, who attended the block parties in the 1980s, recalled that "milling through the crowd, one is likely to find a dozen or more calypso celebrities, all maintaining the easy contact and camaraderie with fans that has become the music's endearing hallmark."[67]

The intensity of calypso and soca activity around Labor Day 1978 was documented in a brief piece in the *Daily Challenge*. Soca options for Labor Day weekend included Sparrow at the Eastern Parkway Arena on Saturday night and at the Parkside Towers on Sunday; Calypso Rose, Swallow, and Syd Joe at the Parkside Towers on Saturday; Calypso Rose with Boyie Lewis and Exodus Brass at the Hotel Grenada on Sunday; Arrow and Swallow with Milo and the Kings at the Harlem Audubon Auditorium; Beckett at Brooklyn's Club Royal; and additional performances by Shadow, Crazy, and Duke at unspecified venues.[68]

WIADCA Survives and Brooklyn Carnival Comes of Age

As the 1970s drew to a close, Brooklyn Carnival rolled on against the backdrop of mounting criticism regarding the event's shoddy organization and WIADCA's inadequate leadership. Basir Mchawi, reporting for the *Daily Challenge*, noted that the 1979 Labor Day parade was "marred by the usual problems of confusion, violence and lack of organization," and complained of having to wait three hours before seeing a single mas band.[69] Peter Noel's account of his Parkway experience for the *Amsterdam News* was even more disconcerting. He described reports of "disruptive gangs . . . on a rampage brandishing pistols and revolvers," snatching gold chains, and assaulting spectators. Homicide detective reports of an unidentified man that had been "allegedly shot by Rastafarians" on Eastern Parkway contributed to the tensions surrounding stereotypes of violent Jamaican behavior at Carnival. According to Noel, before the parade, Lezama had warned that "groups of thugs were out to mar and discredit the West Indian Carnival."[70] Noel's gloomy report was tempered by a second piece in the same issue of the *Amsterdam News*, penned by J. Zamgba Browne under the banner headline "1.5 Million Play Mas: A Big Day in Brooklyn." Browne recounted an enormously successful celebration tainted only by the controversial appearance of Mayor Ed Koch, who had fallen out of favor with New York's black community at that time.[71]

The bottom line was that numbers mattered, and as long as WIADCA could turn out huge crowds that gave the appearance of representing a unified, albeit slightly unruly, constituency, its proprietorship over Carnival could not be denied by city officials or its community rivals. The following year, in an attempt to assuage tensions with the city authorities, WIADCA agreed to a 6:00 p.m. curfew, a doubling of the police presence, a ban on sidewalk disco/sound systems, and significant increases in the sanitation and insurance fees the organization would have to pay the city.[72] The *Daily News* reported that as result of these changes, the 1980 event was smaller (by its estimate only half a million), and more orderly.[73] Sensationalist reports of violence, however, would continue to plague Carnival in the ensuing years, even when incidents occurred after the 6:00 p.m. curfew and away from the official parade route.[74]

For the fall 1982 issue of *Everybody's Caribbean Magazine*, Herman Hall wrote a thoughtful retrospective titled "Inside Brooklyn's Carnival." He listed a litany of WIADCA's ongoing financial and organizational problems and chided board members for lacking sufficient managerial skills and being bereft of creative ideas. Nonetheless, Hall extended both "credit and praise" to Lezama for producing what he characterized as a "superb" event that was "the best in years." Hall's exposé included a detailed account of yet another competing event, a three-day extravaganza billed as the Caribbean Basin Festival that took place on Pier 88 on Manhattan's West Side over the 1982 Labor Day weekend. The event was a failure and, according to Hall, a clear rejection by Brooklyn's Caribbean community of any efforts to move Carnival to an unfamiliar venue outside of the borough. WIADCA was in dire need of reorganization, Hall warned, yet somehow Lezama had again emerged victorious in his efforts to maintain control over Labor Day Carnival.[75]

By the early 1980s, Brooklyn Labor Day Carnival was firmly established as the borough's largest and most prominent cultural event. Lezama and WIADCA had succeeded, despite a plethora of community and external conflicts, in creating a festival aimed at uniting Brooklyn's diverse Caribbean communities under the banner of shared culture and political struggle. While loosely modeled on Trinidad Carnival, WIADCA's four-day celebration differed significantly. The main Eastern Parkway parade became a showcase for competing fancy mas bands, which, as in Trinidad, took to the road accompanied in the early years by steelbands, and later by deejays and amplified bands on mobile sound trucks. But the Brooklyn parade was limited to one afternoon (Labor Day), with participants pressured to adhere to an "official" linear route with prescribed start and end points, and to operate within a specified time frame. Carnival revelers, used to a ritual that lacked centralized authority and structure, were put at odds with city officials, who expected a more orderly, conventional pageant resembling the Saint Patrick's Day, Columbus Day, or Puerto Rican Day parades in Manhattan.[76] In Trinidad, on the other hand, the road processions were spread over two days (Carnival Monday and Tuesday) and were much less structured. Following no prescribed routes, scores of mas bands wound their way through downtown Port of Spain, eventually making their way past the judging stands.[77] By its nature, Trinidad Carnival defied orthodox notions of time and space. Moreover, the most spontaneous and transgressive displays in Trinidad street Carnival occurred in the early Monday morning J'Ouvert (Break of Day) celebrations, a component that was conspicuously absent from Brooklyn's initial Carnival, and that would not materialize until the early 1990s under separate, non-WIADCA sponsorship.

On a more practical level, WIADCA lacked the support of a central government agency, such as Trinidad's National Carnival Council, and was thus dependent almost entirely on volunteers rather than a full-time professional staff. This put the Brooklyn event at a severe organizational disadvantage compared to its Trinidadian prototype. While New York City eventually picked up the costs for security and sanitation, and the Brooklyn Museum offered its grounds and logistical support for the evening concerts, WIADCA struggled continuously with issues of production, publicity, and fundraising. The latter was a constant source of tension with the steelbands, who never felt sufficiently compensated for their contributions to Carnival.

Despite these internal and external adversities, Lezama and WIADCA survived. By the mid-1980s it was clear that Brooklyn's burgeoning Caribbean community demanded a Carnival, and given their growing numbers and political clout, they could not be denied. Brooklyn Carnival, similar to, yet distinct from, its Trinidadian parent, was destined to flourish into the new millennium and beyond.

Carnival Music and Caribbean Cultural Identity in Brooklyn

In addition to organizational and structural differences, Brooklyn's diasporic Carnival addressed a set of discrete cultural and political issues that set it apart from Trinidad's pre-Lenten celebration. During the early post-independence era, Carnival served as a force for forging national art and identity in Trinidad, while in Brooklyn the event mediated the tensions of the migration experience and acculturation into a culturally diverse and at times unwelcoming urban setting. Speaking of the broader Caribbean diaspora, Keith Nurse explained that at times "[overseas] Carnival has emerged as a basis for asserting a pan-Caribbean cultural identity as a mode of resistance in an otherwise alienating environment. The Carnivals have also allowed for integration as well as contestation with the dominant white population in addition to the other immigrant communities within the host society."[78] Moreover, as Philip Scher has suggested, Brooklyn and other overseas Carnivals help migrants remain connected to their native country through the formation of an imagined sense of "transnation" based on a presumed shared history, culture, and homeland—in this case, Trinidad and the adjacent English-speaking islands.[79] In the context of Brooklyn Carnival, steelband and calypso/soca music proved both useful and problematic in three ways: in uniting New York's diverse island populations under a single pan-Caribbean banner; in promoting an atmosphere conducive to the broader social integration of Caribbean people into the fabric of the city; and maintaining tangible connections between the diasporic communities and their Caribbean homelands.

Regarding pan-Caribbean identity, WIADCA was faced with a challenge from the start: there could be no genuine Caribbean Carnival without significant calypso and steelband components, yet these art forms were native to Trinidad and most closely associated with that island. Indeed, the Trinidadian government had been promoting them as forms of national culture since independence in 1963. How, then, could music be used as a means to further WIADCA's "One People" motto? In terms of steelband, there was no straightforward solution, as the steel drum was fiercely defended by Trinidadians at home and abroad as their national instrument. Yet given the instrument's growing popularity in Brooklyn and the emerging bands' potential for recruiting non-Trinidadian islanders into their ranks, WIADCA had no choice but to push forward with a Trinidad-style Panorama. (The history of Brooklyn's Panorama and the role of the steelbands as sites for pan-Island integration will be the focus of the next chapter.)

Turning to the arena of popular music, calypso, soca, and reggae styles also offered opportunities and posed problems for constructing a pan-Caribbean Carnival. While Trinidad rightly claimed calypso as its native music, by the 1970s Trinidadian singers had toured the Caribbean and local scenes had sprung up in their wake, creating a broad appreciation for calypso music among Caribbean Americans hailing from different English-speaking islands. Although its Calypso King of the US competition was short-lived, WIADCA could draw a diverse Caribbean audience to its Labor Day shows by featuring star figures such as Sparrow and Kitchener, and by reaching out to other islands by presenting singers such as Arrow (Monserrat), Swallow (Antigua), Short Shirt (Antigua), and Lord Slim (Grenada), and groups such as the Draytons Two (Barbados), Tabou Combo (Haiti), and Wareika (Jamaica). The inclusion of dance and drum ensembles showcasing the folk traditions from Jamaica, Haiti, Grenada, Costa Rica, and Panama presented additional opportunities to celebrate diverse island music traditions as part of the Labor Day stage shows.

Jamaican reggae was more complicated, however, given its generational tensions and drug-related cultural connotations, which turned off much of the older WIADCA leadership. The WIADCA-sponsored reggae contests never caught on, but the addition of reggae acts to the Labor Day shows, culminating in a 1983 Thursday Reggae Night celebration, was a genuine effort to bring Jamaicans and their music into the fold. And while the banning of street sound systems might be interpreted as a move to tamp down the reggae volume on Eastern Parkway, by 1980 reggae deejays and amplified bands were mounting their equipment on sound trucks and integrating into the road march itself, surrounded by fans sporting Jamaican colors on T-shirts, head scarfs, and flags.[80] Reggae and calypso/soca did more clashing than integrating, but they eventually managed to peacefully co-exist on the Parkway and the Brooklyn Museum stage. Truck-mounted ensembles playing other popular island styles, including spouge from Barbados and konpa/meringue from Haiti, were also appearing on the Parkway by the mid-1970s.[81] "On Labor Day Eastern Parkway becomes the West-Indian crossroads of North America," observed Don Rojas in the *Amsterdam News*. "A Trinidad masquerade band is followed by a Vincentian DJ on a truck and a spirited Haitian music band on a massive float."[82] Calypso and soca ruled, but the musical offerings on the Parkway and the Museum stage grew more diverse as the decade wore on.

In sum, WIADCA's efforts to use music to unify Caribbean New Yorkers had mixed results. The steelbands remained primarily Trinidadian social units that looked to their homeland for inspiration—other islanders could participate, but only by engaging Trinidadian forms, performance practices, and repertories. Popular music offered additional possibilities for accommodating different island performers and styles that appeared on the Parkway and the museum stage. But the result took the form of a musical mosaic rather than a melting pot or salad bowl—to employ popular metaphors of the era—with various national styles competing with, rather integrating with, one another. The different island groups were well represented on the Parkway, but the Trinidadians tended to dance and wave their national flags around their trucks with deejays playing the latest soca hits. Likewise Jamaicans gravitated toward their reggae truck, Haitians toward their konpa truck, Bajans around their spouge/calypso truck, and so forth. Jamaican reggae and Haitian konpa found a place on the Brooklyn Museum stages, but most comfortably with their own separate reggae and Creole night events.

Regarding Nurse's second observation on Carnival as a force of social integration, there is little doubt that Lezama and his WIADCA associates understood that Carnival music presented an opportunity to reach out beyond the confines of the Caribbean community and garner broader appreciation and respect for their culture.[83] In its 1977 Carnival program booklet, WIADCA declared that "the pulsating melodious rhythms of the steel bands" and the "celebrated tunes composed by calypsonians," along with related mas artistry, would "provide opportunities for building bridges of understanding, tolerance, and appreciation between 'You and I,' 'Them and Us,' and all mankind."[84] Members of central Brooklyn's native-born black community no doubt attended the Eastern Parkway parade as spectators, just as Harlem's native black populace had done in previous decades on Seventh Avenue. In addition, a small number of white New Yorkers were drawn to the sounds of steelband and calypso, as was a previous generation that had embraced tropical music during the calypso craze of the 1950s. Based on recent history, Lezama and WIADCA had good reason to speculate that Carnival music might serve as a cultural conduit between New York's Caribbean communities and the city's black and white non-Caribbean populations.In reality, during its initial decade, relatively few non-Caribbean people attended Labor Day Carnival festivities outside of the Eastern Parkway parade, and the music itself was not a significant integrating enterprise in Brooklyn. The organizers, arrangers, and players associated with the Brooklyn steelbands, as well as their followers, were almost exclusively of Caribbean heritage—there were few American blacks or Latinos, and almost no whites, in the bands. Likewise, the audiences for the Brooklyn Museum Panorama competition and calypso/soca stage shows, as well as the various calypso/soca tents and dances taking place in and around Labor Day weekend, were overwhelmingly Caribbean. The big Eastern Parkway parade was, from its inception, a solidly Caribbean event in terms of the members of the participating mas and steelbands, the crews of the deejay trucks, and the throngs of un-affiliated revelers who chipped and wined down the Parkway. Those native blacks and few whites in attendance were by and large curious bystanders, not participants.

There is no way to accurately measure the number of native-born African Americans who turned out for the early Eastern Parkway parades. Media reports described diverse "Caribbean" and "island" crowds, rarely distinguishing between island- and native-born blacks. Given the large crowd numbers and the parade's location in central Brooklyn, however, it is reasonable to assume that significant numbers of African Americans were there as onlookers. Moreover, the steelbands occasionally performed calypso-style arrangements of American tunes in hopes of engaging those black American spectators. Exactly how successful the music was in attracting non-Caribbean listeners is difficult to assess, but there were no reports of native-born blacks seeking to join any of the steelbands.

On the other side of the racial divide, few white New Yorkers, outside of maverick reporters, occasional politicians, and a handful of inquisi-tive onlookers, attended Carnival events. In the 1970s many, if not most, white New Yorkers were reluctant to venture out to experience the music at a rowdy Eastern Parkway road march or at one of WIADCA's nighttime shows. Such events were no doubt perceived to be possibly dangerous, a fear stoked by sensationalist media coverage of Parkway violence that the parade received in the late 1970s. For many of Brooklyn's "white folks," as Wilfred Thomas recalled from his experience at the 1968 gathering, the early Carnival parades with their raucous calypso and steelband music were distasteful examples of blacks "disturbing the peace." Such criticisms were not new, hearkening back to the rhetoric of British colo-nial authorities and their trepidations over early Carnival gatherings in Trinidad.

As a symbolic display of group identity and pride, the Carnival parade and attendant music no doubt helped Brooklyn's Caribbean commu-nity navigate the choppy waters of multicultural urban politics, serving as a unifying force for the borough's diverse Caribbean peoples. But as musical practice, both steelband and calypso/soca remained firmly ensconced within Caribbean transnational, intracultural networks. Put simply, Brooklyn's early Carnival music was performed by Caribbean artists primarily for Caribbean audiences—there is little evidence that it succeeded in drawing a significantly more diverse demographic to Labor Day Carnival, which throughout the 1970s remained primarily an Afro-Caribbean event. Despite WIADCA's hopes, music's power as a force for social integration was limited in the context of Brooklyn Carnival.

Moving from the local to the global, Carnival music was an essential thread that knit together the collective fabric of the Brooklyn-Caribbean transnation. For first-generation Trinidad migrants and those from adja-cent islands with familiarity with steelband and calypso traditions, music proved to be a vital force in maintaining ties to their home countries and easing the stress of geographic dislocation. When Sparrow, Kitchener, and

Shadow performed at Brooklyn's Dimanche Gras, they brought something of the Caribbean with them that deeply touched their migrant audiences. Equally important, Brooklyn's steelbands had a profound impact on the forging of these transnational linkages.

Notes

1. Winston Munroe, interview with author and Les Slater, 8 August 1996; interview with author and Ray Funk, 8 September 2014.

2. Philip Kasinitz, *Caribbean New York: Black Immigrants and the Politics of Race* (Cornell University Press, 1992), pp. 54–59.

3. Gorin letter quoted in Herman Hall, "Celebrate Lionel 'Rufus' Gorin, True Pioneer: Brooklyn's 50 Years of Carnival," *Everybody's Caribbean Magazine* 4, no. 2 (October 2017), p. 18.

4. Clyde Henry, interview with author, 24 April 2015.

5. Hall, "Celebrate Lionel 'Rufus' Gorin," pp. 15–16. The *Antillean Echo* (25 August 1970) also reported that Gorin founded the United West Indian Day Development Association in 1966.

6. The exact dates of Lezama's ascension to power and the name change from the United West Indian Day Development Association (UWIDDA) to the present-day West Indian American Carnival Day Association (WIADCA) are not certain. Lezama's 2007 *New York Times* obituary (27 January 2007) cites 1967 as the date he assumed control. Joshua Guild also offers 1967, but it is not clear whether he is referring to the date that Lezama took over or the year the name change occurred. Don Hill suggests that Lezama took over in the late 1960s and changed the name in order to obtain a permit to parade on Eastern Parkway in 1971. The previous year the *Antillean Echo* (25 August 1970) referred to Lezama as the head of the United West Indian Development Association. The 1971 Carnival program booklet, published to coincide with the first Carnival parade down Eastern Parkway, refers to the sponsoring organization as the West Indian-American Day Association, Inc., with Lezama as chairman. The next two booklets keep this same designation, but the 1974 booklet (and all subsequent publications) identify the organizers as the West Indian-American Day Carnival Association. This evidence suggests that the change from UWIDDA to WIADA probably occurred sometime between the 1970 and 1971 Labor Day Carnivals, and the final change to WIADCA took place before the 1974 event. All subsequent WIADCA Carnival booklets refer to 1967 as the date of the first Carnival sponsored by the organization, suggesting this was the date that Lezama took over from Gorin. See Joshua Guild, *You Can't Go Home Again: Migration, Citizenship, and Black Community in Postwar New York and London* (PhD diss., Yale University, 2007), p. 275; Hill, "History of West Indian Carnival," pp. 50–51.

7. UWIDDA minutes from 8 June 1967 and 22 June 1967 courtesy of Camilla Groin and Herman Hall.

8. Kenneth Pollock, "From Carnival Parade to Political Power," WIADCA Carnival program Booklet, 1978.

9. Determining exactly who participated and where the mid-to-late-1960s Brooklyn block parties and small Carnival parades took place is difficult because there is no press coverage or flyers of Carnival activities from 1964 through 1969. The only written accounts are the above-cited 1967 UWIDDA meeting minutes and the 1978 remembrance of the

1967 parade by Kenneth Pollock. Steelband manager Clyde Durrant, who arrived in Brooklyn in 1966 from Trinidad, recalls a Labor Day Carnival parade in 1967 or 1968 that began on St. Johns Place, went up New York Avenue to Dean Street, and then went west over to the Dean Street–Crown Heights Armory. He recollects that Rudy King's Tropicans and Pops McCarthy's Harlem All Stars were part of the street festivities, and that Syd Joe's Orchestra performed for the Armory dance. The pan players Caldera Caraballo and Clyde Henry recall informal parades on Fulton Street that ended near Franklin Avenue and were followed by a dance at one of the Armories. Caraballo recalls his Moderneers band played. Clyde Durrant, personal interview with author, 27 April 2015; Caldera Caraballo, personal interview with author, 20 June 2014; Clyde Henry, personal interview with author, 24 April 2015.

10. For more on the early contributions of Sparrow, see Gordon Rohlehr, *Calypso and Society in Pre-Independence Trinidad* (Port of Spain: published by the author, 1990), pp. 525–534; and Jocelyne Guilbault, *Governing Sound: The Cultural Politics of Trinidad's Carnival Musics* (University of Chicago Press, 2007), pp. 154–158.

11. "Mas in Brooklyn" by Slinger Francisco, from the LP *More Sparrow More* (1969, RA2020).

12. Wilfred Thomas, "Brooklyn Labor Day Carnival: The Indisputable Facts," *Everybody's Magazine* 39, no. 2 (September 2016). According to *Everybody's* editor Herman Hall, Thomas wrote the piece in 2006. More recently, Thomas reflected that the 1968 and 1969 Carnival parades down Prospect Park West were relatively small affairs, which may explain why they received no press coverage at the time. It was not until the September 1970 parade, which Thomas recalled was considerably larger and louder than the previous two, that the *Caribbean Antillean Echo* covered the event (see notes 13 and 14 below). Wilfred Thomas, phone interview with author, 15 October 2017.

13. "You Can't Miss Mas' in Brooklyn on Labor Day," *Caribbean Antillean Echo*, 8 September 1970.

14. "Glory of Aztecs Best Carnival Band," *Caribbean Antillean Echo*, 15 September 1970.

15. Winston Munroe, personal interview with author and Ray Funk, 4 September 2014, Brooklyn.

16. There has been some confusion as to exactly when the first Carnival parade was held on Eastern Parkway. In 1979 Donald Hill and Robert Abramson reported that Lezama secured a permit for Eastern Parkway in 1969, and Philip Scher reprises the 1969 date of the first Parkway parade. But the evidence from press and the WIADCA Carnival booklet make it clear that the first Eastern Parkway event was not held until Labor Day 1971. Donald Hill and Robert Abramson, "West Indian Carnival in Brooklyn," *Natural History* 88, no. 7 (August–September 1979): 83; Philip Scher, *Carnival and the Formation of a Caribbean Transnation* (University Press of Florida, 2003), p. 80.

17. "Brooklyn Mas: Eastern Parkway to Close for Monday 'Jump Up,'" *Antillean Caribbean Echo*, 28 August 1971; "Brooklyn West Indians Set Labor Day Festival," *New York Amsterdam News*, 28 August 1971.

18. "Serpent Worshippers Wins Best Band on Labor Day," *Antillean Caribbean Echo*, 11 September 1971; "West Indian-American Weekend Carnival a Smash Bash in Boro!," *New York Amsterdam News*, 11 September 1971. Wilfred Thomas, in his 2006 recollections of the 1971 Eastern Parkway Carnival, estimated the crowd at around 5,000. Thomas, "Brooklyn Labor Day Carnival," 2016.

19. "Serpent Worshippers Wins Best Band."

20. Carlos Lezama, "Chairman's Message," WIADCA Carnival program booklet, 1971.

21. Carlos Lezama, "Chairman's Message," WIADCA Carnival program booklet, 1973.

22. Henrietta Johnson Burroughs, "West Indian Festival: A Heritage," *New York Amsterdam News*, 23 September, 1972.

23. Napier Pillai, "It's Labor Day Mas in Brooklyn," *Trinidad Overseas Express*, 11 September 1972.

24. The LCDDD 1973 Carnival Festival was announced in a short piece appearing in the *New York Amsterdam News* (25 August 1973) and a full-page ad in the *Echo* (25 August 1973), which lists the steelpan, calypso, and reggae competitions but makes no mention of a calypso headliner. According to the ad, the event was produced by the LDCCC in association with the New York Department of Parks, Recreation, and Cultural Administration; Medgar Evers College; and Central Brooklyn Model Cities. Horace Morancie, who was a leader of the Models Cities program, clearly had New York City support for the program.

25. "It's Boro Carnival Time, 2nd Straight Weekend," *New York Amsterdam News*, 1 September 1973.

26. Clyde Henry recalled that he and Horace Morancie were able to persuade Kitchener to perform for their event for free. Kitchener had been brought to New York by WIADCA and would perform for their Saturday and Sunday evening Brooklyn Museum shows following his surprise Medgar Evers appearance. Clyde Henry, personal interview with author, 24 April 2015.

27. A "Carnival Extravaganza" produced by the Airport Mechanics C&S Club of New York to be held at the Manhattan Center was announced in the *Antillean Echo* (18 August 1973). The event was scheduled to conflict with WIADCA's Saturday night Kitchener show, and it featured the calypsonians King Wellington, Lord Nelson, and Nap Hepburn, and dance orchestras led by Mano Marcellin and Ron Berridge.

28. J. Zamgba Browne, "It Looked like All the World Was West Indian!: Unity Is Theme as Many Groups March Together," *New York Amsterdam News*, 9 September 1973.

29. Knolly Moses, "Mas' Like Never Before: 1½ Million Crowd Parkway," *Antillean Caribbean Echo*, 18 September 1973.

30. Dalton James, "It Was Like This on Eastern Parkway," *Antillean Caribbean Echo*, 15 September 1973.

31. Judith Cummings, "600,000 Get in Step with West Indian Beat of Brooklyn Parade," *New York Times*, 4 September 1973.

32. Jean Perry, "Parade Organizers Never a Step Behind," *Sunday News*, 16 September 1973.

33. "West Indians Fight over Annual Parade," *New York Amsterdam News*, July 20, 1974.

34. "Big Parade Presents Big Problems, *New York Amsterdam News*, 7 September 1974.

35. Ibid.

36. "West Indian Carnival Fight Continues," *New York Amsterdam News*, 27 July 1974.

37. "One Million Participate in West Indian Parade," *New York Amsterdam News*, 7 September 1974.

38. Don Hill, "New York's Caribbean Carnival," *Everybody's Caribbean Magazine* 5, no. 5 (1981): 35.

39. Grace Lichtenstein, "Mardi Gras Spirit Enlivens Brooklyn," *New York Times*, 3 September 1974.

40. Herman Hall, personal interview with author, 22 July 2014.

41. Slinger "Sparrow" Francisco, phone interview with author, 26 March 2018.

42. Gordon Rohlehr, *My Whole Life Is Calypso: Essays on Sparrow* (Tunapuna, Trinidad, self-published, 2015), p. 17. A recording of Sparrow's 1962 "Sparrow Come Back Home" can be found on YouTube, at https://www.youtube.com/watch?v=6msSm1A3ZEQ.

43. "A Calypso Spectacular," ad listing in the *New York Amsterdam News*, 19 July 1969.

44. "Calypso Carnival at Garden this Weekend," *New York Amsterdam News*, 17 July 1971.

45. The 1971 recording of Lord Kitchener's "Mas in Madison Square Garden" can be heard on YouTube, at https://www.youtube.com/watch?v=gPu3irEPHhQ.

46. "Caribbean Festival," *New York Amsterdam News*, 12 May 1979.

47. "Parks Dept. Asks for $10,000 to Clean Up after Carnival," *New York Amsterdam News*, 27 August 1975.

48. Ray Funk and Michael Eldridge, eds., *Calypso Craze: 1956–57 and Beyond*, booklet accompanying Bear Family CD box set (2014), p. 56.

49. Randolph "Count Robin" Hilaire, personal interview with author, 17 August 2013.

50. Winners of the 1975 US Calypso Competition appeared in the 1976 WIADCA Carnival program booklet.

51. Prince Galloway's biography is drawn from phone interview with Prince Galloway by author, 15 September 2014.

52. Tape of US Calypso Competition recorded by Don Hill, 29 August 1975, WIADCA sponsored show at the Brooklyn Museum.

53. Phone interview with Galloway by author, 15 September 2014. Galloway recorded "Labor Day" with slightly revised lyrics on his own Rosie label in 1983.

54. Winners of the 1976 US Calypso Competition were announced in the *New York Amsterdam News* (18 September 1976) and appeared in the 1977 WIADCA Carnival program booklet. Several singers recalled that additional US Calypso Competitions continued after 1976, but if so they were not under the sponsorship of WIADCA.

55. Hall, interview with author, 22 July 2014.

56. According to WIADCA public relations director Herman Hall, the executive board of the organization was made up of all Trinidadians with the exception of himself and Dr. Emanuel Stanislaus, who were from Grenada, and Gerald Spence, the sole Jamaican representative. Hall claimed that Spence was a friend and co-transit worker of Lezama who had little interest in WIADCA policy decisions. Jamaicans thus had little to no say regarding WIADCA policy and programming decisions. Hall, interview with author, 22 July 2014.

57. According to the 1980 census figures, Jamaicans made up nearly a third of New York's non-Hispanic Caribbean population. They outnumbered New York's Trinidadian population by more than two to one, 93,100 to 39,160. Statistics taken from Kasinitz, *Caribbean New York*, p. 54.

58. Hill, "New York's Caribbean Carnival," p. 35. Eventually a few reggae bands and DJs would join the parade with mobile sound systems mounted on trucks. Philip Kasinitz, "Community Dramatized, Community Contested," in *Island Sound in the Global City: Caribbean Popular Music in New York*, edited by Ray Allen and Lois Wilcken (University of Illinois Press, 1999), p. 104.

59. Don Rojas, "Carnival Is Bacchanal," *New York Amsterdam News*, 10 September 1977.

60. Jennifer Dunning, "Dancing in the Streets Marks Brooklyn's West Indian Fete," *New York Times*, 6 September 1977.

61. Hill, "History of West Indian Carnival," p. 60; Hall, interview with author, 22 July 2014.

62. WIADCA Carnival program booklet, 1975 and 1976.

63. "A Call for Unity among Carnival Artists," *New York Daily Challenge*, 16 August 1978.

64. Listings of the calypso and soca singers who participated in WIADCA-sponsored events at the Brooklyn Museum can be found in the WIADCA Carnival program booklets, 1972–1980.

65. Count Robin, interview with author, 28 May 2015.

66. Peter Noel, "Opening Night of a Calypso Tent in Brooklyn," *New York Amsterdam News*, 29 August 1981. The calypsonian Cro Cro mentions the clashes between Rainbow Terrace and B's Palace in Frank Smith's obituary, "Calypso Godfather Dies," *Trinidad Guardian*, 22 May 2015, http://www4.guardian.co.tt/entertainment/2014-05-22/carnival-2015-and-running.

67. Frank Manning, "Overseas Caribbean Carnivals: The Art and Politics of a Transnational Celebration," *Plantation Society in the Americas* 3, no. 1 (1990): 54.

68. "Sweet-Soca Expression," *New York Daily Challenge*, 31 August 1978.

69. Basir Mchawi, "Labor Day in Brooklyn," *New York Daily Challenge*, 5 September 1979.

70. Peter Noel, "Sabotage at Carnival," *New York Amsterdam News*, 8 September 1979.

71. J. Zamgba Browne, "1.5 Million Play Mas: A Big Day in Brooklyn," *New York Amsterdam News*, 8 September 1979.

72. WIADCA's concessions to city authorities were reported in Dawad Philip, "Is Carnival Dead?," *New York Daily Challenge*, 4 September 1980; and in "W.I. American Day Carnival 13th Annual Weekend," *New York Amsterdam News*, 23 August 1980.

73. Bob Kappstatter, "Carnival, Smaller but Wiser," *New York Daily News*, 3 September 1980. Estimates of crowd sizes varied greatly, with the *New York Amsterdam News* (6 September 1980) reporting over a million for the 1980 Eastern Parkway event.

74. See, for example, Charles Baillou, "Rampaging Youths Mar Labor Day," *New York Amsterdam News*, 12 September 1981. Despite the scandalous headline, Baillou notes that the disruption and vandalism occurred two hours after the 6 p.m. curfew, and much of it off the official Parkway route.

75. Hall, "Inside Brooklyn's Carnival," pp. 12–23.

76. For a comparison of the structure of the Labor Day Carnival parade with that of the New York Puerto Rican Day parade, see Philip Kasinitz and Judith Freidenberg-Herbstein, "The Puerto Rican Parade and West Indian Carnival: Public Celebrations in New York City," in *Caribbean Life*

in New York City: Sociocultural Dimensions, edited by Constance Sutton and Elsa Chaney (Center for Migration Studies in New York, 1987), pp. 340–341.

77. For a comparison of Port of Spain and Brooklyn Carnival road processions, see Scher, *Carnival and the Formation of a Caribbean Transnation*, p. 90. See also Stephen Stuempfle's description of the complex special arrangements of Port of Spain's Carnival, which offered "many possible routes for procession," in Stephen Stuempfle, *Port of Spain: The Construction of a Caribbean City, 1888–1962* (University of the West Indies Press, 2018), p. 215.

78. Keith Nurse, "Globalization and Trinidadian Carnival: Diaspora, Hybridity, and Identity in Global Culture," *Cultural Studies* 13, no. 4 (1999): 680.

79. Scher, *Carnival and the Formation of a Caribbean Transnation*, p.1.

80. Joshua Guild suggests that the banning of sidewalk discos was a conscious attempt by WIADCA to curtail the presence of reggae during the Eastern Parkway parade. Guild, *You Can't Go Home Again*, p. 192.

81. In addition to conventional steelbands, Don Hill reported sighting truck-mounted (calypso) brass bands as well as combos playing Jamaican reggae, Bajan spouge, and Haitian meringues on Eastern Parkway in the mid-1970s. Hill, "New York's Caribbean Carnival," 35.

82. Rojas, "Carnival Is Bacchanal."

83. Herman Hall, for example, reported the steelband's broad appeal outside the Caribbean community, noting its successful reception from the White House to the stages of Lincoln Center and the Kennedy Center. He observed that "across Post-Bicentennial U.S., Americans are developing steelband orchestras." Hall, "The Steelband: A New American Music," *New York Amsterdam News*, 9 September 1978.

84. Ed Anderson and Joseph Lewis, "West Indian-American Carnival Day in Brooklyn," WIADCA Carnival program booklet (1977), p. 18.

5

The Brooklyn Steelband Movement

Winston Munroe, fresh off the plane from Trinidad, had no way of knowing he was on the cusp of Brooklyn's nascent steelband movement when he played in Rufus Gorin's ad hoc Carnival celebration on Labor Day, 1966. After completing a degree at Hunter College and taking a job as an accountant, Munroe joined the Pan Masters, a large steelband that made its debut in the 1971 Eastern Parkway parade. In 1973 the Pan Masters placed first in the recently instituted Labor Day Panorama, a contest that pitted Brooklyn's steelbands in head-to-head competition. By the early 1970s the Pan Masters had joined the ranks of the Tropicans, the Harlem All Stars, the Moderneers, the Highlanders, and the BWIA Sunjets, appearing at WIADCA's Labor Day events and at Carnival dances and fetes across the borough. They also played occasional engagements for white audiences at Greenwich Village clubs, midtown Manhattan concert halls, and suburban parties. In spirit and practice, these bands were extensions of Trinidad's steelband movement that afforded Brooklyn's migrants, now far from home, the opportunity to re-experience their native culture.

The Early Brooklyn Steelbands

The uptick in post-1965 Caribbean migration to Brooklyn led to the influx of skilled steelband players like Munroe, as well as arrangers and tuners with years of experience with the Trinidad bands. As a result, the number and average size of the Brooklyn bands increased dramatically. One such pan man was Leslie Slater (b. 1940), who arrived from Trinidad in 1964 with plans to study journalism and public relations at New York University. An experienced player and arranger for the Trinidad Highlander Orchestra, Slater was immediately recruited to arrange for Kim Loy Wong's Brooklyn Highlanders, a band playing for the Caribbean dances and fetes that were becoming increasingly popular in Brooklyn by that time. But Slater soon joined a second, six-member ensemble, the Trinidad Serenaders, led by another Trinidad expatriate and pan man, Conrad Mauge. Through connections outside of the Caribbean community, Mauge was able to find lucrative work for the band performing primarily for white audiences in the suburbs. Rarely did the two group's repertoires overlap. The Highlanders were interested in Slater's arrangements of the latest calypso tunes from Trinidad, which he was able to keep up with through imported calypso and steelband recordings. By contrast, the Trinidad Serenaders favored simple, Belafonte-style pop-calypsos, and conventional, non-calypso-style arrangements of American popular songs that conformed to white audiences' expectations of exotic steelband music. Tunes such as "Yellow Bird" and "Jamaica Farewell" were popular with white audiences but were not well received at Caribbean dances.[1]

Cliff Alexis (1937–2019) was another influential pan player and arranger who first visited the United States in 1964 as a member of the touring Trinidad National Steel Band. He was eventually able to obtain a four-year US visa, and in 1965 relocated to Brooklyn where he began to arrange for the BWIA Sunjets. At the time the Sunjets were one of the larger bands in Brooklyn, boasting approximately fifteen players and performing at Caribbean dances in Manhattan and Brooklyn, where they alternated sets with a brass band such as Syd Joe's Orchestra. The latest calypso tunes were always in demand, and Alexis recalled friends mailing him the most recent records from Trinidad in order to keep the band's repertoire up to date. And like Mauge and Slater's Trinidad Serenaders, Alexis and his players maintained a group of American pop standards and Belafonte-style calypsos for occasional concerts and engagements at private white parties.[2]

One of the Sunjets' organizers was the aforementioned powerful Caribbean American political figure Horace Morancie. He approached Columbia Records and convinced them to record the band, and in 1966 Columbia issued the LP *Steelband Spectacular/The Sounds of the Caribbean/The Sunjet Serenaders Steelband* (CS 92620). In flowery prose the liner notes celebrate "the sound of the Caribbean . . . the romantic, frolicking beat of the steelband" that "sings 'welcome' to travelers in the friendly accents of the Caribbean." Fifteen pan men, playing on what appears to be an idyllic tropical beach, are pictured on the album's cover. Nowhere, however, does it say that the photograph was taken on Jones Beach, Long Island (about twenty miles east of Brooklyn) rather than the Caribbean. Musically, the album is a compilation of mostly popular American songs, including Gershwin's "Summertime," Bobby Scott and Ric Marlow's "A Taste of Honey," Leonard Bernstein's "Maria," "More—Theme from Mondo Cane," and the "Theme from Exodus"—all set to light calypso rhythms. The decision not to include any of Alexis's contemporary calypso arrangements suggests that the LP was aimed at white, crossover listeners rather than for New York Caribbean audiences who might hire the band for a dance or fete.[3] In retrospect, the Sunjets Columbia LP was a throwback to the calypso craze of the late 1950s rather than an indication of how steelband style and repertoire were developing in Brooklyn by the mid-1960s.

A number of prominent steel-pan builders and tuners became part of the Brooklyn pan scene in the late 1960s, including Michael Enoch, Emanuel "Cobo Jack" Riley, and Ellie Mannette. The most influential of these was Mannette (1926–2018), considered a pioneer in the development of the steel pan in Trinidad. He is widely recognized as the first to sink out the bottom of an oil drum and to successfully groove out diatonic scales, sometime in the late 1940s, and eventually to align the notes in a systematic chromatic configuration.[4] The former leader and tuner for Trinidad's prestigious Invaders steelband, Mannette was brought to New York in 1967 at the behest of Murray Narell and Pete Seeger to establish a steelband program at the Lower Manhattan Settlement House. Mannette settled in Queens, where he maintained his own band, the Trinidad Hummingbirds, which specialized in formal stage performances. But he also tuned for the Brooklynaires and several other Brooklyn bands, and his presence on the scene helped promote higher quality pans among the New York pan community.[5]

By the late 1960s, steelband activity in Brooklyn was on the rise. A number of small ensembles, such as those lead by Mauge and Alexis, continued to perform for more exclusive white audiences, but panists increasingly found work playing for dances and fetes held in the borough's expanding Caribbean communities. These engagements demanded larger ensembles of ten to fifteen individuals with trap drums and additional percussion in order to produce a full sound and rhythmic groove suitable for dancing. When Rudy King moved from Harlem to Brooklyn in the mid-1960s he organized exactly such a band, the Tropicans. Around this time another midsize Brooklyn-based ensemble, the Moderneers, was established by Reynolds "Caldera" Caraballo. A former bandmate of King, Caraballo was a veteran of small stage ensembles, including one that toured with Harry Belafonte in the early 1960s. King's and Caraballo's groups had fluid personnel that could be trimmed down to a small ensemble of five to six players for club, hotel, and suburban party engagements, enlarged to ten to fifteen performers to accommodate Caribbean dances, or expanded to twenty or more musicians for outdoor Carnival processions. Other large bands, including the Pan Masters, the Brooklynaires, and the Sonatas, would soon form to participate in the Eastern Parkway Carnival parade and early Brooklyn Panorama contests.

Steelbands on the Parkway

Exactly how many of Brooklyn's steelbands actually appeared at the first Eastern Parkway parade in 1971 is not certain. Clyde Henry, Rudy King, and Winston Munroe, who were all there, remembered up to half a dozen groups on the road. Winston Wellington, another participant and co-founder of the Brooklynaires, recalled the scene:

In 1971 we went out on Eastern Parkway with a small stage side [twenty players] on a float, being pulled by a car. And in those days we headed up the Parkway, not down like we do now. We started at the Brooklyn Library and heading east, toward the Crown Heights area. I remember we played three tunes—a pop tune, the Osmond's "One Bad Apple," Sparrow's "Queen of the Band," and Sparrow's "Mas in Brooklyn." . . . We played more straight-up arrangements—on the road you had to keep the people jumping. Rhythm is quite important on the road.[6]

Count Robin, a calypso singer and pan player with King's Tropicans, recounted that King's band turned out roughly twenty players, sporting single pans held in place by straps around their necks. Winston Munroe remembered playing with a larger band, the recently constituted Pan Masters. The band consisted of close to seventy-five members, many of whom played multiple steel pans stacked on racks and wagons that were pulled down the Parkway by fans and costumed dancers. Evidently there were no officially designated points along the route for the steelbands to enter or exit the parade. Robin recollected that the Tropicans and the Brooklynaires simply joined the fray at the corner of Kingston Avenue and Eastern Parkway, turning left and inching their way down the Parkway for five blocks toward Lincoln Terrace Park.[7] The structure of the parade was loose, and apparently not all of the steelbands were paired with masquerade bands. Nor were there any formal registration procedures or appearance fees, according to Munroe:

We just went out and played. Pay was unheard of! We went out there and played from the heart—just for the enjoyment. We weren't associated with any masquerade band. The masquerade bands would try and get involved with the steelbands when they were out on the road. When they came out on the road they would join the steelbands, which we were happy for, because we had people following us. It was all informal, no one was hired.[8]

The Pan Masters, he recalled, were awarded a small trophy for "Best Steelband Performance" on the Parkway that year.

Exactly what these early Brooklyn steelbands sounded like is difficult to assess, given the paucity of recorded material. But Wellington's and Munroe's comments provide important hints. By "straight up" arrangements Wellington was referring to simple repetitive verse/chorus forms accompanied by a strong, pulsing beat to "keep the people jumping." The organizational structure was loose and informal, as Munroe suggested, with masqueraders and bystanders spontaneously coalescing around a steelband and literally pushing and pulling the rack-mounted players down the Parkway. Such "pan-on-the-road" performances were modeled after Trinidad's Carnival processions where, in the pre-deejay/sound truck era, steelbands were the primary source of music.[9] On Eastern Parkway, as on Port of Spain's Frederick Street, steelbands played open-ended verse/chorus, percussion-heavy music meant to pull revelers in to what would ideally become a dancing/singing road procession. Such practices exemplify Turino's "participatory performance" model, where formal distinctions between performers and audience members tend to blur.[10] During these moments of intense communal bonding among musicians, masqueraders, and spectators-turned performers, the Carnival procession transforms from conventional parade into social ritual.

Regarding repertoire, Wellington's recollection of the Brooklynaires playing a rendition of the Osmond's 1971 hit song "One Bad Apple" is a reminder that in addition to calypsos, the steelbands occasionally played American pop songs, commonly referred to as "bomb" tunes. Playing steelband arrangements of popular American bomb tunes was common in Trinidad, especially during J'Ouvert. In addition to reprising the Trinidad practice, dropping a bomb in Brooklyn functioned to attract American listeners. Munroe recalled this practice:

> The audience on the Parkway at that time [mid-1970s] was heavily [native-born black] American. In order for them to really participate and feel part of the Carnival you had to play songs they knew. So we would play the basic popular songs you would hear on the radio every day—the R&B songs. And that's when you got the people on the Parkway going crazy, because they had never heard a Michael Jackson song played on a steel drum before. And those people on the side would want to jump in and participate; they would help push the pan down the Parkway.

Tunes such as the Jackson Five's "ABC" and Stevie Wonder's "Sir Duke," were particularly successful in catching the attention of the black Americans who had wandered upon the early Parkway parades.[11]

While bomb tunes were heard on the Parkway, the early Brooklyn bands' repertoires consisted primarily of calypso tunes originating from Trinidad and brought north by migrant players and arrangers, or on recent commercial recordings by the island's most popular calypsonians and steelbands. A premium was placed on rendering the latest tunes, especially those that had competed for the Road March and Panorama titles during that year's Port of Spain Carnival. The demand for new arrangements of the most contemporary calypsos would become increasingly imperative with the advent of Brooklyn's own Panorama.

Establishing a Brooklyn Panorama

For Labor Day 1972, WIADCA's Brooklyn Museum programming was extended to three evenings and included for the first time a steelband Panorama contest. Their 1972 Carnival program booklet lists a Friday evening Panorama Preliminary contest, a Saturday night Steelband

Semi-finals, and a Steelband Finals as part of the Sunday night Dimanche Gras show, which also included a performance by the Mighty Sparrow and presentation of the King and Queen mas band winners. No one can verify if there were enough steelbands for the scheduled preliminary and semi-final rounds, but the *Echo* reported that a $1,000 first prize was awarded to Rudy King's Tropicana Steelband, a $700 second prize to the Pan Masters Steelband, and a $250 third prize to the visiting Boston Silver Stars.[12] WIADCA's decision to add a Panorama contest to the event was clearly an attempt to re-create one of the most popular components of Trinidad Carnival in Brooklyn. Since its inception in 1963, Panorama, along with the national calypso contest, had become a centerpiece of the Port of Spain Savannah Carnival shows leading up to Carnival Monday.[13]

Brooklyn Panorama would eventually become the highlight of the Labor Day stage shows, but there were bumps along the way. Brooklyn's first Panorama was contested by a number of pan players who suspected the official judges' results had been tampered with. They claimed that following the competition, an announcement was circulated identifying the Brooklynaires and the Sonatas tying for first place, the Tropicans taking the second spot, and the Pan Masters and Silver Stars tying for third place. Lezama, they contended, had overturned the judges' decision and declared the Tropicans the winner. Clyde Henry, a spokesperson for the steelbands, was quoted as threatening to take action against Lezama and the WIADCA.[14] Count Robin of the Sonatas and Winston Wellington of the Brooklynaires later confirmed this controversy, recalling that their bands were initially declared the joint winners, with arrangements of the Mighty Sparrow's "Drunk and Disorderly" and "Rope," respectively.[15]

Henry and the steelband men were not the only ones to find fault with the way Lezama and his WIADCA team were running Carnival. The pan arranger Leslie Slater, now an NBC-TV publicist who had helped WIADCA promote the 1971 Labor Day events, broke with the organization and wrote a scathing letter in the *Echo* chastising Lezama and his associates for their overall lack of managerial skills and professionalism. In addition, he criticized WIADCA's Trinidadian inner circle and the organization's overall lack of representation from other islands.[16] Slater would go on to join forces with Henry and Morancie to produce alternative Carnival events.

Horace Morancie's previously discussed 1973 alternative Carnival at Medgar Evers College included a Panorama, but it was a one-night affair with no preliminary rounds.[17] Participating bands included the Pan Masters, the Brooklynaires, the Harlem All Stars, the Sonatas, and the Highlanders. Hue Loy, who played for the Pan Masters that night, recalled that each band was asked to play two numbers, a calypso and a non-calypso piece. The Pan Masters were awarded a trophy for the best steelband performance with Sparrow's "My Connie," arranged by Dave La Barrie, and Beethoven's 5th Symphony, arranged by Lester Harbin. The contest, Henry remembers, was relatively informal and involved no prize money. Henry and his fellow steelband men hoped to further weaken WIADCA by boycotting the Eastern Parkway parade that year, but the effort broke down at the last minute when La Barrie brought the Pan Masters onto the Parkway and other bands followed.[18] WIADCA's 1973 Carnival program booklet lists a Panorama contest for its Friday evening show, but there is no record of a contest at the Brooklyn Museum that year.

In 1974 Clyde Henry and allies attempted to stage another alternative Panorama, this time at the grounds of Boys and Girls High School in Bedford Stuyvesant. Wellington, the Brooklynaires' arranger, recounted what transpired that evening:

> Memories of the steelband Panorama competition of 1974 will remain indelibly etched on the minds of the thousands of pan enthusiasts who attended the show which was held on the grounds of Boys High School on Rutland Road in Brooklyn. Heavily favored and regarded as "the band to beat" by the masses in attendance, we [Brooklynaires] were confident that we would emerge as winners. We played two polished renditions entitled "Mis Mary" and "Baseman." Both were well received by the audience. So thrilling was the band's performance of the exquisite arrangements done respectively by Winston Wellington and Leon Sterling that it seemed to have surpassed our own expectations. Sentiments quickly changed from satisfaction and confidence to frustration, disappointment and anger, because shortly after the pans were removed from the stage, a thunderstorm came and washed out the rest of the show. Demonstrating a sense of urgency were hundreds of persons who formed a sea of humanity rushed to the gates to gain egress and to elude the rain. I could clearly see from my vantage point that the gates were not designed to accommodate a crowd of that magnitude. Within a short period of time most of the people had left the premises. Only a few diehards including myself remained and kept surveillance mainly over the tenor and double second pans because of the susceptibility to pilferage. There was never any official announcement from any of the organizers regarding a postponement or cancellation of the competition. I imagine that by virtue of the fact that the Brooklynaires, which played first and was the only band that was judged but the adjudicators, won in a strict technical sense.[19]

Following the rainout of Henry's Panorama, a few bands competed on Saturday or Sunday night at the Brooklyn Museum, with the Tropicans being declared the 1974 winner.[20] Henry wanted the bands to stay away from Eastern Parkway on Monday afternoon and rally at an alternate site on New York Avenue, but most of the bands opted for the Parkway.[21] Although Henry failed to mount a serious alternative to WIADCA's Panorama, he did succeed in publicly articulating the problems facing Brooklyn's steel-pan community. The costs of putting a band together, finding rehearsal space, hiring a tuner and arranger (usually the only two guaranteed paid positions), and transporting a large band to Eastern Parkway and the Brooklyn Museum were substantial, and few of the bands had sponsorship. The Brooklyn steelbands faced different challenges than did their counterparts in Trinidad, where Panorama was run by a government agency, the National Carnival Council (NCC), which granted prize money and modest appearance fees to the participating bands. In addition, the NCC encouraged private industry to sponsor bands, and by the late 1960s most of the prominent bands had private sponsorship.[22] The logistics and financing of steelbands in Brooklyn would remain an ongoing problem despite WIADCA's efforts to raise more prize money and appearance fees. The following year, Henry established an organization calling itself the Steelband Association of the Americas and threatened to boycott the 1975 and 1976 WIADCA Panoramas, but with no success.[23]

In 1975, for the first time, Panorama received top billing WIADCA's Friday evening show. Stung by the 1973 and 1974 boycotts, Lezama engaged Caldera Caraballo to recruit bands and organize the competition. Although Henry and his SBAA called for a boycott, Caraballo was successful in getting approximately a dozen bands to participate, offering small appearance fees and prize money that included $1,800 donated by the Schaefer Brewing Company.[24] According to the 1976 WIADCA Carnival program booklet, the Brooklynaires took first place (see Figure 5.1), followed by the Silhouettes Steel Orchestra and the BWIA Sonatas Steel Orchestra. In addition, the Tropicans, the Caribe Masquerades, Steel Unlimited, and an unidentified seventh band were listed as runners up.

BROOKLYNAIRES — 1975 Panorama Winners

Figure 5.1. Brooklynaires, 1975 Panorama winners (courtesy of the West Indian American Day Carnival Association).

Brooklyn's Early Panorama Bands

The Tropicans won Brooklyn's first Labor Day Panorama in 1972 with Denzil Botus's arrangement of Sparrow's tune "Rope."[25] In Trinidad, by the mid-1960s, it had become common for steelbands to employ an individual to arrange a popular calypso song and teach it to the group. Arrangers would often choose calypsos with memorable hooks and chorus lines that would be recognizable to audiences and that would lend themselves to the new and larger bands, which now featured multiple sections that could play melodies and countermelodies, strum chords, and lay down bass lines. Panorama bands, which in Trinidad had grown in size up to 100 players, were divided into six or seven sections. The high-range tenor pans usually played the primary melodic line, while the double tenors and double seconds reprised the main melody or contributed countermelodies. The mid-range cello and guitar pans provided chordal accompaniment. Full-sized, fifty-five-gallon drums, arranged in six, nine, or twelve drums-per-player configurations maintained a moving bass line. A trap drummer became the center of the rhythm section, or "engine room," joined by conga drummers, iron players (who struck automobile brake drums with metal sticks), and other hand percussionists.[26]

None of the early Brooklyn bands, with the possible exception of the Pan Masters, were as large as their Trinidad Panorama counterparts. Rudy King's 1972 Tropicans, who paraded on Eastern Parkway and won the Panorama that year, probably numbered between twenty and twenty-five players. In addition, King kept a smaller group of seven or eight players, known as a "stage-side," for parties and stage events. His band consisted primarily of Trinidad-born men, many who were formerly associated with the island's Invaders, Desperadoes, and Starlift steelbands. Rehearsals of the core stage-side members took place in the basement of a St. John's Place building in Crown Heights and moved to a vacant lot on the corner of Nostrand Avenue and Gates Street to accommodate the expanded band for Carnival and Panorama season. The Tropicans employed Emmanuel "Cobo Jack" Riley, formerly of Trinidad's Invaders Steel Orchestra and considered one of the country's top steel-pan builders and tuners, and two experienced arrangers, Denzil Botus (who had played with Trinidad's Desperadoes) and Winston "Mouter Bee" Phillip (who had played with Trinidad's Invaders). Like most of the bands, the Tropicans boasted a broad repertoire of Trinidadian calypsos and American popular tunes, often performed with a calypso beat, although they played primarily calypsos for the Eastern Parkway road march and exclusively calypsos for the Panorama.[27]

Prior to the 1973 Carnival, *Echo* reporter Albert Jones visited the pan yards of the Tropicans, the All Stars Steel Orchestra, and the Pan Masters. The All Stars were organized by arranger Neville Jules, the founder of the Port of Spain's popular Trinidad All Stars. There were rumors that the Trinidad All Stars, who had won the Trinidad Panorama earlier that year, might be coming to New York to compete against their Brooklyn namesakes, although there is no evidence this came to pass. The Pan Masters, who maintained a yard at New York Avenue and Fulton Street, were led by Dave La Barrie, a veteran arranger for the Trinidad Harmonites and the Nutrine Playboys who had come to New York in 1971 to study economics at Hunter College. Jones reported that the Pan Masters was an exceptionally big ensemble, boasting 75 "beaters." They would be providing the music for a band of 500 masqueraders playing "French Sailors Ashore," while the Tropicans were paired with a 300-member mas band with the theme "Fashions of the Roaring Twenties and the Fabulous Fifties." Jones was impressed with the musicianship of all three of the ensembles he sampled, predicting "bands coming from the West Indies would have a hard time getting by our locals in New York."[28]

In addition to the Tropicans and the Pan Masters, Brooklyn's most popular steelbands in the early 1970s were the Brooklynaires and the Brooklyn Sonatas. The Brooklynaires were founded by Winston Wellington, Glen Olivache, and Mervyn James, three former members of Trinidad's famed North Stars Steelband who relocated to Brooklyn in the late 1960s. In 1970 the core group found rehearsal space in a basement on Ralph Avenue and quickly began recruiting other recently arrived players from North Stars as well as former members of Trinidad's Sunjets, Invaders, and Desperadoes orchestras. Winston Wellington and Leon Sterling became the band's arrangers. Wellington (b. 1944), a native of Port of Spain, had experience playing with the North Stars when they toured the United States and England in the 1960s, and had been arranging for the lesser-known Sun Valley Orchestra before migrating to Brooklyn in 1969 to study computer science. The well-connected Horace Morancie became a sponsor of the band, helping them find a larger space for the Panorama rehearsal and prestigious engagements at Manhattan's Hilton Hotel and Lincoln Center. According to Wellington, the stage-side version of the band comprised about twenty players who maintained a broad repertoire that included the latest calypsos from Trinidad as well as American popular songs ranging from Frank Sinatra's "My Way" to contemporary hits such as Isaac Hayes's "Shaft" and Simon and Garfunkel's "Bridge Over Troubled Water." When they played a Caribbean dance in Brooklyn, they organized their material in response to their audience's needs:

At a club or fete, we would play calypsos and a few American pop tunes. Something like "My Way" (slow ballad), maybe early on in the show, not later when things got hot late at night. In the earlier part of the evening we would include that in our repertoire, because in those days the men would like to hold on to their wives, their women, whatever, and dance slowly and so forth, you know? But once it got late in the night, like say at two or three o'clock, when things really got to bouncing, you could hardly go back to that. You'd play more uptempo calypsos and things like that, whatever calypsos were popular that year back in Trinidad. The dancers would break away (separate) and wine to the music, it was amazing![29]

Wellington, who had played under one of Trinidad's most influential arrangers, Tony Williams of the North Stars, was well versed in the latest developments in instrumentation and arrangement and provided the Brooklynaires with their 1975 winning arrangement of Kitchener's "Tribute to Spree Simon."

The Brooklyn Sonatas were formed sometime around 1972 by Count Robin and several other Trinidadian migrants who had played with the Sonatas steelband back in the southern Trinidad town of Gasparillo (see Figure 5.2). Robin began playing with King's Tropicans shortly after migrating to Brooklyn in 1967. He was inspired by his earlier experiences performing with the big Trinidad bands and by the large ensemble that the Pan Masters brought out at the first Eastern Parkway parade in 1971:

And I remember saying, wait a minute, no, I'm going to make my own band. You see we had this band in Trinidad called the Sonatas, and most of the guys hanging around [Brooklyn] were from my village, Gasparillo, in the south of Trinidad. So we decided to re-create the band here. We started rehearsing at 1245 Sterling [Crown Heights], in the basement. I did the building and tuning of the pans, and the arranging . . . . Then we started rehearsing down at Restoration Plaza, on Fulton Street. We could rehearse on the second floor, they

Figure 5.2. BWIA Sonatas on Fulton Street, circa 1982. Photo by Kevin Burke.

had a big open space. Then we moved over to these buildings on New York Avenue and Fulton Street. Restoration and I got buildings for other bands on Fulton near New York—the Pan Masters and Highlanders—they called it "Steelband Alley," you had about four, five, six steelbands there. In these abandoned buildings—but they still kept the electricity on.[30]

The band kept a stage-side of ten to twelve musicians who performed year-round for dances and fetes, and a bigger Panorama band of forty to fifty players. Robin also put together a large road band on racks and wagons that appeared on Eastern Parkway throughout the 1970s. Following the disappointing 1972 Panorama, where their initial victory was overturned by WIADCA officials, the Sonatas continued to compete in the annual competitions and to appear on Eastern Parkway, and in 1976 they received sponsorship from British West Indies Airlines (BWIA). They finally won Panorama in 1981 as the BWIA Sonatas with a rendition of Blue Boy's "Unknown Band," arranged by Hillary Borneo, and in 1982 and 1983 with arrangements by Ken "Professor" Philmore, a young, yet-to-be-discovered pan prodigy whom Robin brought in from Trinidad to arrange for the band.[31]

Early Panorama Musical Arrangements and Performance Practices

Few recordings of Brooklyn's early steelbands exist outside the handful of previously discussed Sunjets and Sonatas arrangements of American standards. But those were produced primarily for mainstream, non-Caribbean audiences and did not accurately represent the aesthetic preferences or arrangements favored by Brooklyn's Carnival steelbands of the period. Recollections of Brooklyn's early pan men suggest that arrangements for the initial Panorama contests consisted of relatively simple repetitive verse/chorus forms learned by ear that were similar to those performed on the road and at dance parties. Changes in Trinidad performance practices would eventually reach Brooklyn and profoundly alter the way the steelbands would arrange their tunes for Panorama. In the years following the establishment of Trinidad's Panorama contest in 1963, the Port of Spain bands began moving toward more complex forms organized by professional arrangers, some of whom had formal Western musical training. By the early 1970s, as Brooklyn's first competitions were taking place, a Panorama style had evolved in Trinidad that placed a premium on complex forms that called for an introduction, the statement of verse and chorus followed by melodic variations of each, key modulations, repetitions of the original theme in a minor key, a rhythmic groove/percussive jam section, and a coda. In addition, speed and precision became highly valued, while improvisation all but disappeared. Panorama arrangements were structurally fashioned after sonata and theme/variation forms common to classical orchestral music, and typically lasted for eight to ten minutes.[32]

According to Winston Munroe, it was Pan Masters arranger David La Barrie who first introduced the sophisticated Trinidadian Panorama style to Brooklyn with his 1973 arrangement of Sparrow's "My Connie."[33] Unfortunately, no known recording of the group performing the song exists. However, in 1975, around the time the Pan Masters split up, La Barrie took a small stage-side of players into a local Brooklyn establishment called Sun Sound Studios. The ensemble consisted of approximately ten players—tenors, double tenors, double seconds, guitars, bass, and trap drums.[34] His arrangement of Sparrow's 1975 recording "Ah Diggin' Horrors" follows a basic verse/chorus structure that one would expect for a road march. But his rendition also includes an introduction built around a melodic motif derived from the verse as well as melodic variations played by the tenor pans the second time that the verse appears. The move from verse to chorus is marked by a pronounced chromatic ascent (CM to C#M to Dm), providing a sense of harmonic movement. Three minutes and twenty seconds in length, the arrangement is not as long or complex as what would have been performed from the Panorama stage. However, the inclusion of the introduction section and the variations on the verse melody reflects the influence of the Trinidad Panorama style that La Barrie would have been familiar with from his time arranging for the Trinidad Harmonites and Nutrine Playboys in the late 1960s. This was no doubt the sort of straightforward arrangement with an intro, outro, verse/chorus, and a dash of melodic variation that a well-rehearsed stage-side band might have used at a dance or concert.

A partial recording of the 1975 WIADCA Panorama competition by Don Hill offers a window into the sound of Brooklyn's early Panorama bands, and clearly demonstrates the influence of the Trinidad Panorama style. That year each band played two pieces, several choosing Kitchener's "Tribute to Spree Simon," the most popular tune of that year's Trinidad Carnival. Kitchener's calypso won the 1975 Road March and Calypso Monarch titles, with arrangements of the tune placing in the top three slots of Panorama. His recording of the piece follows the standard format for calypso arrangements of that time, opening with a band chorus featuring the horns playing a variation on the chorus, followed by his vocal verse and chorus, a repetition of the band chorus, and a second verse and chorus.[35]

The Brooklynaires' winning rendition of "Tribute to Spree Simon" was arranged by Winston Wellington. The piece opens in a somewhat unstable A-flat Minor setting with the tenor pans playing agitated riffs that he composed. The introduction cycles through a series of ascending chords and dramatic runs before settling into a variation of the chorus melody set in the tonic key of B Major. The piece remains in the major tonic key, with the high-range pans alternatively playing variations on the verse and chorus melodies until they drop out and the low range pans take the lead melody. The tension builds as the series of ascending chords modulate up to a new key, E-flat Major. Following a flurry of runs, the piece returns to the verse melody, this time played by the bass pans while the high pans add arpeggiated riffs. After a series of descending and ascending runs, the high pans take back the verse melody and continue with a variation on the chorus, remaining in the new key of E-flat. Next a series of descending chromatic chords brings the piece back momentarily to the original tonic key of B Major before shifting into a final E Major coda. The piece ends on a dramatic strum alternating between E Major and B Major chords before leaving the audience hanging on a final C-sharp Minor chord.[36]

From the perspective of classical music or modern jazz, the harmonic language, thematic variations, and rapid melodic runs employed by Wellington and the Brooklynaires were relatively rudimentary. But the rhythmic nuances and interlocking textures were extremely complex, and the interweaving of Western formal structures and harmonies with African rhythms and textures was remarkably executed. It should be kept in mind that Wellington was working with a group of mostly amateur musicians, few of whom were musically literate or had any background in Western music theory. All parts were taught by ear and the final nine-minute piece completely committed to memory. Spot listening to other performances from Hill's recordings of the 1975 Brooklyn Panorama reveals a similar pattern. The latest Trinidadian calypsos, including Kitchener's "Fever" (by the Brooklynaires), Sparrow's "Do Dem Back" (by the Carib Steel Orchestra), and Shadow's "Bassman" (by Steel Unlimited), were arranged into extended eight- to ten-minute pieces based on Trinidadian Panorama style that included introductions, codas, theme and variations, key modulations, and so forth.

In additional to these musical transformations, the movement of steelbands from the road and dance floor to the formal Panorama stage marked a distinct change in performance practice. Pan-on-the-road, as discussed earlier, was deeply participatory in nature—a successful performance was measured by the pan players' ability to pull masqueraders and bystanders into their orbit and transforming them into co-performers. To accomplish this, their music had to be simple, repetitive, highly rhythmic, and densely textured. In contrast, a Panorama performance on a formal stage separated the musicians spatially, and to a degree sonically, from their audiences—very much in the manner of a staged performance of Western classical music. In Turino's terms, Panorama performance marked the move from a "participatory" to a "presentational" mode, where a designated group was producing music for consumption by a group of spectators who contributed minimally (if at all) to the music/dance performance. More complex arrangements involving multiple and contrasting themes, transparent textures, and variable rhythms were necessary in order to keep the interest of the now relatively passive audience members who were seated and listening, rather than dancing, singing, or playing along.[37]

By the mid-1970s, Brooklyn's Panorama bands were clearly, as Dudley had observed in Trinidad, "privilege[ing] spectacle over participation."[38] For some pan aficionados, especially those who placed a high premium on musical innovation and creativity, these sophisticated Panorama arrangements demonstrated exciting new possibilities for the steel pan as an instrument and the steelband as performance ensemble. For those who were more traditionalist, however, Panorama arrangements were viewed as overly dramatic and formulaic, and lacking in the essential sociality that was at the core of the participatory road and dance performances where they first experienced the music. The squeezing of steelbands off the Parkway and limiting their Carnival role to Panorama led to a high degree of dissatisfaction among some of Brooklyn's pan players and masqueraders, provoking them to eventually establish a J'Ouvert performance venue for pan-on-the-road.

Brooklyn Pan Meets the Rolling Stones

Several months before the 1975 Panorama, the Brooklyn steelbands experienced a rare brush with fame when a representative from the Rolling Stones contacted Daphne Weeks about hiring steel pan players to be part of the group's upcoming concert at Madison Square Garden. Apparently, Mick Jagger had played mas in Trinidad Carnival for several years with Stephen Lee Heung's band and had firsthand street experience with steelband music. The experience inspired Jagger to include a steelband component in the Stones' upcoming June 1975 concerts at Madison Square Garden. Weeks was unable to pull the project together and handed it off to Clyde Henry and his SBAA. Henry was able to persuade the Stones' producers to expand the project to include a mass steelband of 100 players drawn from Brooklyn's top bands. Henry organized the pan players and a small battery of percussionists, who rehearsed together for a week in a garage in East New York, Brooklyn. There Leon Sterling of the Brooklynaires worked out an arrangement of the Stones' song "Sympathy for the Devil." Several days before the show, all the players and their pans were loaded into several trucks and taken north of the city to rehearse with the Stones in an airplane hangar in Newburgh, New York.[39]

The Garden shows stretched over six nights, opening on Sunday, 22 June. The rock critic Dave Marsh, writing for *Rolling Stone* magazine, described an elaborate stage that had been built specially for the occasion—a six-pointed star structure over which 350 ten-foot hydraulically powered conical leaves would fold open to reveal the band. The steelbands were divided into four or five groups and scattered around the entire Garden floor. Marsh recalled that "roving knots of drummers . . . circled the stage," finally gathering at the foot of the structure as the Stones entered with guitars blaring the riff to "Honky Tonk Woman."[40] The *Village Voice* critic Robert Christgau, who was also at the show, reported that "a fierce energy level was being whipped higher by some fancy lighting and the steelbands who had been hired to roam the arena in lieu of an opening act."[41]

Forty years later, none of the steelband players could remember exactly which tunes were played before the Stones took the stage, but given their recollections and the reports by Marsh and Christgau, it seems likely that each of the separate bands was playing its own set of tunes, in road-march fashion, spread far enough apart around the Garden floor that they would not clash with one another. Winston Munroe, one of the players from the Silhouettes, recalled that the entire 100-piece band started at the same area in front of the stage and then split into four or five groups that circulated around the arena. They began with pans on stationary stands, but when they began to move they strapped their pans on in the traditional "pan-around-the-neck" configuration reminiscent of early Carnival bands.[42]

All the players came out to join the Stones in a finale, "Sympathy for the Devil." Christgau noted that the steel drums were so loud the singing was difficult to hear, but then "(Eric) Clapton appeared and ripped off a stunningly filthy solo, the steel rang on, and without intending to . . . I began to get a buzz of transcendence." The pans are barely audible on an unmixed bootleg recording of the final June 27th show, strumming the I–VII–V chord progression as Jagger begins his second verse (2 hour, 24 minute, 8 second mark) before fading into the background of the recording, overwhelmed by the electric guitars and drums.[43] Munroe, however, was adamant that the song was well rehearsed and Sterling's arrangement called for the pans to play both melodic and chordal support parts. For the finale of the initial shows, several lines of players were positioned in front of the stage with pans on racks, while two groups of musicians playing single pans around the neck processed dramatically down the aisles from the back of the arena to eventually join the stationary players in front of the stage. On the last night—the performance at which the bootleg recording was made—a small group of pan players and hand percussionists joined Jagger and the band onstage.[44]

While the Brooklyn pan players were thrilled to be performing in a prestigious venue like Madison Square Garden with the world-famous Rolling Stones, it is not clear that their music was well received by the young rock fans, who, according to Marsh and Christgau, grew restless after half an hour and began to boo and shout for the Stones, when one group of pan players broke into strains of "Satisfaction." This reaction may have been due in part to the lack of amplification, which certainly would have made it difficult for their playing to be heard clearly in the vast reaches of the Garden, and nearly impossible during the encore over the din of the Stones' electric instruments. Jagger may have been well intentioned, but the Stones' incorporation of the steelbands apparently resulted in exotic spectacle more than respectful appreciation for a Caribbean folk music that was foreign to most of the Garden's youthful American audience.

Nonetheless, following the shows, Henry claimed that Jagger was so pleased that he wanted to bring the entire steelband to California for the Stones' Los Angeles appearances in July. But issues with the New York musicians' union and the INS became too complicated, and none of the Brooklyn players made the trip. Although Henry would not discuss numbers, he told George Goodman, Jr. of the *Times* that the band had been well remunerated at union scale. Goodman, however, noted that one of the contractual negotiators told him the steelband musicians' cut was a "pea-sized fraction" of the estimated 1.4 million dollars the Stones would gross for the six-night engagement.[45] Hue Loy of the Harmonies, the only pan player who kept reliable records, documented that the bands were paid a total of $31,000 for the six nights, the Harmonites receiving $5,780 to be divided between twenty players. In addition, Henry noted that an undisclosed portion (perhaps a fifth) of the total payment went to purchase pans to help the fledgling Desperadoes USA band get established.[46]

Desperadoes USA, which would go on to become one of Brooklyn's most successful and enduring bands, had its origins in Exhibit Serenaders, a group that included a number of Trinidad expatriates who had played with the popular Desperadoes Steelband back in Port of Spain. One of those Desperadoes veterans was Denzil Botus (b. 1946), who in 1969 migrated to Brooklyn, where he began playing and arranging for the Tropicans. In 1974 Bertram Asch, another ex-Desperado who helped run the Brooklyn Exhibits, invited Botus to arrange for the band. Although that year's Panorama was rained out and Botus's arrangement of "Jericho" was never performed, he bonded with Asch, and the two, along with a number of other Desperadoes veterans, decided to form their own band under the banner of Despers USA. With a share of the money from the Rolling Stones concert, Botus was able to buy a set of quality steel drums from Ellie Mannette to jump-start the group. In 1978 the band changed its name to Metro Steel Orchestra and placed second in the Panorama with Botus's arrangement of Kitchener's "Pan in the 21st Century." Metro would become a dominant force in the Brooklyn Panorama in the 1980s and early 1990s, when Clive Bradley was brought in to arrange. Botus would return to lead yet another Desperadoes/Metro splinter group that reclaimed the Despers USA moniker and won five consecutive Panorama victories beginning in 1994.[47]

Brooklyn's Steelband Movement Expands as the Trinidad Arrangers Arrive

WIADCA held successful Panoramas over Labor Day weekends in 1976, 1977, and 1978, which were won by the Exhibit Serenaders, Moods Steel Orchestra (an offshoot of the Pan Masters), and the Satisfiers, respectively. Panorama now headlined the Saturday evening Brooklyn Museum Carnival shows each year. Henry and his SBAA apparently tried, unsuccessfully, to hold an alternative Panorama at Boys High School in 1976. Tensions between the steelbands and WIADCA continued to simmer, but in March 1977 Henry resigned and SBAA folded. Later that year, Dawad Philip reported in the *New York Amsterdam News* that most of Brooklyn's steelbands, then represented by no formal association, agreed to participate in Panorama after WIADCA offered them $7,000 in total prize money.[48] WIADCA made further concessions by forming an official Steelband Committee to give the musicians a greater voice in the planning and execution of Panorama.[49]

This upsurge in steelband activity in Brooklyn did not escape the press. For the 1977 Labor Day Carnival season, Philip wrote two review articles for the *Amsterdam News*, chronicling the history of steelband in New York and acknowledging pan pioneers Caldera Caballero, Rudy King, and Lawrence "Pops" McCarthy. Philip concluded that the in-migration of Trinidadians to Brooklyn had created "an atmosphere in steelband music to be compared only with that of Trinidad."[50] Jennifer Dunning of the *Times* characterized that year's Labor Day parade as a festive event that drew 750,000 spectators, noting that many of the mas bands were accompanied by steelbands, including guest stars the United States Navy Steel Band. Above the article is a dramatic picture of the BWIA Sonatas perched on a multi-level float, being pulled down Eastern Parkway, surrounded by throngs of Parkway revelers and several poker-faced policemen (see Figure 5.3).[51]

That same week the *Sunday News Magazine* published a lengthy piece on steelband music in New York, based on Rebecca Morris's interview with Ellie Mannette and visits the reporter made to PS 26 in Brooklyn and the Exhibit Serenaders Fulton Street pan yard. She described the Exhibits, who won the 1976 Brooklyn Panorama, as a fourteen-piece group of Trinidadians between the ages of fourteen and forty-three (their number swelled to around fifty for the Labor Day competition). Morris recounted how Michel Enoch, the tuner and arranger, "moved from player to player, cuing the bass, slowing the double tenors, taking over the cello drums. A steelband arranger must be able to play all the instruments, because *he* is the score. 'I will hear something on the radio and consider it in my

Figure 5.3. BWIA Sonatas on Eastern Parkway, 1977. Photo by Marilynn K. Yee (courtesy of the *New York Times*/Redux).

head—I will know it. Then I put it out on the drums.'" She also reported a lively steelband scene in Brooklyn schools, noting that the District 16 Steelband comprised the best players from ten public schools.[52]

Morris's account of Enoch's instructional method marked the first time that a steel pan arranger received serious attention in the local press. It also confirms that the arranger's role in the process was more than simply scoring out parts for the different sections. Because all instruction at that time was done by ear without the benefit of a written score, the arranger was expected to teach each section leader his or her respective part, to drill individual sections, and finally to coordinate and conduct the entire band during a series of rehearsals that would begin a month or more before Panorama. This was a demanding job, and aside from the tuner, the arranger was the only position in the band that would be guaranteed some form of remuneration for his or her services.

The following week, Knolly Moses, writing for the *Amsterdam News*, penned a substantial piece on Brooklyn's growing legion of steelband arrangers. He interviewed Randolph "Count Robin" Hilaire of the BWIA Sonatas, Michael Scanterbury of Nebulae, Joseph Gerald and Knolly "Panther" Nicholas of Despers USA, and Leon Sterling and Winston Philips of the Brooklynaires. There was general agreement that simple, catchy calypso tunes made the best steelband arrangements, with the chorus, according to Sterling, providing "the moving force in the tune" for the audience. Adopting a composer's mentality, Scanterbury noted his partiality for melodies with gaps so he could add his own material: "the calypso tunes I prefer to arrange are those that have lots of spaces for me to work with."[53]

One arranger Moses did not profile was a young Trinidadian named Len "Boogsie" Sharpe (b. 1953), whose rendition of Lord Kitchener's calypso "Hasely Crawford" had won the 1977 Brooklyn Panorama for the Moods Steel Orchestra. A native of St. James, Trinidad, Sharpe was a pan prodigy who began playing at the age of eight with Crossfire and as a teenager joined the Starlift steelband.[54] In 1971 he helped found Phase II Pan Groove, for whom he made unconventional arrangements that included "daring harmonies and dissonances, creative sound effects like chromatic glissandi, and a 'roughness' and funky rhythmic groove."[55] Inspired by pan arranger/composer Ray Holeman, Sharpe began composing his own original tunes for Trinidad's Panorama and finally won the national Panorama in 1987 with his own piece "Feelin' Nice." Sharpe was just emerging as an innovator in Trinidad's steelband scene when Clyde Durrant of Moods enlisted him to arrange for the Brooklyn band in 1977. Durrant recalled that Sharpe had been visiting Brooklyn that summer and was recruited to arrange the Kitchener tune for Moods. Arrangers now expected to be paid, especially if their efforts placed the band in the top three positions of the competition. Moods won the $4,000 first-place prize in the 1977 Panorama, a third of which, Durrant recalled, went to Sharpe for his arranging and instructional services.[56]

Up to this point, most of the arrangers had been drawn from the ranks of Brooklyn's individual bands. While they had experience playing with Trinidadian bands, few, with the exception of Dave La Barrie, had established reputations as serious Panorama arrangers, and all, including La Barrie, had migrated north to work or study, not to be employed as steelband arrangers. Durrant's recruitment of Sharpe in 1977 marked the first time a visiting Trinidad arranger of some stature was brought in to work with a Brooklyn band, and was a harbinger of things to come. In the late 1970s and 1980s, Durrant recalled, the Moods orchestra enlisted other leading Trinidadian arrangers, including Pelham Goddard (from Trinidad's Exodus steelband) and Jit Samaroo (from Trinidad's Renegades steelband).

The two most important Trinidadian arrangers who would dominate Brooklyn Panorama in the 1980s were Ken "Professor" Philmore and Clive Bradley. Ironically, they each won their first Brooklyn Panoramas in 1982, tying for first place with arrangements for the BWIA Sonatas and the Metro Steel Orchestra, respectively. Like Sharpe, Philmore (1959–2018) was relatively unknown in Trinidad when Count Robin recruited him to arrange for the Brooklyn Sonatas. As a teenager he earned a reputation as a crack player with an exceptional ear while performing first with the Hatters and later with the Fonclaire Steel Orchestra in San Fernando. He was just beginning to develop his arranging skills when Robin brought him to Brooklyn in the summer of 1982 to work on his first Panorama tune. Robin's instincts proved correct, as Philmore's arrangement of Scrunter's "The Will" tied for first that year with Bradley's arrangement of Lord Nelson's "Jenny." Throughout the 1980s, Philmore traveled to Brooklyn every spring, lodging with Sonata's manager Mack Scott and obtaining an official work permit through BWIA, the band's sponsor. He played with the Sonatas stage-side at various functions in and around New York, and during the latter part of the summer he would direct the larger band, preparing for Panorama. Shortly after Labor Day Carnival he returned to Trinidad to work with Fonclaire and eventually as a pan soloist. In addition to his initial 1982 success, he led the Sonatas to Panorama titles in 1983 with Blue Boy's "Rebecca," in 1985 with Crazy's "Soucouyant," in 1988 with Tambu's "This Party Is It," and in 1989 with Tambu's "Free Up." Also like Sharpe, Philmore was a talented pan soloist who performed jazz and pop pieces in various small ensembles, in addition to writing his own calypsos for steel orchestras.[57]

A native of Diego Martin, Trinidad, Clive Bradley (1936–2005) was formally trained in mathematics and self-taught on guitar and piano. After spending several years as a mathematics teacher, he gravitated toward the music business, playing piano and arranging for a dance band before being invited in 1968 to arrange for Desperadoes, one of Trinidad's top steelbands. There he established his reputation by winning Panorama titles with Desperadoes in 1970, 1976, and 1977. By the late 1970s Bradley was spending considerable time in New York, where he first began working with the popular soca singer Lord Nelson, arranging a number of his most successful songs for Charlie's Records and B's Records. For several years he took up residency in Queens while continuing to travel back to Trinidad during Carnival season to work with Desperadoes and eventually other bands. Sometime around 1980 he hooked up with several old Desperadoes bandmates who had migrated to Brooklyn and were playing with a band called the Metro Steel Orchestra.[58] In 1981 they convinced Bradley to direct their Brooklyn band, and he went on to lead Metro to Panorama victories in 1987 with Baron's "Say," in 1990 with Baron's "Tell Me Why," in 1991 with Baron's "This Melody Sweet," and in 1992 with Shadow's "Dingolay."[59]

Bradley's arrangements were famous for their timbral clarity and rousing polyrhythmic groove sections.[60] Garvin Blake, a young pan player at the time who served as Bradley's assistant in the Metro yard, described Bradley as a master orchestrator who could transform simple folk motifs into sophisticated arrangements through his use of advanced chords and phrasing, and his genius at voicing phrases for the different pan sections. "He was a little like Duke Ellington in that sense," Blake mused, "Ellington would play a simple blues, but it didn't sound simple at all because of the way he voiced the parts. That was how Bradley did it."[61]

Philmore's and Bradley's arrangements won nine of ten Brooklyn Panoramas for the Sonatas and Metro, respectively, between 1982 and 1992 (there was no Panorama in 1986). They, along with Sharpe and a handful of others, demonstrated that recruiting Trinidadian arrangers bolstered a Brooklyn band's reputation and its chances of excelling in the Panorama competition. But more importantly, they introduced a high level of musicianship and orchestral sophistication to the Brooklyn steelbands at a critical time in their development. Philmore and Bradley embodied the transnational character of the Carnival music that was emerging in the 1980s, as both won Panorama titles in Brooklyn and Port of Spain, and the latter arranged soca hits for Brooklyn and Trinidad record labels.

The 1978 Panorama was, according to Dawad Philip, the most impressive to date, featuring fourteen New York bands who collectively "demonstrated just how improved overall the steelband movement in the U.S. had become." Philip provided a list of the top five competitors and their choice of songs:

1. Satisfiers: "Warrior" by Calypso Rose
2. Metro Steel: "Pan in the 21st Century" by Lord Kitchener
3. Silhouettes: "DuDu Yemi" by Sparrow
4. Solo Harmonites: "Tell Them" by Explainer
5. Moods: "Social Dora" by Lord Kitchener

Philip characterized the Satisfiers' winning performance as "a tight, clean version, marked with exhilarating junctions and crescendos," while Metro's second-place effort "rumbled with feverish tension bounced from pitch to pitch, from key to key in this marvelous arrangement by Denzil Botus." In keeping with the Trinidad model, all the bands had selected popular calypso songs from that year, and the tunes "DuDu Yemi" and "Pan in the 21st Century," played by the Silhouettes and Metro, had placed first and second at that year's Trinidad Panorama contest, performed by Starlift and Desperadoes, respectively. The references to "exhilarating junctions and crescendos" and the "bounc-[ing] from pitch to pitch, from key to key" confirm that the top Brooklyn bands had incorporated the advanced harmonic and structural forms that had come to dominate the Trinidadian Panorama arrangements of the 1970s.[62]

The 1978 Panorama was also noteworthy for the drama that unfolded between the WIADCA judges and the steelbands. Evidently, after the winners had been announced, it was revealed that one of the judge's score sheets had not been tallied, thus calling the results into question. Philip reported that angry players demanded that the entire $7,000 in prize money be handed over to the SBAA to be evenly distributed among all the participating bands and that the trophy winners be decided by a se- cret ballot of SBAA members.[63] WIADCA ignored these appeals, and once again steelband players were left with deep feelings of resentment toward the Carnival organizers. Tensions between the two groups continued unabated, which may explain why WIADCA opted for smaller "Steel Band Jamboree" presentations rather than more elaborate and expen- sive Panorama contests as part of their 1979 and 1980 Carnival shows.[64] But the desire for a competition did not wane, and WIADCA was able to bring the steelbands back and continue to sponsor the annual Panorama throughout the 1980s and 1990s.

Prior to the 1978 Panorama, manager Hue Loy sat down and made a list of sixteen steelbands that were active in New York at that time. The Brooklynaires, the Sonatas, the Silhouettes, Despers USA, Metro Steel, Satisfiers, Exhibits, the Golden Stars, and the Moods Steel Orchestra were among the larger bands that competed in Panorama and took part in the Eastern Parkway road march. These bands would have thirty to forty players for Panorama, but most maintained smaller, ten-to-fifteen player stage-side bands that would perform year-round for dances, concerts, and fetes. Other bands, including Loy's Solo Harmonites, Wong's Highlanders, and Dem Boys were more modest-sized, ten-to-fifteen-member ensembles that rarely competed in Panorama but would often come out to Eastern Parkway and played all year for community events. Up to this point most of the players were adult men. While a smattering were from Grenada, Guyana, Antigua, and the Virgin Islands, most were from Trinidad, and many had experience playing with well-known bands back home be- fore they migrated to New York. According to Loy, they looked to the big Trinidad Panorama bands as sources of repertoire and to their arrangers for the latest stylistic developments.[65]

The growth of Brooklyn's steelband movement was lauded by Herman Hall, the ex-publicist for WIADCA who in 1977 had launched the Caribbean arts and culture publication *Everybody's Caribbean Magazine*. In 1978 he wrote a piece titled "The Steelbands: A New American Music" for the *Amsterdam News*. Hall observed that "this rapid internationalization of

Figure 5.4. Pulling pan on Eastern Parkway, 1982. Photo by Martha
Cooper (courtesy of City Lore).

steelband is due to its infectious characteristics. One can get high on
steelband music. Like a Baptist revival prayer meeting, it adds spirt and
sound to the body." Specifically, he went on to argue that the expansion of
the music in New York was thanks to the rise of "a new generation of West
Indian-American steel band musicians," and that Brooklyn's Sonatas and
Caribe Masqueraders "were among the best in the world."[66]

It is unlikely that any of the Brooklyn steelbands could have offered
serious competition to the big bands in Trinidad at that time, nor was
WIADCA's single-night Panorama on the same scale as Trinidad's multi-
round competition. Nevertheless, Hall's observation that pan was flour-
ishing in America in general, and in Brooklyn in particular, was undeniable.
By the decade's end, pan music was pervasive at the big Eastern Parkway
parade (see Figure 5.4) and the WIADCA Panorama offered large bands
the opportunity to compete for local acclaim and modest prize money.
The borough's growing Caribbean population was hungry for stage-side
bands to provide music for dances, fetes, and boat rides, while the white
club and suburban party circuit continued to offer occasional employment opportunities for small ensembles.

Brooklyn Steelbands as Transnational Expression and Cultural Identity

In many ways the early Brooklyn bands and the WIADCA Panorama
remained extensions of the Trinidad steelband scene. Nearly all of

Brooklyn's early steelband organizers, tuners, and arrangers were Trinidadians who had some experience playing with bands before they migrated north. Ensembles like the Sonatas, Harmonites, Silhouettes, and Despers USA were founded by groups of migrants who had played together in bands by those names back in Trinidad. They transplanted their knowledge and skills, including the recently emerged Panorama arranging style, to Brooklyn. Repertoires were drawn from the latest Trinidad calypsos, particularly those that had fared well in competition back home. Not surprisingly, there was significant Panorama repertoire overlap between the Brooklyn and Trinidad bands. For example, "Tribute to Spree Simon," "Crawford," and "Unknown Band" won the 1975, 1977, and 1981 contests in Brooklyn and Port of Spain; and "Du Du Yemi" and "Pan in the 21st Century" placed in the top three categories in both 1978 competitions. Eventually, top Trinidad Panorama arrangers, including Sharpe, Philmore, and Bradley, were brought in to work with the more established Brooklyn bands that could pay for their services. Brooklyn's early steelband movement flourished thanks to the ongoing importation of musicians, arrangers, tuners, and musical practices from Trinidad.

In terms of cultural globalization, Trinidad remained the creative epicenter, and Brooklyn the primary receptor, of steelband activity in the 1970s and 1980s. This development represented a poignant example of what Keith Nurse has identified as "globalization in reverse," typical of overseas Carnivals, where developing nations assumed the center-stage and the older industrialized metropoles moved to the periphery of cultural production.[67] The transnational flow of steel pan players and musical practices was relatively unidirectional in the early years of Brooklyn Carnival, as Trinidadian musicians, arrangers, and tuners regularly visited Brooklyn and helped shape the emerging steelband scene. The movement was not totally one-way—occasionally Brooklyn-based expatriates traveled home for Carnival and a few, such as Count Robin, might play with their old bands. But Brooklyn's early steelbands were composed primarily of amateur musicians whose day jobs and student responsibilities rarely afforded them the time or the money to return to rehearse and perform for Trinidad's month-long Carnival Panorama season. Moreover, some players in the bands were on expired visas, making it difficult to move between Brooklyn and the Caribbean without updated papers. And it would be more than a generation before New York–born pan arrangers and players would make an impact back in Trinidad. The transnational Carnival network was more complicated and multidirectional for those singers and musicians involved with the recording and production of commercial calypso and soca music during this period, as the following chapters will explore.

WIADCA hoped that the Brooklyn steelbands could contribute to their mission of creating a Carnival celebration that would unite Brooklyn's diverse Caribbean community. This presented a challenge, given the steel pan's nationalist associations. WIADCA itself did not shy away from this history—its 1974 Carnival program booklet proudly touted Trinidad and

Tobago as "the home of the steelband" and the late Trinidadian Spree Simon as "the genius who invented the greatest musical instrument of the 20th century."[68] This lofty rhetoric had correlates on the ground, as the membership of Brooklyn's larger steelbands was primarily Trinidadian, and several of the groups were direct offshoots of Trinidadian-based bands. This is not surprising, given the extraordinary popularity of the instrument in Trinidad, and the fact that not all of the other English-speaking islands had well-developed steelband scenes in the 1960s and early 1970s. At the time when Brooklyn's steelband movement was emerging, relatively few non-Trinidadian migrants had prior experience playing in steelbands.[69]

On occasion, however, steelbands identified with other islands, such as the Virgin Islands or Carriacou, competed in Brooklyn Panorama. Panists active in the 1970s recalled that individuals from Antigua, Guyana, Grenada, St. Vincent, and the Virgin Islands sporadically played in their bands. All this suggests that there existed an openness to other islanders joining the fold if they were willing to play in bands organized by Trinidadians that performed a Trinidad repertoire chosen and taught by Trinidadian (or Trinidadian expatriate) arrangers. In the 1980s and 1990s, as a new generation of Brooklyn-born Caribbean young people came of age and steel-pan programs became increasingly popular in Brooklyn public schools, more players from other islands would join bands, along with a smattering of native-born African Americans and whites.[70] In the mid-1990s, Gage Averill observed that the steel pan in Brooklyn "now finds itself embraced as a symbol of pan–West Indian identity," and that it "becomes a factor in the negotiation of contrasting visions of Trinidadian, West Indian, and Caribbean American identities."[71] Such an assertion, though subjective and difficult to prove, was certainly in keeping with WIADCA's vision of an inclusive Caribbean Carnival, and it underscored the crucial role the instrument played in the ongoing process of diasporic identity formation. Still, the notion of a pan-Caribbean steelband movement remained an ideal that was far from realized in Brooklyn Carnival's first decade, when transplanted Trinidadians dominated most bands.

While WIADCA was concerned with issues of Caribbean unity and social integration, for first-generation Trinidad migrants and those from adjacent islands with steelband and calypso traditions, music proved to be a powerful force for maintaining ties to home and for developing transnational identity. Especially for Trinidad expatriates, musical practice could be transformed into the celebration of cultural heritage. The process of designating certain musics as signifiers of heritage was in part cognitive, involving a degree of self-conscious selection informed by historical memory and nostalgia. But there were also very real, tangible components involving physical engagement in music-making and dance. That is, Carnival music provided migrants with a space where their home culture could be not only imagined but actually experienced through beating pan with fellow countrymen (and later women) at dances, on the Parkway, or in the Panorama contest. Steel pan was basically an amateur tradition, with plenty of room for participation. In addition to the players themselves there existed a much wider social circle including family, friends, and fans who limed at pan yards during summer rehearsals, who danced to pan music on the Parkway and at fetes, and who listened avidly to Panorama performances. For pan players and their followers, musical performance and attendant dance allowed them to go beyond simply recalling their past by literally re-creating the sublime experience of home. And this process would continue for decades, eventually incorporating a new generation of Brooklyn-born Caribbean Americans, reminding them of who they were and where their families came from. Commenting on her experiences with the Sonatas in the early 1990s, Rachel Buff observed, "At the same time that the band provides a link to an imagined or remembered homeland, its players and administrators are actively involved in creating a culture in diaspora."[72] These musical experiences, coupled with the ability to occasionally travel between Brooklyn and Trinidad to participate in Carnival activities in both sites, helped mediate the tensions of dislocation while fostering a transnational sensibility.

Steelband performance on the road, at fetes and dances, during Panorama competition, and in the pan yards provided Brooklyn's Caribbean migrants with a sonic space to experience their cultural heritage and to connect with one another. Like other Caribbean musics, steelband was a hybrid form, drawing from diverse African, European, American, and Caribbean sources. But given its unique instrumentation and set of performance practices, it stood as a marker of cultural difference. Players and listeners alike understood that steel pan music was specific to Trinidad and its adjacent East Caribbean islands—it was not the music of other New York migrants originally from Haiti, Cuba, Puerto Rico, or the Dominican Republic, nor was it music directly derived from the African American popular genres favored by the city's native black residents. While steelband music was occasionally consumed by non-Caribbean New Yorkers, it was viewed by and large by the general populace and the media as something of an exotic curiosity rather than a serious art form. But the cultural boundary demarcated by calypso and steelband became more porous in the 1980s with the rise of soca music, a style that drew heavily from African American soul and funk as well as rock. The possibilities for cultural crossover seemingly increased as Brooklyn rose to prominence as the international center of soca.

Notes

1. Les Slater, personal interview with author and Ray Funk, 8 May 2015.
2. Cliff Alexis, personal interview with author and Ray Funk, 31 August 2014.
3. Alexis interview, 31 August 2014. Alexis noted that American pop songs set to a calypso beat were part of the Sunjets' repertoire and would be played at Caribbean fetes and dances. But the bulk of the music they played at such events would have been instrumental arrangements of recent calypsos.

4. For more on Ellie Mannette's contributions to the development of steel pan, see Stephen Stuempfle, *The Steelband Movement: The Forging of a National Art in Trinidad and Tobago* (University of Pennsylvania Press, 1995), p. 42; and Andrew Martin, *Steelpan Ambassadors: The US Navy Steel Band, 1957–1999* (University Press of Mississippi, 2017), pp. 33–34.

5. For more on Ellie Mannette's contributions to the development of steel pan, see Stuempfle, *Steelband Movement*, p. 42; and Martin, *Steelpan Ambassadors*, pp. 33–34.

6. Winston Wellington, personal interview with author, 28 May 2015, Brooklyn.

7. Clyde Henry, personal interview with author and Les Slater, 24 September 1996. Rudy King, personal interview with author 1996; Winston Munroe, personal interview with author and Les Slater, 8 August 1996; Count Robin, personal interview with author, 17 August 2013.

8. Winston Munroe, personal interview with author and Ray Funk, 8 September 2014.

9. See Shannon Dudley's account of informal verse/chorus pan arrangements in Trinidad in *Music from Behind the Bridge: Steelband Spirit and Politics in Trinidad and Tobago* (Oxford University Press, 2008), pp. 151–154. Dudley reports that in addition to lively calypsos, American popular tunes set to calypso rhythms and Latin mambos were played by Trinidadian steelbands on the road and at fetes from the 1950s through the early 1970s. See Shannon Dudley, *Carnival Music in Trinidad: Experiencing Music, Experiencing Culture* (Oxford University Press, 2004), pp. 72–76.

10. Thomas Turino, *Music as Social Life: The Politics of Participation* (University of Chicago Press, 2008), p. 26.

11. Phone interview with Munroe, 7 August 2017.

12. "Labor Day Weekend Problems Continue, S/Band Men Angry," *Antillean Caribbean Echo*, 16 September 1972.

13. For more on the history and structure of the Trinidad Panorama, see Dudley, *Music from Behind the Bridge*, pp. 137–139, 176–177; and Stuempfle, *Steelband Movement*, pp. 159–164. Dudley notes that Panorama finals were moved to the prestigious Sunday night Dimanche Gras show in 1968 and were granted the entire Saturday night stage beginning in 1976 due to their increased popularity (p. 176).

14. "Labor Day Weekend Problems Continue, Bandsmen Angry: WIAD Association Disregards Festival Judges' Findings," *Antillean Caribbean Echo*, 16 September 1972.

15. Winston Wellington, interview with author, 29 May 2015, Brooklyn; Count Robin, interview with author, 29 May 2015, South Ozone Park, Queens.

16. "Leslie Slater, A Former Member of West Indian American Day Association, Tells His Side of Why He Resigned in '71," *Antillean Caribbean Echo*, 16 September 1972.

17. Les Slater, Clyde Durant, Clyde Henry, and Hue Loy all recalled that the 1973 Medgar Evers Panorama was a single-night affair with no preliminaries. Interviews with Henry, 24 September 1996; Loy, 12 May 2015; Slater, 8 May 2015; Henry, 24 April 2015. The *New York Amsterdam News* (1 September 1973) reviewed a 24 August Carnival celebration at Medgar Evers College, but only previewed the second week's activities. No report of the 31 August–2 September events exists.

18. Interview with Munroe, 8 August 1996; interview with Henry, 24 April 2015; interview with Loy, 12 May 2015.

19. "Band Spotlight" by Winston Wellington (unpublished manuscript, circa 2012). Personal collection of Winston Wellington.

20. The Specifics of WIADCA's 1974 Panorama are uncertain. Clyde Henry claims the Brooklyn bands were all committed to his rained-out event at Boys High School and did not participate in WIADCA's Panorama (Henry interview, 24 September 1996). The *New York Amsterdam News* (31 August 1974) reported that WIADCA had received a $1,000 donation from Abrahams and Strauss for prize money for the winning steel, and that Schaefer Brewery had given $1,000, half of which was to go to the Tropicans steelband for mobile equipment (pan racks) on the Parkway. The 1975 WIADCA Carnival program booklet includes a picture identifying the Tropicans as the "1974 Panorama Champion" but lists no runners-up or other contestants.

21. Clyde Henry's failure to stage an alternative road march on New York Avenue on Labor Day 1974 is reported by Dawad Philip (*New York Amsterdam News*, 10 September 1977).

22. For more on government and private sponsorship of Panorama steelbands in Trinidad, see Stuempfle, *Steelband Movement*, pp. 142–150, 191–194, and Dudley, *Music from Behind the Bridge*, 217–218.

23. The Steelband Association of the Americas' proposed 1975 Panorama boycott and Henry's objections to WIADICA's mistreatment of the steelbands are reported in the *Caribbean Express* (n.d., circa August 1975); clipping from Clyde Henry's personal collection. Dawad Philip, writing for the *New York Amsterdam News* (10 September 1977), noted that in 1975 Henry and the SBAA opted to participate in the WIADC Panorama, and in 1976 tried unsuccessfully to stage an alternative Panorama at Boys High School field.

24. The proposed boycott by the Steelband Association of the Americas is reported by William Doyle-Marshall in the *Trinidad Express* (n.d., circa August 1975); clipping from Clyde Henry collection. The article noted that WIADCA would offer $1,800 in cash prizes for the top three bands. It is not clear whether any of the bands did boycott the 1975 WIADCA Panorama, and no alternative competition is mentioned.

25. See http://whensteeltalks.ning.com/page/new-york. Denzil Botus claimed he arranged the tune for Tropicans that year, with minor assistance from Winston "Mouter Bee" Phillip. Interview, Denzil Botus with author, 4 June 2015, Brooklyn.

26. Background on the different types of steel pans and their organization in modern steelbands is found in Dudley, *Music from Behind the Bridge*, pp. 279–285; and Gage Averill, "'Pan Is We Ting': West Indian Steelbands in Brooklyn," in *Musics of Multicultural America*, edited by Kip Lornell and Anne Rasmussen (Schirmer Books, 1997), pp. 107–110.

27. Rudy King, personal interview with author and Les Slater, 25 October 1995. Durant interview, 27 April 2015.

28. Albert Jones, "Top Bands Tune Up for Labor Day," *Antillean Caribbean Echo*, 18 August 1973.

29. Winston Wellington, interview with author, 29 May 2015, Brooklyn.

30. Count Robin, personal interview with author, 29 May 2015, South Ozone Park, NY. Hue Loy verified that his Harmonites and the Pan Masters moved into an abandoned building on Fulton Street, plugged into the block's existing electrical system, and created free indoor rehearsal spaces. Apparently the city was in such disarray at the time that neither the absentee landlords nor the city officials objected. Hue Loy, personal interview with author and Ray Funk, 24 February 2015, Port of Spain.

31. Count Robin, interview with author, 29 May 2015, South Ozone Park, NY.

32. See Dudley's discussion of the evolution of the "Panorama formula" in Trinidad in *Music from Behind the Bridge*, pp. 171–172. Gage Averill notes that the borrowing of formal structures from orchestral music for Panorama arrangements was not surprising, as Trinidad steelbands had been playing arrangements of classical pieces since the 1950s. See Averill, "'Pan Is We Ting,'" p. 113.

33. Winston Munroe, personal interview with author and Fay Funk, 8 September 2015, Brooklyn.

34. Dave La Barrie recalls that the recording of "Ah Diggin' Horrors" and "Pan Groove" was made with hopes that Rawlston Charles of Charlie's Records might pick up the single for distribution, but this never came to pass. La Barrie ended up releasing the single on his own label, Damla Records. Dave La Barrie, phone interview with author, 15 May 2015.

35. Lord Kitchener's 1975 recording of "Tribute to Spree Simon" can be heard on YouTube, at https://www.youtube.com/watch?v=UxmPHuirfrg.

36. Tape of Brooklyn Panorama recorded by Don Hill, 29 August 1975, WIADCA-sponsored show at the Brooklyn Museum.

37. Thomas Turino, *Music as Social Life: The Politics of Participation* (University of Chicago Press, 2008), p. 59.

38. Dudley, *Music from Behind the Bridge*, p. 199. This is not to suggest that members of a steelband do not experience a sense of deep connection with one another on the Panorama stage when performing a well-synchronized arrangement. That energy is palpable in a good performance. And, as Dudley notes, in Trinidad Panorama, "despite being separated by the stage," pan players and their audiences "continue to celebrate steelband performances as an expression of community identity and solidarity." This acknowledged, in Brooklyn Panorama, the separation of musicians and audience, and the formal procession of one band after another on stage in front of judges, does not produce the same sense of communal spontaneity that one experiences during street Carnival at J'Ouvert or in the earliest years of the Parkway.

39. Clyde Henry, interview with author and Ray Funk, 3 September 2014, Brooklyn. The story of Clyde Henry organizing the 100-piece steel orchestra for the Madison Square Garden concert was reported in George Goodman, "At Jagger Show, Band Beats to 100 Different Drums," *New York Times*, 25 June 1975.

40. David Marsh, "The Stones Roll On: A Scare in Boston, Success in Toronto, A Slip in New York," *Rolling Stone*, 31 July 1975.

41. Robert Christgau, "It Isn't Only Rock and Roll: The Rolling Stones," *Village Voice*, 30 June 1975.

42. Interview with Winston Munroe by author and Ray Funk, 8 September 2014. Similar accounts of the small bands being positioned around the Garden floor come from interviews with Henry, 3 September 2014, and with Loy, 13 May 2015.

43. "The Rolling Stones Live at the Madison Square Garden [27-6-1975]—Full Show," YouTube posting by George King, 27 May 2013, https://www.youtube.com/watch?v=XAUovDuFelQ.

44. The encore configuration involving the processing pan-around-the-neck players moving toward the stationary players in front of the stage was recalled by Denzil Botus, interview with author, 4 June 2015, Brooklyn, NY. The steel pan players and percussionists on stage with the

Rolling Stones were recalled by Winston Munroe, interview with author and Ray Funk, 8 September 2014.

45. Goodman, "At Jagger Show."

46. Hue Loy, interview with author, 13 May 2015, Brooklyn; Clyde Henry, interview with author and Ray Funk, 3 September 2014, Brooklyn.

47. Denzil Botus, personal interview with author, 4 June 2015, Brooklyn, NY.

48. Dawad Philip, "Quality Performances Mark Panorama 1977," *New York Amsterdam News*, 10 September 1977.

49. The 1977 WIADCA Carnival program booklet lists a committee representing thirteen steelbands.

50. Dawad Philip, "The Evolution of Steelband Music in the U.S.," and "Quality Performances Mark Panorama 1977," *New York Amsterdam News*, 10 September 1977.

51. Jennifer Dunning, "Dancing in the Streets Marks Brooklyn's West Indian Fete," *New York Times*, 6 September 1977.

52. Rebecca Morris, "It's Carnival Time in Brooklyn and the Steelbands Are Tuned Up," *Sunday News Magazine*, 4 September 1977.

53. Knolly Moses, "Steel Band Arrangers: Different Styles, Appeals," *New York Amsterdam News*, 10 September 1977.

54. Dudley, *Music from Behind the Bridge*, pp. 232–235.

55. Ibid., p. 234.

56. Clyde Durrant, personal interview with author, 27 April 2015, Brooklyn.

57. Ken Philmore's biography is drawn from Ken Philmore, phone interview with author, 23 August 2015; and Count Robin, interview with author, 28 May 2015.

58. Brooklyn's Metro Steel Orchestra began in 1975 under the name Despers USA, with a number of expatriate players from Trinidad's original Desperadoes. The band changed its name from Despers USA to Metro Steel in 1978, three years before Bradley began arranging. Ian Franklin, phone interview with author, 23 August 2015.

59. Clive Bradley's biography is drawn from Jon Pareles, "Clive Bradley dies at 69: Arranged Steel-Drum Music," *New York Times*, 1 December 2005; Franklin, phone interview with author, 23 August 2015; and Garvin Blake, interview with author, 24 August 2015, Brooklyn.

60. For a discussion of Clive Bradley's innovative use of harmonic and timbral voicings and polyrhythmic "groove" or "jam" sections in Panorama arrangements, see Dudley, *Music from Behind the Bridge*, pp. 160–162.

61. Blake, interview with author, 24 August 2015.

62. Dawad Philip, "Just Who Are the Winners of 1978 Steelbands Contest?," *New York Daily Challenge*, 7 September 1978.

63. Ibid.

64. The 1979 and 1980 WIADCA Carnival program booklets list "Steelband Jamborees" for their Saturday night Brooklyn Museum stage shows. There were no mentions of Panorama or of any winning steelbands, suggesting that the jamborees were straightforward stage performances by several steelbands rather than formal contests involving multiple ensembles. In their list of New York Panorama Results, the "When Steel Talks/PanOnTheNet" website lists "No Panorama" for the years 1979 and 1980. Surprisingly, given their intense coverage of the event in previous years, the local press made no mention of Panorama contests, nor why the contests did not take place for those two years. The general consensus of

older pan players is that there were no Panorama contests in 1979 or 1980, but no one can recall a formal boycott or other mitigating circumstances. The WIADCA-sponsored Panorama contests at the Brooklyn Museum resumed in 1981.

65. Loy, interview with author, 12 May 2015.

66. Herman Hall, "The Steelbands: A New American Music," *New York Amsterdam News*, 9 September 1978.

67. Keith Nurse, "Globalization and Trinidadian Carnival: Diaspora, Hybridity, and Identity in Global Culture," *Cultural Studies* 13, no. 4 (1999): 683.

68. WIADCA Carnival program booklet, 1974.

69. A thorough history of steelband music in the Caribbean outside of Trinidad has yet to be written, but clearly the nations of Antigua, coastal Guyana, and Grenada had steelband cultures by the early 1970s. Antigua had a venerable steelband tradition dating back to the 1940s, holding its first steelband competition in 1949. "Leroy Gordon, "The Story of Pan in Antigua," When Steel Talks, http://whensteeltalks.ning.com/page/the-story-of-pan-in-antigua.

In 1955 Emory Cook recorded Antigua's famous Brute Force band and released the first commercial recording of steel pan (Cook Records 01042, 1955). Guyana, perhaps due to its close proximity to Trinidad, developed a lively steelband scene in the 1950s, with the iconic figure Roy Geddes establishing a national steelband in 1962. "Godfry Chin, "Rise of the Steelband in Guyana: Tribute to Steelbands before Mash 1970," When Steel Talks, http://www.panonthenet.com/news/2010/mar/guyana-3-24-10.htm; "Roy Geddes—Architect of Guyana's Steel Pan Evolution," *Guyana Chronicle*, 22 March 2015, https://guyanachronicle.com/2015/03/22/roy-geddes-architect-of-guyanas-steel-pan-evolution.

Grenada, while lacking a formal Panorama, had local steelband activity in the 1950s and 1960s.

Herman Hall, interview with author, 21 September 2017, Brooklyn. Other islands had a smattering of steelbands in the 1960s and 1970s, often geared for tourists, but the tradition was not an integral part of local grassroots culture as it was in Trinidad, or to a lesser extent in Antigua, Guyana, and Grenada.

70. Rachel Buff, who was studying Brooklyn steelbands in the early 1990s, reported that despite the Trinidadian nationalist associations of the steel pan, some bands were starting "to attract players in Brooklyn from Caribbean nations without a steel band tradition, as well as some young African-American players." Rachel Buff, *Immigration and the Political Economy of Home: West Indian Brooklyn and American Indian Minneapolis, 1945–1992* (University of California Press, 2001), p. 124. Gave Averill, who participated as a scholar, performer, and judge in various Brooklyn steelband settings in the early 1990s, noted that the bands "almost exclusively consist[ed] of West Indians," referring to Brooklyn migrants originally hailing from the Anglophone Eastern Caribbean. Averill, "'Pan Is We Ting,'" p.122.

71. Averill, "'Pan Is We Ting,'" p. 121.

72. Buff, *Immigration and the Political Economy of Home*, p. 141.

6

The Brooklyn Soca Connection

Comparing overseas Carnivals in 1990, Frank Manning observed that Brooklyn's Labor Day celebration had been dominated by calypso from its inception. In his words, Brooklyn had become, since the late 1960s, "the world capital of calypso" with a calypso season running nearly year-round. He went on to explain that for Brooklyn Carnival-goers, "the real highlight of the festival is the tremendous number of calypso shows and dances that take place before, during, and after the (Labor Day) festival." Manning touted Brooklyn-based Charlie's Records label and the "leading international performers (who) maintain residencies there (in Brooklyn) and visit regularly for shows, recording sessions, and promotional work."[1] While some mas and steelband aficionados might take exception to Manning's assessment that calypso had actually eclipsed their contributions to Brooklyn Carnival, there can be no doubt that calypso and the new variant soca (soul/calypso) were essential hallmarks of the festivities. Equally important, concurrent with the rise of Brooklyn Carnival in the 1970s was the borough's emergence as a vital transnational center for the recording and production of calypso and soca music.

As discussed earlier, Trinidadian musicians and calypso singers had been journeying to New York to record since George "Lovey" Bailey's orchestra and Lionel Belasco arrived in the 1910s and Wilmoth Houdini and Sam Manning became popular singers in the 1920s. Recordings were made and distributed by the large US companies Victor, Columbia, Decca, Okeh, and the American Recording Company. In the postwar years, small American companies such as Cook, Dial, Monogram, and Disc/Folkways occasionally issued records of calypso singers as part of their diverse catalogues of folk and popular music. During the "calypso craze" of the late 1950s, the large US labels RCA, Decca, Capitol, and Columbia dominated the field, although much of their attention was devoted to Harry Belafonte and North American interpreters of calypso. As the commercial craze wound down, so did North American interest in calypso. Only RCA maintained a studio in Trinidad and continued, throughout the early 1960s, to record a handful of the best-known singers including Kitchener, Sparrow, Melody, and Duke. On the other side of the Atlantic, the British independent label Melodisc issued recordings by Kitchener, Invader, and others during the 1950s and 1960s.[2]

Back in Trinidad, the recording business was something of a hodge-podge around the time of Independence in 1963. Trinidad/RCA and Telco/Columbia, which released singles from the late 1950s through the 1960s, maintained relationships with their parent American companies. Meanwhile, dozens of other small, independent, Trinidadian-owned-and-operated labels sprang up. Some were vanity labels founded by individual calypsonians hoping to market their own songs, while a few, including National, Tropico, and Antillana, produced a significant number of singles and LP recordings throughout the 1960s and early 1970s.[3] K.H. Studios, once the RCA facility located in the Sea Lots neighborhood of Port of Spain, and Telco studios, located in Champ Fleurs, became popular re-cording venues.[4] But, in general, the Trinidad recording facilities were not advanced, and master tapes were often shipped to Barbados for pressing.[5] Most troubling for singers and musicians, these small labels lacked ade-quate distribution networks outside of Trinidad and the English-speaking Caribbean. By the mid-1960s, growing overseas Caribbean communities located in North America and England offered potential opportunities for better production and expanded audiences, with New York, and even-tually Brooklyn, taking the lead. Since North American companies had by this time turned their backs on calypso, the job would fall to migrant Caribbean entrepreneurs to establish independent record labels.

Camille Hodge and Camille Records

Camille Hodge (b. 1932) was just such an entrepreneur. Born in St. Thomas in the US Virgin Islands, he arrived in New York as a teenager in 1948. At that time the heart of the city's Caribbean community was still in Harlem, with outposts in the Bronx and Brooklyn, and Hodge ended up settling in with his mother in an apartment on 165th Street in the Bronx. After finishing high school and working odd jobs in the Garment District, he was drafted into the military and spent two years in Korea. Following his discharge from the military in late 1954, Hodge returned to the Bronx and began studying business and accounting and helping to promote a band led by his childhood friend and fellow Virgin Islander, Emile "Milo" Francis.[6]

Milo and the Kings were a twelve-piece dance orchestra from St. Thomas, similar to those led by Syd Joe, MacBeth , and Fats Greene. Though based in the Virgin Islands, the musicians traveled regularly to New York to per-form in Manhattan dance halls, where they played a variety of calypso and Latin styles, depending on the demands of their audiences. Featuring the calypso singer Lord Spectacular and Latin singers Pedro Maldonado and Miguel Morreo, and backed by a rhythm section that included conga, guira, and clave, the ensemble was truly bilingual and bimusical. The band's first two recordings, which Hodge helped distribute locally, were the calypso "The Iceman" and the Latin dance tune "La Pachanga." Convinced of the demand for and the commercial viability of the music, Hodge persuaded Selwyn Joseph, the owner of Harlem's Central Ballroom, to front $3,500 in start-up capital to put together a record label. With an eye toward the English-speaking Caribbean audience, they dubbed their venture CAB Records (Calypso At its Best).

Sometime in late 1964, Hodge brought Milo's orchestra and two additional calypso singers into a studio on the ground floor of the Belvedere Hotel, on West 48th Street in Manhattan. The resulting seven-inch singles recordings, "Dove and Pigeon/Save the Federation" (CAB Records 101) by Lord Nelson, "The Wedding/Loretta" by Prince Galloway (CAB Records 102), and "Lazy Man/New York Situation" by Lord Spectacular (CAB Records 103) were released in 1965.[7] The musical arrangements, Hodge recalls, were worked out by Milo by ear during rehearsal. They exemplify the conventional early 1960s approach to calypso, in which an instrumental band chorus on brass and reeds was followed by a vocal verse, a vocal chorus, another band chorus, and so forth. Most of the songs are introduced with a formulaic eight-bar piano/bass line over a chugging percussion section. Overall, however, the rhythmic pulse is relatively straight, with the bass establishing a plodding on-the-beat pulse. The horn lines are bright and slightly syncopated, and the two Lord Spectacular pieces include brief R&B-style saxophone solos.[8]

Lord Spectacular was a native Virgin Islander who often traveled to New York to sing with Milo and the Kings but who never lived there for an extended period of time. His song "New York Situation" recounts his journey to New York with the band, his frustrations with not finding work, and the unhappiness of life in the city away from his island home and family. In the final verse he nostalgically pleads with potential Caribbean migrants to "think back on your happy years / and you ought to shed tears." He concluded with a challenge: "If a hard and rough time, that's what you looking for / pack up your bundle, come and live in America."[9]

Edward "Prince" Galloway, a St. Croix native whose biography was discussed earlier, had a hand in what would turn out to be Hodge's best-selling calypso record. Following a disagreement with Selwyn Joseph over a botched Lord Melody album, Hodge decided it was time to strike out on his own. He shut down CAB and created the Camille record label sometime around 1965. By this time he had set up his own record shop, Bulrand Records, at 975 Prospect Avenue in the Bronx, and was doing promotional work organizing Caribbean dances. Galloway, meanwhile, in a moment of nostalgic reflection from his Jersey City home, wrote a song he called "Archie Buck Dem Up." The lyrics refer to a favorite St. Croix musician, Archie Thomas, and a local dance called the "buck up." Galloway, on a trip to St. Croix in 1965, premiered the song, and soon after the Archie Thomas ensemble was granted permission to record the piece with lead vocalist Eldred Christian. Upon returning to New Jersey,

Galloway brought the song to Hodge, but following a falling out between the two, Hodge had the Fats Greene orchestra record the piece with vocalist Al Thomas (no relationship to Archie), rather than Galloway, singing the lead.

Hodge and Greene changed Galloway's original title from "Archie Buck Dem Up" to "'Fats' Shake 'Em Up" (see Figure 6.1) The lyrics were modified to celebrate dancers jumping up in Harlem's Renaissance Ballroom (rather than in the Hideaway in St. Thomas), and to reference Greene and other members of his band, including vocalist Al Thomas and saxophonist Pritchard Chessman (rather than Archie Thomas's group from St. Croix). The 1966 Greene recording rocked with a rhythmic drive reminiscent of Archie Thomas's "Buck Dem Up" arrangement, but Al Thomas's vocal with the Greene ensemble was smoother with a less pronounced island accent than Eldred Christian's voice on the original St. Croix recording.[10] As a result the piece had a slightly more polished, R&B feel, so much so that Hodge did not like it at first, fearing it did not sound Caribbean enough for his audience.[11] As it ended up, the piece became a hit in New York

Figure 6.1. *Fats Shake 'Em Up*, Camille Records, 1964.

after Hodge was successful in getting it into rotation on the local R&B radio stations WLIB and WWRL. "'Fats' Shake 'Em Up" was Camille's one and only crossover hit. Exact numbers are nearly impossible to calculate, but Hodge recalled ordering an initial pressing of 5,000 (ten times more than he would usually order for a calypso record) and a 9 July 1966 advertisement in *Billboard Magazine* described the piece as a "Smash Hit in New York. Sold over 50,000." Galloway was given a co-authorship credit along with Hodge, and received a small royalty payout. However, most of the profits went to Hodge, and Galloway was not pleased with the financial arrangement.[12]

The third calypsonian who participated in Hodge's inaugural recording session was Lord Nelson. His career is unusual because he did not begin to sing calypso until after migrating to the United States as a young man. Born Robert Alfonzo Nelson in Plymouth, Tobago, in 1931, Nelson relocated to Port of Spain after high school. He lived with his aunt for several years in the Woodbrook neighborhood, where he played briefly with the Invaders Steel Orchestra. At age twenty-one he migrated to Brooklyn to live with an uncle, and soon after joined the armed services and was sent to Korea. It was in the military that he began to perform as a comedian and calypso singer, covering the popular songs of Sparrow, Kitchener, and Melody.[13]

After leaving the military in 1955, Nelson returned to New York, now with dual Trinidad/Tobago and US citizenship. Recalling his youthful experience with Invaders he joined the Magnets, a Harlem-based steelband. But his talents as a vocalist were quickly recognized, and he soon found himself fronting the band singing popular calypsos for Caribbean and white audiences in the late 1950s, at the height of the calypso craze. Nelson then began singing with Caribbean dance orchestras in Manhattan, including the aforementioned Milo and the Kings, Fats Greene, Claude Brewster, and Bert Samuel (the latter two from the Virgin Islands). He recalled performing in Harlem Carnival, singing with an orchestra perched on a truck that drove up Lenox Avenue, surrounded by dancers. On a trip to St. Croix with Samuels in 1960 or early 1961, Nelson recorded the song "Garrot Bounce," backed by the Bert Samuel band, at a local radio station studio. Nelson released the song on his own Tarco record label in 1962, and in 1967 Camille Hodge would re-release the piece under the title "Garrot Bounce '67." The piece was a high-energy romp, propelled by Nelson's spirited yelps and yips, and punctuated by his off-the-beat vocal phrasing, highlighting his talent for pulling vocal phrases across the standard bar line. The flip side of the record ("Garrot Bounce '67 Part 2") was an instrumental version of the song featuring a series of feverish rhythm and blues saxophone solos.[14]

Sometime in the late 1950s, while performing at the Park Palace dance hall in Harlem, Nelson met the Mighty Sparrow.[15] Upon hearing "Garrot Bounce," Sparrow invited Nelson to come and sing in his Young Brigade tent in Trinidad, marking the first time Nelson had appeared as a calypso singer in his native Trinidad. There he met and befriended the calypsonian

Duke, whom Nelson credits for mentoring him as a calypso songwriter. In 1963 Nelson began recording for Sparrow's National Label and toured the Caribbean as part of his show. He sang in the Port of Spain tents for several years but was declared ineligible for the Trinidadian Calypso Monarch and Road March competitions due to his status as a US citizen.[16] Nelson maintained New York as his home base, regularly touring the Caribbean and eventually Europe and Africa. But like many calypsonians, he found it difficult to make a living as a full-time musician, and for a number of years he worked a part-time job managing a dairy section in the local Waldbaums.

From 1965 through 1974 Nelson recorded several dozen singles and four LPs for CAB/Camille, backed by Milo and the Kings, Fats Greene, Claude Brewster, and Ron Berridge. Most of his early work was in a traditional calypso vein, with simple arrangements done by Milo or the other leaders. But by the early 1970s his songs were reflecting his growing interest in African American R&B and soul. His 1973 LP *This Is Lord Nelson*, for example, included a calypso-style cover of Jean Knight's 1971 Stax Records soul hit "Mr. Big Stuff" (recast by Nelson as "Mrs. Big Stuff"), and "Vero," which featured a melodic bass line and bluesy fills on sax, organ, and trumpet.[17] Similarly, a number of the songs on his 1974 release *Again*, this time backed by the Ron Berridge Orchestra, are accompanied by funk-influenced syncopated bass lines and bluesy organ and saxophone riffs.[18] Nelson's early excursions into R&B and soul music foreshadowed his later work with the arranger Clive Bradley, which would establish him as one of the pioneers of soca music in the late 1970s and 1980s.

Another influential calypsonian who recorded for Hodge was Kelvin "Mighty Duke" Pope (1932–2009). A native Trinidadian, Duke had established himself as a leading calypsonian by winning the coveted Calypso Monarch title an unprecedented four years in a row, from 1968 through 1971. In the 1970s he relocated to Brooklyn, making New York his base for recording and touring, and returning to Trinidad every year for several months during Carnival season. He made his first New York recordings for Camille, which were released on the 1973 LP titled *Message for the Man*. Several of the songs, particularly "Child of the Ghetto," "Thorns of a Blackman," and "This 'V' for Peace," resonated with Caribbean audiences in the islands and in New York, as they addressed controversial issues of social injustice and the need for black unity and pride. This was timely, given the burgeoning Black Power movement, coupled with the venerable calypso tradition of addressing political topics along with Hodge's own outspoken political views on racial inequality. Duke, like Nelson, would go on to record for the Brooklyn record companies discussed below, producing a number of influential calypsos, including his 1986 anti-apartheid anthem "How Many More Must Die" and his 1987 Road-March-winning "Is Thunder."[19]

Hodge released several dozen 45 rpm singles on the CAB label between 1964 and 1965, and sixty singles and several dozen LPs on the Camille label between 1966 and 1978. With the exception of a handful of R&B and reggae sides, this catalogue was exclusively calypso, including, in addition to Spectacular, Galloway, Nelson, and Duke, such prominent artists as Swallow, Inventor, Melody, Lion, Wellington, and Robin, as well as a number of less well-known figures. Most sang in the medium tempo, text-heavy Trinidadian calypso style of the day, although Nelson and Duke were already showing strong interests in incorporating elements of contemporary American popular music into their compositions, portending the soca revolution that was poised on the horizon.

Taken as a whole, Hodge's catalogue is relatively thin compared to those of the Brooklyn-based companies that would soon supplant Camille Records. He did, however, established a model that others would emulate. Hodge demonstrated that by the mid-1960s, an entrepreneurial Caribbean migrant, regardless of which island he or she hailed from, could launch a profitable independent label devoted exclusively to calypso, thanks to the music's growing popularity in the Caribbean and in the burgeoning New York Caribbean market. Direct access to talent posed no problem, as New York was rapidly becoming a destination for calypsonians and Caribbean ensembles. Instrumental groups could be augmented with talented American-born musicians, and the city boasted excellent recording, mixing, and production facilities. Through regular travel back and forth to Trinidad, the Virgin Islands, St. Vincent, and other English-speaking islands, networks could be established for the distribution of New York–produced recordings back to the Caribbean. As the Caribbean population shifted from Harlem and the Bronx to Brooklyn, bolstered by a new wave of migrants who landed in the late 1960s, the stage was set for the emergence of new immigrant-owned record labels that would change the face of the calypso recording industry.

St. Vincentians in Brooklyn: Straker's Records and Frankie McIntosh

Granville Straker (b. 1939), a native of St. Vincent, came to Brooklyn via Trinidad in 1959. Shortly after arriving he took a job as an auto mechanic, and in 1964 he rented a storefront at 613 Nostrand Avenue in the heart of Brooklyn's Bedford Stuyvesant neighborhood. There he opened up a car service and began to pursue his dream of selling records. In addition to American R&B and soul music, which for many years was his mainstay, he began to import Caribbean music from the Samarou, Tropico, and Telco companies in Trinidad. Eventually he began licensing material from Telco, who provided him with a master tape and the rights to manufacture the records in New York. As Brooklyn's Caribbean community grew, so did demand for calypso, and by the early 1970s Straker had three stores in central Brooklyn, along with two in Port of Spain and one in Kingstown, St. Vincent.[20]

In the late 1960s, Straker decided to try his hand at recording calypsonians and establishing his own record label. He purchased a two-track Ampex portable machine, and sometime in 1969 convinced the most popular calypso singer of the day, the Mighty Sparrow, to allow him to record him live at the Blue Coronet club in Brooklyn. The resulting LP, released in 1970 under the title *The Best of the Mighty Sparrow*, presents nine songs performed live by Sparrow and his Troubadours band, which consisted of a rhythm section and a single saxophone. The arrangements were loose, and the vocals were not Sparrow's most memorable, but the recording conveys a relaxed atmosphere and showcases the singer's witty verbal repartee with his audience. Aside from "Love One Another," a call for black unity, the album features mostly humorous and risqué numbers including "Bag of Sugar," "Village Ram," and "Big Bambo." The remnants of the calypso craze are evident in a medley of Belafonte hits "Day-O," "Yellow Bird," and "Jamaica Farewell."[21]

The live Sparrow album sold well enough to encourage Straker to move forward with his record label. Having the popular calypso icon Sparrow as his first Straker's Records release gained him notoriety and helped attract talent, enough so that by 1971 he began to record and issue a series of seven-inch singles. One of the first artists to be featured was the relatively unknown Trinidadian calypso singer Hawthorne Wellington Quashie (b. 1939), who went by the sobriquet King Wellington. He migrated to New York in 1967, picking up various odd jobs while singing in Village clubs at night. Eventually he relocated to Boston where he took a job in a hotel. But Wellington continued to visit Brooklyn, and in 1971 he ventured into Straker's record shop to inquire about making a recording. Straker was impressed with Wellington's songs and invited him to come back and record on his two-track Ampex right there in the store. Straker employed Ron Berridge's band and, with arrangements of Wellington's tunes by Clement Berridge, the sessions unfolded. Wellington recollected:

> So the first recordings with Straker were with a full band, right there in his store on Utica Avenue. I had a song called "Mas for George Baily," and back in those days there was no over-taping—if you made a mistake you had to stop and start over. And I had to sing from Straker's toilet, with the mike chord coming through the door. We only had two tracks, one track for the band, the other track for me. The band was in the front of the store, and I had to shut the toilet door so I wouldn't get feedback through my vocal mike when the band was playing. And I was never satisfied with those songs ["Mas for George Baily" and "Calypso Race"]—we never got locked in, with Berridge's band—we couldn't get the timing right.[22]

Straker quickly abandoned the idea of using his store for a recording studio when he realized there were suitable studios in Brooklyn and in Port of Spain. Later that year Wellington would record "New Calypso Music" in K.H. Studios in Trinidad and Straker would issues the single with "Pretty Baby" by the R&B singer Cheno Fester on the flip side. The 1971 recording of "New Calypso Music" was unusual in that it broke the standard band-chorus/vocal verse/vocal chorus structure, with Wellington calling out solos for the bass, the drums, and a pan player. Although Clement Berridge arranged the piece, Wellington claims that the horn lines and bass solo lines were his, the latter foreshadowing the prominent moving bass parts that would become a hallmark of soca by the late 1970s. When Wellington re-recorded the song in 1974 for the Plek label, he upped the tempo and employed an even more active and syncopated bass that doubled the horn lines before it reached its allotted eight-bar solo. The difference between the two recordings is striking—a sonic record of Wellington's transition from the older calypso to the emerging soca style. Even more notable is his 1973 recording of "Steel and Brass," which ended up on the Camille label. The fast tempo, prominent bass line, electric piano, and compact text describing the anticipated bacchanal to the accompaniment of steel and brass music give the piece a distinctive soca feel, although no one would have labelled it such in 1973.[23]

By 1972 Straker had quit his mechanics job and abandoned his cab service to devote himself full-time to his record label. He began traveling back and forth between Trinidad and Brooklyn, frequenting the Port of Spain Carnival tents in search of fresh singers with new songs. On one such trip in 1972 he met a thirty-year-old school teacher and aspiring calypsonian named Hollis Liverpool, who went by the stage name Chalkdust. Unhappy with his business arrangements with RCA and several Trinidad companies, Liverpool agreed to record several songs for Straker, who brought in Trinidad's premiere arranger, Art de Coteau, to work with Liverpool. By the late 1960s most calypsonians (or their record producers) employed arrangers to compose and score out horn and bass lines, as well as the basic chordal progressions for guitar and keyboard. Musicians were expected to sight-read charts that were passed out at recording sessions and live performances. The horn lines were deemed central to the arranger's craft and an essential component of a song's potential popularity.[24]

De Coteau oversaw the recording in a local Port of Spain studio, and the master tape was brought back to Brooklyn for final mixing and production. In 1973 the LP titled *The Mighty Chalkdust: First Time Around* was released on Straker's Records. Never one to shy away from controversy, Liverpool included a number of songs addressing local Trinidadian politics, including "Af Fraid Karl" (a sarcastic rebuke of People's National Movement Attorny General Carl Hudson-Phillips), "PNM Loves Me," "Our Cultural Heritage," and "Immigration Problems."[25] Nor did Straker balk at Liverpool's social commentary, recognizing the appreciation his Trinidadian and local Brooklyn audiences had for Liverpool's sharp political wit. Liverpool would go on to record more than a dozen albums on Straker's Records, including songs that won him five Trinidad Calypso Monarch competitions.[26]

The dozens of singers whom Straker recorded in the early 1970s performed in the straightforward calypso style that was popular in Trinidad in the 1960s. But the musical tides were changing by the mid-1970s, with the advent of the new soca (soul/calypso) sound that Lord Shorty, Nelson, and others were experimenting with. Early soca was differentiated from calypso by its strong 4/4 rhythmic structure, with accents on second and fourth beats of each measure; emphasis on a syncopated bass line that often incorporates pulse anticipation, anacrusis patterns, and melodic figures; and fast, often frenetic, tempos. In contrast, calypso pieces were based on a two-beat structure that emphasizes a steady bass line and generally exhibited slower tempos. In soca the voice and instruments tended to interlock to form a repetitive rhythmic groove, while in calypso the vocal line was more melodic and prone to improvisation as the text unfolded in a linear, verse-chorus form. Soca lyrics were more apt to address themes of love, sensuality, dance, and celebration, often employing short, repetitive phrases, while traditional calypso songs featured text-dense lyrics filled with witty and occasionally ribald social commentary. And, finally, soca arrangements often foregrounded synthesizers, electric guitars, mechanical drum beats, and additional electronic sounds for timbral effects, which were considered highly inventive in the 1970s.[27] There were a number of transitional songs, most composed by established calypsonians like Kitchener, Sparrow, Duke, and Stalin, which embraced elements of both styles by using basic soca rhythms and instrumental effects to accompany lyrics laden with social commentary and delivered at moderate but danceable tempos.

Straker was quick to recognize these trends. In 1974 the well-known calypsonian Shadow (Winston Bailey) walked into Straker's Frederick Street record shop, guitar in hand and head buzzing with a new song. Straker recalled:

So Shadow came into the store one day and said "Straker, I have something for you to hear." He had his guitar, always had his guitar with him. And he starts to sing—bom-bom-beaty-bom, bom-beaty-bom. I say hold it, start over. He sings again. And that's how it started. He sang two songs at the same time, "Bass Man" and "Come out to Play." I said Kaiso! I want those songs![28]

"Bass Man" was Straker's best-selling single to date, winning the Trinidad Road March title in 1974 (see Figure 6.2).[29] The foregrounding of the melodic bass line, along with the compact, repetitive text, were considered highly innovative at the time, leading Jocelyne Guilbault to suggest that the song brought about a "musical metamorphosis in the calypso sound from the time it was heard in 1974."[30] While Guilbault correctly credits Shadow's arranger Art de Coteau for embracing and popularizing the melodic bass line, it is crucial to note that Shadow composed the original phrases, singing them first to Straker and later to de Coteau, who incorporated them into his arrangement. It was Straker's keen ear that picked up on Shadow's nascent idea for a song and fronted the capital to turn it into a memorable recording. Without Straker, de Coteau probably would never

Figure 6.2. Shadow, *Bass Man*, Straker Records, 1974.

have heard the piece, and indeed it might not have been recorded and gone on to become a transformational calypso and key soca prototype.[31]

Straker's recording and production process quickly evolved into a transnational project. He traveled back and forth between Brooklyn and Port of Spain, establishing contacts with Trinidad-based singers, musicians, and arrangers and befriending Brooklyn's Caribbean expatriate artists. He would record in either Brooklyn or Trinidad, depending on where a calypsonian was based, or when a particular artist might be visiting New York. With the advent of multitracking, sections of a single recording were often done at both locations (for example the horns and rhythm section in a Trinidad studio, the final vocals in a Brooklyn studio). The final mix was almost always completed in a Brooklyn or New York City studio, which, by the early 1980s, offered more sophisticated mixing boards with sixteen- or twenty-four-track capability. As word of New York's superior recording and mixing facilities spread, more singers and musicians came north to record. Meanwhile Straker formed a distribution network that stretched back to Trinidad, Barbados, Jamaica, and other English-speaking Caribbean islands.[32]

In the early years, Straker worked with leading Trinidadian music arrangers Art de Coteau, Ed Watson, and Ron Berridge. De Coteau and Watson frequently traveled to New York with their ensembles to perform

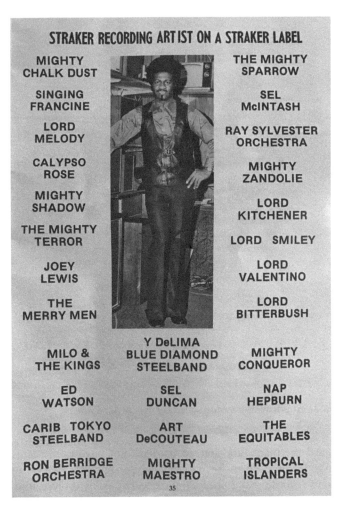

STRAKER RECORDING ARTIST ON A STRAKER LABEL

MIGHTY CHALK DUST	THE MIGHTY SPARROW
SINGING FRANCINE	SEL McINTASH
LORD MELODY	RAY SYLVESTER ORCHESTRA
CALYPSO ROSE	MIGHTY ZANDOLIE
MIGHTY SHADOW	LORD KITCHENER
THE MIGHTY TERROR	LORD SMILEY
JOEY LEWIS	LORD VALENTINO
THE MERRY MEN	LORD BITTERBUSH

MILO & THE KINGS	Y DeLIMA BLUE DIAMOND STEELBAND	MIGHTY CONQUEROR
ED WATSON	SEL DUNCAN	NAP HEPBURN
CARIB TOKYO STEELBAND	ART DeCOUTEAU	THE EQUITABLES
RON BERRIDGE ORCHESTRA	MIGHTY MAESTRO	TROPICAL ISLANDERS

35

Figure 6.3. Granville Straker, 1975 ad (courtesy of the West Indian Day Carnival Association).

and record, while Berridge relocated to the city in 1971 and ran a successful dance orchestra until moving to California in 1976.[33] But Straker found his musical alter-ego in the pianist, arranger, and fellow St. Vincentian Frankie McIntosh (b. 1946). Born in Kingstown, St. Vincent, McIntosh had the benefit of piano lessons and as a young boy played in his father Arthur McIntosh's dance orchestra, the Melotones. The band performed primarily instrumental dance orchestrations of calypso, Latin, and American standards, but members gathered at the McIntosh home on Sunday afternoons for jazz jam sessions. The senior McIntosh, a saxophonist, idolized Illinois Jacquet, Charlie Parker, and Lester Young. After graduating high school and teaching in Antigua for three years, Frankie McIntosh migrated to New York and began studying music at Brooklyn

College in 1968. While earning a bachelor's degree in music at Brooklyn College and an MA in music at New York University, he played keyboards with several Caribbean bands and American R&B and jazz groups.[34]

McIntosh's initial foray into arranging Caribbean music had nothing to do with Straker or his record label. In the summer of 1976, Alston Cyrus, a St. Vincent calypsonian with the stage name Becket, approached McIntosh about reworking several of his calypso arrangements for an upcoming Manhattan boat-ride engagement. The two St. Vincentians hit it off, and shortly after McIntosh arranged his first calypso recordings for Becket's *Disco Calypso* album. Recorded in 1976 and released the following year on the American Casablanca label, the album did not sell well in North America, but one song, "Coming High," was popular in Trinidad, St. Vincent, and Brooklyn. The song was originally titled "Marijuana," but producer Buddy Scott insisted that the title be changed to "Coming High" and that Becket alter the phrase "Marijuana" to the nondrug but sexually suggestive line "Mary do you Wanna"?[35]

Musically, "Coming High" demonstrates key characteristics of early soca: the foregrounded melodic bass line that occasionally doubles the vocal; the prominence of the synthesizer; the compact, repetitive text; and the lengthy break/groove sections in the middle and end of the piece. These rhythmic break sections (3:25–4:00; 7:22–end), built around the breaking down and rebuilding of the instruments and fundamental riffs, were similar to those heard on popular African American funk, soul, and disco recordings of the period. The inclusion of such dance-friendly break/groove sections to extend the length of songs (in this case to 8:22) would become increasingly popular in the soca music of the 1980s. In addition, McIntosh introduced innovations seldom heard in calypso or early soca. Following the initial two verses and choruses, he modulates up half a step (from B-flat to B) into a jazzy-sounding bridge with the synthesizer trading riffs with the double-voiced horns and bass (1:55), before cycling back down to the original key of B-flat. Later in the piece he brings in a bluesy guitar solo (5:35–6:15) by Victor Collins, which flows into another set of horn riffs and a final modulation and bridge.[36]

The following year, 1978, Becket and McIntosh teamed up for a second recording. The LP *Coming Higher* included the song "Wine Down Kingstown," a reference to Carnival festivities in the St. Vincent capital. The prominent bass and synthesizer lines, the rapid tempo, the extended percussion break/groove sections, and Becket's exhortation for listeners to "wine down" (dance) place the piece squarely in a soca vein. As in "Coming High," jazz and blues elements are clearly evident. The piece opens with a syncopated, choppy horn line alternating between the reeds and the brass. The vocal chorus ends with the bass moving through a cycle of fourths from C back to the tonic F-sharp chord (0:40)—a common jazz progression but unusual for calypso or soca. The arrangement is further enlivened by a bop-inflected 24-bar solo played by African American trumpeter Ron Taylor (2:58) and McIntosh's improvised synthesizer figures over punchy horn riffs (3:20). The piece ends on an extended groove section with the horns blasting out a dominant-seven-sharp-nine chord (6:30), a dissonant voicing associated more with Latin jazz or rock than calypso.[37]

Impressed with the Becket recordings, Straker approached McIntosh in 1978 about arranging for his label, and the two would go on to forge a musical alliance that would last for decades. McIntosh became musical director for Straker's Records, organizing a studio band called the Equitables, and arranging for dozens of Straker's calypsonians including Chalkdust, Shadow, Calypso Rose, Winston Soso, Poser, Lord Nelson, Singing Francine, Duke, and King Wellington. As the music moved into the 1980s, McIntosh was at the forefront of the new soca style. He distinguished himself through his innovative horn lines and synthesizer figures, although few of his arrangements reached the harmonic sophistication and jazzy feel of his initial collaborations with Becket. McIntosh admitted that there was pressure from the market to stick to more standard I-IV-V triadic chord progressions and simplified melodies with less improvisation and more emphasis on repetitive dance loops: "In order to sound like Kitchener's Sugar Bum Bum (1978) you had to leave out the 7th and raised 9th chords. You just played simpler things, more accessible to the ear. Harmonies were in decline, in a sort of state of attrition."[38]

McIntosh's use of improvised blues and jazz instrumental solos on his early Becket albums would turn out to be the exception, not the norm, as few soca arrangements in the 1980s foregrounded individual instrumentalists. There were several reasons for this. As Guilbault has suggested, the rise of arrangers in Trinidad who would score out introductions and band-chorus themes led to a de-emphasis on improvised soloing, a practice that was fading from calypso dance bands by the late 1960s.[39] Although the soca songs recorded in the late 1970s and 1980s were often extended tracks of eight or more minutes, much of that time was taken up by written instrumental band/chorus themes and the extended break/groove sections favored by deejays and dancers. Perhaps most importantly, soca, like its parent calypso, remained primarily a vocal music that featured the singer, not the band. This differed significantly from African American R&B, Latin jazz, and salsa, which maintained improvised soloing as central to their musical practices. According to many arrangers and musicians, most calypso and soca singers were not eager to share the limelight with talented instrumental soloists. Backup bands were there to back up, not to compete with the singer.[40]

Despite these trends, McIntosh continued to produce imaginative arrangements that maintained a degree of spontaneity. His 1981 arrangement of Wellington's "Take Your Time" is exemplary. The piece opens with a bright, galloping theme voiced in thirds on the trumpets, with supporting horns moving parallel to the main melody. The trumpets drop out for the final two beats of measure 2 while the saxophones and trombone play a brief ascending phrase to complete a call-and-response figure. The rhythmic groove is anchored in a punchy, syncopated bass line that interlocks with a simple, mid-range guitar phrase that is repeated every four measures. Off-beat piano and synthesizer chords add harmonic and rhythmic support (see Music Example 6.1). The harmonies are built around an elementary I-IV-V7 chord progression, but the texture is dense and the rhythm insistent. Halfway through the piece McIntosh brings in a percussion break with bass solo (3:18–3:40), followed by the staggered entry of the guitar and synthesizer, followed by horns and backup vocals.

Music Example 6.1 Instrumental band introduction by Frankie McIntosh for King Wellington's "Take Your Time." Straker Records, 1981 (transcription courtesy of Frankie McIntosh).

Music Example 6.1 (continued).

Following a final verse and chorus, the piece chugs on with choke-neck guitar improvisations over a heavy dance groove.[41]

McIntosh's arrangement for Chalkdust's 1983 recording for Straker's Records, "Ash Wednesday Jail," is an up-tempo soca with forceful horns, slinky synthesizer fills, and a melodic bass figure that occasionally doubles the horn lines and vocals. Half-way through the piece McIntosh enters with a 16-bar improvised solo (3:08) using a steel-pan sound programmed though his Prophet 5 synthesizer. He recalls having to convince Liverpool to increase the tempo of his original song to create a stronger soca groove.[42] Though skeptical at first, the singer was quite satisfied with the final arrangement, which turned out to be one of his most popular recordings. Liverpool had publicly decried the incursion of commercial soca as a threat to Trinidad's venerable calypso tradition in his popular 1979 Straker recording "Calypso vs. Soca," but he was willing to embrace elements of the new music as long as his lyrical text remained intact.

Liverpool remembers McIntosh being much freer in the studio than older arrangers like Art de Coteau, allowing musicians and singers more input, modifying arrangements on the spot during sessions, and in general leaving room for modest embellishments and improvisation.[43] In McIntosh's words:

> Oh yes, even when I go to a full score, it's never like this is written in stone and we must stick to this. From the first date, if we are playing the rhythm section and I don't think a chord works I will change it. Or I would change the horn line or the bass line in a flash . . . I was quite open to ideas, as long as they worked. So in the studio we might be playing a chart, and someone like [trumpeter] Errol Ince might say "Frankie, do you mind if we do this instead?" I'd say play it and let me hear it. And if I liked it I'd say "bang, go for it!" Then I'd change the music.[44]

McIntosh brought a more flexible, jazz-influenced sensibility to the studio. The Equitables were a cosmopolitan ensemble, composed of musicians from Trinidad, St. Vincent, Barbados, Panama, Puerto Rico, and the United States. Many had experience playing jazz, Latin, R&B, soul, and funk—influences that crept into McIntosh's arrangements at a critical time in soca's development.

Straker had a good ear for spotting talent and recognizing a potential hit song, but when it came to the music itself he always deferred to McIntosh, which is one reason they worked so well together. Occasionally, Straker worked with other arrangers, as was the case with his final big hit, Black Stalin's "Ah Feel to Party," arranged by the Trinidadian trumpeter and bandleader Errol Ince. The song's genesis and development exemplify the transnational nature of soca produc-tion. When Stalin, who was based in Trinidad, came up with the idea for the song, he phoned Ince in New York and sang him the melody. Ince, who had relocated in New York in the 1980s and had worked with Stalin on several previous records, wrote down the melody and proceeded to score out the parts. On his next trip up to Brooklyn, Stalin went in the studio with Ince to set the tempo and work out the background vocals. Ince then organized the recording of the rhythm and horn tracks with his band of Caribbean and American players, and brought Stalin back into the studio several nights later to lay down his final lead vocal. Ince oversaw the final mix, and with Straker's approval the record was mastered, manufactured, and sent back to Trinidad, where it won the 1991 Road March title.[45]

As a business person, Straker, like many ambitious migrants, was a veri-table one-man operation—talent scout, recording/mixing engineer, record distributor, and concert promoter. His catalogue is impressive—although exact numbers are difficult to establish, by the time he had cut back production in the mid-1990s, he had released hundreds of albums and perhaps as many as a thousand seven- and twelve-inch singles.[46] As a cultural broker, Straker moved easily across geographic boundaries to knit together transnational musical networks that helped bind members of Brooklyn's burgeoning migrant communities to their Caribbean homelands while providing new and expanding markets for the music.

Rawlston Charles and Charlie's Records

Rawlston Charles (b. 1946) was a second Brooklyn-based record producer who would emerge as Straker's main rival in the 1970s and 1980s. A native of Delaford, Tobago, he moved to Port of Spain as a teenager, and then, at age twenty-one, migrated to Brooklyn. Charles recalls how he arrived in 1967, carrying a suitcase and a record: "I don't even know why I walked into the plane with that Kitchener album under my arm, . . . but I took up that album and brought it to America with me, not knowing at the time that it was probably a symbol of what my calling would be."[47] Charles found work as an auto mechanic but soon began pursuing his passion for music by spinning records at West Indian fetes in Brooklyn. In 1972 he quit his day job and opened his own shop, Charlie's Records, at 1265 Fulton Street, selling primarily R&B and soul music. Soon he began importing calypso discs from K.H. and other Trinidad-based outlets. Like Straker, he quickly realized that New York offered superior studios and production facilities, and that in the long run it would be more economical to move production north, where the Caribbean audience was expanding and interest by non-Caribbean listeners might be nurtured. In 1973 he established his own label, Charlie's Records, and began traveling back and forth to Trinidad in search of promising calypsonians and their songs.[48] Charles's decision turned out to be well-timed. As the 1970s unfolded, Trinidad's record industry was on the wane and many calypsonians were looking abroad for better opportunities to record, mix, and distribute their music.[49]

One of Charles's first successful projects was to license and distribute Lord Shorty's *Sweet Music* LP in 1976. Often cited as the most important originator of the soca style, the calypsonian Garfield "Lord Shorty" Blackman (b. 1941) consciously attempted to reinvigorate calypso, which by the early 1970s, he claimed, was "dying a natural death" as "reggae was [becoming] the thing."[50] Shorty's original concept was to combine calypso with indigenous Trinidadian East Indian musical instruments and rhythms to form the new style of "sokah"—"so" from calypso and "kah," the first letter of the Indian alphabet and a symbol of Indian rhythm.[51] But in 1976 journalists began to refer to Shorty's style as "soca," jettisoning the East Indian reference and instead stressing the fusion of African American soul music ("so") and traditional calypso ("ca"). Shorty claimed his 1976 hit "Sweet Music" maintained an Indian rhythmic sensibility without the Indian instruments he had used on previous albums (the *dholak* double-headed drum and the *dhantal* metal clapper), but had no objections when a review of the LP lauded his new "soul calypso" sound as "a perfect marriage" of the two styles.[52]

"Sweet Music" was arranged by Ed Watson (b. 1930), a popular Trinidadian bandleader and veteran of Sparrow's Young Brigade calypso tent who had begun arranging for Shorty in 1973.[53] His arrangement, with its minor chordal progression and opening modal synthesizer line feels vaguely East Indian, while Shorty's cool and restrained signing, coupled with the backup vocals, project a haunting quality associated with African American soul balladeers of the period.[54] Shorty, Watson, and Charles all understood that the song had a potential audience beyond Trinidad's Carnival enthusiasts, and Charlie's Records promised to be the conduit to North American audiences.

Linda McArthur Sandy Lewis, aka Calypso Rose (b. 1940), was another highly influential calypsonian to record for Charles during the early years of his label. A native of Tobago, Rose had established herself as the leading female calypsonian of her generation with her 1967 hit "Fire in Me Wire," recorded on Trinidad's National record label. In 1969, under the management of the African American promoter Earl Harris, she came to New York to perform for the Madison Square Garden calypso extravaganzas. In subsequent years Harris would bring her up to play Madison Square Garden and tour other American cities. She became friends with the Trinidadian limbo dancer Merlyn Gill, who owned a house on Glassboro Avenue in Jamaica, Queens, where Rose would stay for months between Mother's Day and Labor Day Carnival. But she would always go back to Trinidad for the Carnival season, winning the Calypso Queen contest consecutively from 1972 through 1976. There she ran into Granville Straker in a calypso tent and agreed to record for him. He set her up with arranger Art de Coteau, and in 1973 Straker released the LP S*plish Splash*.[55]

Meanwhile, Rose had grown disillusioned with the Trinidad Carnival scene, which would not allow her to compete in the prestigious Calypso King contest and denied her the Road March title year after year in spite of popular protest.[56] In 1975 she relocated to Queens and began attending criminology school in New York while continuing to sing at various Brooklyn venues and at Labor Day Carnival. In 1976 she contacted Rawlston Charles and recorded two singles on his label, including "Labour Day Breakaway," which celebrated Brooklyn Carnival, encouraging her man to "mash up Eastern Parkway."[57] In the fall of 1976 she wrote what would be one of her most successful songs, "Give More Tempo":

I was going to school, studying Criminology in Manhattan, and living in Queens. So I would ride the F train every morning, and the sound of the train wheel going takak-taka-taka every morning gave me the idea for the rhythm of the song "Give Me Tempo." So when I was in class and a line would come in my head, and I would ask to go to the ladies' room. And I would go and be dancing and writing the song in my head. So I wrote that song studying criminology, but I never thought it would win the Road March![58]

Though possibly not labeled soca in 1977, in retrospect the piece's rapid tempo, prominent use of the synthesizer, and compact party lyrics exhorting listeners to jam and roll up the streets of San Fernando would soon be hallmarks of the new style.[59]

The story of "Tempo" embodies the transnational nature of calypso/soca production in the 1970s. Accompanying herself on guitar, Rose recorded the lyrics and basic melody of the song onto a cassette tape, which she gave to Charles, who in turn shipped it back to Art de Coteau in Trinidad. On his next trip south, Charles was not satisfied with the arrangement de Coteau had come up with: "I just paid Art de Coteau and all the musicians who worked on the song and took the tape and dumped it in the garbage right there in front of them," he recalled. "Everyone said I was a madman, but I knew what I was hearing in my head and would not settle for less than that."[60] At the prompting of Trinidad studio producer Ellis Chow Lin On, Charles took Rose's original cassette recording of "Tempo" to the then unknown pianist/arranger Pelham Goddard. Goddard arranged and recorded the rhythm section and horns in Trinidad and mailed the tape to Brooklyn, where Rose recorded her lead vocal and Charles added overdubs and oversaw the final mix. "Tempo" won the Carnival Road March title in 1977—a coup for Calypso Rose and Charlie's Records—and marked the beginning of a long and fruitful relationship between Charles and Goddard.[61]

The following year, "Come Leh We Jam" won Rose her second consecutive Trinidad Road March title, and "Her Royal Majesty" and "I Thank Thee" earned her the Calypso Monarch award, marking the first time a woman had taken the title. All three songs were collaborations with Goddard, recorded in Trinidad and Brooklyn and released on Charlie's Records. Using New York as her base of operations, Rose continued to record for Charlie's Records and began to tour nationally and across Europe, Africa, and Central and South America, returning only occasionally to Trinidad, but no longer competing in Carnival competitions. She was one of the few calypsonians of her generation to move beyond the confines of the Caribbean, serving as an international ambassador for the music and a staunch advocate for women's equal participation in calypso and soca.[62]

In the wake of his successful arrangements for Rose, Goddard formed an alliance with Charles. A native of St. James, Port of Spain, Goddard (b. 1946) was a pianist who had taught himself to read music and the rudiments of band arranging through a correspondence course offered by the Berklee College of Music in Boston. In the early 1970s he began arranging for the Third World Steel Orchestra and playing keyboards and arranging for Clive Bradley's Esquires Brass ensemble, which played instrumental versions of calypsos and American R&B and soul tunes. In 1975 Goddard formed a small band, Sensational Roots, which became the studio band for Trinidad's Corral/K.H. Studios. Meanwhile, after hearing an impressive performance by the well-outfitted Jamaican band Baron Lee and the Dragonaires at Trinidad Carnival, Charles decided to invest in Goddard and Chow Lin On's Sensational Roots. He brought them to New York to purchase some $14,000 worth of high-end equipment to beef up their sound and allow them to become a stage as well as a studio group. In return, Sensational Roots changed its name to Charlie's Roots and would go on to become one of the most influential soca bands of the 1980s. Goddard, working through Charlie's Records, established himself as a premier soca arranger of the 1980s, collaborating with David Rudder on his Calypso Monarch–winning "Hammer" in 1986, and arranging a number of winning Road March title songs for Rudder, Blue Boy, and Tambu in the 1980s and early 1990s.[63]

At the same time he was having success with Rose, Charles began working with Lord Kitchener, the most venerated of the older generation of calypsonians. Charles distributed Kitchener's 1977 album *Hot and Sweet*, and later that year went into K.H. Studios with the singer and the arranger Ed Watson to work on a second production that would yield a song many critics contend helped establish the legitimacy of soca. According to Watson, Kitchener was having trouble coming up with a final song to fill out the LP that would be titled *Melodies of the 21st Century*:

Kitchener brought me nine songs to arrange for the album, but he couldn't come up with the tenth song—back then you needed ten for the album. So one day we had been rehearsing the nine songs at my house and I said "Kitch, I have a nice beat, and I'm going to play it and see if you can make something of it." So I played: bum-bum-bum-bum [sings opening synthesizer/bass line]—I played the bass line and the four chord structure on the piano. And he said "I like that. I will make a tune on that today." And in seventeen minutes he made that song! He never stopped to think, he just sang. . . . And he didn't even know that "Sugar Bum Bum" would be the big hit you know. He ended up putting it as the ninth song, on the B side of the album! He wasn't accustomed to that kind of (soca) music.[64]

Charles confirmed that Kitchener was not terribly excited about the new song, but back in the studio he and Watson encouraged the calypsonian to polish and finally record the piece. Watson and Charles brought the tapes back to New York and oversaw the final mix at Manhattan's Music Farms studio. "Sugar Bum Bum" was exceptionally popular when it was released for the 1978 Carnival season. Evidently this was a surprise to Kitchener, but not to Charles, who later recalled, "I knew right away this was[a] hit. Now Kitchener did not see it as a hit, and many of my colleagues did not see it as a hit at first—they said 'No, no, no!' but I said 'Yes, yes, yes!'"[65] The song caused a minor uproar at the Road March title and Calypso Monarch competitions when Roaring Lion and other calypsonians claimed the piece was too far into the soca vein to be considered legitimate calypso.[66] Rose ended up sweeping the competition that year, but "Sugar

Bum Bum" would become Kitchener's best-selling record, and with its success, Guilbault proclaimed that "soca became firmly established as a style."[67] Musically, "Sugar Bum Bum" remained rooted in a calypso form, but its catchy opening melodic bass pattern, airy synthesizer lines (played by Pelham Goddard), and four-beat, cyclical rhythmic pattern provided enough modern soca elements to distinguish it from Kitchener's previous calypso classics. But without Charles's encouragement it is unclear whether the first soca hit recording would have ever seen the light of day.[68]

The success of "Sugar Bum Bum" signaled not only the rising tide of soca music, but also the increasingly vital role that arrangers like Watson would play in shaping the new style. Watson's original bass line and chord pattern inspired Kitchener's vocal melody and lyric. Moreover, his lengthy introduction, built around lushly interwoven bass, synthesizer, and horn lines, provided the song's primary hook. In retrospect one might argue that Watson deserved full co-authorship of the final composition.

With Kitchener and Rose now out front with the new soca style, it was not long before Sparrow, who like Chalkdust had initially expressed his reservations about the new sound, began to come around. In 1979 Charles produced and mixed Sparrow's *New York Blackout* LP, the title song humorously recounting Sparrow's waking up to the shock of the power blackout of 12 July 1977 and the mayhem that ensued on the streets of Brooklyn. Perhaps noting Goddard's and Watson's recent successful embrace of soca with "Tempo" and "Sugar Bum Bum," Art de Coteau set out to create a more up-to-date sound for calypso's most prominent singer. Nearly all the selections are up-tempo, percussion-heavy dance pieces with pumped-up bass figures that often doubled Sparrow's voice and the horn lines. The bass is used most effectively to create strong counterpoint lines and for voice doubling on "First Black Miss Universe" and "Life Down in Hell."[69]

The soca elements are even more evident on Sparrow's next album, *Mighty Sparrow—25th Anniversary*, which was arranged by de Coteau, co-produced by Sparrow and Charles, and released on Sparrow Music in 1979 and on Charlie's Records in 1980. Pelham Goddard's synthesizer lines, which were backgrounded in the *Blackout* LP, are front and center on the *Anniversary* release, evoking a contemporary feeling that mirrored popular funk and disco styles of the era. "Don't Drop the Tempo," for example, is pure soca. Opening with a slinky synthesizer line set in a call-and-response structure with staccato horn riffs, the piece chugs along with an up-tempo dance groove anchored in an anacrusis bass pattern. In case anyone misses the point, Sparrow announces that "this is a new era with people getting soca fever" as he exhorts revelers to "wine faster, grind faster" and finally "don't drop the tempo." But the LP clearly demonstrated that Sparrow's embrace of the new soca instrumentation and styling did not preclude him from continuing to write songs with serious social commentary. "Save the World" is a plea for universal love and social justice; "London Bridge Is Falling Down" offers a satirical rumination about the fall of the British Empire; and "Dead or Alive" recounts the exploits of

Figure 6.4. Lord Kitchener, *Melodies of the 21st Century*, Charlie's Records, 1978.

contemporary global despots Idi Amin of Uganda, Anastasio Somoza Debayle of Nicaragua, Patrick John of Dominica, and the Shah of Iran. Sparrow's early foray into soca showed there was ample space for provocative political messaging and heavy dance grooves in the same song.[70]

Besides addressing international issues, Sparrow would occasionally comment on his local experiences in songs like "I Love New York," which appeared as a twelve-inch "Disco" disc arranged by Art de Coteau and released on Charlie's Records in 1982 (recorded at K.H. Studios, Trinidad, overdubs at Music Farms Studio, NYC, and mixed at Right Track Recordings, NYC). The song's lyrics recount Sparrow's sardonic observations of the city's teachers' and sanitation workers' strikes ("Garbage piled up high / all around me"), as well as the brazen displays of drugs, prostitution, violence, and poverty he encountered on a daily basis. Despite it all, he ironically proclaims in the crooning chorus, "I Love New York," the city he now claimed as his primary residence.[71]

In addition to the best-known Trinidadian calypsonians, Charles also worked with singers from other islands, who sometimes found it difficult to break into the Trinidad recording scene. One of the most important was Rupert "King Swallow" Philo (b. 1946), the best-known calypso singer

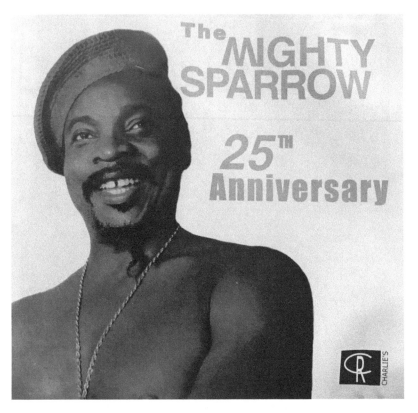

Figure 6.5. Mighty Sparrow, *25th Anniversary*, Charlie's Records 1980.

from Antigua and winner of that country's Carnival Road March title and Calypso Monarch competition on numerous occasions in the 1970s and early 1980s. After capturing his first calypso crown in 1973, Swallow traveled to Port of Spain with hopes of making a recording. There he met Romey Abramson, a producer who handled distribution for Charlie's Records in Trinidad. Abramson was so impressed with Swallow that, on the spot, he called Charles in Brooklyn and convinced him to support a recording of Swallow's winning tune, "March for Freedom." Based on the success of this first venture, Swallow began making a series of LPs for Charles in 1975, working with the arrangers Joey Lewis, Frankie Francis, Ed Watson, and Art de Coteau. The initial recordings were made in Trinidad's K.H. Studios. Swallow recalled that following the recording sessions he would fly to New York, hand deliver the master tape to Charles, and often sit in on the mixing sessions. Charles, he recollected, did more than simply balance the tracks: "Charlie would listen to the master tape and then say 'OK, we can add something to this, we can make this sound better.' So then he would start adding—maybe another guitar, some other fills, maybe a saxophone or other horn lines. And he would even put some effects (reverb, equalizing) on the lead and background vocals, to fill them out. It would always be a good, full orchestration."[72] Swallow's 1979 recording, "Don't Stop the Party," recorded in Trinidad and mixed in New York, was typical. Musically, it was another early de Coteau excursion into soca, featuring a heavy melodic bass line, swirling synthesizer riffs, a bluesy soprano sax solo, and lyrics exhorting dancers to keep the party going at all costs.

By the early 1980s, Swallow was traveling to New York more frequently, often for month-long stints to record, mix, and perform. Typically, he would arrive in Brooklyn sometime in the spring to work on a new recording, aiming to have a release in time for Antigua's August Carnival. He would return home in the early summer months to sing and oversee his own calypso tent, and then rush back to Brooklyn in late August to perform in the WIADCA Labor Day Dimanche Gras show and other Carnival festivities. In September he would travel back to Antigua for a respite, then return to Brooklyn for further recording. After Christmas he would move on to Trinidad for their Lenten Carnival season. In between, he would tour to other Caribbean islands and occasionally to England. Unlike Sparrow, Nelson, Duke, and Rose, Swallow never took up full-time residence in New York, preferring to travel in and out of the city several times a year, staying in an apartment that Charles made available to him. Charles produced some twenty LPs and EPs by Swallow from the mid-1970s through the mid-1990s. In return for this support, Swallow remained loyal to Charles, and unlike most calypso/soca singers did not venture off to record for other labels. Because he could not compete in the prestigious Trinidad Calypso Monarch contest, given his Antiguan citizenship, Swallow was heavily indebted to Charles and Brooklyn Carnival for building his reputation as a singer.[73] He paid homage to his home-away-from-home with a 1988 album titled *Swallow on the Streets of Brooklyn*. Recorded and mixed by Charles in his new Fulton Street studio, the LP included one of Swallow's most popular hits, "Fire in the Backseat," arranged by Frankie McIntosh. The album cover featured a photo of Swallow, perched on a motorcycle on Fulton Street, surrounded by a collage of Brooklyn music club logos and the names of three prominent Brooklyn boulevards: Eastern Parkway, Flatbush Avenue, and Nostrand Avenue.

Early one morning, following an all-night recording session in a midtown Manhattan studio, Swallow and Charles prepared to board the A train to go back to Brooklyn:

There was this guy coming up the stairs from the subway, and we were going down. And this guy says to us: "Hey mon—subway jammed mon!" Which means it was crowded. So Charlie looks at me, and I look at him, and it just got there—subway jam—and the story started popping! So I wrote that song, "Subway Jam," right here in Brooklyn. I just made up the story—like you have all the trains going in different directions—the A, the G, the F. . . . And I was thinking about how Brooklyn was made up of people from all the islands— Antigua, Trinidad, Barbados, you know—and back then most of them did not have cars, so they all rode the subway. So I wanted to get all the different island people involved with the music [the song], so everyone would want a copy.[74]

Around the time of Swallow's New York subway incident, one of his early arrangers, Ed Watson, introduced him to a young and relatively unknown Trinidad arranger named Leston Paul. With Charles's encouragement, Swallow took his subway song to Paul. The resulting "Subway Jam," released in 1981 on Charlie's Records, was a soca masterpiece that highlighted the young arranger's talents. The piece opens with a chugging dance grove underpinned by a syncopated bass guitar line that is doubled on a low register synthesizer. The bass figures interlock with drums, guitar, a bouncy synthesizer mid-register figure, and call-and-response brass and wind lines. The instruments eventually join on a dramatic ascending phrase that leads into Swallow's vocals, which recount a fanciful story of a New York subway station transformed into a huge fete: "Every subway station steaming with action / The place like a disco no train in motion / The man in the booth that's selling the tokens / Leave the booth and come to join in the action." Swallow captures the chaos, energy, and diversity of the subway experience, calling out the home islands of Caribbean New Yorkers partaking in the station revelry: Trinidad, Antigua, Haiti, Barbados, Grenada, Jamaica, St. Vincent, Dominica, St. Lucia, and Monserrat.[75] Unlike the newly arrived immigrant protagonist of Lord Invader's 1946 "New York Subway," who is totally baffled by the modern trains, Swallow's 1980s Caribbean New Yorkers rule the mass transit system.

Swallow's young arranger, Leston Paul (b. 1957), was a native of Port of Spain who grew up in a strict Catholic family that frowned on steel pan yards and calypso tents. His grandfather, Ince Paul, showed him the rudiments of piano technique, and, as a teenager, he took several years of formal piano lessons while teaching himself to play steel pan, drums, and bass by ear. At age nineteen he joined the Tropical Ambassadors dance orchestra, playing piano and eventually arranging the group's material after bandleader Willard Paul provided him with several books on music theory and arranging. This led to a job scoring lead sheets for calypso singers and eventually to his first break in the music business—in 1980 he was asked to arrange the Mighty Duke's *Harps of Gold* album, which was released on the Trinidad Sharc label that year. Rawlston Charles was impressed with Paul's work on the Duke album and invited the young arranger to come to New York to work on projects with Swallow and Kitchener. Paul had been exposed to a great deal of American popular funk and soul music on Trinidad radio stations as a youngster, but being in New York intensified the experience. "Listening to American music really helped me learn a lot about music, the chords, the instruments, the overall arrangements, everything—then actually going to the States opened up a whole new world for me." Paul was impressed with the high quality of the New York studios and the musicians he met there, particularly the American horn players, who he felt were more technically advanced then their Trinidadian counterparts and more capable of properly articulating his complex horn lines.[76]

Paul's bass lines were clearly influenced by American funk and soul styles that emphasized both the percussive and melodic possibilities of the electric bass guitar. For him the bass lines were so important that he often overdubbed them himself after the basic rhythm and horn tracks had been laid down. He referred to this as a "reverse approach" to arranging—that is, a process where the bass was added at the end only after he had totally immersed himself in the basic rhythms, chordal structure, and melodic horn figures of his protean arrangement. When things were going right "the bass lines would just fall out of the sky for me, and I would pick up a bass guitar, grab the engineer, tell him to turn on the recorder, and away we would go."[77]

Paul is probably best known for his collaboration with Monserrat singer Alphonsus "Arrow" Cassell (1949–2010)—with whom Charles began working in 1981. Sometime the following year, Paul and Arrow went into the Eras Studio in New York to record what would turn out to be the most popular soca record of the 1980s, "Hot Hot Hot." Charles was involved in the project during the initial rehearsals, but Arrow eventually decided to hire Paul himself to arrange and oversee the recording sessions. He then released the record on his own Arrow Records label in 1982. A small number of *Hot Hot Hot* LPs were eventually issued on the Charlie's Records label, but the main American distribution went through J&M records, another Brooklyn-based company owned by calypsonian Winston "Gypsy" Peters and his wife Marva Peters.[78] Musically, Arrow and Paul's "Hot Hot Hot" was a quintessential blend of calypso with American funk, soul, and rock, with a brief nod to rap. Paul's seven-minute arrangement opens with a funk-style slap bass trading riffs with rock guitar lines, followed by the catchy "olé, olé" vocal hook and the "Feeling Hot-Hot-Hot" chorus. A I-IV-V-IV chord progression cycles throughout the duration of the song. Paul's snappy brass lines and synthesizer fills enter, leading into Arrow's initial verse. Following a series of verses and choruses comes a percussion break with Arrow and the chorus rhythmically chanting "People in the party, hot hot hot / All the party people say they're feeling hot" [4:18]. After an extended groove section alternating between vocal chant and horn riffs comes a heavy-metal-style guitar solo by Chris Newland, a white American rock guitarist who was brought in especially for the session [6:00]. "Hot Hot Hot" achieved unprecedented popularity in New York, England, and the Caribbean, and reached a wider American and international audience after it was covered by American pop singer David Johansen (under the pseudo-name Buster Poindexter) in 1987.[79]

Paul would eventually go on to work for Michael Gould and B's Records, where he would be recognized, along with Goddard, as one of the top soca arrangers of the 1980s. He was a master of rhythm and texture, skillfully interlocking innovative bass lines with pulsing drums, prominent synthesizer countermelodies, and punchy horn riffs to create groove-based arrangements that were dance-hall favorites. Of all the Caribbean arrangers, he was probably the most influenced by American funk, soul, and rock, and he was always eager to experiment with new sounds and styles.

Frankie McIntosh, while primarily employed as Straker's musical director and arranger, occasionally worked for Charles, who hired him to arrange for several artists, including the Trinidadian calypsonian Winston "Explainer" Henry (b. 1947). Explainer began his career singing in Sparrow's Young Brigade tent in the late 1970s and recording for the Trinidadian labels Semp and Umbala before coming to the United States in 1980. He recalled, "New York at that time was the happening place for calypso. Charlie had all the stars, and staying in Trinidad was not really the in thing—so I went to New York and met Charlie."[80] Charles licensed and distributed Explainer's 1981 LP *One Day*, which had been recorded in Trinidad and included his popular tune "Ras Mas." The following year Charles brought Explainer and McIntosh together in Brooklyn to record *Man from the Ghetto*, which included the tune "Lorraine." Explainer gives much of the credit for the song's success to McIntosh, who took his skeletal melody and lyrics and created the arrangement, and then encouraged him to record it when Explainer favored other new tunes that he felt would be more competitive in Trinidad. McIntosh was proven right—with "Lorraine," Explainer came in second in the Calypso Monarch competition, and it became his best-selling record to date. The song was popular in New York as well, capturing the Caribbean migrants' longing for home and the emotional trauma resulting from the departure of a loved one from Brooklyn back to Trinidad. The lyrics were based on Explainer's actual experience when he announced to his girlfriend (given the pseudonym Lorraine) that he was going back to Trinidad for Carnival and she reacted with tears and by hiding his passport: "Lorraine you better wake up / Ah need ah jet plane to take me non-stop / Ah Can't stay in New York City / When there is sunshine and pan in my country."[81]

Explainer went on to record half a dozen more LPs on Charlie's Records in the 1980s. He recalls with satisfaction the somewhat unconventional business arrangement that Charles worked out with him and other calypsonians. Charles would front the money to record and produce the record. In lieu of any upfront pay or royalties, he would give the stamper of the recording and rights to reproduce the record in the Caribbean to the artist, while he maintained control of the North American and British distribution. All profits of these sales went to Charles, but the artist took all profits from the Caribbean sales after he or she paid to have additional records and jackets manufactured.

In 1984 Charles took a bold step and built a sound studio above his Fulton Street record shop. His move was judicious, as by the early 1980s Trinidad's two record-pressing plants had closed down and few recording studios were operating.[82] Frustrated with the high cost of renting studio time, Charles invested over $100,000 in equipment to create a state-of-the-art recording and mixing facility, including a 32-track Neve 8068 console board that he imported from London (see Figure 6.6). With this equipment Charles had much greater latitude to record and mix on his own schedule. He spent considerable time at the latter, working closely with the sound engineers Eddy Youngblood, Ralph Moss, and Franklin Grant to balance and equalize the tracks to his liking, occasionally adding additional horn and percussion overdubs, including a drum machine track.[83] He viewed mixing as an art, as the final touches that would make a great recording, and by all accounts he had a knack for it. "It was a gift. We all realized that Charlie had an ear," reflected Swallow, who sat in on many of Charles's mixing sessions. "Now he didn't know [read] music or play an instrument—but he knew what he wanted. And he had this natural inclination to realize that this fits with this, that this goes well with that."[84] With the Neve mixing board Charles's recordings became known for their "fat sound," as one musician put it, emphasizing depth and booming bass. [85]

Meanwhile, Charles had bought the adjacent building and set up rehearsal space and living quarters for visiting friends and artists. David Rudder, who would emerge as one of the most influential soca singers of the 1980s and 1990s, recalls visiting Brooklyn for several months around Labor Day throughout the 1980s, staying at Charles's apartment and hanging out around the Fulton Street neighborhood:

> That stretch around Charlie's on Fulton Street was a great action and great energy. It was like the Caribbean, but in another country. And

Figure 6.6. Rawlston Charles in his studio, 1984. Photo by Kevin Burke.

Charlie had a lot of energy—whatever era people had migrated in, that was the space they were stuck in, so to speak. So you would see these different eras of people hanging around by Charlie's studio. You see different aspects of Trinidad, and different generations. There was an energy there, you know? The idea of going to New York was always a big thing for most people around the world, so you looked forward to going up to his studio for a visit.[86]

According to Rudder, he, Goddard, and their band Charlie's Roots still preferred to record in the friendly confines of the Corral Studio in Sea Lots, Trinidad. They did, however, enjoy hanging around Charles's Brooklyn studio, where Goddard would work out instrumental arrangements and Rudder would assist with mixing and arranging background vocals. The group's landmark album, *The Hammer*, which included the 1986 Road March title–winning "Bahia Gayl" and the Calypso Monarch-winning "Hammer," was released on Charlie's Records, while most of the band's albums were on Rudder's own Lypsoland label. But Charles and Rudder had an agreement that the Lypsoland LPs would also have a Charlie's Records number and that Charles would handle distribution in the United States and Europe, while Rudder would concentrate on Trinidad and the Caribbean.

By the mid-1980s, Rawlston Charles's studio had become a destination for singers, musicians, and arrangers from across the English-speaking Caribbean. He possessed a deep understanding of the music and a seemingly innate talent for identifying potentially popular calypso and soca songs, as arranger and longtime collaborator Ed Watson reflected, "Charlie had a good head for the music and a great ear. And you know any tunes that Charlie says will be hitting, ninety out of a hundred will be hits!"[87] Charles would see his business diminish significantly with the advent of CDs and digital pirating in the early 1990s, but for two decades his label put out thousands of sides and promoted the top calypso and soca singers in the business. Surveying his achievements, a 1982 profile in *Everybody's Caribbean Magazine* proclaimed him to be "the most prolific calypso producer in the United States and Trinidad, releasing most calypso records sold in this country, and providing stampers for most calypso records manufactured in Trinidad."[88] Charles never made a deal with a major American or British label that might have led to more significant sales, but he did establish networks of distribution that brought the music out of the Caribbean to North America, Europe, and Africa.

B's Records and J&W Records

The early 1980s saw an increase in demand for calypso and soca recordings, and the success of Straker and Charles as record producers and distributors did not go unnoticed by other ambitious Caribbean businessmen. One such entrepreneur was Michael Gould, a Trinidad native who had success running restaurants in Brooklyn. Sometime around 1980 Gould recruited the calypso singer King Wellington to run a calypso tent for the Labor Day Carnival season. Wellington, with the help of another Trinidadian friend, Kenrick Meade, organized B's Calypso Castle for Gould in a building on Fulton Street, not far from Charlie's Calypso City record store. Based on the success of this initial venture, Gould decided to move into the recording business, founding his own label, B's Records. Beginning in late 1981, with Wellington enlisting talent and Meade organizing recording sessions and record production, the B's label began issuing LP recordings of the popular calypsonians Wellington, Melody, Duke, Nelson, Gypsy, Baron, and Penguin. Gould did not have the depth of musical knowledge or breadth of contacts of a Straker or Charles, but his previous business ventures had left him awash in assets, and he was not hesitant to pay hefty up-front fees for artists and arrangers, or to invest in state-of-the-art studio recording and mixing equipment as well as high-end jacket-art to assure a quality product. Nor did he and his associates shy away from encouraging singers and musicians to expand the new soca sound by borrowing generously from contemporary American soul, funk, and disco styles.[89]

One of Gould's first efforts was to produce the LP *Over and Over and Over Again*, featuring the Mighty Duke. The project was begun by Rawlston Charles in the Sharc Studio in Trinidad, but Gould convinced Charles to sell him the initial tapes and then brought Leston Paul and Duke into Brooklyn's Sound Heights studio to rearrange and re-record much of the original material. Released in 1982, the album sold well and demonstrated the willingness of Duke and Paul to draw on contemporary American music styles. Meade recalls that by the early 1980s, Duke was consciously pursuing a crossover strategy that involved blending his calypsos with American R&B, soul, and rock music. In his liner notes, Meade introduced Duke as "one of the architects of the beat called soca," and predicted listeners would be "intoxicated with the smooth merging to American music and soca in the song 'Is It Groovy Now.'" Indeed the piece pulses to a straight-ahead disco beat and features funk-derived syncopated bass and synthesizer lines, choke-style wa-wa guitar, staccato horn fills, and a smooth background chorus behind Duke's lilting, soulful vocals. Around three minutes into the piece the voices and melodic instruments drop out for a brief percussion break. As the bass returns he rhythmically raps: "I'm a soca man, from soca land / I'm out here with, my soca band / To play for you, is what I do / So this is what I'm asking you." The background vocals respond with the repeated question, "Is it groovy?," followed by an instrumental dance groove section where the band hangs on a single chord and the guitar, horns, and synthesizer rotate funk-style riffs. Together, Paul's instrumental arrangement and Duke's vocals created a disco/funk sound reminiscent of Cool and the Gang and Earth, Wind, and Fire, only with a Caribbean tinge.[90] Other songs on the album are richly textured with Paul's synthesizer lines, played on the Prophet 5, which at the time was state-of-the-art technology not available in Trinidad.[91] He even dispenses with the horns on the funk-infused "Point of Direction" and the reggae-style "Babylon Go Fall," relying solely on interlocking synthesizer themes and riffs to fill out the instrumental sections.

Following the success of *Over and Over*, Gould and Meade recruited Paul to arrange for Poser (1982), Penguin (1983), Baron (1985), and a host of other top calypso and soca singers who rushed to record on the B's label.[92] With Gould rarely involved in studio work, Paul had more freedom in the recording and mixing process than he did with Charles, who took a much more hands-on approach to his productions. The final mixing, which Paul insisted on overseeing, had become increasingly important following the advent of sophisticated multitrack mixing boards that were available in New York studios by the early 1980s. As he explained, "The mix could either make or break a record. You could have the best recording, the best tracks, the best arrangement, and it fails if you have a mix where the levels are not right, the person doesn't know how to bring up certain frequencies that supposed to come up the levels and not putting the right ingredients like the reverb and other effects."[93] By mid-decade, Paul had assumed the main arranging responsibilities for B's Records and had organized his own band, Leston Paul and the New York Connection. The group consisted of a rotating cast of Caribbean and American musicians based in New York, and functioned primarily as a studio band that featured vocalist Lennox Picou singing hits from the previous Carnival season.[94]

Lord Melody was one of the old-guard New York–based calypsonians whom Wellington and Meade convinced to record for B's early on. Toward the end of his illustrious career, Melody's songs began to move away from the traditional calypso style that had made him famous in the late 1950s and 1960s on his earlier Straker recordings. For example, *I Man*, arranged by Art de Coteau and released in the United States on Charlie's Records in 1979, was an early excursion into reggae themes and soca-style accompaniment. Melody recorded his two final albums, *Brown Sugar* (1982) and *Lola* (1983), for B's. The LPs, arranged by Earl Rodney, featured medium-tempo soca rhythms, melodic bass lines, and modest synthesizer fills. On all three albums, Melody's aging but still mellifluous voice remained foregrounded, brimming with clever lyrics and referencing Rastafarian culture with songs like "Rastaman" and "Bob Marley." The title songs to Melody's two B's LPs, "Brown Sugar" and "Lola," drew on contemporaneous soca party themes, celebrating dance and the singer's disco-dancing lovers. As he approached his sixth decade, Lord Melody, one of Trinidad's most venerated calypsonians, had joined Kitchener and Sparrow on the soca train at the behest of Charles and Gould.[95]

Given his affinity for American disco, funk, and soul, Lord Nelson was a natural candidate for Gould's new label. Nelson had recorded for several Trinidad-based companies, as well as for Hodge, Straker, and Charles. But as was the norm for calypsonians, he had no exclusive contract, and thus was receptive to Gould's financial offer to record for B's. By that time Nelson had forged an alliance with the renowned steelband arranger Clive Bradley, who had relocated in New York sometime in the late 1970s.

Bradley arranged Nelson's popular LPs *Black Gold* (1978) and *Disco Daddy* (1980) for Charlie's Records, as well as Nelson's initial two LPs for B's Records, *Family* (1982) and *We Like It* (1983). Nelson recalls how he and Bradley would often collaborate on arrangements, working out instrumental introductions and bridge sections during studio sessions, with Bradley writing out horn and bass lines on the spot and handing them to musicians to play.[96] Bradley was evidently enamored enough with Nelson's songs to arrange "Jenny" (from the *Family* LP) for steelband and win the Brooklyn Panorama competition in 1982.

Like Paul and Nelson, Bradley was strongly influenced by American popular music. "Music Land," on the *Black Gold* LP, opens with heavy syncopated bass and funk-rock guitar and synthesizer licks, climaxing with a sweet-soul vocal chorus describing a magical musical dance land. The title track, "Disco Daddy," thumps to a four/four disco beat over electric piano, synthesizer, and wah-wah guitar and melodic bass accompaniment. "Bald Head Rasta," from the same LP, pulses to a reggae beat anchored by lead bass/synthesizer lines and off-beat organ and guitar hits. "Ah Going to Party Tonight," from *Family*, foregrounds a melodic bass line that doubles the main vocal melody and is repeated throughout a standard band chorus, vocal verse, vocal chorus structure, while jazzy guitar fills by Jeff Medina and bluesy synthesizer/organ runs by Bradley provide R&B shadings. Bradley's arrangement of "Gimme Love," also from the *Family* LP, moves deeper into a contemporary American vein, employing diminished piano chords, broken bass, atmospheric guitar and flute runs, and smooth background vocals to create a light jazz/funk sound to support Nelson's crooning ode to his lover. "Super Star," from, the same LP, opens with an ascending rock guitar line and features psychedelic guitar breaks and dissonant horn riffs interspersed between Nelson's cynical observations on the cult of celebrity. "Mih Lover," one of Nelson's most enduring recordings from *We Like It*, is built around a memorable chorus hook, "Oh, let's have a good good time," and a catchy descending synthesizer line that weaves throughout Nelson's ruminations on love and jealousy. "My Love and I," another light-jazz-tinged love song, opens with a syncopated, staccato vocal chorus and airy flute line, switches to a three-beat pulse (1:15) for a guitar/synthesizer interlude, before returning to the standard four-beat meter for the verse and chorus before winding down with two jazzy guitar solos (3:48 and 4:45). Stylistically, these Bradley arrangements owe as much to American jazz, rock, and funk as they do to calypso. When paired with Nelson's universal themes of love and partying, they were clearly designed to appeal to a wider audience beyond the immediate Caribbean community.[97]

Nelson identified the melodic bass line as the quintessential stylistic marker of soca, a genre he claims to have helped invent without receiving ample credit.[98] Upon listening to his 1983 recording of "Mih Lover," he spontaneously began singing the bass line and went on to explain:

See that's my own bass line. And if you listen properly to most of my calypsos you hear that the bass line has its own melody going on, and I sing over that. That is where soca came from . . . I had the formula. . . . I used to go to Clive Bradley and hum the bass line and he would play it on the piano. In 95% of my songs, it's the bass line that carries the music there that I could sing over. Shorty and Maestro never did that—I was the only one.[99]

Ascribing soca's origin to one individual is dangerous speculation, but there can be no question that Nelson, occasionally dismissed in the Caribbean as the "Yankee calypsonian" due to his permanent expatriate status in New York, contributed immensely to the emergence of the style. More than any other calypso singer of his generation, he succeeded in integrating elements of African American popular music into his distinctive sound.

Like McIntosh and Paul, Bradley brought a mix of musicians into Brooklyn studios to work with Nelson and other B's artists. While the core group of B's studio musicians were originally from Trinidad and adjacent islands, many had relocated to New York to study, play, and record. Some, like Bradley (who played keyboard on many recording sessions), guitarist Jeff Medina, alto saxophonist Eddie Quarless, trumpeter Errol Ince, drummer Earl Wise, and background singer Glenda Ifle, were Trinidad expatriates living full-time in New York during the 1980s. Others, like Paul (who played keyboards and occasionally bass in his recording sessions), guitarists Junior Wharwood and Tony Voisin, drummer Bugs Niles, alto-sax player Roy Cape, and trumpeter Clyde Mitchell, were based in Trinidad and traveled regularly to New York to play and record. But not all the musicians hailed from Trinidad. New York–based bassist Marcelino Thompson and trumpeter Al Demarco were of Panamanian heritage, and saxophonist Charles Daugherty was originally from Jamaica. A number of horn players, including trumpeters Ron Taylor, Mac Gollehon, Chris Albert, and Stanton Davis, trombonists Clifton Anderson and Earl McIntyre, and saxophonists Sam Furnace and Jimmy Cozier, were African Americans whom McIntosh had met through his jazz connections or Bradley had recruited through the musician's union. All these players had considerable firsthand experience performing and recording a wide range of American popular and jazz music, a reality Bradley, Paul, and Nelson believed worked to their advantage as they strove to create more hybrid-sounding soca with crossover potential.[100]

B's Records boasted a host of other Trinidadian calypso/soca singers, including Penguin, Poser, Explainer, Baron, and Singing Francine, as well as singers from other islands, including Short Shirt (Antigua), Red Plastic Bag (Barbados), Wizard (Grenada), and Ron Pompey (St. Vincent), to name a few. Once the label was established, Gould was able to lure three of calypso's biggest old-guard stars, Sparrow, Kitchener, and Black Stalin, to his studios. In late 1983 he recruited Frankie McIntosh to arrange an album for Sparrow titled *King of the World*. Unlike Sparrow's earlier work with Charlie's Records, this album would be recorded in New York at Manhattan's Planet Sound Studios with a mixed group of Caribbean and American musicians. Under McIntosh's direction the selections were all up-tempo soca arrangements with prominent bass figures and synthesizer-driven band choruses. With tongue in cheek, Sparrow sang "Soca Man" over a pulsing soca beat, playfully proclaiming himself to be the king of calypso and not a soca man. Continuing a precedent set in his *25th Anniversary* album, he included several songs that blended elements of soca with calypso-style social commentary, including "Sam P.," his assessment of the early 1980s bribery scandal surrounding the American construction company owner Samuel P. Wallace, and "Grenada," his cynical observations of President Reagan's 1983 invasion of his country of birth. But the most popular song was the high-energy dance piece "Don't Back Back," which featured a memorable chorus hook in which Sparrow half-heartedly beseeches his temptress dance partner to not "wine up" against him. The song proved to be one of his most popular back home, winning the Trinidad Road March title in 1984 and solidifying McIntosh's reputation in Port of Spain as a top soca arranger despite his St. Vincent lineage and permanent Brooklyn residency.[101]

In 1986 Lord Kitchener and Black Stalin agreed to record for B's Records. Kitchener's *The Grandmaster* was overseen by Paul, who by this time was serving as Gould's in-house arranger. The album's most memorable song, "Pan in A Minor," reflects Kitchener's long-standing interest in composing calypsos for and about steel pan—arrangements of his tunes had won fourteen of twenty-one Trinidadian Panoramas from the competition's inception in 1963 through 1985 (there was no Panorama in 1979). The piece opens with a pulsing iron-driven rhythm section evocative of the steel orchestra engine room, followed by a jagged modal line played simultaneously by Len "Boogsie" Sharpe on tenor pan and Paul on synthesizer, flowing into a call-and-response exchange between Sharpe's pan and the horns over a minor harmonic setting (:25). Kitchener's voice enters, jumping to a dissonant pitch and elongating the vowel "a" in the words "change" and "pan." He evokes a haunting tension, proclaiming "You say / to me / you want / a musical cha-a-a-nge / in pa-a-a-n" (:50). As the vocal chorus commands the band to "beat pan," Kitchener calls out various Trinidadian pan virtuosos and steel orchestras (1:20), and Sharpe adds several extended tenor pan solos (2:00; 3:40; 5:38)—unusual inclusions for a calypso or soca recording. The arrangement is an evocative blend of the traditional and the modern sounds, balancing the shimmering timbre of a single acoustic pan against the electronic buzz of the synthesizer. Although steel orchestra arrangements of "Pan in A Minor" placed only second and third in the 1987 Trinidad Panorama (with Boogsie Sharpe's arrangement of his own tune, "This Feeling Nice," taking first place), the piece has been a favorite of steel orchestras ever since.[102]

Black Stalin's *I-Time* LP featured one of his most enduring songs, "Burn Dem." Arranged by Errol Ince and recorded in New York, the song's provocative lyrics beg St. Peter to allow Stalin to help him turn imperialist sinners—Columbus, Hitler, Mussolini, Cecil Rhodes, Ian Smith, Ronald

Reagan, Margaret Thatcher, among others—away from the gates of heaven and "burn dem." Like Sparrow and Duke, Stalin aptly demonstrated that a soca-style song could deliver biting social commentary with popular appeal. "Burn Dem" won the Calypso Monarch for him in 1987, again confirming that calypso and soca songs arranged and produced in Brooklyn would resonate powerfully with fans and critics back in Trinidad.[103]

Between 1982 and 1988, B's Records released over 120 LPs and twelve-inch extended-play discs. But the company could not sustain itself, due in part to shabby business practices by Gould, who was prone to overspending on artist fees, travel, and concert management.[104] He gravitated back to the food and night-club industries, and in 1988 he issued his final recordings on the B's label. At the same time, Leston Paul had begun to work with his uncle, Julian Williams, a native St. Vincentian who had migrated to Brooklyn via Trinidad in the 1960s. Williams was a successful small business owner who, like Rawlston Charles, had a passion for calypso and soca and, according to Paul, a discerning ear for what would make a successful recording. With B's closing down, Williams decided there was room for another Caribbean record company in Brooklyn, and in 1987 he established J&W records with Leston Paul as musical director. Soon after, he opened a record store and recording studio on 2833 Church Avenue in central Brooklyn, and in 1988 he began to issue LPs by Duke, Baron, Errol Asche, and Leston Paul's New York Connection. While J&W releases were limited to about half a dozen LPs a year in the late 1980s and early 1990s, Williams became an important licenser and distributor of soca. J&W was the only one of the early Brooklyn labels to successfully transition to CDs, beginning with Baron's *It's Magic* in 1992.[105] Paul continued to arrange into the 1990s for his own New York Connection band and popular calypso/soca singers Baron, Duke, Kitchener, Nat Hepburn, and Crazy, but there was little new, stylistically, coming out of the J&W studios.

Brooklyn's Golden Age of Soca Production

Brooklyn's reign as the international hub of soca music began in the late 1970s and stretched into the early 1990s. During this period the borough was home to the three most important calypso/soca labels: Charlie's, Straker's, and B's Records. Brooklyn's Platinum Studio, Sound Heights Studio, and Charlie's Records Studio, along with nearby facilities in Manhattan, were recognized as the most advanced recording, mixing, and production facilities, employing the best sound engineers. The four most sought-after soca arrangers—Frankie McIntosh, Clive Bradley, Leston Paul, and Pelham Goddard—either resided in Brooklyn or were in and out of New York, often for extended stays. Sparrow, Rose, Nelson, Duke, and a number of lesser-known calypso/soca singers had made Brooklyn or Queens their base of operations, finding it financially advantageous for recording and touring. Dozens of other singers and musicians cycled in and out of the city between Mother's Day and Labor Day Carnival to record and perform.

While exact numbers are difficult to come by, thousands of singles, twelve-inch EPs, and LP albums were produced in Brooklyn during this period. Likewise, estimating how many of these recordings constituted "hits" in New York and the Caribbean is challenging, but we do know that more than half of the Trinidad Calypso Monarch and Road March title-winning songs from the mid-1970s through the early 1990s were recorded, mixed, or distributed by Brooklyn-based labels, or were arranged by one of the big four arrangers mentioned above. Specifically, these included songs performed by ten of the Trinidad Calypso Monarch winners between 1976 and 1991, and eleven of the Trinidad Road March title-winning songs between 1974 and 1991.[106] In addition, the three most influential soca songs of the period that were not competition winners: Lord Shorty's "Sweet Music," Kitchener's "Sugar Bum Bum," and Arrow's "Hot-Hot-Hot" had production and distribution ties to the New York studios and Brooklyn labels.

After two decades of continuous production—an impressive run for any independent label that never scored a national or international hit—Charles and Straker found themselves cutting back on their LP releases by the mid-1990s. They attempted, with limited success, to transition to CDs. But sales dropped precipitously, crippled by the CD pirating that cheap digital burners had made possible. Around that time the energy was shifting back to Trinidad and Barbados, where improved studio technology facilitated advanced recording and mixing, diminishing the need to go abroad to produce a high-quality record or CD.[107] J&W continued to distribute current soca music, and Straker and Charles maintained their Brooklyn record stores with declining clientele and scaled-back production. Brooklyn's golden age of soca music production, having reached its zenith in the late 1980s, had passed.

The history of Brooklyn's Caribbean record companies reveals a good deal about the transnational dimensions of Carnival music while raising a number of critical questions. What exactly constituted a Brooklyn soca style, and how successful was that style in crossing over to wider non-Caribbean audiences? Who controlled the production of the music, and who benefited financially? How was soca positioned among the other Caribbean diasporic popular musics in New York, and where did it fit into the broader "world music" market? And finally, how did soca, as a hybrid style, mediate boundaries among New York's varied Caribbean migrants and their African American neighbors?

Notes

1. Frank Manning, "Overseas Caribbean Carnivals: The Art and Politics of a Transnational Celebration," *Plantation Society in the Americas* 3, no. 1 (1990): 54.

2. The history of the prewar calypso industry is covered in chapter 2 of this work. Little has been written about the North American calypso

recording industry in the postwar, pre-soca recording era (1945–1975). See Gordon Rohlehr's brief comments on Dial and Cook's recordings in *Calypso and Society in Pre-Independence Trinidad* (self-published, Tunapuna, Trinidad, 1990), p. 524. See also Rohlehr's discussion of Sparrow's early 1960s recordings for RCA in *My Whole Life is Calypso: Essays on Sparrow* (self-published, Tuna Puna, Trinidad, 2015), pp. 15–21. Lord Invader's Disc/Folkways recordings from the 1940s and 1950s, with extensive notes by John Cowley, have been reissued as *Lord Invader: Calypso in New York* (Smithsonian Folkways CD 40454, 2000). Calypso recordings by North American record companies during the "calypso craze" are well documented in *Calypso Craze, 1956–1957 and Beyond*, a CD/DVD set and booklet edited by Ray Funk and Michael Eldridge (Bear Family Records, 2014). Discographic research confirms that RCA issued recordings by Melody (1959–1963), Sparrow (1961–1964), Duke (1961–1964), and Kitchener (1963–1967) during this time. Melodisc, in the UK, issued recordings by Kitchener from 1951 through 1965. See Dmitri Subotsky's Calypso Archives, at https://web.archive.org/web/20080513092643/http:// www.calypsoarchives.co.uk/.

3. For discographies of calypso labels, see http://calypsography.com/ label/. The history of the Trinidadian recording industry has yet to be written. For preliminary background, see Cleve Osborne, "Celebrating 100 years of Vocal Recording of Calypso," at http://caribbeanradiomagazine.com/100-years-of-calypso/.

4. For an account of saxophonist Roy Cape recording with the Frankie Francis band in the Telco Studios in the early 1960s, see Jocelyne Guilbault and Roy Cape, *Roy Cape: A Life on the Calypso and Soca Bandstand* (Duke University Press, 2014), pp. 49–50.

5. Although he had recorded for years at Telco studios in Trinidad, Roy Cape recalls that his first experience in a "professional recording studio" with sound-baffle separation was not until the late 1960s, when Sparrow and his Troubadours band booked time in a New Jersey studio. Guilbault reports that the Telco studio used old Ampex recording machines and was not known for experimenting with recording equipment, as Jamaican studios did in the 1960s. See Guilbault and Cape, *Roy Cape: A Life on the Calypso and Soca Bandstand*, pp. 66–68, 241, n.11.

6. Camille Hodge's biography is drawn from the author's phone interview with her, 15 September 2014; and from Andreas Vingaard, "Interview: Camille E. Hodge," 19 April 2012, available at http:// othersounds.com/interview-camille-e-hodge/.

7. Discographies of CAB and Camille Records can be found at http:// calypsography.com/label/cab/ and http://calypsography.com/label/camille/ ; and at http://calypsoarchives.co.uk/maindirectory/camille.html.

8. Early CAB recordings can be found at these YouTube sites:

- "Dove and Pigeon" by Lord Nelson: https://www.youtube.com/watch?v= MXSFPghOnR0.
- "Loretta" by Prince Galloway: https://www.youtube.com/watch?v= OssN-PGe6i8.
- "New York Situation" by Lord Spectacular: https://www.youtube. com/watch?v=Mo0uyAXEXfs.

9. The 1965 Lord Spectacular recording "New York Situation" on CAB records can be heard on YouTube, at https://www.youtube.com/ watch?v=Mo0uyAXEXf.

10. Fats Greene's 1966 recording "'Fats' Shake 'M Up" on Camille Records can be heard on YouTube, at https://www.youtube.com/watch?v=5y0GHfkIpN8.
Lord Galloway's original song, "Archie Buck Dem Up," recorded by Archie Thomas, can be heard on YouTube, at https://www.youtube.com/watch?v=vawsv35gBnc.
    11. Vingaard, "Interview: Camille E. Hodge," p. 4.
    12. Phone interview with Edward Galloway by author, 15 September 2014.
    13. Lord Nelson's biography is drawn from interview with Lord Nelson by the author, 22 August 2013, Brooklyn, NY; liner notes to *Nelson: When the World Turns Around* (Shanachie CD 64024, 1990); and Randall Grass, liner notes to *When the Time Comes: Rebel Soca* (Shanachie CD 64010, 1988).
    14. A discography of Lord Nelson's recordings can be found at http://calypsoarchives.co.uk/maindirectory/Lord%20Nelson.html.
The original 1962 recording of Nelson's "Garrot Bounce" on the Traco label (and later reissued as Camille 113) can be heard on YouTube, at https://www.youtube.com/watch?v=dPldg8YQ-qg.
    15. Nelson was not certain about the exact date that he was introduced to Sparrow at the Park Palace, but he recalls the popular calypso he was singing that year was "Dear Sparrow," which was released in 1958. Personal conversation with author, 17 November 2017.
    16. Grass, *When the Time Comes*, CD Notes, 1988.
    17. Lord Nelson recordings can be found at the following YouTube sites:

- "Mrs Big Stuff": https://www.youtube.com/watch?v=ofI2zIkZhrg.
- "Vero": https://www.youtube.com/watch?v=83JXAdjV1BM.

    18. Listen, for example, to the melodic bass line and syncopated horn riffs on "Gemma Gone" from Nelson's 1973 Camille *Again* album, which can be heard on YouTube, at https://www.youtube.com/watch?v=3OImv89zyVo&list=PLzAHco1bfApsA-HFXrdhcR-c2KvQNYbNg&index=8.
    19. Mighty Duke's biography is drawn from

> Wayne Bowman, "A Long Life in Calypso: The Might Duke Is Dead," *Trinidad Express*, 7 February 2011, http:// www.trinidadexpress.com/ news/ A long_ life_ in_ calypso- 115469854.htm; "Kevin 'Might Duke' Pope Passes Away," *Trinidad and Tobago News Blog*, 22 January 2009, http:// www.trinidadandtobagonews.com/ blog/ ?p=848; and "Chalkdust's Eulogy for the Mighty Duke," 25 January 2009, http:// www.trinisoca.com/ Duke/ 220109b.html.

> A discography of Mighty Duke's recordings can be found at http:// calypsoarchives.co.uk/maindirectory/Duke.html.
Duke's recordings can be heard at the following YouTube sites:

- "Child of the Ghetto": https://www.youtube.com/watch?v=Su2rOIzaw3A.
- "How Many More Must Die": https://www.youtube.com/watch?v=Gt58Znw8g6g.
- "Is Thunder": https://www.youtube.com/watch?v=IizX-cnOV_Q.

    20. Granville Straker's biography is drawn from interview with Granville Straker by author, 18 July 2013, Brooklyn; and Bill Nowlin, liner notes to *Best of Straker's: Ah Feel to Party* (Rounder CD 5066/67, 1996).

21. Sparrow's live 1969 recordings at Brooklyn's Blue Cornet can be heard on the CD reissue *The Best of the Mighty Sparrow* (Straker's Records GS7772CD, 1995).

22. Hawthorne "King" Wellington Quashie, personal interview with author and Ray Funk, 12 August 2013. Wellington's "Calypso Race" (Straker's Records, 1971), recorded in Straker's Utica Avenue store with a slightly out-of-synch lead vocal and horn lines, can be heard on YouTube, at https://www.youtube.com/watch?v=EwK7BqYga8Y.

23. King Wellington recordings can be heard on the following YouTube sites:

- "New Calypso Music" (Straker's Records, 1971): https://www.youtube.com/watch?v=Ha6bXztctx0.
- "New Calypso Music" (Plek/Charlies, 1974): https://www.youtube.com/watch?v=expTLL68D-w.
- "Steel and Brass" (Camille Records, 1973): https://www.youtube.com/watch?v=3r06CnXMgeY.

24. For an informative discussion of the contributions of early calypso arrangers Frankie Francis and Art de Coteau, see Jocelyne Guilbault, *Governing Sound: The Cultural Politics of Trinidad's Carnival Musics* (University of Chicago Press, 2007), pp. 138–154.

25. The 1973 Straker recording of Chalkdust's song "Ah Fraid Karl" can be heard on YouTube, at https://www.youtube.com/watch?v=zoz1DpCQuBo.

26. Liverpool's Calypso Monarch–winning songs recorded for Straker's Records were "Three Blind Mice" and "Ah Put on Meh Guns Again" in 1976; "Juba Dubai" and "Shango Vision" in 1977; "Ah Can't Make" and "My Kind of Worry" in 1981; "Chauffeur Wanted" and "Carnival Is the Answer" in 1989; and "Kaiso Sick in de Hospital" and "Misconceptions" in 1993.

27. For a discussion of the stylistic characteristics of soca that differentiate it from calypso, see Shannon Dudley, "Judging 'By the Beat': Calypso versus Soca," *Ethnomusicology* 40, no. 2 (Spring/Summer 1996): 269–298. For further analysis of the underlying rhythmic structures that characterize soca—particularly the pulse anticipation and anacrusis patterns—see Selwyn Ahyoung, "Soca Fever!: Change in the Calypso Music Tradition of Trinidad, 1970–1989" (MA thesis, Indiana University, 1981, pp. 232–233).

28. Straker Interview, 18 July 2013.

29. Exact numbers of record sales are difficult to come by. Straker recalls that a calypso hit in the 1970s might have sold somewhere around 15,000 copies. Nowlin, *The Best of Straker's* (CD, 1996). Likewise, Rawlston Charles of Charlie's Records estimated that 15,000 records constituted a "big hit" in the 1970s and 1980s. Interview with Rawlston Charles by author, 17 September 2013, Brooklyn. And Kenrick Meade of B's Records confirmed that 10,000–15,000 records constituted a good sale in the early 1980s. Interview with Kenrick Meade by author, 29 March 2015, Brooklyn. These numbers probably do not reflect total sales, as they take into account only the records sold directly by the Straker's, Charlie's, and B's labels themselves; often additional records were produced and sold in the Caribbean and England through various licensing agreements. David Rudder, for example, estimated that Charlie's Roots' popular *Golden Calabash* (1985) and *Hammer* (1986) LPs sold between 20,000 and 30,000 copies in Trinidad and throughout the Caribbean, where the band controlled distribution, but had no idea how many additional copies were

sold by Rawlston Charles, who controlled distribution of the LPs in North America and Europe. Phone interview with David Rudder by author, 18 December 2014.

30. Guilbault, *Governing Sound*, p. 159.

31. The 1974 Straker recording of Shadow's "Bass Man" can be heard on the CD reissue *Best of Straker's: Ah Feel to Party* (1996).

32. A discography of Straker's Records can be found at http://calypsoarchives.co.uk/maindirectory/strakers.html.

33. For more on Berridge's time in New York, see Guilbault and Cape, *Roy Cape: A Life on the Calypso and Soca Bandstand*, pp. 69–71.

34. Frankie McIntosh's biography is drawn from interview with Frankie McIntosh by author, 23 July 2013, Brooklyn; and "Frankie McIntosh," http://www.basementrecordings.com/asp/bamn/mcintosh.htm. See also Ray Allen, "The Brooklyn Soca Connection: Frankie McIntosh and Straker's Records," *American Music Review* 44, no. 1 (Fall 2014), http://www.brooklyn.cuny.edu/web/academics/centers/hitchcock/publications/amr/v44-1/allen.php.

35. Alston Becket Cyrus, interview with author and Ray Funk, 19 August 2013, Brooklyn.

36. A recording of Becket's 1977 "Coming High" on Casablanca Records can be found on YouTube, at https://www.youtube.com/watch?v=9gbG2eaHkl4.

37. A recording of Becket's 1978 "Wine Down Kingstown" on the Cocoa label can be found on YouTube, at https://www.youtube.com/watch?v=dk-4lId73GU.

38. Interview with McIntosh, 23 July 2013.

39. Guilbault and Cape, *Roy Cape: A Life on the Calypso and Soca Bandstand*, pp. 92–93.

40. Arrangers Leston Paul and Frankie McIntosh, along with tenor sax player Charles Dougherty, were adamant about the point that calypso and soca singers were selfish in their demands that they, and not instrumentalists, were the center of attention on recordings and live shows. Private conversations with author.

41. A recording of King Wellington's 1981 "Take Your Time" on Straker's Records is available on YouTube, at https://www.youtube.com/watch?v=3FP50kR0YoI.

42. Interview with McIntosh, 23 July 2013. A recording of Chalkdust's 1983 "Ash Wednesday Jail" on Straker's Records can be heard on YouTube, at https://www.youtube.com/watch?v=AG2UP_RACXU.

43. Interview with Hollis Liverpool by author, 5 October 2014, Brooklyn.

44. Interview with Frankie McIntosh by author, 24 October 2014, Brooklyn.

45. Interview with Errol Ince by author, 23 February 2015. Port of Spain, Trinidad. A recording of Stalin's 1991 "Ah Feel to Party" on Straker's Records can be heard on *Best of Straker's: Ah Feel to Party* (Rounder CD 5066/67, 1996).

46. Straker told Rounder Record producer Bill Nolin that he estimated producing "some 600 to 700 albums, maybe in excess of 1,000 twelve inches, and 'oh my gosh, two or three thousand singles.'" Liner notes, *Best of Straker's* (1996).

47. Wayne Bowman, "Charlie and His Roots: Tobago's Rawlston Charles," *Caribbean Beat Magazine* 93 (September/October 2008), http://caribbean-beat.com/issue-93/charlie-and-his-roots#axzz3XOzlpo2d.

48. Rawlston Charles's biography is drawn from interview with Rawlston Charles by author, 17 September 2013, Brooklyn; and Bowman, "Charlie and His Roots," 2008. A partial discography for Charlie's Records can be found at http://www.discogs.com/label/61879-Charlies-Records.

49. Guilbault cites Trinidad record producers who complained that the local facilities for recording and pressing records were diminishing precipitously throughout the 1970s, leading calypsonians to "go to New York to make their recordings in state-of-the-art studios." Only after a 1983 change in import levy regulations did the Trinidad recording industry begin to recover. Guilbalult, *Governing Sound*, pp. 55–56. The decline in Trinidad record production in the 1970s and early 1980s correlates precisely with the expansion of Brooklyn calypso and soca production by Straker's and Charlie's Records.

50. Roy Boyke interview, *Carnival Magazine*, 1979, quoted in Ahyoung, "Soca Fever!," p. 98.

51. Guilbault, *Governing Sound*, p. 173.

52. *Caribbeat*, 1976, p. 37; quoted from Ahyoung, "Soca Fever!," p. 101.

53. Interview with Ed Watson by author and Ray Funk, 20 February 2015, Port of Spain, Trinidad.

54. Lord Shorty's 1976 recording of "Sweet Music" for Charlie's Records can be heard on YouTube, at https://www.youtube.com/watch?v=RiR40bhzJDI.

55. Calypso Rose's biography is drawn from an interview with Calypso Rose by author, 23 July 2014, Queens, NY; Hope Munro, *What She Go Do: Women in Afro-Trinidadian Music* (University of Mississippi Press, 2016), pp. 97–106; and Guilbault, *Governing Sound*, 2007, pp. 102–111.

56. Guilbault, *Governing Sound*, pp. 106–107.

57. Calypso Rose's 1976 recording of "Labour Day Breakaway Part 1" for Charlie's Records can be heard on YouTube, at https://www.youtube.com/watch?v=5MFNheHtXYo.

58. Interview with Calypso Rose by author, 23 July 2014, Queens, NY.

59. Calypso Rose's 1977 recording of "Give More Tempo" for Charlie's Records can be heard on YouTube, at https://www.youtube.com/watch?v=wIBTAdQThNQ.

60. Bowman, "Charlie and His Roots."

61. Interview with Charles, 17 September 2013; interview with Rose, 23 July 2014.

62. Munro, *What She Go Do*, pp. 103–107.

63. Pelham Goddard's biography is drawn from interview with Pelham Goddard by author and Ray Funk, 20 February 2015, St. James, Trinidad; and Anthony Ferguson, "Pelham Goddard: The Making of a Musical Maestro," *We Beat Magazine* 5 (June 2005): 8–12. Goddard's winning Road March tunes included "Soca Baptist" and "Rebecca" with Blue Boy in 1980 and 1983, respectively; "Bahia Girl" with David Rudder in 1986; "Free Up" with Tambu in 1989; "This Party It Is" with Tambu in 1990; and "Get Something and Wave" with Super Blue in 1991.

64. Interview with Watson, 20 February 2015.

65. Interview with Rawlston Charles by author, 5 February 2015, Brooklyn.

66. Ahyoung, "Soca Fever," p. 102.

67. Guilbault, *Governing Sound*, p. 174.

68. A recording of Lord Kitchener's 1978 "Sugar Bum Bum" can be heard on YouTube, at https://www.youtube.com/watch?v=0X2ZHqTw3Wo.

69. Recordings from Sparrow's 1977 LP *New York Blackout* on Charlie's Records can be heard at these YouTube sites:

- "New York Blackout": https://www.youtube.com/watch?v=gh5RVjZjdA0.
- "First Black Miss Universe": https://www.youtube.com/watch?v=D9L5KbHu2Qk.
- "Life Down in Hell": https://www.youtube.com/watch?v=HbPrENAH6g4.

70. Recordings from the 1980 LP *Might Sparrow—25th Anniversary* on Charlie's Records can be heard at these YouTube sites:

- "Don't Drop the Tempo": https://www.youtube.com/watch?v=3ymoTcYjR1E.
- "London Bridge is Falling Down": https://www.youtube.com/watch?v=4Zm1HyqQg9c.
- "Dead or Alive": https://www.youtube.com/watch?v=AHIJJmTRbYE.

Interestingly, Sparrow and de Coteau kept these and other songs on the album at a medium tempo, thereby allowing Sparrow's lyrics to be easily comprehensible.

71. A recording of Sparrow's 1982 "I Love New York—Part 1" on Charlie's Records can be heard on YouTube, at https://www.youtube.com/watch?v=zNYxKjxQTyQ.

72. Quote and biographical information are drawn for Rupert "Swallow" Philo, interview with author, 4 September 2015, Brooklyn. See also Jean Forrester-Warner, "Don't Stop the Party—Mighty Swallow," *Socca News*, 28 May 2011, http://www.socanews.com/articles/article.php?Don-t-Stop-the-Party---Mighty-Swallow-252#.Ves-KX0wy70.

73. For a number of years Swallow traveled annually from his home in Antigua to Trinidad during Carnival season to sing in the calypso tents and record at K.H. Studios. But as a noncitizen he was barred from competing in the prestigious Trinidad Calypso King competition, and his songs were not considered for the Road March competition.

74. Philo, interview, 4 September 2015.

75. Recordings of Swallow can be heard at the following YouTube sites:

- "Don't Stop the Party" (1979, Charlie's Records): https://www.youtube.com/watch?v=5WWtJzUPn0A.
- "Subway Jam" (1981, Charlie's Records): https://www.youtube.com/watch?v=UEJsc3sj4Pc.

76. Leston Paul's biography and quotes are drawn from interview with Leston Paul by author and Ray Funk, 21 February 2015, Mt. Lambert, Trinidad.

77. Ibid.

78. There is not total agreement regarding the details of how Arrow's recording "Hot Hot Hot" was produced and distributed. My story draws from accounts related by Rawlston Charles, interview with author, 5 February 2015. Brooklyn; Leston Paul, interview, 21 February 2015; and Winston "Gypsie" Peters, interview with author and Ray Funk, 23 February 2015, Port of Spain, Trinidad. Sadly, Alphonsus "Arrow" Cassell, the one

individual who could offer a definitive account on the song's production and distribution, passed away in 2010.

79. A recording of Arrow's 1982 "Hot Hot Hot" on Arrow Records/ Charlie's Records can be heard on YouTube, at https://www.youtube.com/ watch?v=OkGgdIBX1to.

80. Interview with Explainer by author, 25 February 2015, Port of Spain.

81. A recording of Explainer's 1982 "Lorraine" on Charlie's Records can be heard on YouTube, at https://www.youtube.com/watch?v=aijYM34KZc4.

82. Guilbault, *Governing Sound*, p. 56.

83. Interview with Ralston Charles by author, 5 February 2015, Brooklyn.

84. Interview with Swallow, 4 September 2015.

85. Interview with Charles Dougherty by author, 15 January 2015, Brooklyn.

86. Phone interview with David Rudder by author, 18 December 2014.

87. Interview with Watson, 20 February 2015.

88. R. B. Wilk, "Charlie's Calypso City," *Everybody's Caribbean Magazine* (March/April 1982): 42.

89. Background on B's Records is drawn from an interview with Kenrick Meade by author, 22 August 2013, Brooklyn, and an interview with Hue Loy by author, 24 February 2015, Trinidad. Loy worked for Meade in the 1980s, organizing recording sessions and overseeing distribution.

90. Duke's recording of "Is It Groovy Now" appears on the LP *Over and Over and Over Again*, with liner notes by Kenrick Meade (B's Records, B's-R1009, 1982).

91. Kenrick Meade recalls Leston Paul's excitement at first encountering a Prophet 5 synthesizer in at Brooklyn's Sound Heights studio at a recording session in the early 1980s. Meade was amazed that it only took Paul about fifteen minutes to program the new keyboard with a variety of sophisticated sounds. Interview with Kenrick Meade by author, 30 March 2015.

92. A discography of B's Records can be found at http:// calypsoarchives.co.uk/maindirectory/Bs.html.

93. Interview with Paul, 21 February 2015.

94. See Leston Paul and the New York Connection's first three releases for B's Records: *Soca Invasion* (1985), *Soca Destruction* (1986), and *Eruption* (1987).

95. Lord Melody's recordings can be heard at these YouTube sites:

- "Rastaman" (Charlie's Records, 1979): https://www.youtube.com/ watch?v=rxNqD3SiKbc.
- "Brown Sugar" (B's Records, 1982): https://www.youtube.com/ watch?v=oFJyFDhHApY.
- "Lola" (B's Records, 1983): https://www.youtube.com/watch?v= T6gTW0YzMhk.

96. Interview with Lord Nelson by author, 28 March 2015, Jamaica, NY.

97. Lord Nelson's late 1970s and early 1980s recordings arranged by Clive Bradley can be heard at these YouTube sites:

- "Music Land" (1978, Charlie's Records): https://www.youtube.com/ watch?v=lgbKnkogg6c.
- "Disco Daddy" (1980, Charlie's Records): https://www.youtube.com/ watch?v=p9wTcw-0RXo.

- "Bald Head Rasta" (1980, Charlie's Records): https://www.youtube.com/watch?v=FwyFA-pmwEY.
- "Ah Going to Party Tonight" (1982, B's Records): https://www.youtube.com/watch?v=COGBJCi5IUE.
- "GimmieLove" (1982, B's Records): https://www.youtube.com/watch?v=-guc366SqAM.
- "SuperStar" (1982, B's Records): https://www.youtube.com/watch?v=4DFtpJJ-jfo.
- "MihLover" (1983, B's Records): https://www.youtube.com/watch?v=wNXNlIlWuG0.
- "My Love and I" (1983, B's Records): https://www.youtube.com/watch?v=O6Qyu1_00mc.

98. Nelson recalls sitting around a club in Tobago sometime in the late 1970s, chatting with Lord Shorty about the need to "improve calypso and to take it abroad. . . . We wanted to see if we could crossover this calypso thing and do something different—we wanted to reach everyone, the world." He claims it was during this conversation that he, Nelson, coined the word "soca" in reference to his calypsos that "had so much soul in them . . . my music was so Americanized." Interview with Nelson, 28 March 2015, Jamaica, NY.

99. Ibid.

100. The musicians listed here are drawn from the back of various album covers from Charlie's and B's Records. Thanks to Frankie McIntosh, Charles Dougherty, and Kenrick Meade and for identifying the musician's individual nationalities.

101. Sparrow's 1983 recordings on B's Records can be heard at these YouTube sites:

- Soca Man: https://www.youtube.com/watch?v=nYf3NP2YIK0.
- "Sam P": https://www.youtube.com/watch?v=y128DHS0glE.
- "Grenada": https://www.youtube.com/watch?v=HWlTUm11oEs.
- "Don't Back Back": https://www.youtube.com/watch?v=yR6Evk8IASc.

102. A recording of Lord Kitchener's 1987 "Pan in A Minor" on B's Records can be heard on YouTube, at https://www.youtube.com/watch?v=DGPwBXUKK7I.

103. A recording of Black Stalin's 1987 "Burn Dem" on B's Records can be heard on YouTube, at https://www.youtube.com/watch?v=2ScLFqhHXwQ.

104. Kenrick Meade recalls that Gould often paid artists extravagant money upfront that neither Charles nor Straker could match, and that he was often cavalier with expenses. Interview with Kenrick Meade, 30 March 2015. Hue Loy, who replaced Meade at B's in 1985, recalled a similar pattern of sloppy financial management. Interview with Hue Loy, 24 February 2015.

105. Background on J&W records is drawn from an interview with Frankie Roberts, 16 January 2015, Brooklyn; and an interview with Paul, 21 February 2015. Roberts worked for Julian Williams on and off during the 1990s and 2000s. Paul is Williams's nephew and served as J&W's music director and main arranger.

106. Select Trinidad Calypso Monarch Winners (1976–1991):

- 1976—Chalkdust: "Three Blind Mice" and "Ah Put Meh Guns On," Straker's Records, arranged by Art de Coteau.
- 1977—Chalkdust: "Juba Dubai" and Her Majesty," Straker's Records, arranged by Art de Coteau.

- 1978—Calypso Rose: "I Thanks Thee" and Her Majesty," Charlie's Records, arranged by Pelham Goddard.
- 1981—Chalkdust: "Things That Worry Me" and "I Can't Make It," Straker's Records, arranged by Frankie McIntosh.
- 1984—Penguin: "We Living in Jail" and "Soft Man," B's Records, arranged by Leston Paul
- 1985—Black Stalin: "Ism Schism" and "Wait Dorothy Wait," Charlie's Records.
- 1986—David Rudder: "The Hammer" and "Bahia Girl." Charlie's Records, arranged by Pelham Goddard.
- 1987—Black Stalin: "Burn Dem" and "Mr. Pan Maker," B's Records, arranged by Errol Ince
- 1989—Chalkdust: "Chauffeur Wanted" and "Carnival Is the Answer," Straker's Records, arranged by Frankie McIntosh.
- 1991—Black Stalin: "Black Man Feelin' to Party" and "Look on the Bright Side," Straker's Records, arranged by Errol Ince.

Select Trinidad Road March Title Winners (1974–1991):

- 1974—Shadow: "Bass Man," Straker's Records, arranged by Art de Coteau.
- 1977—Calypso Rose: "Tempo," Charlie's Records, arranged by Pelham Goddard.
- 1978—Calypso Rose: "Come Leh We Jam," Charlie's Records, arranged by Pelham Goddard.
- 1980—Blue Boy: "Soca Baptist," Charlie's Records, arranged by Pelham Goddard.
- 1983—Blue Boy: "Rebecca," Charlie's Records, arranged by Pelham Goddard.
- 1984—Sparrow: "Doh Back Back," B's Records, arranged by Frankie McIntosh.
- 1986—David Rudder: "Bahia Girl," Charlie's Records, arranged by Pelham Goddard.
- 1987—Mighty Duke: "Thunder," Lem's Records, arranged by Frankie McIntosh.
- 1989—Tambu: "Free Up," Charlie's Records, arranged by Pelham Goddard.
- 1990—Tambu: "We Ain't Going Home," Charlie's Records, arranged by Pelham Goddard.
- 1991—Super Blue: "Get Something and Wave," Charlie's Records, arranged by Pelham Goddard.

107. For example, by the mid-1990s, Eddy Grant's Barbados-based Ice Records, with its sophisticated Blue Wave recording studio, was producing LPs and CDs by many leading soca artists, including Sparrow, Kitchener, Calypso Rose, Stalin, Duke, Super Blue, and others. See Guilbault and Cape, *Roy Cape*, pp. 115–117.

7

Brooklyn Soca as Transnational Expression

The Brooklyn-based, independent record companies run by Caribbean entrepreneurs Rawlston Charles, Granville Straker, and Michael Gould helped usher in the transition from calypso to soca. Moreover, their international production and distribution apparatuses marked soca as a transnational music from its inception. But not all Trinidadian musicians and critics were enamored by this new soca sound or its overseas production and distribution. Some worried publicly that the commercialization of traditional calypso through the incorporation of what they identified as "foreign" popular styles—specifically elements of American soul, funk, and R&B, and Jamaican reggae—would compromise the integrity of Trinidad's most distinctive musical expression. Equally troubling was the concern that production and distribution of the music might fall to North American and British record companies, which would reap the lion's share of the profits. Gordon Rohlehr, while stressing calypso's long history of self-reinvention, warned that the new soca ran the danger of embracing the "ethos of popular music" and becoming "a kind of fast food, mass-produced, slickly packaged, and meant for rapid consumption and swift obsolescence."[1] Hollis "Chalkdust" Liverpool, known for his biting satirical calypsos, decried the commercialization of the art form in his 1979 song "Calypso vs. Soca." Liverpool warned his fellow calypsonians not to give in to the temptation of making music for foreign markets and tourists, exhorting them to embrace their native culture and sing calypsos for their own people: "If you want to make plenty money and sell records plenty here and overseas / Yes, well plan brother for de foreigner, compose soul songs and soca, do half lease / But if you are concerned about your roots / anxious to pass on your truths, to the young shoots dem youths / and learn of the struggle of West Indian people / If so, yuh got to sing calypso."[2]

In 1983 the calypsonian Willard "Lord Relator" Harris raised the specter of cultural imperialism, grousing over the expansion of overseas soca record production in a song aptly titled "Importation of Calypso": "The music that you jump to and play mas today / is now mass produced in the USA

/ It is a bad blow, for Trinidad and Tobago / The records will show, we are now importing our own calypso."[3]

The concerns of Rohlehr, Liverpool, and Harris were, on one hand, well founded, given the way the calypso craze had played out in in the 1950s under the control of United States recording companies that favored pop arrangements by American singers over songs performed by native Caribbean calypsonians. On the other hand, their perspective does not adequately account for the growing market for calypso and soca among overseas Caribbean audiences, or the impact of the Caribbean-owned and run independent labels, as discussed in the previous chapter. Brooklyn's rise to prominence as a center of soca production in the 1980s could not be reduced to a North American, corporate hijacking of Third World music. The reality on the ground—in the Brooklyn recording studios and record stores, on Eastern Parkway and at Crown Heights fetes, and even back in Trinidad—was more complicated. Understanding the cultural politics of Brooklyn soca and its commercial crossover potential demands a critical examination of the local record producers' control over production and distribution that was, at times, in tension with desires of the artists they sought to promote. These questions of control and agency necessitate further attention to issues of stylistic transformation, lyrical content, soca's location vis-à-vis other popular diasporic world musics, and the interplay of musical hybridity and cultural identity.

A Brooklyn Soca Style?

Judging exactly what constituted a Brooklyn soca composition is difficult because of the complex production configurations made possible by increased international travel and the new multitracking technology. Straker, Charles, Gould, and their representatives spent considerable time moving back and forth between New York and the Caribbean, establishing connections with singers, musicians, arrangers, and recording facilities at both sites. Many of their songs became transnational productions. Calypso Rose's 1977 "Tempo" was exemplary—written in New York by a Trinidad expatriate, arranged in Trinidad, recorded in Trinidad (rhythm and horn sections) and New York (lead vocals), mixed in New York, and distributed through a Brooklyn-based company with networks in Trinidad and throughout the Caribbean, North America, and Great Britain. Was it a Brooklyn creation, a Trinidad creation, or both?

This transnational production process, coupled with increased availability of American music in Trinidad, further complicated Brooklyn's position as the primary site of artistic production. All the important singers, musicians, arrangers, and record producers were born and reared in Trinidad, St. Vincent, the Virgin Islands, or other English-speaking East-Antillean islands. There is no doubt that the absorption of black American R&B, soul, funk, and disco styles was essential to the transformation of calypso to soca during the 1970s and the 1980s. Just how much of this mixing was due to direct contact with black American and Latin music in New York, however, and how much was from simply listening to recordings and radio broadcasts of American music on local stations in Trinidad, is difficult to assess. Leston Paul grew up hearing black American pop music on the radio during the 1960s and 1970s in Trinidad, but he claimed that coming to New York and experiencing the music firsthand was personally transformative. Rawlston Charles was familiar with American music as a young man in Trinidad, but he had to immerse himself in the R&B, soul, and funk music that were his bread-and-butter sales when he first opened his Brooklyn record store in 1972. As a youngster in St. Vincent, Frankie McIntosh heard his father's band play American jazz pieces learned from records and written scores imported from the United States, but he only became a practicing jazz performer after settling in Brooklyn. Likewise, there is no way to quantify how much black American and Latin influences seeped into the music of Sparrow, Rose, Nelson, Duke, and other New York/Brooklyn-based singers, due to their proximity to the city's diverse music cultures. Worth noting, however, is that Nelson, the singer most responsible for bringing funk and disco directly into soca, was the one artist who began his singing career in New York, not Trinidad, and who continued throughout his life to call the city home.

Would soca have happened if there had been no Caribbean diaspora and subsequent establishment of Brooklyn-based record companies? Probably, but the music's stylistic evolution and economic viability were greatly enhanced by activity in Brooklyn during its formative years. Rather than thinking in terms of a distinctive Brooklyn soca style, we might better view the music's development in the context of an ongoing cultural dialogue, as a transnational expression anchored in Trinidadian tradition but indelibly shaped by overseas musical influences. This assessment finds validation when seen through the lens of calypso's evolution. As Rohlehr has noted, calypso has repeatedly reconfigured itself by incorporating foreign musical styles and instrumentation since its nineteenth-century inception as an amalgamation of African, French, and British folk music traditions, and its twentieth-century pre-WWII engagement with New Orleans and big band American jazz influences.[4] Thus, the soca of the 1980s, which grafted elements of black American soul, funk, and jazz music onto Trinidadian calypso, can be envisioned as another stage in the music's rich history of continuous transformation through contact with outside musical influences.

Soca evolved in a transnational milieu, but the music that developed in Brooklyn never strayed too far from its Trinidad roots. While Brooklyn's Labor Day Carnival and its calypso/soca recording industry were expanding during the 1970s and 1980s, the pre-Lenten Trinidad Carnival back home remained the vital creative wellspring to which singers, musicians, arrangers, and fans continuously returned. The ease and frequency of international travel and phone communication, coupled with advances in mass media, facilitated the transnational musical connection between New York and the Caribbean. This explains, in part, why, despite the cross-cultural musical exchange that was crucial to soca's stylistic development, no grand synthesis of soca and American popular music occurred during this period. McIntosh's occasional excursions into jazz, and Nelson's, Bradley's, and Paul's fascination with funk and disco aside, no enduring styles of soca-jazz, soca-funk, or soca-rock took hold in Brooklyn or in Trinidad in the 1980s. Certainly there was nothing akin to the rich fusion of Cuban and Puerto Rican popular styles with black American jazz that gave birth to mambo in the 1950s, and to boogaloo and salsa in the 1960s. Likewise, despite the fact that Jamaicans, Haitians, Nuyoricans, and Dominicans were living side by side with Trinidadian and other English-speaking Caribbean people in Brooklyn, their musical styles remained relatively distinct and separate. Trinidadian soca and Jamaican reggae would clash, not merge, as their competing sound trucks rolled down Eastern Parkway on Labor Day. Indeed, the truly innovative hybrids, such as chutney soca and raga soca, that developed in the late 1980s and 1990s, respectively, came primarily out of Trinidad and the Caribbean, not from Brooklyn or other diasporic communities.[5] The tenacity of the Trinidadian-based calypso and soca in culturally heterogeneous Brooklyn belies both theories of cultural homogenization via assimilation and of radical hybridization via cross-cultural exchange with other close-proximity migrant groups.

Soca and World Music

In retrospect, the tendency of Brooklyn soca not to drift too far from its Trinidadian moorings cut both ways. On the one hand, the music maintained a degree of insularity that limited its crossover appeal to wider North American and European audiences—certainly nothing close to the international popularity reggae had come to enjoy in the 1970s and 1980s. While Straker, Charles, and Gould did expand the audience to include North American and British Caribbean migrant consumers, they did not establish agreements that would have ceded control to major North American, European, or international companies in return for potential increases in distribution and sales. This frustrated many soca singers, who envied the success of their Jamaican counterparts and blamed the Brooklyn-based producers for not pursuing more lucrative international distribution agreements. On the other hand, Straker, Charles, and Gould did manage to keep the production and distribution of the music within a Caribbean network, a stark contrast to the North American hegemonic domination of the industry during the 1950s calypso craze. The resulting benefits of the independent Brooklyn-based labels maintaining control were two-fold. Musically, the core aesthetic values of Trinidadian-based soca were preserved with little watering down or appropriation by non-Caribbean artists. Financially, the profits, meager as they may have been, remained largely within the transnational Caribbean community.

The fact that no significant distribution deals were struck between Brooklyn's Caribbean record companies and larger North American or European labels is somewhat curious, given the overall surge of interest in global music by the recording industry in the 1980s. Soca's rise to prominence coincided with efforts by US and UK companies to capitalize on the growing market demographic of cosmopolitan, globally minded consumers who had tired of their rock and pop offerings. In 1987 a group of British independent label owners developed a new marketing category they dubbed "world music," in hopes of more effectively packaging non-Western, hybrid pop styles for UK and North American audiences.[6] The term quickly stirred controversy over the possible effects of commodifying local music traditions for international consumption. Some critics worried that such activity could lead to the kind of cultural imperialism alluded to by Liverpool's and Harris's previously cited calypsos—one fraught with the potential for appropriation and exploitation by the Western music industry and the popular artists they represented. Others argued that local music cultures might be revitalized as new markets opened up to support recording and touring, while select artists might serve as cultural ambassadors and social activists for their homelands.[7]

Genres classified as world music in the late 1980s and 1990s were, according to Jocelyn Guilbault, "mass-distributed worldwide yet associated with minority groups and small or industrially developing countries." Stylistically, they combined "local musical characteristics with those of mainstream genres [rock, soul, and other popular styles consumed primarily by English-speaking North American and European audiences] in today's transitional music related industry."[8] Soca, as a hybrid meld of "local" Trinidad traditions and elements of North American "mainstream" styles, certainly met the musical criteria. With its authentic Caribbean roots, a slate of professional singers, and an ample catalogue of recorded material, Trinidadian soca appeared to be well positioned to gain a boost from the world music wave. But such was not the case. Evidently the major record companies were not as enamored with soca's Carnival-centered, party lyrics and repetitive, heavily synthesized instrumental accompaniments as they were with the messianic messages of reggae or the deep rhythmic grooves and improvisatory practices of Latin and African styles. But equally important, the small Brooklyn- and Caribbean-based companies that had been recording and distributing most of the music throughout the 1980s remained staunchly independent. Without the backing of major or well-established independent record labels with sophisticated distribution apparatus—save London and Mango/Island Records' brief associations with David Rudder and Arrow in the late 1980s— soca's efforts to penetrate the international markets remained severely hampered. A few American independent labels specializing in folk and roots music, most notably Rounder and Shanachie Records, dabbled briefly in soca with compilation and reissue releases, but their interest was short-lived and their handful of soca releases paled in comparison to their catalogue of reggae material.[9] Independent labels that discovered

Trinidad Carnival music tended to be more interested in reissuing old ca- lypso recordings with extensive liner notes aimed at niche audiences of collectors and roots music aficionados rather than in exploring the con- temporary soca sound.[10]

Nor did soca manage to attract well-known mainstream artists to serve as conduits or interpreters of the music for Western audiences, as, for example, Paul Simon and the Talking Heads did for various African pop styles.[11] The world music movement of the 1980s and 1990s may have gotten a handful of records by the best-known soca artists into the "World" and "World Beat" bins of specialty record shops, and onto select compila- tion releases, but there was limited impact on overall international distri- bution and sales. Ironically it was the music of the earlier calypso craze, which consciously drew upon American folk and pop music idioms and benefited tremendously from the backing of major US record companies, that was successfully marketed as a popular "world music," although the term had not been coined back in the 1950s.

Soca Lyrics: Local and Universal

Writing soca lyrics with broad Caribbean audience appeal and cross- over potential presented something of a dilemma, whether the process unfolded in Brooklyn, Trinidad, or within the transnational network. How deep into local subject matter could the songwriter go? Were migrants in the diaspora interested in current goings-on in Trinidad or Antigua, and vice versa? Must lyrics be exclusively oriented toward exhortations to dance and party, or could serious social and political issues be addressed, and if so should those issues be of local or universal consequence?

With the exception of a few notable pieces by Chalkdust and Sparrow, most of the material produced or distributed by the Brooklyn labels, and the body of songs written by New York–based singers, did not deal with local Trinidad politics or events other than the big Carnival celebration. Rather, they followed the general trends of dance-oriented soca that downplayed text-heavy narratives and social commentary. Lyrical themes tended to ad- dress the more general subjects of love, sensuality, dance, and celebration (often tied to some aspect of Carnival), and occasionally broader issues of universal social justice. This was part of a conscious strategy to attract in- ternational crossover audiences. Not surprisingly, however, given the ven- erable calypso tradition of local reporting and commentary, songs about experiences in New York occasionally cropped up, most notably Sparrow's "NY Blackout" (1977), "I Love New York" (1982), and "Crown Heights Justice" (1991), and Swallow's "Subway Jam" (1981). More common were songs celebrating the excitement and revelry of Brooklyn Carnival, such as Sparrow's "Mas in Brooklyn" (1969), Rose's "Labour Day Breakaway" (1976)," and Galloway's "Labor Day" (1976/1983). While enjoying a degree of popularity with Brooklyn audiences, these songs had limited currency in Trinidad and around the Caribbean.

As noteworthy as the themes the singers did address were those they did not. With the exception of Explainer's 1982 "Lorraine," Brooklyn soca songs did not reflect the sort of nostalgic longings for the Caribbean homeland that were common in early Puerto Rican, Dominican, and Haitian songs by New York–based migrants.[12] There was certainly no shortage of songs about Trinidadian Carnival that were marketed for New York and Caribbean audiences, but those written by the New York expatriates Wellington ("Steel and Brass," 1973) and Rose ("Tempo," 1977), and even Explainer's "Lorraine," tended to look forward with anticipation to attending the event back home, not backward with romantic sentimentality over a bygone era or vanishing tradition. Rather than pining for home, the New York–based singers and their fans appeared ready to hop on a plane and head back to the Caribbean, a geographic locale from which many did not feel a sense of permanent displacement. These songs attest to their eagerness to attend Trinidad Carnival, and upon their return to re-create the party in the new diasporic space as a way of cementing cultural connections between their old and new homes. But the Carnival-centered subject matter placed limitations on the broader marketability of such songs outside of Caribbean networks and the Carnival season.

Sparrow's 1991 "Crown Heights Justice" is an intriguing example of a song that attempted to cast a local Brooklyn, non-Carnival event into the wider arena of social justice. Sparrow chronicled the story of Galvin Cato, a young Guyanese boy who was killed in August of that year when a Hasidic driver's car jumped the curb turning off of Eastern Parkway. The event sparked several days of rioting in Crown Heights that included the murder of a young Hasidic scholar, Yankel Rosenbaum, by a group of black youths. Sparrow's lengthy narrative placed the calamity in the context of long-simmering tensions between the Crown Heights Hasidic Jewish and Caribbean communities resulting from gentrification and the perceived unequal treatment of the latter by state officials and the NYPD. But he moved on to broader issues, noting the similar historical struggles Jews and blacks had endured, respectively, during the Holocaust and slavery, and beseeching both sides to reconcile: "Pain and sufferin' we have borne / Blacks and Jews should live as one / Here life is great / No swastikas, no slave masters / Instead of dat is endless fight / Where we live here in Crown Heights."[13]

Sparrow's anthem-like chorus was built around a lofty proclamation: "all we want is justice, we should be living in peace."[14] While "Crown Heights Justice" stands as one of Sparrow's most poignant lyrics, and his call for equality for people of color certainly had strong historic and contemporary resonance, the song did not sell well. Charles, who recorded and co-produced the song with Sparrow, lamented this situation:

The song had serious messages, it had long lyrics, but it really wasn't a dance piece. A lot of calypso buyers said it was a nice song but you couldn't get down with it, it wasn't too much for dancing and bacchanal and everything—it was more of a listening, educational historical thing about what's going on in the community around us. In the end, it wasn't a big seller, but it was an incredible piece.[15]

Although the song's "justice" chorus was a catchy hook, overall the tempo was slow, the band section was not well developed, and the lengthy verses tended to drag out. While the lyrics looked good on paper, without the insistent dance beat the song never caught on, particularly back in the Caribbean, where conflict between Hasidic Jews and Trinidadians was not a burning issue. Raising the local to the universal was not always easy, even for a master calypsonian like Sparrow.

In contrast to "Crown Heights Justice" was another release on Charlie's Records that won the 1991 Trinidad Road March, Super Blue's "Get Something and Wave." Recorded and mixed in Charles's Brooklyn studio and arranged by Pelham Goddard, the song was an uptempo romp whose lyrics proclaimed, "This Carnival is Bacchanal!" and exhorted revelers to "break away" and wave their flags and bandanas. The song was extremely popular in Trinidad and Brooklyn that year, suggesting that by the early 1990s, danceability was trumping lyrical content.[16] A strong groove and catchy hook accompanying repetitive Carnival-oriented party lyrics were apparently the essential ingredients for a soca song to sell well among both Caribbean and diasporic audiences. Even so, "Get Something and Wave" was too local in its association with Carnival to be a crossover success. The failure of soca's lyrics to consistently deliver more compelling, universal social commentary or deeper insights into the mysteries of love relations—as reggae and R&B were able to do—hampered its ability to reach wider, non-Caribbean black and white audiences.

Brooklyn Soca and Globalization

These patterns of musical style, international marketing, and diasporic song content are useful in assessing the dynamics of cultural globalization. As previously discussed, Keith Nurse was correct in asserting that overseas Trinidad Carnivals challenged outmoded center-periphery models of globalization based on an oversimplified one-way flow of cultural products from First World centers to Third World peripheral societies. Overseas Carnivals, Nurse contended, turn the original model on its head by "facilitat[ing] the centering of the periphery."[17] Brooklyn soca fits this model of reverse globalization in many ways. Nearly all the singers, musicians, arrangers, and producers were expatriates or visiting transnationals who brought Carnival music from the Caribbean (now the central cultural source) to New York (now the peripheral cultural receptor).

Nurse provides a useful point of departure, but the history of Brooklyn soca underscores the need for a more nuanced approach that stresses the dialogical movement of cultural actors and their expressions among Caribbean homeland(s) and their diasporic communities. Specifically, the exchange of cultural capital between Trinidad and Brooklyn was circular and not simply a unilateral-reverse flow, thereby further blurring distinctions between what constituted the center and what constituted the periphery. Here Nurse's provocative query—"Who is globalizing whom?"—becomes the essential question.[18] While Trinidad remained the undisputed font of Carnival culture, Brooklyn was by no means a passive periphery. The borough emerged as the nexus of the new soca sound, and as an essential component of the international Carnival complex that supplied vital creative and economic support that helped keep the original Trinidad center afloat. Singers, musicians, arrangers, and record producers moved fluidly between Port of Spain and Brooklyn. Their widely circulated recordings, often jointly produced in both sites, linked diasporic communities in North America and the UK with the Caribbean.

Rather than viewing this sort of transnational musicing in terms of center-periphery binaries or First World/Third World hierarchies, Guilbault has suggested that soca artists and their recordings "articulate a transnational social, musical and political field that spans and bounds the experiences and attitudes of Caribbean people living in Caribbean nation-states and elsewhere [in the diaspora]."[19] Similarly, looking over the biographies of transnational musicians like the Ethiopian jazz vibraphonist Mulatu Astatke, Simon Frith has proposed that "the concept of globalization, with its intimations of the inexorable forces of history and/or capital, should be replaced in the discussion of world music by an understanding of networks—globalization from below as it were."[20] Such cultural fields and networks are knit together by multidirectional flows of artists among multiple geographic sites for musical production and performance. Moreover, musical activity within these fields and networks can be understood as both a response to and cause of global decentralization. Regarding the latter, in her study of New York's Chinese American music communities, Su Zheng has argued that diasporic music-making "destabilizes the center with its worldviews, aesthetics, and cultural forms," and eventually can "contribute to the dynamics of a 'global culture' sustained in part by the joining of transnational networks of people, ideas, and cultural products diffused from the 'rest' to the 'West.'"[21] The dynamics of overseas Carnivals further undermined this "West/rest" dichotomy, not only because the cultural exchange had grown increasingly circular, but also because, demographically, the diasporic metropoles that once constituted so much of the "West" had become so full of the "rest."

Circular approaches to globalization that downplay center-periphery hierarchies have increasingly become the norm in assessing the movement of musical production and practice across international borders, particularly when considering the post-1965 period. But as Mark Slobin and Gage Averill warn, any such transnational models must remain flexible, since the experiences of different cultural groups in the diaspora and their conceptual relationship to their homeland may vary radically, depending on the specifics of historical conditions and recent social circumstances.[22] Thus, within New York's broader Caribbean diaspora, one finds both similarities and disparities in the way island-specific styles were produced and distributed inside and outside their communities.

Soca versus Reggae versus Salsa versus Konpa

Soca never enjoyed the global popularity that reggae and salsa achieved in the 1970s and 1980s—there were no soca equivalents to Bob Marley and Jimmy Cliff, or to Tito Puente and Ruben Blades. Stylistically, soca lacked reggae's hard-edged, electric guitar/bass-driven sound and ganga-tinged messages of spiritual and political liberation that were so appealing to American and British rock audiences of the era. Nor did it offer the virtuosic instrumental work and improvisational flourishes that drew international fans to Latin jazz and salsa. Spanish lyrics presented a challenge to salsa's crossover possibilities, but its close ties to Latin dance, an expression that was easily commodified and sold as a viable recreational activity in a way that Carnival dancing was not, broadened its appeal to urban non-Latino audiences in North America and Europe. Perhaps the overall soca sound was simply too bright and bouncy for the cynical times, and the lyrics too Carnival-oriented for non-Caribbean audiences. In addition to these musical qualities, the recording and distribution of soca and the other island-specific styles impacted their global reach and crossover potential.

Jamaican ska, rocksteady, and reggae were heavily indebted to American R&B and rock music of the 1950s and 1960s. Reggae became extremely popular among New York's Jamaican community and carved out a small niche in the Brooklyn Carnival complex, but New York did not develop into an important center for reggae recording and production outside of Jamaica in the 1970s. Much of the early ska, rocksteady, and reggae was recorded in Jamaican studios and issued on small local labels by producers Coxsone Dodd of Studio One, Duke Reid of Treasure Island, and Prince Buster of Voice of the People. While a great deal of innovative work in mixing and dubbing went on in these Jamaican studios, local labels had limited distribution outside of Jamaica, with the exception of occasional agreements with independent British companies.[23] It was London-based Island Records, founded by Chris Blackwell, that catapulted reggae into the international arena with Bob Marley's crossover album successes *Catch a Fire* (1972), *Natty Dread* (1974), and *Exodus* (1977). In the early days of rocksteady and reggae, Jamaican artists seeking international exposure tended to head for England, where Blackwell and Emil Shalit, the owner of Melodisc/Blue Beat, had already established a sophisticated recording and production apparatus.[24] Not until the early 1980s, when the Jamaican migrant Philip Smart opened HC&F Recording Studio in Freeport, Long Island, was there a viable Jamaican record-production company in New York. It was only in the late 1980s that the legendary producer Coxsone Dodd finally moved his operations to Brooklyn.[25]

Latin music has a long and venerable history in New York. Drawn by the city's superior recording, broadcast, and club opportunities, many of the best Cuban and Puerto Rican musicians migrated to New York in the 1930s and 1940s. The city became a crucible for the evolution of Latin jazz in the 1940s, with expatriate Cuban bandleaders and arrangers Machito, Mario Bauza, and Chico O'Farrill merging Cuban son with African American big band swing. In the postwar years, New York's large Puerto Rican population came to dominate the Latin music scene, with Nuyorican bandleaders Tito Puente and Tito Rodriguez popularizing the mambo style in the 1950s and early 1960s. This set the stage for the emergence of salsa in the late 1960s, with a younger generation of Nuyorican musicians led by Willie Colon, Ray Barretto, and the Fania All-Stars. In the late 1960s and early 1970s, the innovative Dominican bandleaders Johnny Ventura and Wilfrido Vargas brought their new style of pop merengue to the city's growing Dominican migrant communities in Washington Heights and Brooklyn.[26] The recording history of these genres is complex. A good deal of early Latin jazz appeared on New York–based jazz labels such as Verve and Impulse, while popular mambo orchestras were recorded by American majors RCA and United Artists, as well as by the New York–based independent labels Seeco (founded in 1944), Tico (founded in 1948), and Alegra (founded in 1956). But it was Fania Records (founded in 1964), under the direction of Dominican American Johnny Pacheco and Italian American Jerry Masucci, that would come to be known as the "Latin Motown." Fania grew to dominate the scene in the 1970s, the period when grassroots salsa was in ascension and the major American labels had lost interest in Latin music.[27]

As Fania's star began to fade in the 1980s, Nuyorican/Dominican Ralph Mercado launched RMM records in hopes of reaching a more bicultural and bilingual Latino audience.[28] With a large pool of New York–born and expatriate musicians to draw from, and a substantial New York Latin market, the producers of Fania and RMM did not have to journey to the Caribbean in search of fresh talent, as their soca counterparts were prone to do. The experience was slightly different with regard to the Dominican Republic, where the local Karen and Kubaney companies, which offered modern studios and recording engineers sensitive to merengue aesthetics, recorded much of the island's music.[29] Broadly speaking, New York reigned over the Latin music recording industry from the 1940s through the early 1990s, when Miami emerged as the center of contemporary salsa and Latin popular music. Control of production was spread over a spectrum of cultural actors working for the major American record companies and for independent labels owned and operated by various configurations of Latinos, non-Latinos, and joint ventures between the two.[30] While the majors and RMM were the most attuned to crossover possibilities, Fania remained committed to the tipico barrio style and its Nueva York Latin audiences.[31]

The experiences of Haitian musicians and record producers in Brooklyn during the 1960s and 1970s were closer to those of Straker, Charles, and

Gould and the Brooklyn soca singers. The Haitian businessman Joe Anson moved his Ibo Records label from Port au Prince to Brooklyn in the late 1950s, and in the mid-1960s Haitian beauty-shop operator Marc Duverger opened up a record shop in Brooklyn and began recording visiting Haitian bands.[32] Gage Averill describes a transnational production process in which the producers "imported raw musical materials (tracks and mixes) from Haiti for pressing and distribution in the United States and exported them back to Haiti."[33] By the 1970s, Brooklyn had become the hub of the Haitian music business with the small labels Mini and Rotel Records joining Ibo. Meanwhile, the island's most popular konpa bands, Tabou Combo and Skah Shah, migrated to New York, where they cut their latest recordings with disco beats and funk horn lines, employed African American horn players for recording sessions and gigs, and occasionally sang in English.[34] With deteriorating economic and social conditions in Haiti, musicians and record producers became more dependent on the Haitian overseas communities in New York and Paris, occasionally achieving modest crossover sales in France.

In sum, the migration of these Caribbean popular musics to New York was essential to their development and emergence as transnational expressions. All demonstrated a degree of hybridity in their mixing of indigenous Caribbean forms with elements of American jazz and popular music styles, a process that was accelerated by the significant numbers of Caribbean musicians, arrangers, and record producers who relocated in New York, where they established vibrant community music scenes. Latin jazz, salsa, and reggae proved to be the most innovative and enduring. In terms of production and distribution, Jamaican musicians ceded a degree of control to British and American record companies, thereby enhancing their potential for international marketing and crossover sales. New York's salsa musicians moved within overlapping Latino- and non-Latino-controlled production settings, achieving their most sustained success among the rapidly expanding, Spanish-speaking urban audiences in the United States, South America, and the Caribbean. Sales to the English-speaking crossover market were relatively limited. Haitian konpa producers and artists, like their soca counterparts, maintained considerable control over production and distribution of their music, but in doing so they sacrificed more international exposure and expanded sales opportunities.

Brooklyn's soca scene shared many similarities with adjacent New York Caribbean communities in terms of musical practice and, in some cases, musical production and distribution. But the one indispensable cultural factor that differentiated Brooklyn soca from the rest was the music's unbroken ties to Carnival celebrations in Trinidad and abroad. Trinidad Carnival had continued to expand in the post-Independence era, and by the late 1970s overseas Carnivals in Brooklyn, London, Toronto, Miami, and other Caribbean islands were offering viable employment networks for singers, musicians, and arrangers that were not available to musicians from other Caribbean nations that lacked indigenous Carnival celebrations.

The Trinidad and Brooklyn Carnivals provided a fertile environment for soca to emerge and flourish, yet inadvertently confined the music largely to seasonal Caribbean and overseas-Caribbean audiences. Brooklyn soca music, along with the steelband music discussed in the previous chapter, can only be fully understood in the context of Carnival, which fundamentally set them apart from the musical expressions of New York's Jamaican, Haitian, Puerto Rican, Dominican, and other Caribbean communities.

Musical Hybridity and Cultural Identity

Musical miscegenation has been a touchstone of creativity across the Caribbean for centuries. In the innumerable combinations of African, European, and American musical elements were threads of commonality that reflected a shared Afro-Caribbean legacy, as well as subtle and nuanced distinctions that led to the emergence of island-specific musical traditions such as the popular styles discussed above. The role these varied musics played in the negotiation of social identity was equally complex, for as Nederveen Pieterse has argued, hybridity can problematize cultural boundaries.[35] In terms of diasporic music, hybrid styles could unite and divide members of heterogeneous urban migrant communities. Soca, for example, provided a kind of cultural boundary between the recently arrived Caribbean migrants and their African American neighbors in central Brooklyn, much as calypso, decades earlier, had demarcated difference between native-born blacks and foreign-born Caribbean islanders in Harlem. That boundary was certainly porous, thanks to a shared African heritage that allowed native-born and Caribbean blacks to listen to, dance to, and appreciate one another's music. But there was no question that the calypso and soca music performed at clubs and dances, especially in conjunction with Carnival festivities, coded Caribbean, not African American. Carnival music allowed migrants to unite around a common Caribbean heritage and to distinguish themselves culturally from the surrounding African American community, which, in Harlem, had favored jazz and R&B, and later in Brooklyn identified with R&B, soul, funk, and rap. This was a cultural distinction seldom made by the white New Yorkers, who, naively, tended to assume a homogenous black population.

Just as music could bring English-speaking Caribbean migrants together, it could also segregate them by providing island-specific cultural expressions. Brooklyn's Jamaicans tended to favor reggae, Bajans spouge, Haitians konpa, and Trinidadians, Antiguans, St. Vincentians, and Grenadians soca (and particularly the soca popularized by singers from their native island—Swallow from Antigua, Becket from St. Vincent, etc). Carnival provided the intercultural space for island migrants to dialogue and compete musically while waving their flags and sporting their national colors on T-shirts and bandanas. The Parkway was one great Caribbean Sea, but individual islands remained sonically and visually prominent. Participants danced under the umbrella of a pan-Caribbean celebration, but that dance was simultaneously communal and rivalrous. Carnival organizers were delighted and vexed by the paradox that musics could concurrently unify (we are all one Caribbean people) and divide (we are Trinidadians with our soca, they are Jamaicans with their reggae, those people are Bajans with their spouge, etc.) the larger Caribbean community. In Brooklyn such hybrid musics helped mediate the cultural boundaries as individuals struggled to sort out their multiple identities as Americans, as black Americans, as Caribbean people of African ancestry, and as migrants with island-specific affiliations.

Returning to the concerns of Rohlehr, Liverpool, and Harris, a cultural politics that addresses the processes of production, distribution, and consumption must be considered when assessing the consequences of musical hybridization. Harlem calypsos were fresh blends of early Trinidadian calypso with American jazz and Tin Pan Alley that resulted in creative new forms. Although distribution was under the control of American record companies, the performers were Trinidadian singers and musicians, and their records were consumed primarily by Caribbean New Yorkers and their brethren back in the islands. Elements of the equation flipped during the calypso craze of the 1950s, with American appropriators and their record companies garnering most of the profits from so-called Manhattan calypsos that were marketed primarily at to non-Caribbean North American and European audiences. But the situation turned once more in the 1980s with soca, when the performers, audiences, and record producers were all Afro-Caribbean, and the music evolved as a deep indigenous expression of Brooklyn and Trinidad Carnival. There were no Andrews Sisters or Kingston Trio interpreters in that round. Soca was being mass produced in the United States, as Harris observed in his calypso, but this time by and for Caribbean people, not by and for foreigners, as Liverpool warned. This all suggests that when it comes to music in the diaspora, the processes of hybridity and cultural crossover can never be assumed a priori to be beneficial or to be deleterious, but rather unpredictable—the results can be culturally affirming or culturally exploitive, or even both. Every case must be evaluated on its own merits with scrutiny paid to what Nederveen Pieterse identifies as "the *terms* under which cultural interplay and crossover take place" that recognize "the actual unevenness, asymmetry, and inequality in global relations."[36]

Liverpool's own recording career is a case in point. The lyrics to his 1979 song "Calypso vs. Soca" posited sharp binaries between what he perceived to be authentic calypso and commercially tainted soca that were aimed at local Trinidad and foreign audiences, respectively (see Figure 7.1). But his choice of musical accompaniment, along with the actual production and distribution of his records, suggests otherwise. Dissatisfied with his initial attempts to work with RCA's Trinidad affiliate and other local labels, Liverpool eventually teamed up with Granville Straker. As a result, most of his 1970s–1990s material was produced and distributed on the Brooklyn-based Straker label. Liverpool spent considerable time in and out of New York and his records were marketed in Brooklyn and

Figure 7.1. Chalkdust, *Calypso vs. Soca*, Straker's Records, 1979.

other overseas sites as well as in Trinidad. His song lyrics remained solidly in the traditional calypso mold, often addressing controversial political issues and local Trinidad subject matter. He did not, however, hesitate to collaborate with Brooklyn's top soca arranger, Frankie McIntosh, who set many of his songs to heavy soca beats replete with flashy synthesizer fills and pulsing melodic bass lines.[37] His record sales were modest and he had no crossover hits. Liverpool did, however, control his own musical content, and politically he preferred that production and distribution were through a Brooklyn-based Caribbean independent label, rather than a North American–run multinational like RCA. As a singer and composer who was deeply committed to indigenous culture, Liverpool was inherently skeptical of foreign and commercial influences. Yet he was willing to plunge into the transnational arena and embrace musical hybridity, but only on his own terms.

While Labor Day Carnival proved vital to Brooklyn's emergence as a center of soca music production, the winding down of the borough's soca recording industry in the 1990s had little immediate effect on local Carnival events. The Eastern Parkway parade continued to attract expansive crowds, while the Brooklyn Museum Panorama contest and Dimanche

Gras shows consistently drew large and enthusiastic audiences. And even as his record and CD sales plummeted, Charles could take solace in his lively Fulton Street block party that brought throngs of eager fans to Fulton Street to rub shoulders with famous calypsonians. But the disappearance of the steelbands from the Parkway and the increased commercialization of the parade, with its heavy emphasis on mediated contemporary music and glitzy modern costumes, was a growing concern for some Carnival traditionalists. In response, a second road procession known as J'Ouvert (Break of Day) was coalescing and would soon become an important component of the Labor Day Carnival weekend. J'Ouvert, championed by the proponents of Trinidadian heritage, would bring the steelbands and older masquerading traditions back to the road during the early hours of Carnival Monday morning.

Notes

1. Gordon Rohlehr, *A Scuffling of Islands: Essays on Calypso* (San Juan, Trinidad: Lexicon Trinidad, 2004), p. 11.
2. Chalkdust's recording of "Calypso vs. Soca," arranged by Art de Coteau, is found on his LP *Calypso vs. Soca* (Straker's Records GS 2224, 1979).
3. Lord Relator's recording of "Importation of Calypso" is found on his *Nostalgia* LP (R.A.P.E. Records 0003, 1983).
4. Rohlehr, *A Scuffling of Islands*, pp. 374–380.
5. For background on chutney soca (the result of the fusion of East Indian traditions with Afro-Trinidadian soca in the 1980s) and raga soca (the result of the reinfusion of Jamaican dance hall and reggae elements into soca in the 1990s), see Jocelyne Guilbault, *Governing Sound: The Cultural Politics of Trinidad's Carnival Musics* (University of Chicago Press, 2007), pp. 175–182; and Shannon Dudley, *Carnival Music in Trinidad: Experiencing Music, Expressing Culture* (Oxford University Press, 2004), pp. 95–102.
6. Simon Frith, "The Discourse of World Music," in *Western Music and Its Others*, edited by Georgina Born and David Hesmondhalgh (University of California Press, 2000), pp. 305–306.
7. For critical discussions of the world music debate, see Frith, "The Discourse of World Music," pp. 305–322; Jocelyn Guilbault, "World Music," in *The Cambridge Companion to Pop and Rock*, edited by Simon Frith, Will Straw, and John Street (Cambridge University Press, 2001), pp. 176–192; and Su Zheng, *Claiming Diaspora: Music, Transnationalism, and Cultural Politics in Asians/Chinese America* (Oxford University Press, 2010), pp. 32–36.
8. Jocelyn Guilbault, "On Redefining the 'Local' Through World Music," *The World of Music* 35, no. 2 (1993): 36.
9. See, for example, *When the Time Comes: Rebel Soca*, compiled and annotated by Gene Scaramuzzo (Schanachie 64010, 1988); and *Best of Straker's: I Feel to Party*, compiled and annotated by Randall Grass (Rounder CD 5066/67, 1996).
10. See, for example, *Calypso Pioneers: 1912–1937*, compiled and annotated by Dick Spottswood and Don Hill (Rounder CD 1039, 1989); *Lord Invader: Calypso in New York*, compiled and annotated by John Cowley (Smithsonian Folkways CD 40454, 2000); and *West Indian Rhythm: Trinidad Calypsos, 1938–1940*, compiled and annotated by

John Cowley, Don Hill, Dick Spottswood, and Lise Winer (Bear Family BCD16623 CD Box, 2006).

11. For a critical discussion of Paul Simon's controversial 1986 *Graceland* recording project with South African musicians, see Steven Feld, "Notes on 'World Beat,'" in *Music Grooves*, edited by Charles Keil and Steven Feld (University of Chicago Press, 1994), pp. 238–246; and Louise Meintjes, "Paul Simon's Graceland, South Africa, and the Mediation of Musical Meaning," *Ethnomusicology* 34, no.1 (Winter, 1990): 37–73.

12. For examples of nostalgia songs written by Puerto Rican and Dominican migrants, see Peter Manuel, "Representations of New York City in Latin Music," in *Island Sounds in the Global City: Caribbean Popular Music and Identity in New York*, edited by Ray Allen and Lois Wilcken (University of Illinois Press, 1998), pp. 24–34. For examples of nostalgia songs written by Haitian migrants, see Gave Averill, "'Mezanmi, Kouman Nou Ye? My Friends, How Are You?': Musical Constructions of the Haitian Transnation," in *Ethnomusicology: A Contemporary Reader*, edited by Jennifer Post (Routledge, 2006), pp. 262–264.

13. "Crown Heights Justice" was recorded and mixed in Brooklyn by Rawlston Charles and Sparrow and released on Charlie's Records (SCR 3571, 1991). A recording of the song can be heard on YouTube, at https://www.youtube.com/watch?v=lqsirp9vDKk.

14. Sparrow's call for justice was apparently aimed at Brooklyn's Caribbean migrants of color, as his song makes no mention of the murder of the Hasidic student Yankel Rosenbaum. See Philip Kasintz's interpretation of the lyrics in "Community Dramatized, Community Contested: The Politics of Celebration in the Brooklyn Carnival," in Allen and Wilcken, *Island Sounds in the Global City*, pp. 106–109.

15. Rawlston Charles, interview with author, 5 February 2015, Brooklyn.

16. Super Blue's "Get Something and Wave" was recorded and mixed in Brooklyn by Rawlston Charles and released on the LP *Super Blue and the Love Band 10th Anniversary* on Charlie's Records (BCR 3538, 1990). A recording of the song can be heard on YouTube, at https://www.youtube.com/watch?v=UzC6wTEZZxs.

17. Keith Nurse, "Globalization and Trinidadian Carnival: Diaspora, Hybridity, and Identity in Global Culture," *Cultural Studies* 13, no. 4 (1999): 685

18. Ibid., 683.

19. Guilbault, "World Music," p. 188.

20. Frith, "The Discourse of World Music," p. 319.

21. Zheng, *Claiming Diaspora*, p. 289. The internal quote is from James Clifford, *The Predicament of Culture: Twentieth-Century Ethnography, Literature, and Art* (Harvard University Press, 1988), p. 273.

22. For more on the importance of exploring the connections, real and perceived, between host and homeland countries in diasporic music studies, see Mark Slobin, *Subculture Sounds: Micro Musics of the West* (Wesleyan University Press, 1993), pp. 64–65, and Averill, "Mezanmi, Kouman Nou Ye?," p. 262.

23. For more on the history of Jamaican producers and early record labels, see Peter Manuel, *Caribbean Currents: From Rumba to Reggae* (Temple University Press, 1995), pp. 154–159; and Dave Thompson, *Reggae and Caribbean Music* (Backbeat Books, 2002), pp. 305–318.

24. Chris Blackwell began recording music in Jamaica in the late 1950s, but in 1962 he moved his operation, Island Records, to London, where he continued to record and market Jamaican music to British and eventually

international audiences. An ancillary Island label, Trojan Records, specialized in Jamaican ska, rocksteady, and early reggae beginning in 1967. In the 1970s Blackwell formed distribution deals with various major US companies, including Atlantic, Capitol, and Warner Brothers, and in 1989 he sold Island Records to Polygram. See Lloyd Bradley, *This Is Reggae Music: The Story of Jamaica's Music* (Grove Press, 2000), pp. 412–414, 430–431; and https://www.discogs.com/label/8377-Island-Records.

25. Thompson, *Reggae and Caribbean Music*, p. 310.

26. A useful overview of Latin music in New York is found in John Storm Roberts, *The Latin Tinge: The Impact of Latin American Music on the United States* (Original Music, 1979). See also Juan Flores's account of postwar Latin music in New York and the importance of New York–based record labels and artists for the emergence of the salsa style in *Salsa Rising: New York Latin Music of the Sixties Generation* (Oxford University Press, 2016).

27. For more on the history of Tico, Alegre, Seeco, and Fania Records, see Deborah Pacini Hernandez, *Oye Como Va!: Hybridity and Identity in Latino Popular Music* (Temple University Press, 2010), pp. 24–33; Manuel, *Caribbean Currents*, pp. 72–75; and Flores, *Salsa Rising*, pp. 62–72, 175–207.

28. For more on the history of RMM Records, see Hernandez, *Oye Como Va!*, pp. 147–149.

29. For a brief history of the recording industry in the Dominican Republic, see Paul Austerlitz, *Merengue: Dominican Music and Dominican Identity* (Temple University Press, 1997), pp. 97–98.

30. New York's influential independent Latin music labels were owned by a mix of Latinos and non-Latinos—Fania by Dominica-born Johnny Pacheco and Italian American Jerry Masucci; Tico by Jewish American George Goldner; Seeco by Jewish American Sidney Siegel; Alegre by Nuyorican Al Santiago and Jewish American Ben Perlman; and RMM by Nuyorican/Dominican Ralph Mercado. By the 1990s most of these companies had folded and many of the major US record companies had established Latin music divisions. See Hernandez, *Oye Como Va!*, pp. 15–33, 147–149.

31. Hernandez, *Oye Como Va!*, pp. 31, 148.

32. For background on Brooklyn's early Haitian music recording business in Brooklyn, see Gage Averill, "Moving to the Big Apple: Tabou Combos Diasporic Dreams," in *Island Sounds in the Global City: Caribbean Popular Music and Identity in New York*, edited by Ray Allen and Lois Wilcken (University of Illinois Press, 1998), p. 144.

33. Gave Averill, *A Day for the Hunter, A Day for the Prey: Popular Music and Power in Haiti* (University of Chicago Press, 1997), p. 23.

34. Averill, "Moving to the Big Apple," p. 141–147.

35. Jan Nederveen Pieterse, *Globalization and Culture: Global Mélange* (Rowman & Littlefield, 2015), pp. 101.

36. Ibid., p. 79.

37. Listen, for example, to Frankie McIntosh's soca-infused arrangements on Liverpool's recordings *With a Bang* (Straker's Records GS 2243, 1983), *Port of Spain Gone Insane* (Straker's Records GS 2267, 1986), and *Chalkdust: The Master* (Straker's Records GS 2283, 1988).

8

J'Ouvert in Brooklyn
Revitalizing Carnival Tradition

That whole thing broke down on the Parkway—because of the trucks and deejays, steel pan could not be heard. . . . And there was no competition, no prize money, no nothing. So why should a steelband go out there? And knowing that we were responsible for Labor Day—but no kind of respect—they just pushed us aside, they narrowed us to Panorama.

—Earl King, founder of J'Ouvert City International[1]

J'Ouvert is different here in Brooklyn with no deejays or amplification. It's certainly more authentic and old school here than in Trinidad—having pan as the main instrument entertainment here in Brooklyn.

—Arddin Herbert, director and arranger of the CASYM Steel Orchestra[2]

The pan men Earl King and Arddin Herbert recount an extraordinary story of cultural revitalization within Brooklyn's Caribbean community. The establishment of a Brooklyn J'Ouvert celebration in the 1990s brought a vital component of Trinidadian Carnival into the diasporic mix, taking its place alongside the Eastern Parkway parade, the Panorama and Mas Band competitions, and the Dimanche Gras stage show. This chapter will flesh out the emergence of Brooklyn J'Ouvert, focusing on how a group of Trinidadian migrants revived a century-old celebration to create an event that appeared to some, as Herbert noted, to actually be "more authentic and old school" than what was going on back in Trinidad at the time. Brooklyn J'Ouvert was no doubt derived from its parent Trinidad celebration, but like many diasporic expressions, it took on a life of its own.

For more than a century, J'Ouvert "Break of Day" processions have marked the opening of Carnival in Trinidad. Held in the predawn hours of Carnival Monday, J'Ouvert evolved from the nineteenth-century Canboulay festivals—the nighttime celebrations where former slaves gathered to masquerade, sing, and dance in commemoration of their emancipation.[3]

When the tradition was incorporated into Trinidad's pre-Lenten Carnival, J'Ouvert became an arena for African-derived percussion, witty satire singing, sardonic costuming, and, more recently, lively steelband music.[4] In contrast to the bright, fancy pageantry of Monday and Tuesday afternoon Carnival, J'Ouvert's gruesome devils and mud-covered revelers personify what Stephen Stuempfle has called the "underworld dimension of Carnival . . . grim and sinister characters, dirty and coarse costumes, and aggressive verbal and physical action."[5] Historically, J'Ouvert's demonic and satirical masquerading, coupled with dense percussion and steel pan music, manifest Carnival's deepest challenge to order and authority, and for the Trinidadian novelist Earl Lovelace, the essence of the emancipation spirit.[6]

J'Ouvert was never a component of Harlem's Labor Day Carnival, nor was it part of the official Brooklyn celebration during the 1970s and 1980s. Indeed, up to the time of this writing, the West Indian American Day Carnival Association (WIADCA) has not sponsored any sort of J'Ouvert event as part of its Labor Day Carnival festivities. In the initial years, Carlos Lezama and his associates had their plates full trying to fund and produce the Eastern Parkway parade and the attendant Brooklyn Museum concerts. Taking on an additional event—one that would have certainly raised significant security concerns given its 3:00 a.m. start time and tradition of transgressive hijinks—was no doubt more than they felt they could handle. Lezama was personally supportive of the initial efforts to establish a Brooklyn J'Ouvert, assisting the organizers in negotiating the original parade route with the Brooklyn 67th Precinct Police and often attending the event.[7] But he shied away from any official involvement or sponsorship. In retrospect, WIADCA's failure to add a steel pan-friendly J'Ouvert component to their Labor Day Carnival, coupled with its lack of incentives for steelbands to participate in the Eastern Parkway parade, further strained the organization's already tense relationship with Brooklyn's steel pan community.[8] A separate organization would be needed to coordinate J'Ouvert and bring Brooklyn's steelbands back into street Carnival.

Steelbands and Sound Trucks on the Parkway

Steelbands were the primary source of music in the early years of the Brooklyn Carnival, providing the rhythmic groove for participants to chip and wine down Eastern Parkway. But by the late 1970s, as the parade grew in size and sound trucks became more plentiful, acoustic steelbands became increasingly unnecessary, and, for some, an impediment to a smooth-running Carnival parade. Collectively feeling "disrespected," as J'Ouvert founder and pan man Earl King put it, the pan players found themselves being pushed off the Parkway. The rise of soca music was one of the culprits. Soca's dense bass lines and mechanical drum rhythms reflected a new, high-volume musical sensibility. Record-spinning deejays and amplified brass bands, mounted on large trucks and broadcasting over powerful sound systems driven by portable generators, produced extraordinarily loud, bass-heavy dance music that no conventional steelband could come close to matching. When mounted on flatbed trucks, the new sound systems were easily integrated into Carnival street processions without hindering the forward progress of the large mas bands. The results were devastating for acoustic steelbands that could not take advantage of the new technology. "The whole thing broke down on the Parkway," King recalled with frustration:

> It didn't make any sense. Guys would come out with their steelband, and they [the WIADCA organizers] wanted you to come in the last part—they say you moving too slow. If you were in the front you would slow things down too much. So you are in the back—you have to wait until all these big mas bands—Hawks and Buroketes and Sesame Flyers—all go by, before you could come down the street. And if you find yourself between two deejay trucks you cannot be heard.[9]

Martin Douglas, the president of the United States Steelband Association (USSA) and a veteran player with Invaders USA reflected, "The steelbands just couldn't fit in between the deejays and their heavy electric equipment anymore; after your ears acclimate to the loudness, there was no way you can hear steel pan."[10] Herman Hall recalled that steelbands were not always welcomed on the Parkway because critics claimed that they "slowed down" the parade—which of course, in the spirit of Carnival, they did.[11]

The transition from acoustic steelbands to deejays and heavily amplified live band music was slow but steady. Don Hill, writing about his experiences on Eastern Parkway in the mid-1970s, reported a mix of steelbands and live combo/brass bands perched on trucks, with the latter playing Trinidadian soca and calypso, Jamaican reggae, Bajan spouge, and Haitian pop meranges.[12] In 1982 Hall, in a lengthy Carnival review for his *Everybody's Caribbean Magazine*, reported on music by two steelbands and a number of truck-mounted discos, the latter "blasting" the latest soca hits. One mas bandleader told Hall he spent $3,000 out-of-pocket to rent a large truck with audio system, generator, and musicians.[13] When I first began attending Carnival in 1984, the music was roughly evenly divided between steelbands and trucks with deejays or amplified live bands. By the late 1980s Philip Kasinitz noted that mas bands were more likely to employ deejays with loud sound systems than traditional steelbands.[14] Gage Averill complained that the steelband he was following at the 1990 Carnival could hardly be heard over the din of amplified soca.[15] The *New York Times*, in a 1991 account of Carnival, reported that "[a] succession of flatbed trucks carried bands and enormous loudspeakers" down Eastern Parkway.[16] Writing for the *Carib News* in 1994, Michael Roberts concluded that the steelbands on the Parkway had been "upstaged" by deejays with high-tech sounds systems.[17] Newspaper accounts of the Parkway celebration in the mid- and later 1990s increasingly focused on deejays and sound systems rather than steelbands:

> And Eastern Parkway will be the scene of the deejay clash as huge speakers, state-of-the-art amplified sounds and high-tech systems will blast the soca music to the delight of millions who will be chipping down Eastern Parkway for Labor Day. Without the deejays there is no party.[18]

By the late 1990s pan had nearly disappeared from the Parkway. Of the twelve bands competing in the 1999 Brooklyn Panorama, I observed only Despers USA coming out for the Labor Day Monday parade.

These events in Brooklyn tended to mirror those in Trinidad, but with some noteworthy variations. Carnival researcher Jeffrey Thomas observed "a gradual but steady decline in steelbands' participation during Carnival season at social gatherings (called 'fetes') and on Carnival days" since the early 1970s.[19] Much of the responsibility for the latter, he surmised, rested with the large sound trucks, on which

> both [amplified] brass bands and D.J.'s are driven slowly through the streets, high above the crowds on huge flatbed trailers. Steelbands have not been able to compete with the volume, mobility, or convenience of the brass bands and D.J.'s, and have clearly forfeited their place as the favored music of most large Carnival mas bands today.[20]

Thomas went on to note, "Whereas steelbands used to provide the most popular music to accompany revelers from dawn on Monday morning until Tuesday midnight, they now confine themselves mostly to the period of Carnival known as J'Ouvert morning, with a handful of bands appearing on Tuesday to play a mas."[21] Other observers reported that by the late 1970s the numbers of steelbands playing for large mas bands were rapidly diminishing as Trinidadian pan players increasingly turned their attention toward the big Panorama competition and the elaborate preparations it demanded.[22] Earl Lovelace blamed the decline of steelbands on the road on this singular focus on Panorama—a controlled, sit-down performance space that to his ear fostered music "frozen in the mode of the European classics" and stripped of its original participatory and rebellious emancipation spirit. "It [steelband] cannot allow itself to be sidelined to a single tune a year—a hundred men and women in a band playing a single tune while the youth disappear into the Socarama arena to find a music to sing them and speak for them."[23]

Trinidad's National Carnival Commission (NCC), taking note of these developments, in 1996 instituted a steelband-on-the-road competition in hopes of luring pan players back onto the streets during Carnival Monday and Tuesday. This "state-sponsored nostalgia competition," as Philip Scher characterized the effort, did manage to bring more steelbands out that year, but in the long run the results have been modest at best, with sound trucks to this day continuing to dominate the daytime masquerading.[24] This acknowledged, the decline of steelbands from Port of Spain's daytime Carnival was not as dramatic as their near disappearance from the Eastern Parkway parade. In the late 1980s, Stuempfle observed, "[m]any steelbands continued to come out for these two days" (Carnival Monday and Tuesday), albeit "without the large numbers of followers they once enjoyed." On Monday and Tuesday evenings they appeared at smaller competitions in downtown Port of Spain and for the Last Lap gathering that marked the close of Carnival festivities.[25] In the 1980s and 1990s there were still a number of street performance opportunities open to Trinidad's steelbands, but they did not rule the big daytime Carnival processions the way they had in decades prior. The sheer size of Trinidad Carnival allowed more room for steelbands than did its Brooklyn counterpart. In Port of Spain the numerous steelbands, mas bands, and sound trucks could take multiple routes as they converged on the Savannah judging stands and the downtown area. Nor were they generally under strict schedules. This looser structure, spread over two full days, allowed more space for steelbands and sound trucks to avoid constant collisions and conflict with one another (although this certainly occurred). Contrast this to Brooklyn, where all the steelbands, mas bands, and sound trucks where squeezed into one parade route for a single afternoon event that began around noon and ended with a firmly enforced 6:00 p.m. curfew.

Such restrictions on the Parkway help explain in part why steel pan players increasingly pushed for the establishment of a J'Ouvert component for Brooklyn Carnival. With the growing hegemony of the sound trucks by the late 1980s, the Brooklyn steelbands found their opportunities for participation in Carnival becoming increasingly restricted to Panorama. While the Panorama competition and prize money were, as in Trinidad, alluring to many, they did not satisfy the desires of some pan players and their followers to bring steelband music back to the streets. The drive to reunite pan and "playing mas" eventually led to the emergence of a new component for Brooklyn Carnival—the Monday morning predawn J'Ouvert celebration.

J'Ouvert Grows in Brooklyn

There are reports dating back to the late 1970s of informal groups of Dimanche Gras revelers processing through the streets of Flatbush in the early hours of Labor Day morning. One version of this history was chronicled in 1997 by J'Ouvert's founders:

In the 70's the idea of J'Ouvert in New York came about from an inner hunger for the totality of Carnival. One morning in an impromptu moment after enjoying " Dimanche Gras" in the back of the Brooklyn Museum, Janet "Flagwoman" Lewis, Michael "Scanty" Scanterbury, our local calypsonian, and Lion and the Naturals, took to the streets with their Cuatros and Iron Instruments. Defying the rules, five o'clock Labor Day morning, dancing and chipping to the rhythms of calypso music. As Flagwoman recalled, someone gave her a flag and she led the band down the road. People were hanging out their windows, buses and cars stopped. They were amazed at what was taking place.[26]

Not until the mid-1980s, recalled King, did steelbands become involved in J'Ouvert activities. It was during the early hours of Labor Day morning (circa 1985) that a few members of the Pan Rebels Steel Orchestra— then a pan-around-the-neck band—ventured out from their pan yard on Woodruff Street near Flatbush Avenue and began playing on the sidewalk, attracting a crowd of all-night partygoers.[27] Tony Tribuse, a member of Pan Rebels, recalled that a group of fifteen pan players and masqueraders dressed in pajama costumes began moving down Flatbush Avenue. The group picked up other late-night revelers from neighborhood parties and dance halls, and returned to their pan yard with a crowd of nearly one hundred.[28] The Pan Rebels repeated the performance for several years, and eventually were joined by the Golden Stars Steel Band, the Metro Steel Orchestra, and the JuJu Jammers mas band. By the late 1980s, a small group of steel and mas bands were processing around Flatbush and Bedford Avenues early Labor Day morning, staking out an informal route through the heart of Brooklyn's Caribbean community.

As the impromptu J'Ouvert celebration grew, participants realized they would need to create a more formal structure to avoid conflict with the authorities. In 1994 Earl King, with the help of community organizer Yvette Rennie, established J'Ouvert City International (JCI), a not-for-profit organization meant to coordinate the J'Ouvert event. With the assistance of local politicians and the police of Brooklyn's 67th Precinct, the organization was granted permission (although not an official permit) to parade from Woodruff Street up Flatbush Avenue, across Lefferts Avenue (later changed to Empire Boulevard), and down Nostrand Avenue to Linden Boulevard, beginning at three o'clock on Labor Day morning. In order to facilitate control over the event, the police eventually requested that JCI move the opening of J'Ouvert to Grand Army Plaza. Since 1999 the J'Ouvert route has begun at the plaza, moved south on Flatbush Avenue, east across Empire Boulevard, and south on Nostrand Avenue.[29]

To attract more pan and mas bands, King and Rennie established J'Ouvert competitions. In 1994 viewing sights were set up along the route in front of sponsoring businesses, including Alan's Caribbean Bakery, Scoops Ice Cream Parlor, and Mike's International Restaurant. Trophy awards were given for the best steelband calypso (won by the Metro Steel orchestra performing "Bionic Fever") and mas costume (won by the Three Men and a Lady mas band portraying "Anything Red").[30] The following year small cash prizes were offered. In 1997 first, second, and third place cash awards were given for best calypso tune (won by Invaders USA playing Swallow's "Misbehave"), bomb tune (won by CASYM playing the pop song "Falling in Love"), mas band costume (won by Roy Pierre and Associates portraying "Canboulay"), and individual male and female costumes.[31] In 1998 a special "old" calypso category was established for steelbands.

The allure of late night/early morning revelry with steelbands and mas competitions led to a rapid increase in the size of Brooklyn J'Ouvert. The 1994 event was large enough to attract press attention. Under the banner headline "1994 J'Ouvert Winners Feted at Club Prestige," the *Daily Challenge* featured a two-page photo spread with the winners of the steelband and mas competitions posed with JCI's organizers.[32] A *Carib News* review of that year's festivities, boldly headlined "J'Ouvert Is Alive!," reported that eleven ole mas bands and nine steelbands had participated in J'Ouvert.[33] The following year, serving as JCI's public relations officer, Rennie described a crowd of approximately 50,000 watching twelve steelbands, nine of which were accompanying small mas bands. Among them were the Silhouettes Steel Orchestra, whose rack-mounted pans "were pulled by die-hard pan people" bringing back "memories of the old days when steelbands controlled Carnival."[34] In the 1996 J'Ouvert I observed a dozen steelbands, each accompanied by mas bands or groups of individual masqueraders. JCI listed sixteen steel and fifteen mas bands in its 1997 program booklet and I saw roughly that number at the 1998 and 1999 gatherings.[35] By 2000 they claimed to have registered twenty steelbands.[36]

Some of the bands mounted their pans on racks and carts with wheels that enabled them to be pushed and pulled along by their supporters as noted above by Rennie (see Figure 8.1). Others were positioned on low

Figure 8.1. Pulling pan during J'Ouvert, 1999. Photo by Martha Cooper (courtesy of City Lore).

trailers pulled by small trucks, and a few were perched higher off the ground on floats or on the beds of flatbed trucks. The first two configurations kept the musicians and their pans close to the ground and the J'Ouvert revelers who surrounded them, blurring the distinction between artists and audience and creating a communal atmosphere and intense sonic space evocative of early Carnival processions.[37] Arddin Herbert, the leader of the CASYM steelband, favored having his supporters pull the band mounted on racks and wheels: "I found that to be much better than being on a float above everyone else because to me it takes the revelers out of the actual experience. You are high above them and they are looking up, versus having them right there pushing those racks and pans and being right next to you and looking inside your pan seeing what you are doing. I prefer that from an interactive perspective."[38] Herbert's concerns echo those of Trinidad Carnival critics, including Lovelace, who was deeply troubled that "steelbands which used to be pushed through the streets of Port of Spain now ride on trucks—some like floats, high up above the emancipation jouvay jam in which they used to be central."[39]

Early J'Ouvert crowd size estimates varied, ranging from official police figures of 50,000 for the 1996 and 1997 events, to JCI's claim of 200,000.[40] The *Times*, covering J'Ouvert for the first time in 1997, estimated that 50,000 Carnival-goers participated in early morning "rogue parades known as Ole Mas."[41] The Borough Community Affairs Department of the Brooklyn NYPD offered crowd estimates of 80,000–100,000 in 1998 and close to 200,000 in 1999.[42] The *Daily News* predicted that a crowd of nearly a half-million would attend the 1999 J'Ouvert, a gathering that "many purists in the West Indian community consider to be the real parade."[43]

Brooklyn's early morning J'Ouvert celebration, like the Eastern Parkway spectacle, reflected the chaotic revelry of Trinidad Carnival while attempting to maintain some semblance of a parade with a prescribed route, as required by the city's authorities. Bands and individuals slowly wound their way through the streets packed with dancing spectators and participants. The atmosphere was loose, with bystanders moving in and out of the procession uninhibited. However, there were significant differences between the Eastern Parkway and Flatbush events. JCI's official policy, as stated in their 1995 program booklet was "Steelpan music only." A JCI 1998 flyer reminded participating J'Ouvert bands that there would be "Steelband Music Only—No Amplified Steelband or deejays."[44] The deejays and sound trucks that dominated Eastern Parkway were explicitly banned from J'Ouvert—initially only unamplified steelbands were allowed to register and participate; eventually unamplified rhythm bands were encouraged to join.[45] "We allow no deejays at J'Ouvert," Rennie told the *Carib News* in a 1999 interview. "We want to preserve the tradition of J'Ouvert and ole mas. This event has always been accompanied by steelband music."[46] King elaborated:

J'Ouvert puts pan in the spotlight. You see, pan got lost on the Parkway when the big sound systems and deejays took over. So we were determined to do something to preserve pan, to let our children know where Carnival really comes from. So in J'Ouvert it's just pan and mas bands, no deejays invited. Now people are remembering the joy you can get by taking your time and playing mas with a steel band, just inching up the road, pushing pan. We're trying to revive that whole thing."[47]

JCI's message was reprised by Vinette Pryce of the *Amsterdam News*: "For many folks, the daytime parade has become too overburdened by sound systems. They favor live pan music. For a few years now the panmen have boycotted the Eastern Parkway event for the same reason. J'Ouvert has become the alternative."[48] Interestingly, the Brooklyn J'Ouvert organizers preached and enforced a pure pan orthodoxy that did not at that time (nor has it ever) exist in Trinidad. While some players and nationalist culture brokers bemoaned the decline of pan on the streets of Port of Spain, there was never an official ban on deejays or brass bands with sound systems in Trinidad's J'Ouvert. By the 1980s, acoustic steelbands and amplified deejays were part of the early morning J'Ouvert mix, despite the tendency of the latter to sonically overwhelm the former.[49]

Like its Eastern Parkway predecessor, Brooklyn's J'Ouvert began as a spontaneous grassroots movement, emerging from the pan yards and streets of East Flatbush. It was the pan players and ole mas enthusiasts—not government officials, cultural specialists, or commercial sponsors—who organized the earliest J'Ouvert celebrations. JCI came about somewhat after the fact, when growing crowds necessitated an organizational body to coordinate efforts with the police. King was himself a pan player with no previous community organizing experience. He, Rennie, and their associates remained a loosely organized group with few political connections and limited access to government or corporate funding sources. JCI negotiated the parade route and schedule with the 67th Precinct Police, attempted to register the mas and steelbands, and set up modest competitions with judging sites in front of local sponsoring businesses. But in the early days the organization did not have complete control over who participated—in keeping with the spontaneous spirit of J'Ouvert, many musicians and masqueraders simply "showed up," unannounced and unregistered, to play mas. JCI was, however, able to assert authority with its "pan only" policy that kept J'Ouvert free of deejays and amplified bands. In doing so the organizers saw themselves as preserving essential components of the traditional Carnival they had grown up with in Trinidad but that were now vanishing from Brooklyn's official WIADCA-organized events.

Steelbands and Rhythm Sections on the Road at J'Ouvert

The steelbands played a variety of tunes during the four-hour J'Ouvert procession. Each band would likely play a bomb tune (a non-calypso pop tune or classical piece arranged with a calypso beat), one or more old calypsos, and possibly a simplified arrangement of their current Panorama tune. The J'Ouvert bomb and old calypso selections, in contrast to the more complex, multi-section Panorama arrangements, followed a relatively simple verse/chorus structure with a steady, moderately slow, pulsing beat and extended percussion jam sections, and sometimes a familiar sing-along chorus. CASYM's arranger Herbert, who participated in Brooklyn's Panorama contests and J'Ouvert celebrations throughout the late 1990s, summed up his approaches to the two performance settings:

> J'Ouvert is different from Panorama, which is geared toward a dramatic stage presentation. J'Ouvert is repetitive, on the road, people are moving, chipping along to a slower tempo. . . .The arrangements are simpler—they have to be more danceable and singable. The audience needs to hear that melody or counter melody and gravitate to it quickly, and be part of it, sing it, and remember it. So when it comes around again they are like, "yes." That as opposed to the more complicated Panorama arrangements that can fly over the heads of so many people. You might say J'Ouvert is a more condensed style—for a bomb tune I might begin with a verse/chorus, followed by a second verse/chorus with some slight variation, a bridge, a jam session, and end by repeating the initial verse/chorus. It's over in three or four minutes. I would use all those things for my Panorama arrangement, plus more melodic variations, a key modulation, a minor key section, and some sort of dramatic ending. The Panorama piece would have a faster tempo and last for maybe ten minutes.[50]

Unlike the Panorama arrangements that require weeks, or even months, of rehearsal, J'Ouvert bomb tunes were often pulled together in a single practice session.[51] J'Ouvert steelbands, genrally ranging from ten to twenty-five players, were smaller than their Panorama counterparts, and usually featured an expanded percussion section. The traditional steelband "engine room" is augmented by friends and J'Ouvert merrymakers beating cowbells, bottles, iron brake drums, and various homemade instruments. The result is a loose, densely percussive sound meant to propel street dancers. The J'Ouvert style is more "free spirited" and "less regimented" than what one would hear at Panorama, observed pan man Douglas.[52]

Bomb tunes quickly became a part of the Brooklyn J'Ouvert mix. Prizes were awarded to the CASYM and Moods Steel Orchestras for their respective renditions of Mozart's *Messiah* and "Our Day Will Come" in 1994.[53] Rennie reported bomb arrangements of "Impossible Dream," "Overjoyed," "Mr. Bojangles," Albert Keteberg's classical "Monastery Garden," and "America the Beautiful" at the 1995 J'Ouvert.[54] Given the bomb's popularity in Trinidad and Brooklyn J'Ouvert, JCI decided to create a separate bomb category as part of their competitions. The 1996 contest was won by

CASYM with an arrangement of Roberta Flack's 1973 recording "Killing Me Softly."[55] In 1997 bomb tune awards were given to CASYM for "Falling in Love," All Stars USA with a medley of "Impossible Dream" and "Try a Little Tenderness," and the Invaders Steel Orchestra for their arrangement of the Supremes hit "Back in My Arms Again."[56] American popular songs from the 1960s and 1970s were favored for bomb arrangements in Brooklyn, bringing something of an Americana oldies aura to the contest.

In Trinidad, the rendering of such "foreign" bomb tunes was somewhat controversial, with the nationalist-leaning NCC insisting that only calypsos be played at the Panorama competition. But many Trinidadian pan players were attracted to European classical and American pop songs given their diverse musical interests and aesthetic preferences, and because they welcomed the creative challenge of reinterpreting international material for local tastes.[57] In any case, the bomb has remained a favorite in Trinidad's J'Ouvert, and it quickly became a mainstay in Brooklyn. Perhaps the bomb took on yet another level of significance in Brooklyn's diasporic community by offering a site for a musical dialogue between Afro-Caribbean New Yorkers and members of their broader host society. Brooklyn's pan players proclaimed, through their J'Ouvert bomb arrangements, that they were willing to listen to, appreciate, and even play American music, but on their own instruments (steel pans), in their own style (with a calypso beat), and for their own purposes (dancing and masquerading for their Carnival). Several bands, including CASYM, maintained an active repertoire of bomb-style arrangements of classical and popular tunes for performances during the year at cultural festivals and indoor concerts where their audiences would include many non-Caribbean listeners.

In addition to steelbands, smaller all-percussion groups, known as "rhythm bands" formed an important part of Brooklyn's J'Ouvert soundscape. Some were impromptu assemblages of individuals beating hand-held metal brake drums, bottles, bells, sticks, and shakers. Others were more elaborately organized units consisting of multiple percussionists mounted on small trailers or floats who performed with a designated mas band. One of the earliest such groups was the Rhythm Masters, founded by Tony Reece (b. 1956), a native of the Belmont neighborhood of Port of Spain who came to Brooklyn as a teenager in 1971. By the late 1970s Reece was "knocking" his iron brake drum behind Roy Pierre's mas band on Eastern Parkway and at fetes where percussionists would play along with deejays spinning the latest calypso hits. In the 1990s he organized a small quartet to entertain at fetes, and sometime in the late 1990s he brought the Rhythm Masters out for Brooklyn J'Ouvert. He recalled that the group consisted of approximately eight percussionists playing iron brake drums (set out on stands with individual performers playing several irons at once), conga drums, timbales, a large skin "boom" drum, a two-note bass oil drum known as a "dudup," a metal scratcher, and a gourd shaker knows as a "shekere." The Rhythm Masters had been hired to provide the dance groove for mas band whose members crowded around the low float that carried the musicians slowly down the road.[58]

Groups like Reece's Rhythm Masters were organized around the principle of stacked, interlocking rhythms similar to Afro-Caribbean drum ensembles and tamboo bamboo bands that accompanied early Carnival street processions.[59] The fixed ground beat is provided by the low register boom drum and dudup, and by the mid-register congas. The higher register iron brake drums and timbales freely improvise or "cut" over the other instruments and then return to their own fixed rhythmic patterns. The metal scratcher and shekere provide high-register fixed patterns and occasional rhythmic ornamentations. Reece explained that he and his fellow percussionists would develop different rhythmic patterns, which he referred to as "tempos" or "choruses," derived from the underlying ground beat of particular soca songs. The band would cycle between four or five of these tempos for several hours during J'Ouvert, sometimes punctuating transitions with abrupt "stops" and precise unison riffs. The reciprocal relationship between the musicians and Carnival revelers was essential, as Reece observed: "We are pure percussion—percussion turning rhythm into music for people to dance to. . . . And in J'Ouvert we would feed off the dancers and masqueraders and the more we would feed them the more they came [and followed our band]." Like Rennie and the J'Ouvert City organizers, Reece and his cohorts were also consciously aware of the African roots of their percussion music. "We call it ancestral" he explained. "Our ancestors were drummers—we come out of that African goat skin drumming. So, when we start to play we get into a certain zone. . . . And you listen to the rhythm, we call it that 'jumbie.' It's like a spiritual groove—you understand? It makes everything synch together. So yes, it goes back to the roots of it all."[60]

There were only a handful of rhythm sections in the J'Ouvert celebrations of the late 1990s. The road at that time was dominated by the previously described steelbands.[61] But the number grew steadily, prompting JCI to add a rhythm band competition to its sponsored events in the early 2000s. Dudley has noted a similar proliferation of rhythm sections in Port of Spain J'Ouvert around that time, suggesting that such performances "reenact the resourceful and defiant innovations of the early steelband."[62] Port of Spain's best-known group, the Laventille Rhythm Section, was formed in the mid-1980s and eventually became a regular fixture in J'Ouvert, with what one observer described as "an instantly powerful sound that evoked the ancestral homeland of Africa."[63] While Reece and his present band, the Kutters Rhythm Section, still enjoy playing at deejay parties, performing on the road in J'Ouvert holds deeper cultural implications: "Now in New York that's what it's about—rhythm coming down the road—it's the culture. . . . So now we can show the essence of J'Ouvert the way it's supposed to be—rhythm and pan, going out in all its glory."[64]

Ole Mas and J'Ouvert Costumes

Along with steelband and rhythm sections, ole mas costumes and political satire dominated the early Brooklyn J'Ouvert celebrations.[65] In keeping with the J'Ouvert traditions of humor and the macabre, individuals played mud mas (covering their bodies with mud), dressed in old rags, painted their faces, bodies, and costumes, and covered themselves with white powder and flour. Many masqueraded as devils, witches, ghosts, and goblins, while others donned satirical outfits and carried signs with humorous political commentary. Traditional Dame Loraine (usually played by cross-dressing men) and midnight robber characters sporadically appeared. Tubs of mud were actually wheeled down Flatbush Avenue, with revelers stopping every so often to smear fresh muck on each other and on innocent bystanders. Buckets of paint also appeared and creative costumes were splattered on the spot.

Organized mas bands portrayed specific themes or characters, such as devils (red, white, and black), Indians, master/slaves, and African warriors. Some bands provided witty political commentary. For example, in 1998 the Wingate Originals played a satire mas they called "Clinton Turn de White House Red!" A wagon-mounted model house bearing the inscription "Scandal in the White House" was wheeled along by band members smeared in red paint. Men, cross-dressed as Monica Lewinsky, carried lewd placards proclaiming, "Bill and I had an oral arrangement" and "I never inhaled, I only smelled it." (See Figure 8.2.)

Figure 8.2. Wingate Originals, Brooklyn J'ouvert, 1998. Photo by Keith Getter.

In 1999 the Wingates presented "We're Not Takin Dat," which featured biting commentary through costumes and signs on current events, including the Abner Louima torture case; the Amadou Diallo "41 bullet" shooting; the brutal dragging death of James Byrd Jr. in Jasper, Texas; the school mass shooting in Columbine, Colorado; and racial profiling on the New Jersey Turnpike. Several members demonstrated their discontent with the health industry by wheeling a fake corpse through the crowd on a portable bed, surrounded by paint-smeared doctors and nurses who continued to prescribe beer and liquor to the victim. The *Times* interviewed a man "dressed in a swine's mask and police uniform and waving a plunger above his head," clearly another reference to the cruel treatment of Abner Louima at the hands of the New York City Police. "This is Giuliani's plantation now, but even so the police could not stop us," he declared defiantly to the reporter.[66] In keeping with the Trinidad J'Ouvert tradition, these sorts of satirical and transgressive enactments, often accompanied by rhythmic drumming and steelband music, found a comfortable place in Brooklyn's new break-of-day celebration.

Perhaps the most innovative costumes were designed by Roy Pierre, who won the J'Ouvert costume competition three years in a row. In 1997 he presented a Canboulay theme based on traditional African and slave motifs. His 1998 costumes deftly combined Trinidadian folklore characters with American Halloween themes. Entitling his presentation "Jumbie Jamborie," his costumes included rainbow jab jabs (devils), moko jumbies, soucousyants (female vampires), diablesses (temptresses with cloven feet), and Douens (spirits of dead children), as well as witches, black cats, mummies, and Medusa figures. While popular with his followers and the competition judges, Pierre's costumes were considered by some to be too elaborate for J'Ouvert.

JCI's efforts to reunite mas bands and steelbands on the road were undeniably successful. The organization claimed to register nineteen mas bands for the 1998 J'Ouvert. Ten of them were directly sponsored by a steelband (e.g., the CASYM mas band was sponsored by the CASYM Steel Orchestra), eight hired separate steelbands (e.g., the E&K Associates mas band employed the Despers USA steelband), and the Style and Associates mas band used their own "Rhythm Jammers" section.[67] In 2000 JCI reported registering twenty-three mas bands—thirteen had hired steelbands, seven were directly sponsored by steelbands, and three employed rhythm sections.[68]

These sorts of organized mas bands, accompanied by a steelband or a rhythm section, were common, but the majority of J'Ouvert revelers opted for simpler, more spontaneous displays—a bit of body paint, flour or talcum powder on hair and face, a splattered T-shirt, a flag bandana, or a funny hat. Many others, dressed in ordinary summer shorts and tops, lined the sidewalks, occasionally mingling with the costumed throng in the center of the street where they risked getting smeared with powder, paint, or oil. Although there was a slow but steady procession along the prescribed route, many people appeared to wander with friends—eating, drinking, dancing, and simply enjoying the music and mas.

These modest, often homemade J'Ouvert costumes stood in stark contrast to regalia worn by members of the big fancy bands that dominated daytime Eastern Parkway mas. The largest of these bands, such as Borokeetes, Hawks, and Sesame Flyers, boasted hundreds of members who donned brightly colored, sequined, elaborately designed costumes, the most impressive of which resembled small floats. Occasional ole mas characters—jab jab devils, midnight robbers, "bad behavior" sailors, etc.—showed up on the Parkway, but they were few and far between, dwarfed by the large bands of fancy costumes (see Figure 8.3). The ole

Figure 8.3. Fancy costume on Eastern Parkway, circa 1981. Photo by Martha Cooper (courtesy of City Lore).

mas costuming, like unamplified steelbands, migrated away from the Parkway toward J'Ouvert.

J'Ouvert Pan-on-the-Road: Aesthetics and *Communitas*

The newly established J'Ouvert celebration provided Brooklyn's steelbands with an unfettered forum for their art, one that afforded them an immediate and direct connection with their audience while reuniting them with traditional mas bands. The initial success and growth of Brooklyn J'Ouvert reveals much about the aesthetic preferences, deep-rooted performance practices, and concerns over cultural heritage and identity shared by many Brooklyn Caribbean migrants as they struggled to negotiate the forces of tradition and modernity in Carnival. Regarding the music itself, issues of acoustics proved paramount. Pan players and serious fans were quick to attest that steelbands sounded best live, close up, where one could hear clearly the interlocking melodic lines and rhythmic phrases and feel the intense physicality of the groove as fellow players "beat pan." Listening to steelbands on recordings or from afar over outdoor sound systems simply could not replicate the sonically satisfying experience of occupying the intimate space surrounding a live band on the road during Carnival, at a fete or dance, or in the pan yard. This became increasingly difficult by the early 1990s, with diminishing opportunities on the Parkway and at dances, and with pan yard rehearsals given over to the endless part-drilling required in preparation of the increasingly complex Panorama tunes.[69] The competition itself remained an option for playing or hearing live steelband music during Carnival, but the acoustic environment behind the Brooklyn Museum was not ideal. Bands performed on a high stage set back from seated listeners who experienced a somewhat muddy combination of live and mediated sound broadcast over loudspeakers. Miking large steelbands to create a full and balanced sound was difficult, and in the early years sound reinforcement equipment was not of the highest quality. Thus, the newly established J'Ouvert, with its non-amplification, pan-only policy, provided the only sonic space in which pan music could literally be "heard in Carnival," as Herbert declared, free from din of deejay-driven sound systems and the distorted mediation of Panorama. "Steel pan music in the early morning is the best thing to my ears; everything else is still and you're hearing pure pan—it's like birds in the forest," reflected the costume designer Burtrum Alley.[70] For many of Brooklyn's pan players and fans, there was no substitute for the aurally satiating experience of being on the road for J'Ouvert.

In addition to these acoustic considerations, J'Ouvert performance provided an environment where pan players and their supporters could experience the deep sense of social interconnectedness and existential immediacy that lie at the heart of Carnival ritual. Pan-on-the-road processionals were highly participatory in nature, aiming to minimize artist-audience distinctions by encouraging all present to join the performance as masqueraders, dancers, singers/chanters, and hand percussionists. The state of communal ecstasy that ensued during peak surges of performances was akin to Victor Turner's "spontaneous *communitas.*" During the most intense moments of the J'Ouvert procession, participants might come together in what Turner described as "a flash of lucid mutual understanding on the existential level."[71] That is, densely packed throngs of pan players, percussionists, masqueraders, and dancers could experience the suspension of time and the rush of union with their fellow revelers. Or, as pan man Martin Douglas put it, "people used to be all in the middle of the band, pushing the racks and such. They would be totally involved, closer, part of the band—we'd say 'We moving now' and they would push the racks down the road. There was more camaraderie back then."[72] Such "moving together and sounding together in a group," in Turino's view, could foster not only camaraderie, but further a "deeply felt similarity, and hence identity, among participants."[73] This sense of shared Afro-Caribbean identity, experienced through mutually understood cultural performance, was palpable during J'Ouvert, and central to its success.

Carnival participants no doubt experienced similar intense moments of communal mas in the fancy bands that followed the sound system trucks on Eastern Parkway. Indeed, the physical intensity of the amplified music's volume and throbbing bass could surround and seduce, literally transforming individual participants into a singing, dancing throng. But live musicians played a limited role in this unity—steelbands were absent while deejays and amplified soca bands were spatially removed, positioned high above revelers on flatbed trucks. This feeling of communal transcendence for listeners was also difficult to achieve during the Panorama, where performer/audience lines were strongly demarcated by the formal stage setting. Brooklyn Panorama was presentational in mode, a spectacle drawing a clear distinction between the artists on stage and the seated audience and judges for whom they performed. In Brooklyn there was no equivalent to the North Stands in the Port of Spain Panorama, where working-class revelers created their own rowdy fete in between competing bands by "beating dudups and iron and wailing down the place," as Lovelace observed.[74] By the late 1990s, J'Ouvert had supplanted the Parkway as the only dedicated cultural space where musicians, masqueraders, and revelers could commingle as equals in Carnival performance. J'Ouvert's *communitas* fostered a sublime synergy that united Brooklyn's Caribbean revelers in the rebellious spirit of Carnival.

J'Ouvert Pan-on-the-Road: Nostalgia and Heritage

Brooklyn J'Ouvert quickly evolved into an occasion for pan enthusiasts and lovers of ole mas to commune and pursue their passions. But when viewed through the lens of history, the event's cultural significance runs even deeper. J'Ouvert proffered the opportunity for Trinidadian migrants who had arrived in the 1960s and 1970s to indulge their nostalgic desires for an idealized Carnival of their youth. Nostalgia, as Scher points out, played a vital role in the ongoing construction of a transnational consciousness among Trinidadians in the diaspora, serving as "a way of re-membering not only the past but the cultural forms that presumably existed coterminously with the place and space of their occurrence." Those cultural forms were essential to constructing, in his words, a "nostalgic collective memory" among migrants in Brooklyn.[75] Pan man Douglas explained it this way:

> You're here in America, you're not home in Trinidad. So you're bringing the culture to America as far as J'Ouvert is concerned. . . . This is a nostalgic feeling, like back home in Trinidad when J'Ouvert started at five in the morning you could hear the cocks crowing and you hear the bands coming and the sun starts coming up and everyone is having a good time. . . . In the old days a lot of people [in Brooklyn] didn't have green cards and they couldn't go home for Carnival. . . . You know, you come from Trinidad and you can't go home for Carnival, so this is where you are going to enjoy, this is your Carnival.[76]

This interplay of nostalgia, memory, and diasporic identity is best understood through a process of self-conscious cultural selection by which pan-on-the-road and ole mas came to be designated as forms of cultural heritage. Barbara Kirshenblatt-Gimblett has argued that select musical practices take on a cultural gravitas that raises them to the level of heritage precisely because they are perceived to be endangered and in possible need of "protection," "enshrinement," and, as King suggested, "revival."[77] The goal of J'Ouvert was to perpetuate those musical practices associated with an "authentic, old-school" Carnival experience that, as Herbert described, was no longer available on Eastern Parkway, or for that matter in Trinidad. Scholars have grown increasingly wary of terms such as "revival" and "authenticity," arguing they are slippery cultural constructs based on the self-conscious interpretation of the past.[78] But JCI's leaders were deploying exactly this sort of selective historical editing when they designated steel pan and ole mas as powerful cultural symbols that were believed to be in danger of disappearing from Brooklyn Carnival. Of course, there was no evidence back in the 1990s that the steel pan as an instrument was on the decline or in any way in danger of going extinct—indeed, the pan continued to evolve in new and creative ways in the hands of innovative Panorama arrangers and skilled soloists. What was in danger of being lost, in JCI's view, was the history of the instrument and the original practice of playing pan-on-the-road. Their 1995 program booklet made this crystal clear, proclaiming the organization's goal of "the maintaining and preserving of Caribbean art, culture, and heritage (steelband, calypso, and mas). Our programs are designed to educate and teach young people about the origin and history of our culture." The booklet contains a thumbnail sketch of the steel pan, tracing its roots to earlier Carnival "dustbin cover and biscuit tin" bands and tamboo bamboo percussion groups.[79]

Nostalgia and heritage thus nested comfortably together in the diaspora—the desire to re-experience an imagined past coupled with a self-conscious preservationist ideology provided agency for JCI's initial project. The enactment of heritage through the establishment of a "pan only" J'Ouvert celebration allowed nostalgia to move from feeling to praxis. The invocation of culturally significant expressions associated with home and pre-migration times—especially those expressions now perceived to be imperiled by rapidly modernizing forces—helped to mediate the stress of geographic and temporal dislocation that had led to nostalgia in the first place. Strikingly, by the mid-1990s there appeared to be as much, if not more, concern over the loss of pan-on-the-road among members of Brooklyn's diasporic community than there was back in Trinidad, where a number of road venues—though diminished from earlier decades—still remained viable. The Trinidad NCC's attempt to bring steelbands back to the 1996 daytime Carnival notwithstanding, a pan-only policy was never instituted for J'Ouvert or any other component of Port of Spain's road Carnival.

Scher observed that in order "to cultivate and perpetuate a cultural heritage," a constituency of the Borough's older masqueraders chose to return to Trinidad to play a nostalgic sailor's mas.[80] But rather than returning home in search of their cultural heritage, a coalition of steel pan expatriates created a safe space within Brooklyn's Carnival complex for pure pan-on-the-road, willfully defending the tradition from the encroachment of amplified bands and deejays. Heritage in the diaspora proved to be a powerful force that led to the revitalization of an older pure pan cultural practice that, ironically, by the mid-1990s no longer existed in such unadulterated form in Trinidad. Brooklyn's transnationals could and did assuage their nostalgic yearnings by occasionally returning home for Carnival, but they also sought to cultivate their cultural heritage in East Flatbush. And, thanks to JCI, they did precisely that.

J'Ouvert and the Revitalization of Trinidad-Style Carnival

The preservation of pan-on-the-road and ole mas was at the core of a broader revitalization movement to reclaim at least a portion of Brooklyn Carnival as a Trinidadian/Caribbean celebration. JCI and its followers feared that the Eastern Parkway parade was veering away from its roots toward an increasingly multicultural, political, and commercial spectacle. While Trinidadian Carnival continued to provide the basic model for the Labor Day celebration, there was a steady encroachment of other Caribbean and African American influences. This is not surprising, given the multicultural nature of central Brooklyn and the variety of Caribbean groups participating in Carnival, the complex nature of New York City's ethnic politics, and WIADCA's stated mission of uniting the borough's diverse Caribbean people around a shared culture of Carnival. The Caribbean press at that time was quick to pick up on this narrative. A 1996 editorial in the *Carib News* argued that Carnival "serves as an integrative force, bringing together the different national groups from the Caribbean" and listed a dozen islands that had become, in theory, "integrated" through Brooklyn Carnival.[81] The wider cultural and political implications were made explicit the following week: "The Carnival Celebrations are a source of pride for Blacks in this country. The creativity, imagination, and splendor reflect the cultural strength of the Caribbean."[82] New York City's vote-hungry politicians, much to the delight of Carlos Lezama and his WIADCA associates, contributed to the official discourse of unity by proclaiming Carnival a distinctive creation of New York's rapidly growing Caribbean community. In 1992 Mayor David Dinkins placed Brooklyn Carnival in the context of the 178 ethnic groups that make up New York City's "glorious cultural mosaic," proclaiming that none "shine more gloriously than the segment represented by the Caribbean community."[83] His successor, Mayor Rudolph Giuliani, alluded to the parade's multicultural nature by calling it "an ethnic fest that demonstrates the diversity of New York."[84] In his zeal to broaden the cultural net to include African American and even white New Yorkers, the Jewish-American Brooklyn Borough president Howard Golden declared, "You don't have to be from the Caribbean to enjoy this [Carnival]. All Americans can take pride in what's happening today. This is a symbol of living together, respecting each other."[85] Thus, observed Philip Kasinitz, by the 1990s Carnival in New York "vacillate[d] between its Trinidadian roots and its pan-Caribbean agenda."[86]

For some participants, the Parkway Carnival had apparently drifted too far from its Trinidadian moorings into a pan-Caribbean Sea. In response to these concerns, JCI, whose leaders were all Trinidad expatriates, made sure to locate specific Trinidadian Carnival expressions at the center of their J'Ouvert project. Their 1997 program booklet announced their determination to preserve "three Caribbean art forms originating from Trinidad and Tobago: steelband, calypso, and mas."[87] The larger mission, "to educate and teach young people about the origin and history of our culture," left little doubt as to whose culture needed preservation. As the 1995 program booklet recounted, Brooklyn's J'Ouvert's "sweet steelband music" and old mas costuming made "Flatbush Avenue resemble Frederick Street in Trinidad," a reference to a center of Carnival action in downtown Port of Spain.[88] The issue of national loyalty is further clarified in the JCI 1997 program booklet that offered the lyrics to the Trinidad and Tobago National Anthem, followed by those of the Star Spangled Banner (both to be sung at the organizations' annual awards meeting).[89]

Trinidad's position as the epicenter of Caribbean Carnival culture did not, however, preclude JCI's founders from recognizing the global dimensions of Carnival J'Ouvert and their connections to a broader Afro-diasporic heritage. Like WIADCA's organizers, they too walked a fine line between Trinidadian and pan-Caribbean concerns, stressing the "merging cultures from diverse backgrounds" as central to their education mission.[90] Rennie noted that steelbands made up of migrants from St. Lucia, St. Vincent, and Grenada had participated in J'Ouvert: "We are Caribbean people who come here and bring our culture. So you might hear a steelband playing Jamaican reggae music, and you might hear some Haitian rhythms. It's a celebration of different cultures."[91] Evidently, a variety of musical styles could be accommodated, as long as they are played on the Trinidad steel pan or Afro-Caribbean drums. Linkages between the steel pan and African traditions were made explicit—the pan was identified as Trinidad in origin, but an instrument that "grew out of a struggle by people of the African race to maintain our freedom and identity."[92] Rennie later reflected, "The African drumming has always been there in Trinidad, and always in the steelband, in the engine room. Drums are imbedded inside us, it's part of our African history that we are extremely proud of and it naturally fit into the J'Ouvert idea."[93] JCI's recognition of African roots was made clear in the design of its J'Ouvert program booklet logo that embedded the images of a steel pan in its "J" and an identifiably African mask in its "C." The organization's decision to add a rhythm band contest to its roster of events reflected a further conscious nod to African ancestral traditions. JCI was willing to broaden its Trinidad-centric discourse to acknowledge and celebrate the contributions of other Caribbean islands as well as Africa, but always in the context of history and heritage, a sensibility they found increasingly waning in the Eastern Parkway parade. The steel pan offered an ideal cultural symbol for this mission. It was simultaneously recognized as the national instrument of Trinidad, a product of a centuries-old process of blending African and European musical antecedents, and the centerpiece of a transplanted Afro-Caribbean art form that flourished in twice-diasporized communities in Brooklyn.

Specific site location was another crucial factor for JCI. Consider the geographic aspects of Brooklyn Carnival. Eastern Parkway, locally referred to as "Caribbean Parkway," formed one of the northern boundaries of the borough's Afro-Caribbean community in the 1990s. Eastern Parkway was the border area where the English-speaking Caribbean islanders, Haitians, and Hasidic Jews of Crown Heights met the African Americans of Bedford Stuyvesant and the Irish, Jews, and yuppies of Park Slope. The J'Ouvert celebration, on the other hand, took place south of Eastern Parkway, at the intersection of the Crown Heights, Flatbush, and East Flatbush neighborhoods, deep in the heart of Brooklyn's Afro-Caribbean community. The original route, beginning at Woodruff Avenue and running up Flatbush Avenue, across Empire Boulevard, and down Nostrand Avenue, was lined with Caribbean produce stores, roti shops, restaurants, bakeries, social clubs, dance halls, record stores, and Spiritual Baptist storefront churches. Half a dozen mas camps were located along the route, and eight pan yards are within a few blocks. In 1997 a NYC "J'Ouvert City" street sign was added to the intersection at Flatbush and Woodruff Avenues, officially honoring the original starting point for the J'Ouvert celebration. By moving the action from the Parkway down to Flatbush,

Caribbean migrants in general, and Trinidadians in particular, asserted their domain over J'Ouvert.

Brooklyn's Caribbean migrants—old and young, Caribbean and American-born—had multiple and sometimes overlapping motivations for participating in J'Ouvert. The event's original organizers and their supporters saw the occasion as a way of preserving and promoting what they perceived to be their endangered Trinidadian heritage and reclaiming Carnival as their own. Nostalgia motivated a number of middle-aged and older Trinidadians seeking to re-experience their memories of the old-time Carnival of their youth. Serious pan players enjoyed the novelty of beating pan-on-the-road in a participatory Carnival street setting, where their un-mediated music could be intimately shared. And, not surprisingly, many Caribbean and African American youths were simply drawn to the excite-ment of an all-night street fete.

J'Ouvert and Eastern Parkway: Tradition and Modernity

Reviewing this evidence might lead to the conclusion that Brooklyn's J'Ouvert and Eastern Parkway celebrations evolved in divergent trajectories with seemingly disparate social functions. J'Ouvert was Trinidadian, traditional, and community-based, evoking deep Carnival symbols to reinforce a sense of shared cultural heritage. Eastern Parkway, by contrast, reflected a multicultural, modern, and commercial sensibility by showcasing the most contemporary pop styles, proclaiming a unity among diverse Caribbean and African American peoples, and providing New York's politicians and private businesses with a forum to advertise their goods and services. However, like many cultural dialectics, J'Ouvert and the Parkway ultimately circled back to complement one another by serving two interrelated community needs: J'Ouvert strengthened internal cohesion and reinforced in-group identity, while the Parkway provided public display and cultural validation in a larger arena. Many participants saw no contradiction in the two events, and some chose to participate in both. The *Times* profiled a middle-aged West Indian mother who attended J'Ouvert to cheer on her teenage children who play in the Invaders Steel Orchestra, and later showed up on the Parkway to play mas with a fancy band.[94] Herbert confirmed that many young players in his CASYM steelband enjoyed the raucous excitement of beating pan on J'Ouvert morning, and after catching a few hours of sleep head to the Parkway to jump up to soca and reggae-spinning deejays.[95] For these individuals and many like them, J'Ouvert merely became another choice in the kaleido-scope of Carnival options—old and new—available to them.

The emergence of J'Ouvert in Brooklyn in the 1990s underscored the incredible dynamism of the modern, urban Carnival, and its tendency to seek an equilibrium between innovation and tradition. Brooklyn Carnival, like its Trinidadian parent, was constantly evolving, adapting new elements of popular culture, while striving to maintain its traditional roots. The forces of modernity and globalization pushed Carnival to embrace new technologies, the latest popular music styles, mas themes based on contemporary media images, corporate sponsorship and tourism, and the politics of multiculturalism. Simultaneous with this was the urge to preserve, and where necessary to revive, core African-derived participatory traditions. In the case of Brooklyn, the innovations of the Parkway were balanced to a degree by the revitalization of pan-on-the-road and ole mas traditions in J'Ouvert. There was room in the larger Carnival complex for deejays blasting high-decibel soca and pan players beating unmediated calypso; for amplified brass-band-backed calypsonians and acoustic Afro-Caribbean rhythm bands; and for fancy band masqueraders in space-age costumes and J'Ouvert revelers in muddy rags.

This is not to suggest that in Carnival innovative and traditional practices must be separated by time and space, with the latter occurring exclusively at J'Ouvert, and the former only on the Parkway. They existed simultaneously, side by side. Steelbands often played original arrangements of the latest soca hits during J'Ouvert, while the contemporary, amplified soca on the Parkway was deeply rooted in Afro-Caribbean traditions of improvisation, call and response, and rhythmic drive. J'Ouvert's ole mas costumes were sometimes highly individualistic creations that commented on contemporary social events, while more traditional ole mas characters such as devils and midnight robbers occasionally showed up on the Parkway. But by the turn of the new millennium, Brooklyn Carnival's more traditional expressions gravitated toward the J'Ouvert celebration, while the Parkway remained the primary arena for the display of modern forms.

This intersectionality of tradition and modernity in Carnival music should come as no surprise. Cultural historians have challenged the validity of the tradition-modernity binary, re-envisioning the former as dynamic and contemporary rather than as static and antiquated. In the words of Henry Glassie, tradition is an emergent process, the "artful assemblies of materials from the past, designed for usefulness in the future."[96] Tropes of recombining the old with the new, of balancing convention and change, of hybridizing the oral and the written, and of creolizing multiple cultural forms have been part and parcel of Afro-diasporic musical practice for centuries. Lawrence Levine has observed, for example, that the evolution of enduring black American genres such as jazz, blues, and gospel reflected "not merely the emergence of the new but the revitalization of the old," through a "complex process of shifting emphases and reaffirmations: of permitting certain new traits to permeate but of simultaneously re-emphasizing specific traditional loyalties and characteristics."[97] Looking more broadly across the black Atlantic diaspora, Paul Gilroy has argued that "tradition . . . does not stand in opposition to modernity" nor can "Africa, authenticity, purity, and origin" be blithely dichotomized with "the Americas, hybridity, creolization, and rootlessness." Diasporic musical forms gain their power from "a doubleness," he contended, through "their unsteady location simultaneously inside and outside of the conventions, assumptions, and aesthetic rules which distinguish and periodise modernity."[98]

Brooklyn Carnival, with its own ambiguous relationship to modernity, occupied such a location at the turn of the new millennium. The celebration boasted a complex constellation of expressive forms drawing energy from innovators eager to generate "the new" while simultaneously seeking creative reinvigoration and spiritual nourishment from "the old." With the establishment of a bona-fide J'Ouvert component, members of Brooklyn's Carnival community embraced tradition without abandoning innovation. Each Labor Day, during the predawn light on Flatbush Avenue and flowing into the bright afternoon sunshine on the Parkway, Brooklyn's Caribbean pan players, percussionists, deejays, soca bands, and calypsonians, along with masqueraders of all stripes, celebrated their culture by straddling past, present, and future. In doing so they challenged Western conventional notions of modernity by underscoring the vital role tradition continued to play in contemporary urban culture. Tradition and innovation were not such strange bedfellows in the cauldron of Carnival.

Notes
1. Earl King, interview with author and Ray Funk, 6 September 2014.
2. Arddin Herbert, phone interview with author, 14 March 2017.
3. Errol Hill, *The Trinidadian Carnival: Mandate for a National Theater* (University of Texas Press), pp. 23–31.
4. Ibid., pp. 84–99; Stephen Stuempfle, *The Steelband Movement: The Forging of a National Art in Trinidad and Tobago* (University of Pennsylvania Press, 1995), pp. 203–204.
5. Stuempfle, *Steelband Movement*, p. 204
6. Earl Lovelace. "The Emancipation Jouvay Tradition and the Almost Loss of Pan," in *Carnival: Culture in Action—The Trinidad Experience*, edited by Mila Riggio (Routledge Press, 2004), p. 187.
7. According to J'Ouvert City International's communications director and later president Yvette Rennie, in 1994 Carlos Lezama assisted her and J'Ouvert founder Earl King in discussions with Brooklyn's 67th Precinct Police regarding the initial parade route. She also recalled that Lezama attended the event regularly "to give J'Ouvert his blessing." Lezama's daughter, Yolanda Lezama-Clarke, confirmed that her father assisted King and Rennie and was a "huge supporter of J'Ouvert." Yvette Rennie, interview with author, 11 May 2017, Brooklyn; and Yolanda Lezama-Clarke, phone interview with author, 5 July 2017. Lezama was given an award for his service at the 1994 J'Ouvert City International Annual Award Dinner. He is pictured with his award in a photograph spread under the banner "1994 J'Ouvert Winners Feted at Club Prestige." *Daily Challenge*, 19 October 1994.
8. Journalist Herman Hall and JCI organizer Earl King both reported that ongoing tensions between WIADCA and Brooklyn's steelpan community contributed to the need for a separate organization to organize a J'Ouvert event that would attract the borough's steelbands. Herman Hall, interview with author, 18 January 2000; King, interview, 6 September 2014.
9. King, interview, 6 September 2014.
10. Martin Douglas, interview with author, 29 July 1998, Brooklyn.

11. Herman Hall, interview with author, 18 January 2000, Brooklyn.

12. Donald Hill, "New York's Caribbean Carnival," *Everybody's Caribbean Magazine* 5, no. 5 (1981): 35.

13. Herman Hall, "Inside Brooklyn's Carnival," *Everybody's Caribbean Magazine* 6, no. 7 (1982): 18, 19, 21.

14. Philip Kasinitz, *Caribbean New York: Black Immigrants and the Politics of Race* (Cornell University Press, 1992), p.145.

15. Gave Averill, "'Pan Is We Ting': West Indian Steelbands in Brooklyn," in *Musics of Multicultural America*, edited by Kip Lornell and Anne Rasmussen (Schirmer Books, 1998), p. 117.

16. John Kifner, "In Brooklyn, Steel Drums and a Truce," *New York Times*, 3 September 1991.

17. Michael Roberts, "Carnival in the Year 2000," *Carib News*, 6 September 1994.

18. Michael Roberts, "Deejays on Parade," *Carib News*, 7 September 1999.

19. Jeffrey Thomas, "The Changing Role of the Steel Band in Trinidad and Tobago: Panorama and the Carnival Tradition," *Studies in Popular Culture* 9, no. 2 (1986): 96.

20. Ibid., p. 101.

21. Ibid., pp. 102–103.

22. For more on the decline of steelbands in Trinidad's street Carnival due to the proliferation of sound trucks and the obsession with Panorama, see Stuempfle, *Steelband Movement*, pp. 161–163; and Shannon Dudley, *Music from Behind the Bridge* (Oxford University Press, 2008), p. 138.

23. Lovelace, "Emancipation Jouvay Tradition," pp. 192–193.

24. Philip Scher, *Carnival and the Formation of a Caribbean Transnation* (University Press of Florida, 2003), pp. 154–155.

25. Stuempfle, *Steelband Movement*, pp. 162, 204–205. For example, he reported that the Desperadoes steelband turned out for the 1988 Tuesday Carnival with a large group of masqueraders playing a traditional sailors' mas (p. 204).

26. A description of informal J'Ouvert activities in Brooklyn's Flatbush neighborhood is found on the inside cover of the J'Ouvert City International program booklet, Volume 2, 1997.

27. Earl King, interview with author, 9 September 1996. See also J'Ouvert City International program booklet, Volume 2, 1997.

28. Tony Tribuse, interview with author, 4 July 1998.

29. King, interview, 9 September 1996.

30. J'Ouvert City International program booklet, Volume 1, 1995.

31. J'Ouvert City International program booklet, Volume 2, 1997.

32. "1994 J'Ouvert Winners Feted at Club Prestige," *Daily Challenge*, 19 October 1994.

33. "J'Ouvert Is Alive!," *Carib News*, 5 September 1995.

34. Yvette Rennie, "1995 Labor Day: J'Ouvert Morning Memories and the New York Steelbands," http://www.carnaval.com/archive/ny/ny96/jouvert.htm.

35. J'Ouvert City International program booklet, Volume 2, 1997.

36. J'Ouvert City International program booklet, Volume 5, 2000.

37. Keeping the pans close to the ground on racks or a low trailer puts them on the same level as the masqueraders and creates a more satisfying sonic experience, as the sound bounces off the road and back up into the immediate space. When pans are mounted six feet or higher above the

crowd on floats or on flatbed trucks, the sound dissipates more rapidly and musicians and revelers lose the feel of being physically immersed in the music.

38. Herbert, phone interview, 14 March 2017.

39. Lovelace, "Emancipation Jouvay Tradition," p. 193.

40. J'Ouvert City International program booklet, Volume 2, 1997.

41. Randy Kennedy, "At 30, Caribbean Festival Is Bursting at Seams," *New York Times*, 2 September 1997.

42. These crowd estimates are based on the author's conversations with a representative of the Borough Community Affairs Department of the Brooklyn NYPD, September 1999.

43. Don Singleton, "Parade's Wild Twin," *New York Daily News*, 5 September 1999.

44. JCI flyer announcing the 1998 J'Ouvert celebration. Courtesy of Earl King.

45. J'Ouvert City International program booklet, Volume 1, 1995.

46. Yvette Rennie, quoted in interview, *Carib News*, 7 September 1999.

47. King, interview, 9 September 1996.

48. Vinette Pryce, "Lewinsky, Political Hopefuls and Others Enjoy Caribbean Parade," *Amsterdam News*, 9 September 1998.

49. Stuempfle notes that the J'Ouvert masqueraders he observed in the late 1980s employed deejays and brass bands as well as steelbands. *Steelband Movement*, p. 203. Dudley recounts that the Pandemonium steelband with whom he was performing during the 1989 Port of Spain J'Ouvert had to stop playing and wait for a "gut wrenchingly loud" sound truck to move on before they could continue. *Music from Behind the Bridge*, p. 14.

50. Herbert, phone interview, 14 March 2017.

51. Herbert of the CASYM Steel Orchestra reported that he would wait until the Sunday afternoon following the Saturday night Panorama competition to teach his players the simple bomb arrangement. They would go home for dinner and rest, and regroup to push off to play J'Ouvert around 2:00 a.m. Monday morning. Herbert, interview with author, 7 July 1997, Brooklyn. Dudley reports a similar experience playing with the Pandemonium steelband in Trinidad in 1989, when arranger Clive Bradley taught the band two simple verse-chorus calypsos and a bomb tune ("Whiter Shade of Pale") the Sunday afternoon in between Panorama and J'Ouvert. See Dudley, *Music from Behind the Bridge*, p. 13.

52. Douglas, interview, 29 July 1998.

53. J'Ouvert City International program booklet, Volume 1, 1995.

54. Rennie, "1995 Labor Day Memoires."

55. Interview with Herbert, 7 July 1997.

56. J'Ouvert City International program booklet, Volume 2, 1997.

57. For historical background on the bomb tune and the various political controversies it has occasioned, see Stuempfle, *Steelband Movement*, pp. 113–114; and Dudley, *Music from Behind the Bridge*, pp. 119–135.

58. Tony Reece, interview with author, 29 March 2017, Brooklyn.

59. For more on early drum and tamboo bamboo Carnival bands, see Dudley, *Music from Behind the Bridge*, pp. 33–35.

60. Interview with Reece, 29 March 2017.

61. In the 1999 Brooklyn J'Ouvert, I observed twelve steelbands and two rhythm bands. In the 2000 J'Ouvert, I observed eighteen steelbands and three rhythm bands.

62. Dudley, *Music from Behind the Bridge*, p. 262.
63. David Katz, "Du dup and Djun-djuns: The Laventille Rhythm Section," *Caribbean Beat* 94 (November–December 2008), http://caribbeanbeat.com/issue-94/du-dup-and-djun-djuns#axzz4d0W86NOu; Shereen Ali, "Laventille Rhythm Section: Going Strong after 30 Years," *Trinidad and Tobago Guardian*, 3 March 2015, http://www.guardian.co.tt/article-6.2.375897.a2c424f56a.
64. Interview with Reece, 29 March 2017.
65. The descriptions of J'Ouvert costumes are based on the author's observations at the 1996, 1998, 1999, and 2000 Brooklyn J'Ouvert celebrations.
66. Kennedy, "At 30, Caribbean Festival Is Bursting at Seams."
67. J'Ouvert City International program booklet, Volume 3, 1998.
68. J'Ouvert City International program booklet, Volume 5, 2000.
69. Pan yards offered a superior sonic space to experience unmediated music close up, but most of the rehearsal time is spent learning and drilling parts for the Panorama tune. Most bands would only run through their full final arrangements on the last few nights before Panorama, leading frustrated pan enthusiasts to madly traverse Brooklyn, running from yard to yard on those final evenings leading up to Panorama to hear the full arrangements up close.
70. Burtrum Alley, interview with author, 4 September 1998, Brooklyn.
71. Victor Turner, *From Ritual to Theatre* (New York: Performing Arts Journal Publications, 1982), p. 48.
72. Martin Douglas, interview with author, 12 August 2017, Brooklyn.
73. Thomas Turino, *Music as Social Life: The Politics of Participation* (University of Chicago Press, 2008), p. 43.
74. Lovelace, "Emancipation Jouvay Tradition," p. 192.
75. Scher, *Carnival and the Formation of a Caribbean Transnation*, p. 160.
76. Interview with Douglas, 12 August 2017.
77. Barbara Kirshenblatt-Gimblett, "Sounds of Sensibility," in *American Klezmer: Its Roots and Offshoots*, edited by Mark Slobin (University of California Press, 2002), p. 133.
78. For a critical review of the use of the terms "authenticity," "revival," and "tradition" with regard to the study of folk and vernacular music, see Ray Allen, "In Pursuit of Authenticity: The New Lost City Ramblers and the Postwar Folk Music Revival," *Journal of the Study of American Music* 4, no. 3 (2010): 277–306.
79. J'Ouvert City International program booklet, Volume 1, 1995.
80. Scher, *Carnival: The Formation of a Caribbean Transnation*, p. 162.
81. "Our Culture—Much to Celebrate," *Carib News*, 3 September 1996.
82. "West Indian Carnival, More Than a Big Jump-Up," *Carib News*, 8 September 1996.
83. Merle English, "Two Million Celebrate West Indian-American Day," *New York Newsday*, 8 September 1992.
84. Merle English, "Colorful Festivities Mark West Indian Day Carnival," *New York Newsday*, 8 September 1998.
85. English, "Two Million Celebrate West Indian-American Day."
86. Philip Kasinitz, "Community Dramatized, Community Contested," in *Island Sounds in the Global City: Caribbean Popular Music and Identity in New York*, edited by Ray Allen and Lois Wilcken (University of Illinois Press, 1998), p. 102.

87. J'Ouvert City International program booklet, Volume 2, 1997.

88. J'Ouvert City International program booklet, Volume 1, 1995.

89. J'Ouvert City International program booklet, Volume 2, 1997.

90. J'Ouvert City International program booklet, Volume 1, 1995.

91. Yvette Rennie, personal interview with author, 11 May 2017, Brooklyn.

92. J'Ouvert City International program booklet, Volume 1, 1995.

93. Rennie, personal interview, 11 May 2017.

94. Somini Sengupta and Garry Pierre-Pierre, "A Tradition Remade in Brooklyn: West Indians Prepare a Lavish, and Popular, Pageant," *New York Times*, 5 September 1998.

95. Interview with Herbert, 7 July 1997.

96. Henry Glassie, "Tradition," *Journal of American Folklore* 108 (1995): 395. For additional critiques of the tradition-modernity dichotomy, see the essays in Trevor Blank and Robert Glenn Howard, *Tradition in the Twenty-First Century: Locating the Role of the Past in the Present* (Utah State University Press, 2013), especially pp. 1–21.

97. Lawrence Levine, *Black Culture and Black Consciousness: Afro-American Folk Thought from Slavery to Freedom* (Oxford University Press, 1977), p. 189.

98. Paul Gilroy, *The Black Atlantic: Modernity and Double Consciousness* (Verso, 1993), pp. 198–199.

9

"We Jammin' Still"

Brooklyn Carnival in the New Millennium

Trinidad's 2017 road march, a full-throttle soca/EDM rollick titled "Full Extreme," dominated Brooklyn's Carnival that summer. Written by vocalist and producer MX Prime (Edghill Thomas) and recorded by the production team Ultimate Rejects, the anthem became the tune of choice for deejays at fetes and on the Parkway, and for many of the Panorama and J'Ouvert steelbands. The song's infectious hook exhorted Carnival revelers to keep the party going despite ever-mounting social and economic woes: "Oh God the treasury, could burn down / We jammin' still, we jammin' still! / Economy, could fall down / We jammin' still, we jammin' still!"[1]

The message of perseverance in troubling times was immediately understood back in Trinidad as a reference to that nation's battered economy, resulting from the collapse of the oil market. In Brooklyn it no doubt touched on another set of anxieties as the Caribbean community braced for escalating waves of xenophobia and anti-immigrant hysteria promulgated by the new Trump administration. But in a less obvious and unintended way, the song resonated metaphorically on the occasion of Brooklyn Carnival's 50th Anniversary. Carnival had survived in the face of a multitude of financial, political, and organizational obstacles for five decades, and New York's Caribbean community was still jamming to soca and steelband music on Labor Day weekend.

Marking its 50th anniversary, WIADCA touted its 2017 Labor Day festivities as "North America's largest outdoor festival," attracting over two million attendees to its five-day celebration.[2] Over the previous two decades, the press continued to portray the event as the city's largest outdoor celebration, cementing Brooklyn Caribbean Carnival's stature as an iconic New York cultural attraction.[3] Brooklyn Carnival grew increasingly institutionalized since the 1990s, with its overall size and structure remaining relatively unchanged. WIADCA continued to coordinate most aspects of the festivities. Following Carlos Lezama's death in 2007, the organization was taken over by his daughter, Yolanda Lezama-Clarke, and in 2012 Trinidad expatriate Thomas Bailey became president. In 2016 WIADCA's first non-Trinidadian, William Howard, assumed the presidency, and following his passing in 2018, Ionie Pierce became the first Jamaican woman to head the organization. Longtime members Angela Sealy and Jean Alexander, both originally from Trinidad, continued to serve in the powerful positions of board chairperson and secretary/marketing director, respectively. WIADCA's upper echelon has remained primarily older, first-generation Trinidadian (with the exception of African American Howard and the recently arrived Jamaican American Pierce).

The organization's motto—"One Caribbean/One People/One Voice"—and its 2017 mission statement sounded familiar: "To promote, develop and celebrate Caribbean culture, arts, history and traditions through year-round programs which culminate with a week-long display of festivities and a grand finale Carnival parade expanding our cultural reach throughout the world."[4] The five-day Labor Day festival continued to feature a series of calypso and reggae shows, a Panorama, a Kiddie Carnival, and a Dimanche Gras show (with costume winners and calypso/soca luminaries) staged outdoors behind the Brooklyn Museum. The Monday afternoon Carnival parade down Eastern Parkway, featuring scores of fancy mas bands and mobile sound trucks, remained the highlight of the festivities. WIADCA received significant sanitation and security support from the city and NYPD, as well as modest funding from city and state government and private sources. But the organization still operated with a skeletal, mostly volunteer staff, and with the exception of the parade, its events were not widely publicized outside the community.

The Monday Carnival parade continued to attract large crowds, but the number of spectators appears to have declined slightly. Reliable figures are difficult to come by, because the NYPD no longer releases crowd estimates. WIADCA and the press claimed as many as two to three million attendees in the 1990s and 2000s, but some observers feel that number dropped in the years leading up to 2017. Press accounts, lacking police crowd estimates, reported "thousands" rather than "millions" of participants.[5] Herman Hall, who has been active in promoting and writing about Brooklyn Carnival since the early 1970s, claimed that the crowd sizes had been going down since their peak in the late 1990s. For 2017 he estimated less than a million on the Parkway.[6] The decline, he speculated, was due to a number of factors, including an aging first-generation immigrant population that no longer had the energy to venture out to Eastern Parkway, and a younger generation of Brooklyn-born Caribbean Americans who were put off by the strict enforcement of the "no alcohol" policy on the Parkway that was instituted in the 1990s.[7] In addition, in recent years expatriates have been attracted to better-promoted Carnivals back in Barbados, Grenada, Antigua, St. Lucia, and St. Vincent (all of which are held in the summer prior to Labor Day), thereby reducing the necessity of attending the Brooklyn celebration in order to experience Carnival.[8]

Over the years the Eastern Parkway procession gradually came to resemble a more conventional parade. Although it was not as orderly as New York's Columbus Day or St. Patrick's Day parades, the event adhered to a strict noon to six o'clock schedule and a single prescribed route. Politicians, civic organizations, and sponsors still ambled down the Parkway to mark the official opening of the parade prior to the waves of mas bands and sound trucks. Most notably, miles of metal crowd-control fences tightly lined both sides of the entire Parkway route, preventing observers from "jumping the line" onto the road to mingle with the mas bands and sound trucks. As a result, what was once participatory ritual increasingly took on the aura of presentational spectacle. Bystanders could no longer easily push and pull pan as they did in the 1970s and 1980s, or chip and wine with the mas bands and sound trucks as they did in the 1990s and early 2000s. The call-and-response trope was less effective when the latter was barricaded off from the former.

Brooklyn Carnival's other main attraction, the Monday-morning pre-dawn J'Ouvert celebration, continued to operate completely independent of WIADCA in 2017. The event was still coordinated by J'Ouvert City International, now under the leadership of Yvette Rennie, who took over from the late Earl King in 2015. J'Ouvert continued to attract audiences of several hundred thousand who appreciated the steelbands, rhythm bands, and ole mas costuming free of deejays and sound trucks. Violence, however, has marred the occasion in recent years. Following several well-publicized shootings that took place around the event in 2015 and 2016, a steady stream of negative press coverage led some critics to call for J'Ouvert's dissolution.

Music remained central to all the festivities. It is difficult, indeed impossible, to imagine Brooklyn Carnival without deejays dropping the latest soca and reggae hits over high-volume sound systems, and steelbands going head-to-head on the Panorama stage and on the road during J'Ouvert. But the soundscape has changed since the 1970s. The audience for traditional, lyric-centered calypso has aged and diminished, as it has in Trinidad. Calypso, at least in New York, appears to be headed toward enshrinement as cultural heritage music that will need public subvention or private patronage to survive. While soca has persisted as the dance and road music of choice for younger Caribbean New Yorkers, Brooklyn is no longer a center of the music's production. The newer style, dubbed "power soca," is played at a considerably faster tempo than the music Charles, Straker, and Gould produced in the 1970s and 1980s, and the lyrics have become increasingly condensed into repetitive exhortations for dancers to wave and wine.[9] In a 2010 interview Rawlston Charles spoke regrettably of the loss of melody and nuanced lyrical content in the new soca: "With our music [today] it's all about hands in the air, waving and jumping. This is fast food music; there is no identity."[10] Meanwhile, the steelbands that remained active in Panorama, summer fetes, and J'Ouvert continued to attract modest numbers of young people into a vital grassroots music scene. Some of the bands extended their activities beyond Carnival season, maintaining year-round stage-side ensembles for cultural and educational events. Carnival music in Brooklyn managed to survive, and in some corners flourished, despite a plethora of ongoing financial and logistical challenges.

Brooklyn Soca Farewell

Most of the new soca hits heard across Brooklyn each summer were released six months prior in order to coincide with Trinidad's Carnival season. But unlike the prewar Harlem calypsos and 1980s Brooklyn soca songs, today's tracks are no longer recorded, produced, and distributed from New York. B's Records folded in the late 1980s, and Charlie's, Straker's, and B&W Records have released no new material in recent years. As of this writing, Rawlston Charles still runs his record store and studio on Fulton Street, where he sells old calypso and soca vinyl and CDs, but his recording studio is presently used primarily by contemporary hip-hop and R&B artists. Granville Straker has also maintained his store on Utica Avenue, but it serves mainly as a computer repair shop and meeting place for Straker and his old friends. The B&W Records store on Church Avenue was, up until early 2018, one of the few retail outlets that continued to sell calypso and soca releases on vinyl and CD.

One Brooklyn-based label that has released new calypso and soca material over the past two decades is Hometown Music, run by the Trinidadian producer Jamal Talib (b. 1946). A native of Port of Spain, Talib moved back and forth between Trinidad and New York in the 1970s and 1980s before settling in Brooklyn in 1990. In 1997 he opened up Hometown Music and Studios in a storefront on Bedford Avenue, around the corner from Charlie's Calypso City. Unlike Charles and Straker, Talib went after the emerging CD market. Hometown's output has been limited in comparison to its established competitors, restricted to annual calypso and soca compilations of local New York singers under the titles *Real Kaiso* and *Platinum Soca*. In addition, Hometown has released a small number of individual CDs featuring the singers Brown Boy, Crazy, and Wellington, as well as a tribute to Calypso Rose. All recording and mixing are done on the premises, supervised by Talib. His studio band, the Hometown Squad, is led by the Trinidad guitarist Jimmie Brown, the one-time accompanist for Sparrow and member of Super Blue & the Love Band.[11]

In recent years Talib's primary market for his limited line of CDs has been Trinidad, where he returns annually for Carnival season. He confirms that most calypso and soca production today takes place in Trinidad, unlike "back in the day when Trinidad didn't have many studios and 95% of the recording and production went on here in Brooklyn." Advanced computers and software have allowed for more home recording, and less expensive recording and mixing technology has led to a proliferation of small studios in Trinidad. Many soca artists can now produce their own music, uploading the product for online streaming and producing cheap

CDs that they sell at gigs or give away for promotion. Following broader trends in the music industry, Caribbean record shops are bypassed and have become obsolete. Talib sees his own business as a victim of downloading, just as Charles and Straker claimed that CD pirating in the 1990s led to the demise of their record labels. With dwindling sales, Talib decided for the first time in over twenty years not to release any CDs in 2017, and he admitted that the future of his label was in question.[12]

Since 2004 Talib has run an annual calypso tent during the week leading up to Labor Day Carnival. Held at medium-sized venues in central Brooklyn, including Club Tropical Paradise on Utica Avenue, Restoration Plaza Theater on Fulton Street, and the Black Lady Theater on Nostrand Avenue, the shows have followed a traditional calypso tent format, with an emcee who introduces up to a dozen singers backed by the Hometown Squad band. Other tents, sponsored by the independent producer Herman Hall and the Sesame Flyers International organization, have competed with Talib's Kaiso House. Hall's 2012 tent was held for seven nights at Club Tropical Paradise. Calypso and soca acts were both featured, including appearances by old-favorites Sparrow, Calypso Rose, Swallow, Becket, and Count Robin, as well as a menu of less well-known local singers, all accompanied by the Sunshine Band. In hopes of attracting a younger audience, Hall added a World Soca Monarch competition to the program.[13] The Sesame Flyers tent, mounted initially in 2000, featured a multi-night New York Calypso Monarch contest for local singers. Two of the winners, Mervyn "Dr. Witty" Carter and Lloyd "QP" Cupido, went on to perform in the prestigious Trinidad Calypso Revue and Classic Russo tents in 2013.[14] These efforts suggest that in the new millennium, Brooklyn audiences have continued to support live performances of traditional calypso and classic soca, but the fan base for such sit-down shows was clearly aging and shrinking.

While acknowledging that calypso tents may soon be a thing of the past, Talib and Hall contend that a younger generation of Brooklyn-born fans continues to embrace live and deejay-mediated soca. In terms of live music, the Hometown Squad, along with Brooklyn-based calypso/soca groups the Sunshine Band, Lambert and the Matadors, and the Request Band, play regular club gigs in Brooklyn and Queens during Carnival Season and tour to Boston, Washington, Miami, and the Caribbean. They specialize in accompanying calypso and soca singers, but also play reggae, R&B, and American pop tunes. The Request Band consists of younger players at the forefront of the contemporary soca style. They have worked closely with singer Allistair "Rayzor" McQuillkin, a Brooklyn-based Trinidadian who has a growing following in New York and on the international soca circuit. His single "Da Weekend" was well received in Carnival 2017. In 2018 Rayzor teamed up with another Brooklyn-based Trinidad expatriate soca singer/producer, Kevon "Yankey Boy" Heath, on the popular Carnival release "Throw Powder."[15]

New York's legendary calypso-turned-soca singers Sparrow, Calypso Rose, and Lord Nelson have remained active and widely recognized as the most influential living practitioners of the art form. Sparrow toured internationally until a 2013 stroke slowed him down. Heralded as the undisputed king of calypso, he continues to appear in New York and Trinidad Carnival events, where he performs with a surprisingly strong octogenarian voice. Lord Nelson has maintained his residency in Jamaica, Queens. Now in his eighties and sporting a cane, he sings his classic soca hits for Carnival shows in Brooklyn and Trinidad and has finally gained recognition as one of the originators of the early soca style. Calypso Rose has enjoyed something of a renaissance of late with her 2016 album, *Far from Home*. A collaboration with the French singer Manu Chao and released by the France-based Because Music label, the recording won the "World Music Album of the Year" award from the Victoire de la Musique, the French equivalent of an American Grammy. In her late seventies, Rose still tours Europe and the Caribbean from her base in Queens. Sparrow, Nelson, and Rose received lifetime achievement awards in 2013 from the Consulate General of the Republic of Trinidad and Tobago in New York.[16]

Of the pioneering soca arrangers, only Frankie McIntosh has maintained his full-time residency in Brooklyn. In semi-retirement, he has continued to arrange and perform with a small Caribbean jazz-oriented quartet that often includes the pan soloist Garvin Blake. He was honored with a national postal stamp by his native St. Vincent and the Grenadines, and in 2015 he received a "Sunshine Award" for his contributions to Caribbean art and culture. Leston Paul and Pelham Goddard live and work in Trinidad. Paul still composes, arranges, and runs his own recording studio from his Mt. Lambert home outside of Port of Spain. Goddard also operates a studio in St. James while remaining active as a keyboardist and as the main arranger for Trinidad's Exodus Steel Orchestra. By the late 1990s Clive Bradley had cut back on his soca arranging and relocated to Trinidad. There he arranged for the Desperadoes steelband while continuing to visit Brooklyn each summer to arrange for the Pantonic steelband up until his death in 2005. Not surprisingly, without a critical mass of singers composing new songs and studios to record and produce the music, Brooklyn has ceased to be the magnet that it once was for talented young arrangers.

It is doubtful that Brooklyn will re-emerge as a center of soca music in the near future. Decentralization of production and distributions has done much to nullify New York's once privileged position as a nexus of the music recording industry. Few younger, island-born soca artists, save Rayzor and Yankey Boy, have chosen to relocate in New York, as did the early Harlem calypsonians or the modern calypso/soca stars Sparrow, Melody, Rose, Nelson, and Duke. Perhaps most telling is the fact that Brooklyn, despite its robust second and third generations of Caribbean migrants, has yet to produce a single influential soca artist or arranger. Soca will no doubt remain popular in New York, but probably as seasonal music with limited appeal beyond the Caribbean community.

The Steelbands Soldier On

Brooklyn's steelband movement has persevered since the turn of the millennium. The rise of a new generation of young players and arrangers bodes well for the future of the art from, but the bands continue to face serious obstacles, both financial and logistical, which impede growth and foster stagnation. The annual WIADCA-sponsored Panorama remains the primary showcase for Brooklyn's large steelbands. In recent years, between seven and ten large bands (50–100 players) have competed for first, second, and third prize in the Labor Day weekend Brooklyn Museum concert. These numbers are down from the early 2000s, when fifteen bands competed in 2001 and eighteen bands in 2002.[17] Over the years the structure of the WIADCA's Panorama has not changed and remains identical to the Trinidad contest—a formal staged concert where each band rolls up a ramp onto the stage while the soca version of their tune thunders over the loudspeakers. Bands play eight-to-ten-minute arrangements that adhere to what has become the standard Panorama formula of introduction/theme and variation/key modulation or dramatic switch from major to minor mode/percussive jam session/return to main theme/coda. In the wee hours of the morning the judges announce the results, sparking pandemonium among the winners and their supporters.

Placing first, second, or third in the contest was worth more than bragging rights. Financing a large steelband for Panorama has become an increasingly expensive endeavor—as much as $20,000, according to USSA president Martin Douglas.[18] Few bands have private sponsors, unless, like CASYM and Sesame Flyers, they are part of a larger not-for-profit community organization. The $4,500 appearance fee that each band has received in recent years does not fully cover the costs of renting space for rehearsal, paying an arranger and tuner, purchasing additional instruments, building and maintaining the pan racks, and truck rentals for transporting instruments from the pan yard to the Brooklyn Museum. In 2017, the largest and most competitive bands hoped to win some portion of the $20,000 (first place), $15,000 (second place), or $10,000 (third place) prize money to help defray their expenses.

Issues of prize money and sound quality have continued to plague Brooklyn's Panorama and intensified decades-old tensions between WIADCA and the steelbands. The latter, unable to negotiate a satisfactory arrangement with WIADCA, staged their own Panoramas in 2001 and 2002 under the aegis of the USSA. They could not sustain the effort on their own, however, and after co-sponsoring the contest in 2003, they returned the reins fully to WIADCA, which has been the sole sponsor ever since. The steelbands occasionally threatened to boycott WIADCA's Panorama, most recently in 2017, claiming that WIADCA had not paid them their full prize money for Panorama 2016 (the boycott failed).[19] The USSA, unlike Pan Trinbago in Trinidad, has yet to succeed in uniting Brooklyn's steelbands and forcing WIADCA to let them play a more active role in the planning and executing of Brooklyn Panorama.

Poor sound reinforcement has often marred the Panorama listening experience. The founders of the website When Steel Talks (WST), longtime Panorama observers and critics of WIADCA, have voiced concern over this problem over the years. The Brooklyn Museum Panorama stage is not, they rightly pointed out, the best place to hear the bands, given the poor quality of the sound system. WST characterized the experience as a nightmare where "[s]weet pan becomes something out of a horribly-engineered, heavy metal Black Sabbath concert." They recommended listeners visit the pan yards or the side-stage warm-up sessions to hear the "playing abilities and sonic qualities of their instruments."[20]

On top of these financial and production maladies, Brooklyn's steelbands have faced the increasing encroachment of neighborhood gentrification. During the summer months, bands had traditionally rented or squatted in neighborhood parking lots, vacant lots, semi-abandoned buildings, and light industrial spaces in the Crown Heights and Flatbush neighborhoods that were in close proximity to Eastern Parkway and the Brooklyn Museum. But such sites became increasingly difficult to negotiate as Brooklyn developers gobbled them up for potential new residential or retail spaces. During the Carnival season of 2000, Pan Rebels, Metro, and the Nu-Tones steel orchestras were harassed and eventually ousted from a row of abandoned buildings on Parkside Avenue by city authorities at the behest of property developers. The buildings, located in the heart of Caribbean Flatbush, were less than a mile from Eastern Parkway, and had been used as rehearsal spaces since 1994.[21] Rising rents for outdoor spaces, coupled with complaints from non-Caribbean newcomers over noisy rehearsals and late-night gatherings, forced several of the bands to move their pan yards out of residential neighborhoods and into the more industrialized far reaches of East Brooklyn. Around 2010 the D'Radoes steelband relocated to a block in East New York where city garbage trucks and buses were stowed. In 2014 Metro Steel was forced to move from a convenient Crown Heights parking lot to a dirt lot in eastern Brownville, several miles from the Brooklyn Museum. A few bands were able to negotiate public school yards and church halls for rehearsals, but these spaces face restrictions on food and alcohol sales (a modest source of income for the bands), and the former must be totally cleared the day after Labor Day Monday for the opening of the school year. Frustrated with the problems many of the bands were having finding reasonably priced, outdoor rehearsal spaces in Crown Heights and Flatbush, USSA's Martin Douglas told the *Times* in 2015, "It's disturbing." The central Brooklyn neighborhoods from which the pan yards were being systematically evicted were "the heart of the steel-pan world in North America."[22]

Despite these difficulties, the New York steelbands have persisted. According to Douglas, the USSA had twenty-three members registered in 2017. Most were Brooklyn-based, with outliers in Long Island, Philadelphia, and Boston. Some of the older bands, such as the Sesame Flyers, Metro

Steel, and Dem Stars, have dropped out of the Panorama competition in recent years, while newcomers like Pan Evolution have cropped up. In addition to the large Panorama bands, Brooklyn's steelband community boasts a number of smaller stage-side bands, including the New York Pan Stars, Hearts of Steel, Pan Liberty, and the Legend Stars, that play for year-round parties, cultural events, and J'Ouvert.[23] The current Panorama and stage-side bands have a healthy population of younger players (teens through early twenties), and in some cases memberships that are at least half female. Many of the teenage players came into contact through family connections, but some were exposed to the music through afterschool steel pan programs, and a few through church steelbands. The exact demographics of the Brooklyn bands are difficult to estimate, but certainly the majority of players are Afro-Caribbean, with a small number of African Americans and a handful of white participants.[24] The Trinidadian (or US-born players of Trinidadian parentage) presence has remained strong, but bands increasingly have included first-, second-, and now third-generation Antiguans, Guyanese, Jamaicans, St. Lucians, Grenadians, Bajans, and St. Vincennes.[25] Most bands are no longer derived from or formally associated with a parent Trinidad steel orchestra, although some of the older players maintain connections. In short, Brooklyn's steelbands have passed the tradition down to more heterogeneous, second and third generations of New York–born Afro-Caribbean youth. The increased diversity of island representation and female participation differs noticeably from the original bands from the 1960s and 1970s that were dominated by male Trinidadian migrants, and is in keeping with WIADCA's mission of creating a more pan-Caribbean Carnival.

Evidence that a younger, New York–born cohort has taken up their parents' pan culture is the success of the recently instituted Youth Pan Festival. The block-party-style event was first produced in 2014 by the Carlos Lezama Archives and Caribbean Cultural Center, run by the late Lezama's daughter, Yolanda Lezama-Clarke. The competition, held in Crown Heights the week before Carnival, attracts six to eight bands made up exclusively of players under the age of twenty-two. The bands, spread out along the street (with no stage or sound system), compete against one another with well-rehearsed Panorama-style arrangements as the judges move their table from band to band throughout the afternoon. A modest $1,500 first prize is announced at the close of the contest.[26] The pan experience for these New York–born players certainly differs from that of their Caribbean-born parents. Having grown up in Brooklyn, for them steelband music lacked the deep nostalgic associations that it evoked for the first-generation immigrants who created Brooklyn Carnival. Why then did they become involved? The youth bands have provided sites for socializing and creative activity, explained Sparkle Demming, the Trinidad-born organizer and captain of the New York Pan Stars. "But heritage is important, too," she reflected. "Young people might join a band because they knew their uncle or grandfather played steel pan, but they don't know anything about the instrument. So, it's partly a matter of cultural pride, for these second- and third-generation Brooklyn-born kids connecting with where their families came from, and where they come from."[27] The hundreds of young people who participate annually in the Youth Pan Festival appear to have embraced the instrument as a component of their own personal heritage and clearly take great pleasure in performing that heritage in public.

Trinidad has remained the source for the tunes played at the Brooklyn Panorama and Youth Pan Festival, and overlap in the most popular tunes in the Brooklyn and Port of Spain contests is not unusual.[28] Following practices dating back to the 1980s, when big-name Trinidadians were brought to Brooklyn, a fresh crop of top Trinidad arrangers, including Duvone Stewart, Terrance Marcelle, Amrit Samaroo, Seion Gomez, and Leon Foster Thomas have been recruited each August to work with the Brooklyn bands.

In recent years a new generation of American-born arrangers of Trinidadian parentage has emerged. Andre White (b. 1990), Odie Franklin (b. 1988), and Kendall Williams (b. 1986) have distinguished themselves in Brooklyn's Panorama as well as in competitions in Trinidad, London, and Toronto. White, a native of Freeport (a Long Island town twenty miles east of Brooklyn) and a graduate of Boston's Berklee College of Music, grew up playing with the Adlib steelband. He began arranging for the band as a teenager and in 2008 became the youngest arranger to win Brooklyn's Panorama. He led Adlib to subsequent victories in 2011 and 2012, and in 2011 won London's Notting Hill competition with the Mangrove steelband. In the past few years he has been called to Trinidad to arrange for WITCO Desperadoes, Tamana Pioneers, and most recently the Pamberi Steel Orchestra. Since 2016 he has arranged for a band he helped to organize, the Brooklyn-based Pan Evolution, and performed as a soloist in his own small jazz ensemble.[29] Williams was born in Brooklyn and reared in Miami where his parents played with the Miami South Stars. After graduating from Florida Memorial University where he studied under Dawn Batson, he returned to New York and earned a master's degree in percussion and music theory from New York University and is pursuing a PhD in music composition at Princeton University. Williams has arranged for Brooklyn's Crossfire steelband (2013–2016) and CASYM orchestra (2017–2018) as well as several of Trinidad's smaller bands.[30] Franklin grew up around Brooklyn pan yards and started playing at a young age under the tutelage of his father, Clement Franklin, who was the longtime captain/tuner of Despers USA. He first arranged for the band in 2011 and has continued to do so while pursuing his music studies at the Borough of Manhattan Community College.[31]

White, Williams, and Franklin represent a new breed of steelpan arrangers. Trained in Western music theory and the harmonic language of jazz, they notate their scores with Sibelius software to organize and facilitate the arranging/composition process. This also allows them to share parts with musically literate players who come into town at the last minute to play with their bands (although most of the instruction is done aurally in the pan yard—the majority of their players do not read music or prefer to learn by ear). It is too soon to speculate about the emergence of a "Brooklyn" style of arranging, but these three young arrangers have been pushing the conventional boundaries of Panorama tunes thanks to their wide-ranging musical tastes and advanced training in harmonic and rhythmic theory.

In 2013 Williams, Franklin, and another Brooklyn-born musician, Marc Brooks (b. 1985), teamed up to arrange for the Brooklyn Steel Orchestra (BSO), an all-Brooklyn group that was put together to audition for *America's Got Talent* on NBC television. With the trio serving as arrangers, the BSO competed in Trinidad's 2015 International Conference and Panorama (ICP). The band came in fourth in the ICP competition, the only non-Trinidadian band to place among the top eight finishers. So impressive were the trio's arranging talents that they were hired to work with the south Trinidad Skiffle steelband in 2015 and 2016, and again in 2018 when they placed second in the Large Band Panorama category.[32] The international success of the BSO trio and White has been a shot in the arm for Brooklyn's reputation as a center of steelband music. Trinidad's scene continues to eclipse all steelband activity in the diaspora, but these Brooklyn-born émigré sons have made their presence felt back home and in London. As New York–born arrangers become more enmeshed in the transitional Carnival circuit, the cultural currents become increasingly multidirectional.

J'Ouvert has remained the sole venue for pan-on-the-road performance in Brooklyn. "Any steelpan player who has not experienced playing on the road surrounded by an adoring and soulful audience has been deprived of one of the greatest musical performance opportunities ever," proclaimed the WST website following the 2008 celebration. The unique Brooklyn J'Ouvert experience, it was observed, allowed players to "connect to the African traditions that stretch back over the centuries."[33] Despite this ringing endorsement, the number of steelbands has dropped from the early 2000s, when JCI reported twenty participating groups.[34] The number of bands hovered in the low teens for a decade, only to decrease to eight (2015), eleven (2016), and eight (2017 and 2018) in recent years. Only two of ten competing Panorama bands came out for J'Ouvert in 2015, three of ten in 2016, three of eight in 2017, and three of seven in 2018.[35] The decline in the number of bands playing J'Ouvert might signal a waning of interest on the part of younger players who are eager to head to the Parkway for the afternoon parade. But there are probably additional factors, including the increased expense of bringing bands out on the road, media reports of deadly violence along the route, and the increased police presence that some feel has dampened the J'Ouvert spirit.

There has been a marked increase in the number of J'Ouvert rhythm bands since their initial appearance in the 1990s. JCI reported eleven bands competing in its 2013 rhythm competition, eight in 2014, five in 2015, six in 2016, seven in 2017, and six in 2018. These numbers do not include numerous informal groups of percussionists who did not register to compete in front of the judges. The renewed interest in rhythm bands may reflect a growing consciousness and revitalization of African percussion traditions that undergird much Canboulay-derived J'Ouvert ritual. On the more practical side, compared to a steelband a rhythm section is easier to transport and cheaper for a mas band to hire. In any case, JCI's steelband and rhythm–only policy has been upheld since the mid-1990s, with little resistance from deejays or sound truck proponents. Occasionally, Indo-Trinidad tassa drumming bands or Haitian rara ensembles show up. Although their music is not directly related to Carnival, their acoustic, highly percussive styles are comfortable fits for Brooklyn J'Ouvert.[36]

Additional performance sites for the steelbands have cropped up during Brooklyn Carnival season. In recent years a number of the bands have sponsored a pan yard fete in July or early August to raise money and ramp up interest among their supporters. Known as "band launches," these weekend evening events attract five or six stage-side units (15–20 players each), who are allotted roughly half-an-hour each to perform. Each band stakes out a corner of the pan yard and runs through four or five numbers, including several calypso/soca tunes and at least one bomb. Some premiere a shortened version of their upcoming Panorama tune. In between bands, a deejay spins the latest soca tunes while audience members eat, drink, and socialize. While the bands are not formally competing with one another, their members are clearly checking each other out. There is an air of tension and excitement as the audience gathers close to the musicians, often wining and singing along with the tunes. Band launches provide an opportunity to hear full, unmediated pan up close, before the bands fall into their nightly drilling routines leading up to Panorama. They further galvanize the community of pan players and supporters while providing spaces where musical ideas can be informally exchanged and critiqued.[37]

The prognosis for the future health of Brooklyn's steelbands is mixed. On the one hand, the bands continue to attract significant numbers of Caribbean Americans, including a younger generation of players and arrangers who have embraced pan as a creative and culturally meaningful activity. Pan-on-the-road may never return to Eastern Parkway, but it is alive and well in Brooklyn's J'Ouvert, offering a pure-pan experience that at present cannot be found in any other major urban Carnival. On the other hand, the high cost of equipping and maintaining a large-scale Panorama band in Brooklyn is becoming increasingly prohibitive, resulting in a decline in the number of competing bands in recent years. Unless WIADCA and the USSA can come together to find more reliable public, corporate, and individual funding streams, the future of the large Panorama bands, and Brooklyn Panorama itself, will remain in jeopardy.

Brooklyn Carnival 2017

Brooklyn's 50th Anniversary Carnival unfolded according to the script that had been followed for decades.[38] The Eastern Parkway parade attracted a large crowd of spectators for the usual fair of fancy mas costume bands wining to high-volume soca and reggae pumped from sound trucks. Ramajay Mas dominated the costume competition, winning the large adult band category with a troupe of players festooned with colorful feathers, beads, and bikinis. Their presentation was appropriately entitled for fancy mas, "Opulence—The Art of Luxury." Hundreds of vendors lined the Parkway selling their food and wares behind metal barricades that kept them and the rest of the spectators off the road and away from the mas bands and sound trucks. Dignitaries at the head of the parade included Governor Cuomo, Mayor de Blasio, and Jamaican American assemblyman Rick Perry. Looking for support for his 2017 re-election campaign, de Blasio proclaimed that "what hundreds and hundreds of thousands of people of Caribbean descent have done for New York City has made us greater."[39] The mayor had used the earlier occasion of WIADCA's pre-parade breakfast to push back against President Trump's threat to do away with the Deferred Action for Childhood Arrivals (DACA) program, calling on Congress to enact a new and comprehensive Dream Act.[40] Carnival has remained a site for political discourse, attesting to the power Brooklyn's Caribbean community still commands.

Amid continuing tensions between WIADCA and the USSA, the 2017 steelband season opened on a positive note with a series of successful steelband and mas band launches at pan yards and camps across the borough. The launch in D'Radoes' yard on August 6th was exemplary—seven stage-side bands entertained an enthusiastic audience for more than four hours. Hundreds of fans moved around the yard from band to band, carefully listening and later debating which of the groups was most prepared to win the Panorama competition. In between band performances, deejays from Get Loose Music dropped the latest soca tunes, creating a seamless Carnival soundscape. Acoustic steelpan and mediated soca settled comfortably together in a high-spirited community performance, and D'Radoes raised a few dollars. A similar scene unfolded in the Pagwah mas band's launch two weeks prior. In preparation for their J'Ouvert performance, the band's leader, Michael Manswell, led a traditional Canboulay procession with call-and-response singing over a battery of African and tassa drummers accompanied by iron percussion. Among the chants heard was the refrain, "we jammin' still," from the previously cited popular soca tune "Full Extreme." Following the procession, a deejay took over, accompanied by the drummers and iron players. Traditional Canboulay chanting and modern deejay soca shared the stage and were fully embraced by the Pagwah band and its supporters.

The August 24th Youth Pan Fest was an undisputable success. Eight bands competed, including stage-sides of the larger Panorama bands CASYM, Pantonics, Pan Evolution, Harmony, and Despers USA. The latter took first place with an arrangement of "Full Extreme." Following the structure of the main Panorama, the recording of the original soca tune was broadcast prior to each band's performance in order to pump up the players and crowd. The young players' familiarity with the original mediated soca hit clearly contributed to their eagerness to render the tune live on steel pan. Their energy was palpable and their enthusiasm surely reassuring to the organizers, whose goal was to preserve and nurture the steelband tradition in Brooklyn.

While soca dominated the band launches and fetes, two traditional calypso tents were held in the week leading up to Labor Day. The Brooklyn Kaiso House, staged at a small theater on Nostrand Avenue in Crown Heights, was organized by Talib. Over four nights, more than a score of calypsonians performed to the accompaniment of the live Hometown Squad brass band. Headliners Lord Nelson, Super Blue, Cro Cro, and Funny were joined by Dr. Witty, Mudada, Flyman, and a host of less well-known local singers. The opening night drew an audience of close to two hundred, predominantly older, fans. A second tent, organized by the New York Kaiso Brigade, was held down the road on Parkside Avenue. Unlike Kaiso House, the Brigade tent lacked a live band, with singers performing over prerecorded tracks. Talib was pleased with the opening night turnout and the spirited reception his singers received, but expressed concern that the aging audience for such traditional, sit-down calypso tents was rapidly diminishing. He was not certain his Kaiso house operation would be financially sustainable in the future.[41]

The old-guard calypsonians-turned-soca singers headlined the WIADCA Sunday evening Dimanche Gras show. The program might have been promoted as a return the 1980s golden age of Brooklyn soca, with Mighty Sparrow, Calypso Rose, Lord Nelson, David Rudder, and Swallow. The event was not well attended and the appreciative audience was predictably older. Larger, younger crowds were drawn to the Thursday evening show "Reggae Unda Di Stars," headlining Cocoa Tea and Stephen Ragga Marley, and the Friday night "Brass Fest" that featured Trinidad soca stars MX Prime of Ultimate Rejects, Farmer Nappy, Blaxx, and Lyrikal, along with the Brooklyn-based Rayzor and the Request Band. In a nod toward island diversity, the packed program also featured singers from Antigua, St. Vincent, St. Lucia, Barbados, Grenada, and St. Croix. Why the Friday night event was promoted under the old-fashioned banner of a Brass Fest, rather than as a modern Soca Fest, is curious and underscores the struggles the WIADCA organizers have had in connecting with younger audiences.

Brooklyn's 2017 Panorama took an unexpected and somewhat troubling turn. The Saturday night competition was rained out, although not canceled in advance despite ominous weather forecasts predicting the arrival of the remnants of Hurricane Harvey. The result was hundreds of irate ticket holders sitting in the rain until 10:00 p.m. while the Philadelphia Pan Stars stood on stage for nearly an hour before the postponement was finally announced. Seven of the ten bands showed up the next afternoon for the rescheduled Panorama, only to find that the raised stage behind the Brooklyn Museum was not available because of insurance and staffing issues. Quickly shifting gears, the bands reorganized in a side area and decided to play at ground level, without sound reinforcement.

The outcome of this makeshift arrangement clearly pleased the audience, which surrounded the bands for an up-close, unmediated pan experience. However, at the end of the competition it was announced that, inexplicably, there would be no judging of the event (although the judges had been present from the onset) and no awarding of the first, second, or third place prizes. Each of the seven participating bands would be paid only their $4,500 performance fees. This news was not well received, especially coming on the heels of the previous year's unresolved squabble over unpaid prize money. The favored D'Radoes (winners of the 2016 and 2015 Panoramas) and the well-rehearsed CASYM, Pan Evolution, and Despers USA bands, all of whom had reason to expect their share of prize money, were particularly irked. The botched 2017 Panorama underscores long-running problems between WIADCA and the Brooklyn steelbands.[42] WIADCA continued to struggle to raise sufficient funds through ticket sales and grant subvention to guarantee the prize money they promise to Panorama contestants. The steelbands, facing the rising expenses of mounting a Panorama band, were still unable to speak with one voice to negotiate a better financial arrangement or to organize a full boycott if a fair agreement could not be reached.

A great deal of media attention fell to the 2017 J'Ouvert celebration, due to the high-profile violence that had plagued the event over the past two years. In 2015 Carey Gabay, a lawyer for the Cuomo administration, was shot and killed in crossfire between rival gangs while walking home from J'Ouvert. In response, Mayor de Blasio and the NYPD vowed to beef up security in 2016, but again violence erupted, resulting in the deaths of a seventeen- and twenty-two-year-old along the route.[43] This led to an outcry from critics, including New York 1 and *Daily News* journalist Errol Louis, himself of Trinidadian lineage. Louis characterized J'Ouvert as simply a big party with "hundreds of hundreds of thousands of people out roaming the streets at four o'clock in the morning." J'Ouvert, he surmised, was some "sort of a cultural invention. What's been invented can be altered or uninvented or frankly rooted out if necessary."[44] Even the usually supportive *Times* warned that if violence continued in 2017, then J'Ouvert should be shut down.[45] Faced with the very real possibility of having the event canceled, JCI negotiated a new set of rules with the NYPD, which included moving the start time up from 4:00 a.m. to 6:00 a.m., increased police security, metal detector check points, frozen zones along the route, and a no-alcohol policy.[46] Some agreed with this compromise, including Carey Gabay's widow, Trenelle, who saw the measures as necessary to insure a safer J'Ouvert, a cultural event that she still supported. Ms. Gabay joined other activists, including City Council Representative Jumaane Williams, in casting the issue into the broader context of gun control. "J'Ouvert did not take him (Carey) away from me," she painfully recounted. "Gun violence did."[47]

Predictably, not everyone was pleased with these changes. The loss of the magical darkness to dawn transition, which could only be experienced with the traditional 4:00 a.m. start, was troubling for some. Despers

USA arranger Odie Franklin complained to the *Times* that the later start time "dishonored" the tradition of the culture.[48] Michael Manswell of the Pagwah mas band was concerned that the costumed members of his group had to be individually wanded as potential criminals before entering the parade area. He told an AP reporter, "Those of us really involved in J'Ouvert are not creating this violence and we shouldn't be punished or forced to change."[49]

In the end, J'Ouvert 2017 took place without incident.[50] Some participants told the press that the excessive security created a police-state atmosphere that stifled the spirit of the celebration. The *Times* reported that the gathering had been "sapped of its usual energy," and the *Daily News* quipped that the later start time had taken the "*joie de verve* out of Brooklyn's *J'Ouvert*."[51] While the crowd appeared somewhat smaller than in past years, there was no shortage of exuberant art and play on the streets. Fifteen masquerade bands, eight steelbands, and seven rhythm bands participated in the JCI-organized competitions along the route. These numbers are roughly in keeping with the turnout of registered bands over the previous few years, with a slight decline in steelband participation.[52] Hundreds, perhaps more than a thousand, revelers donned homemade, raggedy costumes accented with paint and powder. There were appearances by oil-drenched jab jab devils, midnight robbers, cross-dressing Dame Lorraine figures, and other traditional ole mas characters. The Oil Downeres band lampooned President Trump and his wall with a mas titled "Dey Showing Their True Colors." Crowds thronged around the Philadelphia Pan Stars, D'Radoes, and Pan Evolution, who came in first, second, and third, respectively, in the steelband calypso competition. Revelers wined and sang along to "Full Extreme," performed by the Philadelphia Pan Stars and D'Radoes. Significantly, the new security measures did not include the barricades used on Eastern Parkway to separate spectators from participants. Once individuals had passed through a checkpoint they were free to meld in with the musicians and masqueraders on the road. The core communal and participatory spirit was preserved, at least for J'Ouvert 2017 (see Figures 9.1, 9.2, and 9.3.).

Brooklyn Carnival Moves On

Will Brooklyn's Caribbean community still be jamming fifty years from now? Pessimists surmise that creeping gentrification, WIADCA's shaky organizational structure, lack of sufficient public and private financial support, the high costs of mounting steel and mas bands, and fear-mongering on the part of the press will lead to the inevitable dissolution of Brooklyn Carnival. This is certainly within the realm of possibility. The dip in crowd size at the Eastern Parkway and J'Ouvert parades, the decrease in the number of steelbands participating in Panorama and J'Ouvert, and diminishing attendance at Dimanche Gras and traditional calypso/soca tents might suggest that Carnival, having reached its zenith around the

Figure 9.1. Pan Liberty at Brooklyn J'Ouvert, 2017. Photo by Ray Allen.

Figure 9.2. Jab-Jab Devils at Brooklyn J'Ouvert, 2017. Photo by Ray Allen.

Figure 9.3. Brooklyn J'Ouvert costumes, 2017. Photo by Christopher Mulé (courtesy of City Lore).

turn of the new millennium, has been on the decline of late and is possibly on its way out.

But history suggests that any dire predictions of Brooklyn Carnival's imminent demise are premature. Carnival has endured for nearly two centuries in Trinidad and surrounding islands, and wherever a critical mass of Afro-Caribbean migrants landed and established a beachhead, Carnival soon followed and flourished. Such has been the case in Harlem, Brooklyn, Toronto, London, Miami, and dozens of other locales in North America and Europe, in addition to the proliferation of Carnival celebrations throughout the Caribbean itself. In New York, ever since Rufus Gorin played bat mas in his Harlem apartment and Wilmoth Houdini recorded his first calypso back in the 1920s, island people have found a way to celebrate. By nature, Carnival has been a flash point for controversy and has had to survive numerous attempts by colonial and contemporary civic authorities to shut down or curtail its transgressive play. Yet Carnival has persevered through the Canboulay riots of 1883, the Crown Heights riots of 1991, the shooting-mired Brooklyn J'Ouverts of 2015 and 2016, and countless lesser confrontations. The British and American occupiers outlawed Trinidad Carnival during World War II, but the celebration resurfaced in 1946, stronger than ever. When the New York powers-that-be shut down Harlem Carnival in 1961, a new generation of migrants nimbly reconstructed the tradition in Brooklyn, where it has endured as a vibrant display of Caribbean culture and identity for half a century. Carnival was and continues to be deeply embedded in the Caribbean cultural DNA.

Exactly what form Brooklyn Carnival will take in the future, and if it will even stay in Brooklyn proper, remains to be seen. Like its Trinidadian parent, Carnival in the diaspora has evolved and will no doubt continue to do so. Dame Lorraine dances foreshadowed Harlem's Seventh Avenue parade, an event that began as a civic and ethnic pageant, but quickly morphed into genuine street Carnival with the introduction of the new steelbands and more elaborate masquerading. After too many clashes with the authorities, the action moved across the river, following the influx of new migrants, to Eastern Parkway and the Brooklyn Museum, where mobile sound trucks and soca eventually supplanted pan-on-the-Parkway and old-fashioned calypso tents. Brooklyn's steelband movement thrived, and when pushed off the Parkway, it responded by establishing a pan-only J'Ouvert that became a repository for grassroots Carnival traditions.

Carnival's protean nature, particularly its ability to respond to the rapidly changing urban and media landscapes by accommodating the old and the new, has been its greatest strength, and one it will need to draw on as the twenty-first century continues to unfold. If the current wave of gentrification continues to erode the Caribbean hegemony of central Brooklyn, Carnival may move again, possibly to Queens or Long Island, where Caribbean communities continue to proliferate.[53] Perhaps the old proposal to relocate the Eastern Parkway parade to Manhattan's Fifth Avenue will be resurrected for reconsideration. Whether WIADCA and JCI will continue to exert exclusive authority over Labor Day Carnival and J'Ouvert is uncertain. Perhaps a new organization, or some wing of the city government, will eventually assume the helm. Decentralization may pave the way for a broader coalition of public and private entities to coordinate activities around Labor Day.[54] Such restructuring might inject new life into Panorama and Dimanche Gras, events that are currently in need of rejuvenation. Another possibility is that WIADCA, which has survived a seemingly endless series of challenges and controversies for half a century, may reconstitute itself with a younger and more diverse leadership. What changes the newly elected president, the Jamaican American Ionie Pierce, will bring to the table remain to be seen.[55]

Likewise, the face of the Carnival transnation will no doubt continue to evolve. Advances in transportation and communications led to deterritorialization, which in turn allowed singers, musicians, arrangers, mas costume makers, and Carnival fans to move more readily between Trinidad, the global center of Carnival production, and its various outposts in the Caribbean, North America, and Europe. The future shape of these cultural networks will be telling, for Trinidad's Carnival entrepreneurs and artists have become increasingly dependent on North American and European diasporic communities to provide markets for their goods and a cohort of expatriate tourists to return home to support the main Trinidad attraction. The Brooklyn, Toronto, and London celebrations have taken on their own unique qualities, but currently remain firmly tethered to the Trinidad center. Reverse globalization rules for the moment, although the flow of cultural capital is circular, not one-way, and will continue to readjust itself depending on changing economic conditions in Trinidad and immigration policies abroad.

However these local and global networks develop, there is little question that music will remain omnipresent in twenty-first-century Brooklyn Carnival. For the immediate future, grassroots steelbands will no doubt continue to fulfill a vital creative and cultural niche within the Caribbean community, and the deep-seated desire for competition will probably keep some form of Panorama contest alive. Soca, or its next iteration, should deliver the soundtrack for Carnival fetes and road marches via live band, deejay-mediated, live vocals over prerecorded tracks, or perhaps some yet-to-be-conceived form of presentation. Participatory steelband and soca performances promise to provide the vital social and sonic space for Caribbean transnationals, both island- and American-born, to bond together around a shared cultural heritage and to artfully challenge a status quo system that continues to subordinate people of color in Brooklyn. Through public performance of Carnival music, Caribbean people will remind their black and white American neighbors that they have arrived and are now permanent citizens of New York City's global mélange.

Notes

1. A 2017 recording of the Ultimate Rejects' "Full Extreme" can be heard on YouTube, at https://www.youtube.com/watch?v=rpxExb0qYbA.

2. "President's Message" in the 2017 WIADCA Carnival program booklet. WIADCA's decision to celebrate 2017 as its 50th anniversary apparently dates the genesis of the organization back to 1967, when Rufus Gorin acquired a permit to hold a Carnival parade in Crown Heights. Gorin actually incorporated the United West Indian Day Development Association in 1966. As outlined in chapter 4, the name was changed to the West Indian American Day Association in 1971 when Carlos Lezama became chairman and the first Eastern Parkway Parade and the accompanying Brooklyn Museum evening events were staged. The organization changed its name to the current West Indian American Day Carnival Association in 1974. Given this history, Herman Hall has suggested that 2017 should celebrate Rufus Gorin and UWIDDA, while 2021 should commemorate Lezama and WIADCA's 50th anniversary. See Herman Hall, "Celebrate Lionel Rufus Gorin, True Pioneer: Brooklyn's 50 Years of Carnival," *Everybody's Caribbean Magazine* 40, no. 2 (October 2017): 14–18.

3. In 2007 and 2008 the *Times* and the *Daily News*, respectively, reported that Carnival organizers were estimating three million attendees at the Eastern Parkway parade. The *Times* proclaimed the event "New York's biggest parade." See Robert McFadden, "They Call It Labor Day, but They Celebrate Calypso and Summer's End," *New York Times*, 4 September 2007, https://www.nytimes.com/2007/09/04/nyregion/04parade.html; and Jane H. Furse and Chad Smith, "West Indian American Day Carnival Parade Lets Revelers Soca Up Fun," *New York Daily News*, 31 August 2008, https://www.nydailynews.com/new-york/west-indian-american-day-carnival-parade-lets-revelers-soca-fun-article-1.324218.

4. West Indian American Day Carnival Association, "About Us," http://wiadcacarnival.org/about-us/.

5. "New York Caribbean Carnival Parade Unites Thousands to Celebrate Diversity on Brooklyn Streets," *New York Daily News*, 4 September 2017, http://www.nydailynews.com/new-york/brooklyn/thousands-celebrate-diversity-n-y-caribbean-carnival-parade-article-1.3468944.

6. Herman Hall, "A Disgraceful 50th Carnival Anniversary," *Everybody's Caribbean Magazine* 40, no. 2 (October 2017): 20.

7. Herman Hall is correct that the generation of immigrants who created Brooklyn Carnival in the 1970s is rapidly aging out. But the size of New York's overall English-speaking Caribbean community grew rapidly in the ensuing decades and has been relatively stable since the turn of the millennium. Working with 1980 US Census figures, Philip Kasinitz reported nearly 300,000 non-Hispanic Caribbean New Yorkers, 183,900 of whom were from the four largest English-speaking countries of Jamaica, Trinidad, Guyana, and Barbados. Using US Census estimates from the late 1990s, Nancy Foner reported the number of immigrants from those four locales had more than doubled by 1998, to roughly 435,000. According to the American Community Survey, numbers for those four locales have decreased only slightly to 418,596 in 2010 and 423,935 in 2015. Moreover, these figures do not include the growing legions of second- and third-generation Caribbean–New Yorkers (whose exact numbers are difficult to extract from the census data). Taken as a whole, New York's foreign and native-born Caribbean population, whose members might potentially participate in Carnival, has grown substantially since the first Eastern Parkway parade in 1971 and appears to be in no immediate danger of significant decline. See Philip Kasinitz, *Caribbean New York: Black Immigrants and the Politics of Race* (Cornell University Press, 1992), p. 54; and Nancy Foner, "Introduction: West Indian Migration to New York, an Overview," in *Islands in the City: West Indian Migration to New York*, edited by Nancy Foner (University of California Press, 2001), p. 4.

8. Herman Hall, interview with author, 21 September 2017, Brooklyn. Hall's estimate of the smaller crowd size in 2017 is based on his experience walking up and down the Eastern Parkway parade route while covering the event for radio station WLIB. His conjectures on the general decline in attendance of the Labor Day events are based on his years of personal observations and numerous conversations with Brooklyn Carnival participants.

9. For example, Super Blue's first 1980 hit on Charlie's Records, "Soca Baptist," lilts along at a modest 120 BPM tempo, while the singer offers his humorous observations on the musical similarities between a Spiritual Baptist prayer meeting and a Carnival bacchanal. Compare this to his 2013 Road March–winning song, "Fantastic Friday," which races at a 160 BPM tempo while proclaiming over and over "the bouncing start" for the weekend party. "Soca Baptist" is available on YouTube, at https://www.youtube.com/watch?v=_c2wF4M9gnU, and "Fantastic Friday" is at https://www.youtube.com/watch?v=59s6CRVCoqU.

10. Glenville Ashby, "Rawlston 'Charlie' Charles," *West Indian American Day 2010* Carnival program booklet, p. 3.

11. Jamal Talib, interview with author, 15 September 2017, Brooklyn.

12. Ibid.

13. Michelle Edwards, "Calypso 'N Soca," *Caribbean Life*, 22 August 2012, https://www.caribbeanlifenews.com/stories/2012/8/2012_08_21_sub_revue_tent.html.

14. "Sesame Flyers International 2013 Caribbean Carnival Calypso Spectacular," Streets of New York 411 Inc., 4 July 2013, https://streetsofnewyork411.com/2013/07/04/sesame-flyers-intl-2013-caribbean-carnival-calypso-spectacular/.

15. "Archived: NYC in the House! Request Band's Rayzor Returns to T&T with New Music," *EbuzzNews*, 17 October 2016, http://ebuzztt.com/nyc-in-the-house-request-bands-rayzor-returns-to-tt-with-new-music/. "Two NYC Musicians Rep Hard *for* T&T Soca," *Trinidad Guardian*, 20 January 2018, http://www.guardian.co.tt/lifestyle/2018-01-20/two-nyc-musicians-rep-hard-tt-soca; "Yankey Boy Keeping It Positive," *Trinidad & Tobago Guardian Online*, 30 November 2015, http://www.guardian.co.tt/lifestyle/2015-11-30/yankey-boy-keeping-it-positive.

16. "Lord Nelson, Calypso Rose and Sparrow honored by Consulate General in New York," Government of the Republic of Trinidad and Tobago, 4 September 2013, http://www.news.gov.tt/content/lord-nelson-calypso-rose-and-sparrow-honoured-consulate-general-new-york#.Wc0GfNgpC70.

17. Brooklyn Panorama participation reached its peak in the early 2000s with fifteen steelbands competing in 2001, eighteen in 2002, and fifteen in 2003. In those years WIADCA and the USSA sponsored competing (2001 and 2002) or joint (2003) Panoramas. From 2009 to 2018, under exclusive WIADCA sponsorship, the numbers of steelbands that participated in Brooklyn Panorama are as follows:

2018: 7
2017: 8
2016: 10
2015: 10
2014: 11
2013: 10
2012: 10
2011: 11
2010: 10
2009: 10

For a complete list of all participating Brooklyn Panorama bands from 1973 on, see the When Steel Talks (http://www.panonthenet.com/history/NewYorkResults.htm) and Panscore (http://panscore.com/competitions/new-york-panorama) websites.

18. Martin Douglas, interview with author, 12 August 2017, Brooklyn.

19. "New York Steel Orchestras to WIADCA—Pay Up in Full, or No 2017 Panorama," When Steel Talks, http://www.panonthenet.com/news/2017/aug/no-money-no-2017-nypanorama-8-21-2017.htm; Douglas, interview 12 August 2017.

20. "New York 2011 Steel Orchestra Panorama in Review," When Steel Talks, http://www.panonthenet.com/panorama/2011/new-york-review-2011.htm.

21. Philip Noel, "Giuliani Declares War on Carnival," in *Why Blacks Fear America's Mayor: Reporting Police Brutality and Black Activist Politics under Rudy Giuliana* (iUniverse, 2007), pp. 337–341.

22. Colin Moynihan, "Steel Bands in Brooklyn Struggle for Space," *New York Times*, 7 July 2015.

23. For a portrait of one such stage-side band, see "Legend Stars Steel Band in Play for 2011," When Steel Talks, https://whensteeltalks.ning.com/forum/topics/legend-stars-steel-band-in-play-for-2011.

24. A few white faces can be observed in a number of the Brooklyn Panorama bands, but they are anomalies, as the bands remain heavily Afro-Caribbean in personnel. Over the past five years a group of half-a-dozen Oberlin College graduates and veterans of that school's steelband program have played for one of the Brooklyn bands, most recently Despers USA.

25. The demographics of the Brooklyn steelbands is an area that requires more extensive quantitative research. On a qualitative level, Martin Douglas, the president of the USSA and a longtime observer of the local scene, suggests that today's Brooklyn's steelbands are considerably younger and more diverse in terms of island representation than they were when he arrived from Trinidad in the 1980s. In those days, he recalls, the large bands were still dominated by older Trinidad men. Martin Douglas, phone interview with author, 1 October 2017. My informal conversations with members of Brooklyn's Despers USA, CASYM, Crossfire, D'Radoes, and the New York Pan All Stars confirm this pattern.

26. "New York Youth Pan Fest Showcases Steelpan Talent," When Steel Pan Talks, http://www.panonthenet.com/news/2016/sep/junior-pan-fest-2016.htm/.

27. Sparkle Demming, phone interview with author, 10 September 2018.

28. "Different Me" won both the Port of Spain (Desperadoes) and New York (D'Radoes) 2016 Panoramas. "Full Extreme" won the Port of Spain (Trinidad All Stars) 2017 Panorama and was played by four of the ten bands in the New York 2017 Panorama.

29. Andrew Martin and Ray Funk, "Andre White Does It Again," *Caribbean Live*, 12–18 October 2012; Andre White, personal interview with author, 1 September 2017, Brooklyn.

30. Kendall Williams, personal interview with author, 26 August 2017, Brooklyn.

31. Odie Franklin, personal interview with author, 26 August 2017, Brooklyn.

32. Ray Allen and Ray Funk, "The GQ Arrangers: Three Competitive Collaborators," *Trinidad and Tobago Guardian*, 7 September 2017, https://www4.guardian.co.tt/life-lead/2017-09-07/gq-arrangers.

33. "J'Ouvert 2008 in New York: Steelbands, Pan Music, and Rhythm Sections Rule the Streets," When Steel Talks, http://www.panonthenet.com/news/2008/sep/ny-jouvert-9.05.08.htm.

34. J'Ouvert City International program booklet, Volume 5, September 2000.

35. The numbers of participating Panorama and J'Ouvert steelbands are calculated from the results of J'Ouvert City's annual pan and rhythm contests, which are found on the When Steel Talks and Pancore websites. Steelbands appearing at both Brooklyn Panorama and Brooklyn J'Ouvert over the past six years are as follows:

2018: Philadelphia Pan Stars, D'Radoes, Despers USA.
2017: Philadelphia Pan Stars, D'Radoes, Pan Evolution.
2016: Philadelphia Pan Stars, D'Radoes, Despers USA.
2015: D'Radoes, Despers USA.
2014: D'Radoes, Despers USA, Crossfire, Adlib, Metro Steel, Sonatas.
2013: D'Radoes, Despers USA, Crossfire, Adlib, Pantonic.

36. The Pagwah mas band usually includes Indo-Trinidad tassa drummers along with African skin drums and iron in its rhythm band. For

an account of DJA-Rara's participation in the 2010 J'Ouvert, see Kareem Fahim, "After Tough Year, New York's Haitians Gather," *New York Times*, 6 September 2010.

37. "New York Pan Stars Open New York Steelband Summer Season with a Bang," When Steel Talks, 4 July 2017, http:/www.panonthenet.com/news/2017/Jul/pan-stars-launch-7-4-2017.htm.

38. In addition to cited press accounts and web sources, the information in this section is drawn from my own observations of Brooklyn's 2017 Carnival. I attended the Eastern Parkway and J'Ouvert parades, the rained-out and non-judged Panoramas, the Youth Pan Fest, band launces for D'Radoes and Pagwah, and the Brooklyn Kaiso House calypso tent. I also spent time at the pan yards of D'Radoes, Despers USA, Pan Evolution, and CASYM.

39. Molly Crane-Newman, John Annese, and Andrew Keshner, "A Day to Celebrate," *New York Daily News*, 5 September 2017.

40. H. Nazan Osik, "Mayor Bill de Blasio Sends a Message to President Trump and Marches in the West Indian Day Parade," *Turkish New York*, 12 September 2017, https://www.nkendiken.com/2017/09/05/mayor-bill-de-blasio-sends-a-message-to-president-trump-and-marches-in-the-west-indian-day-parade/.

41. Talib, interview, 16 September 2017. Talib was able to run his 2018 Kaiso Tent with moderate success.

42. A scathing review of the 2017 Panorama is found on the When Steel Talks website: "The Ugly, the Uglier and the Ugliest—New York 'Panorama' 2017," http://www.panonthenet.com/news/2017/sep/ny-panorama-in-review-9-6-2017.htm.

43. Naikita Stewart and Michael Schwritz, "2 Killed at Brooklyn Festivities Despite Heightened Security," *New York Times*, 6 September 2016.

44. Nathan Tempey, "Officials and Activists Demand an End to J'Ouvert Following Violence," *Gothamist*, 6 September 2016, http://gothamist.com/2016/09/06/jouvert_uncancellable.php.

45. "Last Hope for Peace at Brooklyn's Big Party," *New York Times*, 30 August 2017, https://www.nytimes.com/2017/08/30/opinion/brooklyn-west-indian-violence.html?mcubz=0. Responding to Mayor de Blasio's remarks about a few bad apples spoiling the celebration, the *Times* editors noted, "At some point, though, bad apples can define the entire barrel."

46. Ashley Southhall, "Safety Plan for J'Ouvert in Brooklyn Borrows from New Year's Eve Tactics," *New York Times*, 21 August 2017.

47. Widow of Carey Gabay Calls for Safe J'Ouvert and Gun Sanity," *New York Daily News*, 3 September 2017.

48. Ashley Southhall, "As Excitement Builds for J'Ouvert, So Do Hopes for Peace," *New York Times*, 31 August 2017.

49. Colleen Long, "NYC Tries Fencing in Often-Violent Caribbean Celebration," Associated Press, 3 September 2017, http://www.washingtontimes.com/news/2017/sep/3/nyc-tries-fencing-in-often-violent-caribbean-celeb/.

50. Media reports falsely linked several Sunday night neighborhood shootings to J'Ouvert. These events actually took place before and away from the route to J'Ouvert. For example, a *New York Post* headline on 5 September announced, "Bullets Fly at J'Ouvert: Bloodshed Despite Changes." A close read of the article reveals that the shooting occurred at

5:00 a.m., an hour before the J'Ouvert procession began, and more than two miles from the start of the parade route.

51. Ashley Southall, "J'ouvert Spared Violence Amid Heightened Security Effort," *New York Times*, 4 September 2017, https://www.nytimes.com/2017/09/04/nyregion/jouvert-brooklyn-parade.html; Esha Ray and Nicole Hensley, "Ire at J'Ouvert Tight Security," *New York Daily News*, 5 September 2017.

52. The numbers of participating J'Ouvert mas bands, steelbands, and rhythm sections are found on the When Steel Talks website (panonthenet.com). According to this source, the numbers of mas bands that participated in Brooklyn J'Ouvert from 2013 to 2018 are as follows:

2018: 12 bands
2017: 15 bands
2016: 17 bands
2015: 13 bands
2014: 19 bands
2013: 13 bands

The numbers of steelbands that participated in Brooklyn J'Ouvert in this period are as follows:

2018: 8 bands
2017: 8 bands
2016: 11 bands
2015: 8 bands
2014: 14 bands
2013: 13 bands

The numbers of rhythm sections that participated in Brooklyn J'Ouvert in this period are as follows:

2018: 7 bands
2017: 7 bands
2016: 6 bands
2015: 5 bands
2014: 8 bands
2013: 11 bands

53. While Brooklyn remains home to New York's largest English-speaking Caribbean population, the community has become increasingly spread out across the New York metropolitan area since the turn of the millennium. According to the 2015 American Community Survey, 44 percent (194,247) of New York's Caribbean population born in Jamaica, Trinidad, Guyana, Grenada, and Barbados live in Brooklyn, 37 percent (162,499) live in Queens, and 16 percent (71,537) live in the Bronx. The 2015 American Community Survey reports that 55 percent (46,517) of New York's Trinidad-born residents live in Brooklyn, 33 percent (28,260) in Queens, and 8 percent (6,485) in the Bronx. In addition 4,484 Trinidad immigrants live just outside the city limits in New York State's Nassau County, and 9,659 in the nearby New Jersey counties of Bergen, Essex, Hudson, and Union.

54. As of this writing, WIADCA and J'Ouvert City continue to coordinate most of the Labor Day Carnival activities. However, in recent years there have been increasing signs of Carnival decentralization and expansion. For example, the previously mentioned Youth Pan Festival (organized by

the Carlos Lezama Archives and Caribbean Cultural Center and taking place the weekend before Labor Day) and steelband and mas camp launches (organized by individual bands and taking place throughout July and August) have become important components of the Carnival season. A number of independent calypso and soca shows continue to be staged around the Labor Day weekend. In addition, members of Brooklyn's individual island communities have begun to organize their own summer heritage-day festivals that include Carnival-related activities. The 2018 Grenada Day festival, held at Brooklyn's Boys and Girls High School field a week before Labor Day, included performances of Jab Jab drumming and masquerading, traditions central to the Port of Spain and Brooklyn J'Ouvert celebrations.

See Gerry Hopkin, "Grenada Day 2018 in NYC Set for August 26," *Caribbean Life*, 23 August 2018, https://www.caribbeanlifenews.com/stories/2018/8/2018-08-24-sub-grenada-day-nyc-cl.html; and John Alexander, "Barbados Festival Day Is a Hit in Canarsie," *Brooklyn Daily Eagle*, 12 July 2017, https://brooklyneagle.com/articles/2017/07/12/barbados-festival-day-is-a-hit-in-canarsie/.

55. See Vinette Pryce's commentary on the challenges Pierce, as a female Jamaican native, will face as the head of WIADCA, in "Jamaican Woman Will Preside Over WIADCA—a First, *Caribbean Life*, 21 August 2018, https://www.caribbeanlifenews.com/stories/2018/8/2018-08-24-vkp-inside-life-cl.html.

References

Ahyoung, Selwyn. 1981. *Soca Fever!: Change in the Calypso Music Tradition of Trinidad, 1970–1989*. MA thesis, Indiana University.

Allen, Ray. 1999. "*J'Ouvert* in Brooklyn Carnival: Revitalizing Steel Pan and Old Mas Traditions." *Western Folklore* 58 (3–4): 255–277.

Allen, Ray. 2010. "In Pursuit of Authenticity: The New Lost City Ramblers and the Postwar Folk Music Revival." *Journal of the Study of American Music* 4 (3): 277–306.

Allen, Ray. 2014. "The Brooklyn Connection: Frankie McIntosh and Straker Records." *American Music Review* 44 (1): 9–14.

Allen, Ray, and Les Slater. 1998. "Steel Pan Grows in Brooklyn: Trinidadian Music and Cultural Identity." In *Island Sounds in the Global City: Caribbean Music in New York*, edited by Ray Allen and Lois Wilcken, 114–137. Urbana: University of Illinois Press.

Allen, Ray, and Lois Wilcken. 1998. "Introduction: Island Sounds in the Global City." In *Island Sounds in the Global City: Caribbean Music in New York*, edited by Ray Allen and Lois Wilcken, 1–6. Urbana: University of Illinois Press.

Alleyne-Dettmers, Patricia. 2005. "The Relocation of Trinidad Carnival in Notting Hill, London, and the Politics of Diasporisation." In *Globalisation, Diaspora and Caribbean Popular Culture*, edited by G. T. Ho and Keith Nurse, 64–89. Kingston, Jamaica: Ian Randle.

Anderson, Jervis. 1981. *This Was Harlem: 1900–1950*. New York: Farrar, Straus and Giroux.

Appadurai, Arjun. 1990. "Disjuncture and Difference in the Global Cultural Economy." *Public Culture* 2 (2): 1–24.

Austerlitz, Paul. 1997. *Merengue: Dominican Music and Dominican Identity*. Philadelphia: Temple University Press.

Averill, Gage. 1997a. *A Day for the Hunter, A Day for the Prey: Popular Music and Power in Haiti*. Chicago: University of Chicago Press.

Averill, Gage. 1997b. "'Pan Is We Ting': West Indian Steelbands in Brooklyn." In *Musics of Multicultural America*, edited by Kip Lornell and Anne Rasmussen, 101–130. New York: Schirmer Books.

Averill, Gage. 1998. "Moving to the Big Apple: Tabou Combos Diasporic Dreams." In *Island Sounds in the Global City: Caribbean Popular Music* and *Identity in New York*, edited by Ray Allen and Lois Wilcken, 138–161. Urbana: University of Illinois Press.

Averill, Gage. 2006. "'Mezanmi, Kouman Nou Ye? My Friends, How Are You?': Musical Constructions of the Haitian Transnation." In *Ethnomusicology: A Contemporary Reader*, edited by Jennifer Post, 262–264. New York: Routledge.

Basch, Linda, Nina Glick Schille, and Cristina Szanton Blanc. 1994. *Nations Unbound: Transnational Projects, Postcolonial Predicaments, and Deterritorialized Nation-States*. New York: Routledge.

Blank, Trevor, and Robert Glenn Howard. 2013. *Tradition in the Twenty-First Century: Locating the Role of the Past in the Present*. Logan: Utah State University Press.

Bowman, Wayne. 2008. "Charlie and His Roots: Tobago's Rawlston Charles." *Caribbean Beat Magazine* 93 (September/October), https://www.caribbean-beat.com/issue-93/charlie-and-his-roots#axzz5ioEtqucB.

Buff, Rachel. 2001. *Immigration and the Political Economy of Home: West Indian Brooklyn and American Indian Minneapolis, 1945–1992*. Berkeley: University of California Press.

Chambers, Iain. 1993. "Travelling Sounds: Whose Center, Whose Periphery?" In *Otherness and the Media: The Ethnography of the Imagined and the Imaged*, edited by Hamid Naficy and Teshome Gabriel, 205–210. Langhorne, PA: Harwood Academic.

Cowley, John. 1996. *Carnival, Canboulay and Calypso: Traditions in the Making*. New York: Cambridge University Press.

Cowley, John. 2006. "West Indies Blues: An Historical Overview 1920s–1950s." In *Nobody Knows Where the Blues Come From*, edited by Robert Springer, 187–263. Jackson: University of Mississippi Press.

Davis, Susan. 1986. *Parades and Power: Street Theatre in Nineteenth-Century Philadelphia*. Berkeley: University of California Press.

Denning, Michael. 2015. *Noise Uprising: The Audiopolitics of a World Musical Revolution*. New York: Verso.

Dudley, Shannon. 1996. "Judging 'By the Beat': Calypso versus Soca." *Ethnomusicology* 40 (2): 269–298.

Dudley, Shannon. 2004. *Carnival Music in Trinidad: Experiencing Music, Expressing Culture*. New York: Oxford University Press.

Dudley, Shannon. 2008. *Music from Behind the Bridge: Steelband Spirit and Politics in Trinidad and Tobago*. New York: Oxford University Press.

Feld, Steven. 1994. "Notes on 'World Beat.'" In *Music Grooves*, edited by Charles Keil and Steven Feld, 238–246. Chicago: University of Chicago Press.

Ferguson, Anthony. 2005. "Pelham Goddard: The Making of a Musical Maestro." *We Beat Magazine* 5 (June): 8–12.

Filene, Benjamin. 2000. *Romancing the Folk: Public Memory and American Roots Music*. Chapel Hill: University of North Carolina Press.

Flores, Juan. 2016. *Salsa Rising: New York Latin Music of the Sixties Generation*. New York: Oxford University Press.

Foner, Nancy. 2001. "Introduction: West Indian Migration to New York." In *Islands in the City: West Indian Migration to New York*, edited by Nany Foner, 1–22. Berkeley: University of California Press.

Frith, Simon. 2000. "The Discourse of World Music." In *Western Music and Its Others*, edited by Georgina Born and David Hesmondhalgh, 305–322. Berkeley: University of California Press.

Funk, Ray, and Michael Eldridge. 2014. *Calypso Craze, 1956–1976 and Beyond*. Booklet to Bear Family CD box BCD 16947 GK.

Funk, Ray, and Donald Hill. 2003. "Will Calypso Doom Rock 'n' Roll?: The U.S. Calypso Craze of 1957." In *Trinidad Carnival: The Cultural Politics of a Transnational Festival*, edited by Garth Green and Philip Scher, 178–197. Bloomington: Indiana University Press.

Gibbs, Craig Martin. 2015. *Calypso and Other Music of Trinidad: 1912–1962*. Jefferson, NC: McFarland.

Gilroy, Paul. 1993. *The Black Atlantic: Modernity and Double Consciousness*. Cambridge, MA: Harvard University Press.

Glasser, Ruth. 1995. *My Music Is My Flag: Puerto Rican Musicians and Their New York Communities*. Berkeley: University of California Press.

Glassie, Henry. 1995. "Tradition." *Journal of American Folklore* 108 (430): 395–412.

Goldsmith, Peter. 1998. *Making People's Music: Moe Asch and Folkways Records*. Washington, DC: Smithsonian Institution Press.

Gordon, Max. 1980. *Live at the Village Vanguard*. New York: Da Capo Press.

Grass, Randall. 1988. *When the Time Comes: Rebel Soca*. CD Booklet, Shanachie CD 64010.

Green, Garth, and Philip Scher. 2007. *Trinidad Carnival: The Cultural Politics of a Transnational Festival*. Bloomington: Indiana University Press.

Guilbault, Jocelyn. 1993. "On Redefining the 'Local' through World Music." *Worlds of Music* 35 (2): 33–47.

Guilbault, Jocelyn. 2001. "World Music." In *The Cambridge Companion to Pop and Rock*, edited by Simon Firth, Will Straw, and John Street, 176–192. New York: Cambridge University Press.

Guilbault, Jocelyn. 2007. *Governing Sound: The Cultural Politics of Trinidad's Carnival Musics*. Chicago: University of Chicago Press.

Guilbault, Jocelyn, and Roy Cape. 2014. *Roy Cape: A Life on the Calypso and Soca Bandstand*. Chapel Hill, NC: Duke University Press.

Guild, Joshua. 2007. *You Can't Go Home Again: Migration, Citizenship, and Black Community in Postwar New York and London*. PhD diss., Yale University.

Hall, Herman. 1982. "Inside Brooklyn's Carnival." *Everybody's Magazine* 6 (7): 12–23.

Hall, Herman. 2017. "Celebrate Lionel 'Rufus' Gorin: Brooklyn's 50 Years of Carnival." *Everybody's Caribbean* 4 (2): 14–18.

Hall, Stuart. 1981. "Notes on Deconstructing the Popular." In *People's History and Socialist Theory*, edited by Raphael Samuel, 227–240. New York: Routledge Press.

Hall, Stuart. 1991. *Myths of Caribbean Identity*. Coventry, UK: University of Warwick, Center for Caribbean Studies.

Hernandez, Deborah Pacini. 2010. *Oye Como Va!: Hybridity and Identity in Latino Popular Music*. Philadelphia: Temple University Press.

Hill, Donald. 1981. "New York's Caribbean Carnival." *Everybody's Magazine* 5 (5): 33–37.

Hill, Donald. 1993. *Calypso Calaloo*. Gainesville: University Press of Florida.

Hill, Donald. 1994. "A History of West Indian Carnival in New York to 1978." *New York Folklore Quarterly* 20 (1–2): 47–66.

Hill, Donald. 1998. "I Am Happy in This Sweet Land of Liberty: The New York Calypso Craze of the 1930s and 1940s." In *Island Sounds in the Global City: Caribbean Popular Music in New York*, edited by Ray Allen and Lois Wilcken,74–92. Urbana: University of Illinois Press.

Hill, Donald. 1999. *Lionel Belasco: Good Night Ladies and Gents.* CD booklet, Rounder CD 1138.

Hill, Donald, and Robert Abramson. 1979. "West Indian Carnival in Brooklyn." *Natural History* 88 (7): 72–85.

Hill, Errol. 1972. *The Trinidad Carnival.* Austin: University of Texas Press; 2nd ed., 1997. London: New Beacon Books.

Ho, Christine, and Keith Nurse. 2005. "Introduction." In *Globalization, Diaspora, and Caribbean Popular Culture*, edited by Christine Ho and Keith Nurse, vii–xxiv. Kingston, Jamaica: Ian Randle.

Holder, Geoffrey. 1957. "The Fad from Trinidad." *New York Times Magazine*, 21 April.

Kasinitz, Philip. 1992. *Caribbean New York: Black Immigrants and the Politics of Race.* Ithaca, NY: Cornell University Press.

Kasinitz, Philip. 1998. "Community Dramatized, Community Contested: The Politics of Celebration in the Brooklyn Carnival." In *Island Sounds in the Global City: Caribbean Music in New York*, edited by Ray Allen and Lois Wilcken, 93–113. Urbana: University of Illinois Press.

Kasinitz, Philip, and Judith Freidenberg-Herbstein. 1987. "The Puerto Rican Parade and West Indian Carnival: Public Celebrations in New York City." In *Caribbean Life in New York City: Sociocultural Dimensions*, edited by Constance Sutton and Elsa Chaney, 327–349. New York: Center for Migration Studies.

Kirshenblatt-Gimblett, Barbara. 1995. "Theorizing Heritage." *Ethnomusicology* 39 (3): 367–380.

Kirshenblatt-Gimblett, Barbara. 2002. "Sounds of Sensibility." In *American Klezmer: Its Roots and Offshoots*, edited by Mark Slobin, 129–173. Berkeley: University of California Press.

Levine, Lawrence. *Black Culture and Black Consciousness: Afro-American Folk Thought from Slavery to Freedom.* New York: Oxford University Press, 1977.

Li, Xiaofan Amy. 2017. "Introduction: From Exotic to the Autoexotic." *PMLA* 132 (2 March): 392–396.

Lovelace, Earl. 2004. "The Emancipation Jouvay Tradition and the Almost Loss of Pan." In *Carnival Culture in Action: The Trinidad Experience*, edited by Milla Cortez Riggio, 187–203. New York: Routledge Press.

Manning, Frank. 1990. "Overseas Caribbean Carnivals: The Art and Politics of a Transnational Celebration." *Plantation Society in the Americas* 3 (1): 47–62.

Manuel, Peter. 1995. *Caribbean Currents: From Rumba to Reggae.* Philadelphia: Temple University Press.

Manuel, Peter. 1998. "Representations of New York City in Latin Music." In *Island Sounds in the Global City: Caribbean Popular Music and Identity in New York*, edited by Ray Allen and Lois Wilcken, 22–43. Urbana: University of Illinois Press.

Martin, Andrew R. 2011. "A Voice of Steel through the Iron Curtain: Pete Seeger's Contributions to the Development of Steel Band in the United States." *American Music* 29 (3): 353–380.

Martin, Andrew R. 2017. *Steelpan Ambassadors: The US Navy Steel Band, 1957–1999*. Jackson: University Press of Mississippi.

Meintjes, Louise. 1990. "Paul Simon's Graceland, South Africa, and the Mediation of Musical Meaning." *Ethnomusicology* 34 (1): 37–73.

Mitchell, Joseph. 1939. "Houdini's Picnic." *New Yorker*, 6 May.

Munro, Hope. 2016. *What She Go Do: Women in Afro-Trinidadian Music*. Jackson: University Press of Mississippi.

Nederveen Pieterse, Jan. 2015. *Globalization and Culture: Global Mélange*. New York: Rowman & Littlefield.

Ngô, Fiona I. B. 2014. *Imperial Blues: Geographies of Race and Sex in Jazz Age New York*. Durham, NC: Duke University Press.

Nowlin, Bill. 1996. *Best of Straker's: Ah Feel to Party*. CD Booklet, Rounder CD 5066/67.

Nurse, Keith. 1999. "Globalization and Trinidadian Carnival: Diaspora, Hybridity, and Identity in Global Culture." *Cultural Studies* 13 (4): 661–690.

Nurse, Keith. 2004. "Globalization in Reverse: Diaspora and the Export of Trinidad Carnival." In *Carnival Culture in Action: The Trinidad Experience*, edited by Milla Cortez Riggio, 245–254. New York: Routledge.

Osofsky, Gilbert. 1971. *Harlem, the Making of a Ghetto*. 2nd ed. New York: Harper Torchbook.

Pearse, Andrew. 1956. "Carnival in Nineteenth Century Trinidad." *Caribbean Quarterly* 4 (3–4): 175–193.

Phillip, Lyndon. 2007. "Reading Caribana 1997: Black Youth, Puff Daddy, Style and Diasporic Transformations." In *Trinidad Carnival: The Cultural Politics of a Transnational Festival*, edited by Garth Green and Philip Scher, 102–135. Bloomington: Indiana University Press.

Putnam, Lara. 2013. *Radical Moves: Caribbean Migrants and the Politics of Race in the Jazz Age*. Chapel Hill: University of North Carolina Press.

Ramnarine, Tina. 2007. *Beautiful Cosmos: Performing and Belonging in the Caribbean Diaspora*. London: Pluto Press.

Roberts, John Storm. 1979. *The Latin Tinge: The Impact of Latin American Music on the United States*. New York: Oxford University Press.

Rohlehr, Gordon. 1990. *Calypso and Society in Pre-Independence Trinidad*. Port of Spain, Trinidad: published by the author.

Rohlehr, Gordon. 2004. *A Scuffling of Islands: Essays on Calypso*. San Juan, Trinidad: Lexicon Trinidad Ltd.

Rohlehr, Gordon. 2015. *My Whole Life Is Calypso: Essays on Sparrow*. Tunapuna, Trinidad: published by the author.

Scher, Philip. 2003. *Carnival and the Formation of a Caribbean Transnation*. Gainesville: University Press of Florida.

Shapiro, Steve. 2012. *Lovey's Original Trinidad String Band*. CD Booklet, Bear Family Records CD BCD 16057 AH.

Silverman, Carol. 2012. *Romani Routes: Cultural Politics and Balkan Music in Diaspora*. New York: Oxford University Press.

Slobin, Mark. 1993. *Subcultural Sounds: Micromusics of the West*. Hanover, NH: Wesleyan University Press.

Slobin, Mark. 2003. "The Destiny of 'Diaspora' in Ethnomusicology." In *The Cultural Study of Music*, edited by Martin Clayton, Trevor Herbert, and Charles Middleton, 284–296. New York: Routledge.

Stuempfle, Stephen. 1995. *The Steelband Movement: The Forging of a National Art in Trinidad and Tobago*. Philadelphia: University of Pennsylvania Press.

Stuempfle, Stephen. 2018. *Port of Spain: The Construction of a Caribbean City, 1888–1962*. Kingston, Jamaica: University of West Indies Press.

Sutton, Constance. 1997. "The Caribbeanization of New York City and the Emergence of a Transnational Socio-Cultural System." In *Caribbean Life in New York City: Sociocultural Dimensions*, edited by Constance Sutton and Elsa Chaney, 15–30. New York: Center for Migration Studies.

Thomas, Jeffrey. 1986. "The Changing Role of the Steel Band in Trinidad and Tobago: Panorama and the Carnival Tradition." *Studies in Popular Culture* 9 (2): 96–108.

Thompson, Dave. 2002. *Reggae and Caribbean Music*. London: Backbeat Books.

Turino, Thomas. 2008. *Music as Social Life: The Politics of Participation*. Chicago: University of Chicago Press.

Turner, Victor. 1982. *From Ritual to Theatre*. New York: Performing Arts Journal Publications.

Wald, Elijah. 2002. *Josh White: Society Blues*. New York: Routledge.

Waterman, Richard. 1973. "African Influences on the Musics of the Americas." In *Mother Wit from the Laughing Barrel: Readings in the Interpretation of African American Folklore*, edited by Alan Dundes, 81–94. Englewood Cliffs, NJ: Prentice Hall.

Waxer, Lisa, ed. 2002. *Situating Salsa: Global Markets and Local Meaning in Latin Popular Music*. New York: Routledge.

Zheng, Su. 2010. *Claiming Diaspora: Music, Transnationalism, and Cultural Politics in Asians/Chinese America*. New York: Oxford University Press.

Personal Interviews
(with author unless otherwise indicated)

Alexis, Cliff: 31 August 2014, Brooklyn (with author and Ray Funk).
Alley, Burtrum: 4 September 1998, Brooklyn.
Blake, Garvin: 24 August 2015 Brooklyn.
Botus, Denzil: 4 June 2015, Brooklyn.
Byran, Don, Sr.: 7 September 2014, Harlem (with author and Ray Funk).
Caraballo, Reynolds "Caldera": 9 June 1996, Brooklyn.
Charles, Rawlston: 17 September 2013, Brooklyn; 5 February 2015, Brooklyn.
Cyrus, Alston "Becket": 19 August 2013, Brooklyn (with author and Ray Funk).
Dougherty, Charles: 15 January 2015, Brooklyn.
Douglas, Martin: 1 October 2017 (phone); 12 August 2017, Brooklyn; 29 July 1998, Brooklyn.
Demming, Sparkle: 10 September 2018 (phone).
Durrant, Clyde: 27 April 2015, Brooklyn.
Francisco, Slinger "Sparrow": 26 March 2018 (phone).
Franklin, Ian: 23 August 2015 (phone).
Franklin, Odie: 26 August 2017, Brooklyn.
Galloway, Edward "Prince": 15 September 2014 (phone).
Goddard, Pelham: 20 February 2015, St. James, Trinidad (with author and Ray Funk).
Hall, Herman: 21 September 2017, Brooklyn; 22 July 2014, Brooklyn; 18 January 2000, Brooklyn.
Henry, Clyde: 24 April 2015, Brooklyn.
Henry, Winston "Explainer": 25 February 2015, Port of Spain, Trinidad.
Herbert, Arddin: 14 March 2017 (phone); 7 July 1997, Brooklyn.
Hilaire, Randolph "Count Robin": 28 May 2015, South Ozone Park, Queens; 17 August 2013, South Ozone Park, Queens (with author and Ray Funk).
Hodge, Camille: 15 September 2014 (phone).

Ince, Errol: 23 February 2015, Port of Spain, Trinidad.

King, Earl: 6 September 2014, Brooklyn (with author and Ray Funk); 9 September 1996, Brooklyn.

King, Rudy: 25 October 1995, Brooklyn (with author and Les Slater).

La Barrie, David: 15 May 2015 (phone).

Lewis, Linda McArthur Sandy "Calypso Rose": 23 July 2014, Queens.

Lezama-Clarke, Yolanda: 5 July 2017 (phone).

Liverpool, Hollis "Chalkdust": 5 October 2014, Brooklyn.

Loy, Hue: 24 February 2015, Port of Spain, Trinidad; 12 May 2015, Brooklyn.

McIntosh, Frankie: 23 July 2013, Brooklyn; 24 October 2014, Brooklyn.

Meade, Kenrick: 22 August 2013, Brooklyn; 29 March 2015, Brooklyn.

Munroe, Carlton: 8 August 2016, Brooklyn.

Munroe, Winston: 8 August 1996, Brooklyn (with author and Les Slater); 8 September 2014 (with author and Ray Funk).

Nelson, Robert Alfonzo "Lord": 22 August 2013, Brooklyn; 28 March 2015, Jamaica, Queens.

Paul, Leston: 21 February 2015, Mt. Lambert, Trinidad (with author and Ray Funk).

Peters, Winston "Gypsie": 23 February 2015, Port of Spain, Trinidad (with author and Ray Funk).

Philmore, Ken "Professor": 23 August 2015 (phone).

Philo, Rupert "Swallow": 4 September 2015, Brooklyn.

Quashie, Hawthorne "King Wellington": 12 August 2013, Long Island (with author and Ray Funk).

Reece, Tony: 29 March 2017, Brooklyn.

Rennie, Yvette: 11 May 2017, Brooklyn.

Roberts, Frankie: 16 January 2015, Brooklyn.

Rudder, David: 18 December, 2014 (phone).

Slater, Les: 8 May 2015, Brooklyn (with author and Ray Funk).

Straker, Granville: 18 July 2013, Brooklyn.

Talib, Jamal: 15 September 2017, Brooklyn.

Thomas, Wilfred: 15 October 2017 (phone).

Tribuse, Tony: 4 July 1998, Brooklyn.

Watson, Ed: 20 February 2015, Port of Spain, Trinidad (with author and Ray Funk).

Wellington, Winston: 28 May 2015, Brooklyn.

White, Andre: 1 September 2017, Brooklyn.

Williams, Kendall: 26 August 2017, Brooklyn.

Index

Guyana, 85, 89,
141–42n64, 142n69
Gypsy, 99

Haitian music
konpa, 103, 104, 199–200, 201–2
transnational production of,
199–200
Haiti, emigration from, 85
Hall, Herman
on broad steelband
appeal, 111n83
on Brooklyn Carnival crowd
sizes, 236, 255n7, 255n8
on Brooklyn steelband
movement, 133–34
on calypso tents, 1, 239
on commemorative celebration
dates, 254n2
on funding for Dimanche
Gras, 92–93
New York Reggae Contest
promoted by, 96
on steelbands in Eastern
Parkway parade, 209
on WIACDA ethnic
makeup, 109n56
on WIACDA tensions, 96,
101, 230n8
World Soca Monarch
competition, 239
on younger soca audiences, 239
Hall, Stuart, 4, 6, 43
Hammer, The (Rudder), 172
"Hammer" (Rudder),
162–63, 172
Harbin, Lester, 117–18
Harlem, demographics of, 85
Harlem All Stars (a.k.a.
Tropitones), 69–70, 86–87,
106–7n9, 117–18
Harlem calypsos, 75–76
Harlem Carnival
Brooklyn Carnival based on, 77,
84–85, 253
calypso contests, 32
calypso craze and, 75
calypso performances at, 147
crowd sizes, 70–71, 81–82n68
cultural expression at, 73–74
Dame Lorraine Galas (*see* Dame
Lorraine dances)
diverse audience for, 33

diverse audiences of,
27–28, 73–74
emergence of, 3, 32–33,
64–65, 253
end of, 72–73, 77, 82n77
evolution of, 3–4
organizational challenges of,
70–71, 72, 73
police tensions, 72, 82n77, 253
racial stereotypes and, 74
Seventh Avenue Street Parade
(*see* Seventh Avenue Street
Parade)
transnational character of, 77
uniqueness of, 27–28
"Harlem Night Life" (Houdini), 44
Harlem Seen through Calypso Eyes
(Houdini), 44
Harmonites, 92–93, 127–28,
132, 133
Harris, Earl, 161
Harris, Ed, 8
Harris, Willard. *See* Lord Relator
Hart-Celler Immigration Reform
Act (1965), 85
"Hasely Crawford" (Kitchener),
130, 134–35
Hayes, Roland, 45–46
HC&F Recording Studio,
Freeport, 198
Heath, Kevon "Yankey Boy," 239
hegemony, musical, 43, 54–55n51
"He Had It Coming" (Houdini), 44
Henderson, Fletcher, 38–39
Henry, Clyde
on Brooklyn block parties,
106–7n9
Brooklyn Panorama judging
controversy, 117, 139n20
on Crown Heights block
parties, 85–86
Eastern Parkway Parade
performances, 114
LDCCC involvement, 90
rival efforts to WIADCA, 90, 91–
92, 108n26, 117–19, 128
Rolling Stones concert,
126, 127–28
Henry, Winston. *See* Explainer
Hepburn, Nap, 94–95, 99
Herbert, Arddin
on Brooklyn J'Ouvert, 207, 213–
14, 215–16, 222, 224–25

soca (soul/calypso) music,
Brooklyn (*Cont.*)
production/distribution, 4, 77,
143–44, 149, 153, 178–79, 190–
91, 203–4, 237–39
singers as focus of, 156, 183n40
as transnational expression, 159,
162, 190–93, 196–97, 200–1
soca (soul/calypso) music,
influences shaping
Calypso Rose, 239–40
Charles, 22, 163–64
Charlie's Records, 9, 143, 162,
189, 192
Duke, 148–49
Granville, 22, 152
McIntosh, 156, 159
Nelson, 148–49, 175–76,
187n98, 239–40
Shadow, 2, 152
Shorty, 160–61
Sparrow, 239–40
transnational production
process, 190–91
Trinidad Carnival, 191–92, 200–1
Watson, 164
Wellington, 150–51
world music, 192
soca (soul/calypso) music, Trinidad
history of, 2, 148–49
recording of, 22–23, 238–39
transnational roots of, 16
Socarras, Alberto, 38
"sokah," 160–61
Songs to Trinidad (1946), 52n13
Sound Heights Studio,
Brooklyn, 178–79
sound trucks
at Eastern Parkway parade, 97,
98*f*, 101, 103, 207, 208–10
in London, 26
prohibited at Brooklyn
J'Ouvert, 214
tension over use, 26, 97,
207, 208–9
in Trinidad Carnival, 25–26, 101
Sparrow (Slinger Francisco)
Brooklyn Carnival
performances, 86–87, 88–89,
92–93, 97–98, 99–100, 116–17
Brooklyn/Queens as hub
for, 178–79
calypso craze and, 83n83

calypso tent performances, 99
career highlights, 1, 86–87
collaboration with Nelson,
147, 181n15
Madison Square Garden
performances, 93–94, 99
National Label, 147
political lyrics of, 23–24, 164–65,
176–77, 205n14
recordings, 83n83, 143–44, 150,
165*f*, 176–77
soca influenced by, 239–40
soca projects, 164–65,
176–77, 239–40
transnational circulation of,
3, 92–93
Sparrow—25th Anniversary (1979),
164–65, 165*f*, 176–77, 185n70
Spence, Gerald, 109n56
"spontaneous *communitas*,"
19–20, 222–23
spouge, 201–2
Stanislaus, Emanuel, 109n56
"Steel and Brass" (Wellington), 195
"Steelband Alley," 122–23
Steel Band Association
of Americas (SBAA),
118–19, 139n24
"Steelband Jamborees," 133,
141–42n64
steelband music, Antigua,
141–42n64
steelband music, Grenada,
141–42n64
steelband music, Guyana,
141–42n64
steelband music, Trinidad
arrangement style, 138n9
arrangers, 120, 128, 134–35, 244
band sizes and sections, 120
"bomb" tunes, 116
as epicenter of steelband music,
135, 244, 245
as essential component of
Carnival, 67
hybridization in, 18–19
musical development of, 18–19
musical genres embraced by, 19
pan-on-the-road era, 21
participatory performance
of, 22–23
presentational performance,
21, 140n38

WIADCA. *See* West Indian
    American Day Carnival
    Association
Wilhelmina, Gale, 49
Williams, Eric, 23–24
Williams, Eugene, 35–36, 52n13
Williams, Julian, 178
Williams, Jumaane, 249
Williams, Kendall, 244–45
Williams, Tony, 122
"Wine Down Kingston"
    (Becket), 155–56

Wingate Originals, 219*f*, 219–20
"wining" (dancing), 8, 155–56
Wise, Earl, 176
Wong, Kim Loy, 56n72, 112–13
world music, 193–94

Yankey Boy, 239
Youngblood, Eddy, 170–71
Youth Pan Festival, 243–44, 247–
    48, 259–60n54

Zheng, Su, 197

Printed in the USA/Agawam, MA
November 3, 2021

783577.029